The Europeanisation of International Family Law

N.A. Baarsma

The Europeanisation of International Family Law

T·M·C·ASSER PRESS

Springer

N.A. Baarsma
Kolfstraat 19
9717 GP Groningen
The Netherlands
e-mail: nynkebaarsma@hotmail.com

ISBN 978-90-6704-742-5 e-ISBN 978-90-6704-743-2

DOI 10.1007/978-90-6704-743-2

Published by T.M.C. ASSER PRESS, The Hague, The Netherlands, www.asserpress.nl

Produced and distributed for T.M.C. ASSER PRESS by Springer-Verlag Berlin Heidelberg

Cover design: eStudio Calamar, Berlin/Figueres

Printed on acid-free paper

Springer is part of Springer Science+Business Media (www.springer.com)

Preface

This book deals with the Europeanisation of international family law. Over the last decade the European Union has shown increasing interest in the field of international family law. This is not surprising, since the growing mobility of citizens as a result of the free movement of persons has led to a consequential rise of the formation and dissolution of international families. More and more questions of private international law therefore arise.

International family law is an area that is predominantly regulated by national law. Currently the national choice of law rules of the EU Member States are more and more displaced by common European rules, which will thus entail considerable changes. The nature and reasons of the changes brought about by the transition from a national to a supranational choice of law approach are discussed in one particular field of international family law: the termination by dissolution of marriages and marriage-like registered partnerships. The current Dutch and the proposed European choice of law rules on divorce are examined and compared.

Although common European choice of law rules in the field of contractual and non-contractual obligations and maintenance obligations have been established rather smoothly, the establishment of common choice of law rules on divorce has met with a lot of resistance. A long process of negotiation followed, but ultimately the Council had to admit that all possibilities for a compromise on the establishment of a common choice of law on divorce had been exhausted. For the first time in the history of the European Union, the mechanism of enhanced cooperation will be applied.

However, the process of Europeanisation of international family law will most certainly continue. Therefore, the concluding chapter produces a number of recommendations on the development of (a theoretical foundation of) the European system of international family law, starting from the principles and objectives of European law.

Groningen, January 2011 — Nynke Baarsma

Contents

List of Abbreviations

Art.	Article(s)
BW	Burgerlijk Wetboek (Civil Code, The Netherlands)
BGB	Bürgerliches Gesetzbuch (Civil Code, Germany)
CEFL	Commission on European Family Law
Cf.,	Compare, Conform
CFI	Court of First Instance
Chap(s)	Chapter(s)
CLAD	Choice of Law Act on Divorce
CLARP	Choice of Law Act on Registered Partnerships
CMLR	Common Market Law Review
COREPER	Comité des représentants permanents
COSAC	Conférence des Organes Spécialisés dans les Affaires Communautaires et Européennes des Parlements de l'Union européenne
diss.	dissertation
EC	European Community (Treaty)
ECHR	European Convention on Human Rights
ECJ	European Court of Justice
ECR	European Court Reports
ECtHR	European Court of Human Rights
ed./eds.	editor(s)
e.g.	*exempli gratia* (for example)
EPEC	European Policy Evaluation Consortium
et al.	*et alii* (and others)
et seq	*et sequens* (and further)
EU	European Union
EuR	Europarecht
EuZW	Europäische Zeitschrift für Wirtschaftsrecht
ff	following
FJR	Tijdschrift voor Familie- en Jeugdrecht
Hof	Gerechtshof (Court of Appeal, The Netherlands)

HR	Hoge Raad der Nederlanden (Supreme Court of The Netherlands)
ICCPR	International Covenant on Civil and Political Rights
ICLQ	International and Comparative Law Quarterly
ibid.	*ibidem* (from the same source)
i.c.	*in casu* (in this case)
i.e.	*id est* (that is)
IFL	International Family Law
IPR	Internationaal Privaatrecht (Private International Law)
IPRax	Praxis des internationalen Privat- und Verfahrensrechts
MJ	Maastricht Journal of European and Comparative Law
MvA	Memorie van Antwoord (Memorandum of Reply)
MvT	Memorie van Toeliching (Explanatory Memorandum)
n.	note
NILR	Netherlands International Law Review
NIPR	Nederlands Tijdschrift voor Internationaal Privaatrecht
NJ	Nederlandse Jurisprudentie
NJB	Nederlands Juristenblad
NJCM	Nederlands Juristen Comité voor de Mensenrechten
No(s).	Number(s)
NTBR	Nederlands Tijdschrift voor Burgerlijk Recht
NTER	Nederlands Tijdschrift voor Europees Recht
NV	Nota naar Aanleiding van het Verslag (Memorandum in reply to the parliamentary report)
NVvR	Nederlandse Vereniging voor Rechtspraak (Netherlands Association for the Administration of Justice)
NvW	Nota van Wijziging (Memorandum of Amendment)
OJ	Official Journal of the European Communities/European Union
p.	page
PACS	Pacte Civil de Solidarité
para(s)	paragraph(s)
PIL	Private International Law
RabelsZ	Rabels Zeischrift für ausländisches und internationales Privatrecht
Rb.	Rechtbank (Court of First Instance, the Netherlands)
Recueil des Cours	Recueil des Cours de l'Académie de droit international de La Haye
RCDIP	Revue Critique de Droit International Privé
Sect(s).	Section(s)
SEW	Sociaal Economische Wetgeving
spec.	specifically
Stb.	Staatsblad van het Koninkrijk der Nederlanden (Dutch Bulletin of Acts, Orders and Decrees)
Stcrt.	Staatscourant (Dutch Government Gazette)

TFEU	Treaty on the Functioning of the European Union
Trb.	Tractatenblad (Dutch Bulletin of Treaties)
v.	versus
Vol.	Volume
W.	Weekblad van het Recht
WCE	Wet Conflictenrecht Echtscheiding (See CLAD)
WCGp	Wet Conflictenrecht Geregistreerd Partnerschap (See CLARP)
WPNR	Weekblad voor Privaatrecht, Notariaat en Registratie
ZEuP	Zeitschrift für europäisches Privatrecht
ZGB	Zivilgesetzbuch (Civil Code, Switzerland)

Chapter 1
Introduction

The language of love is said to be universal: love brings people together from across the world and is oblivious to boundaries. However, from a legal perspective things are not so straightforward; law is, on the contrary, often strongly bound by borders. Especially when an international marriage breaks down complicated cross-border disputes can arise.

1.1 Research Background

Most people live in the country of which they possess the nationality. In the majority of family law disputes there are therefore no international elements to consider: the dispute is brought before one of the courts of that state and a decision is made on the basis of the substantive laws of that country.

However, the situation is somewhat different when the parties do not live in the same country, do not possess the same nationality or do not possess the nationality of the country in which they live. Throughout the world the substantive family laws vary and it may, consequently, make a great difference to the courts of which country an international family law dispute is brought.

As a result of the existing differences in substantive family law, private international law is of considerable importance. First of all, it decides which state's courts have jurisdiction over a subject-matter. Secondly, private international law determines which law is to be applied. Bearing in mind that, depending on which court is seised, the rules for determining the applicable law can lead to the application of different substantive laws and hence a different outcome of the proceedings, it thirdly has to be ensured that the resulting judgment is nevertheless recognised and enforced in the other states concerned. These three issues are dealt with through private international law. However, each state currently has its own system of private international law, which involves that these systems (may) differ

N.A. Baarsma, *The Europeanisation of International Family Law*,
DOI: 10.1007/978-90-6704-743-2_1, © T.M.C. ASSER PRESS, The Hague,
The Netherlands, and the author 2011

greatly.[1] Private international law in Europe has, consequently, been described as 'a jungle that can confuse even Europeans and that an outsider without guidance may easily become lost in.'[2]

Within the European Union, the Member States' courts are faced more and more frequently with cases of international family law. The free movement of persons, one of the fundamental freedoms of the European Union (Article 45 *et seq* TFEU), has resulted in the increased mobility of citizens in the last few decades. The increasing mobility of Union citizens in turn has led to a consequential rise of formation and dissolution of international families. Moreover, in addition to the European integration, globalisation has resulted in the residence of many third country nationals on the territory of the European Union.[3] With these facts in mind, it is foreseeable that the number of cross-border family relationships is only set to rise.[4]

Currently the Member States of the European Union largely autonomously provide for rules on private international law. These national rules of the Member States are yet more and more displaced by common European rules. In the field of private international law the EU is gaining more and more ground: private international law is, so to say, being 'Europeanised'.

Private international law seems to be the instrument *par excellence* to bridge the existing differences in the substantive laws of the Member States: it presupposes the diversity of national laws and attempts to manage that diversity by means of coordination.[5] Within the EU the progressive integration incites to the establishment of a common system of private international law.[6] Furthermore, also the European motto 'united in diversity' requires a system of coordination of the laws of the Member States which is compatible with the free movement of persons,

---

1 On some issues of international family law international conventions have been established by for example. the Hague Conference on Private International Law, the Commission Internationale de l'État Civil and the Council of Europe. See Schulz 2007, pp. 278–279 for an enumeration of the international conventions that have been established in the field of family law. However, as every sovereign state is free to decide whether or not to ratify one or more of these conventions, their application may be fairly limited (cf., the 1978 Hague Convention on Matrimonial Property Regimes, which has 3 contracting states) or even very broad (cf., the 1980 Hague Convention on International Child Abduction, which has 81 contracting states).

2 See Reimann 1995, p. xxi. However, the situation has gradually changed: by the introduction of the Rome I, Rome II, Brussels I and the Brussels II*bis*-Regulations and the Maintenance Regulation private international law in Europe is becoming more uniform and less of a jungle.

3 While the definition of globalisation varies depending on the context of analysis, it generally refers to an increasing interaction across national boundaries that affects many aspects of life: economic, social, cultural and political. See: http://www.genderandhealth.ca/en/modules/globalization/globalization_what_is-01.jsp.

4 Cf., Dethloff 2003, pp. 37–39.

5 See *inter alia* Kreuzer 2001, p. 98; Remien 2001, p. 63; Fallon/Francq 2004, p. 266.

6 Cf., De Vareilles-Sommières 1998, pp. 136–137: '*dans la conception qui prévaut actuellement de l'Europe communautaire, un renforcement de l'intégration de l'ordre communautaire implique un renforcement de la coordination des ordres des États-Membres, autrement dit que plus de Communauté appelle plus de droit international privé.*'

goods, services and capitals within the European Union.[7] Private international law respects the existing diversities between the laws of the Member States and solves possible conflicts between them.[8] The respect for the diversity of national systems is the leading principle of the European integration in the field of justice.[9]

The European legislative activities in the field of family law that are 'under construction' are, 'in the political rhetoric of the European Union', claimed to be essential for integration in Europe and aim to stimulate the free movement of EU citizens throughout the Union.[10] It is presumed that the existing differences in family law among the Member States of the EU are an obstacle for the free movement of persons. Citizens refrain from moving from one Member State to another if they fear that it might affect their family status and rights.[11] The establishment of a European system of international family law is considered to be necessary so as to overcome this obstacle. The Treaty on the Functioning of the European Union provides for the competence of the EU legislature in the field of judicial cooperation in civil matters (Article 81 TFEU).

Unification of European international family law would be superfluous if sufficient uniform substantive family law would already exist. However, currently no such law exists. It is, moreover, not to be expected that a uniform substantive family law will soon come about.[12]

In 1998 the Study Group on the European Civil Code was set up with the aim of drafting a binding European Civil Code. Family law has nevertheless been excluded from the scope of this Code.[13]

Many regard family law as a field of law that is unsuitable for international unification: family law is based on social and cultural norms and values that vary too much from one legal system to another.[14] It is a field of law that requires considerable sensitivity and care. The deeply rooted nature of family law within

---

[7] In 2004, the motto was included in the failed European Constitution (Article I-8 on the EU's symbols) and it now appears on official EU websites.

[8] See equally Poillot-Peruzzetto 2005, p. 33.

[9] Communication from the Commission to the European Parliament and the Council, An area of freedom, security and justice serving the citizen, COM(2009) 262 final, p. 11. See also Article 4(2) EU-Treaty, which purports to respect 'the national identities of the Member States'. See further *infra* Sect. 8.4.2.2.

[10] Cf., Jänterä-Jareborg 2003, p. 194.

[11] See Tenreiro/Ekström 2003, p. 187.

[12] Cf., Fallon 1998, p. 400: *'L'heure n'est certainement pas à une unification des règles matérielles sur le mariage, le divorce ou la filiation.'*

[13] See Von Bar 2001, spec. pp. 130–131; Hesselink 2006.

[14] Cf., De Oliviera 2000. Draft Council report on the need to approximate Member States' legislation in civil matters of 29 October 2001, adopted on 16 November 2001, Document No. 13017/01 JUSTCIV 129, p. 3, where the Council states that family law is 'very heavily influenced by the culture and traditions of national (or even regional) legal systems, which could create a number of difficulties in the context of harmonisation'. However, others have strongly opposed this 'cultural constraints argument'; see e.g. Antokolskaia 2009.

the Member States is a primary difficulty for the European Union in this area of law and, as will be shown below, in the area of private international law as well.

Although there seems to be a growing support for harmonisation of substantive family law within the EU, such harmonisation is hardly feasible. Despite the 'European Principles of Family Law'[15] and the other academic initiatives[16] that have been developed, there is no denying that still many differences in substantive family law exist.[17] Furthermore, there is as yet no legal basis for harmonisation of substantive family law, as the EU lacks competence in this respect.[18] But also politically speaking, far-reaching harmonisation — let alone unification — of substantive family law is not (yet) feasible at the European level. In this study, it has consequently been presupposed that irrespective of whether the harmonisation or unification of substantive family law in the European Union is desirable, it is evidently not feasible.

As seen above, the European Union's motto is 'united in diversity'; this goal requires the respect of the multiplicity of legal norms in Europe. Uniform private international law rules are therefore the ultimate solution: such rules respect the existing diversities in the laws of the Member States and they solve possible conflicts between them.[19]

Is the establishment of a European system of private international law then to be seen as an interim measure, to provide an intermediate level of ordering, with the view that it will ultimately lead to a substantive unification of law?[20]

Although it cannot be excluded that the unified private international law may very well play a transitory role, its importance should neither be overlooked nor undermined.[21] With the harmonisation or unification of substantive family law

[15] In September 2001 the Commission on European Family Law (CEFL) was established, see: http://www.ceflonline.net/. The CEFL has so far developed principles regarding divorce and maintenance between former spouses and regarding parental responsibilities. Principles regarding property relations between spouses are currently being prepared.

[16] See e.g. Schwenzer and Dimsey 2006. See also Killerby 1996, noticing some harmonising tendencies particularly arising from the European Convention on Human Rights.

[17] See on the unification or harmonisation of substantive family law in general *inter alia* Boele-Woelki 1997; Antokolskaia et al. 1999. In this context it seems worth noting that even in federal states, such as the USA, the need to harmonise substantive family law has never arisen; see Baratta 2005.

[18] Cf., the following statement in the Discussion Paper of the Informal Justice and Home Affairs Council of 14–16 January 2007 held in Dresden, p. 1: 'Harmonising the provisions of substantive family and succession law is not an option, because the requisite legal foundation in the EC Treaty is lacking. This would not be desirable anyway: The diverse values inherent in national family and succession law represent a key aspect of Europe's cultural diversity.' See further Pintens 2003, p. 22; Dethloff 2004, p. 565.

[19] See Thue 2007, p. 95. See also Muir Watt 2005, p. 9.

[20] See Koch 1995. See also Van Erp 2002.

[21] Cf., Curry-Sumner 2005, p. 533.

evidently still many years away — suppose that it will ever come about — cross-border family relationships require legal certainty right now. Such certainty can to a large extent be achieved through uniform private international law rules.

Even though the unification of international family law is not such a vexed question as the unification of substantive family law, it still is a very sensitive subject, politically as well as legally.[22] The Member States are zealous for the protection of their competences and conceptions on family and on family law.

The Europeanisation of international family law thus poses a great challenge for the EU legislature, who has to find a fair and just way of dealing with international family matters across Europe. The European legislature can by no means trespass upon the roots, heritage and valuable traditions of the separate Member States.

1.2 Demarcation of Research

It is clear that international family law will be Europeanised. According to the Hague Programme, instruments in the field of family law including divorce, maintenance and matrimonial property should be completed by the year 2011.[23] With the Maintenance Regulation and the Hague Protocol determining the law applicable to maintenance obligations, the Brussels II*ter*-Proposal and the Green Paper in the field of matrimonial property the establishment of such a common system is more and more taking shape. Besides, issues such as personal status, names and adoption have been mentioned as future areas of Union action in the field of private international law.[24]

For an area that is currently predominantly regulated by national law, Europeanisation will in all probability entail considerable changes. This research examines the nature and reasons of these changes in one particular field of international family law: the termination by dissolution of marriages and marriage-like registered partnerships. Divorce is the first field of family law in which the European legislature made attempts to unify the choice of law: in July 2006 the European Commission proposed the introduction of common choice of law rules on divorce. In order to assess the methodological consequences of the change from a national to a supranational choice of law approach, the Dutch choice of law rules on divorce and on the termination of registered partnerships will be compared to the proposed European choice of law rules on divorce contained in the Brussels

---

[22] Substantive law and private international law are often to a large extent interrelated: if the substantive law supports a certain policy, this policy is often reflected in the choice of law rules as well. See on this interconnection in general *inter alia* Siehr 1973; De Boer 1993.

[23] The Hague Programme, p. 13. However, the objectives set out in the Hague Programme seem to be too ambitious; it is not to be expected that the mentioned instruments are completed in 2011.

[24] See Communication from the Commission to the Council and the European Parliament establishing for the period 2007–2013 a framework programme on Fundamental Rights and Justice, COM(2005) 122 final, p. 67.

II*ter*-Proposal. The aim of studying this subject-matter in a comparative way is to unravel and to analyse the differences and similarities between these two choices of law systems. As far as there are differences between these systems, why do the European choice of law rules differ from national ones? Can such differentiation be justified and explained in light of specific European aims and objectives?

Subsequently, the aim is to determine whether and to what extent the establishment of a supranational European system of international family law alters — or should alter — the traditional choice of law methodology underlying the national systems of international family law. A number of directions as regards the methodology of European international family law at large are deduced from the European attempt to unify the choice of law on divorce. This study consequently results in a look into the future with respect to the methodological aspects of the European system of international family law that is being established as a whole.

The research is confined to the question of which state's law should be applied in a cross-border case by the competent court, i.e. the choice of law.

As already observed above, the field of private international law deals with three kinds of questions. First is the question of *jurisdiction*: which state's courts are competent to rule on a certain case? Second is the question of *choice of law*: which state's law is applicable to a certain case? Third is the question of *recognition and enforcement* of foreign judgments: under what circumstances can foreign judgments rendered by the courts of another state be recognised and enforced? Although these three questions are (strongly) interrelated,[25] the main focus of this study lies on the choice of law; the issues of jurisdiction and recognition and enforcement will be discussed only where the circumstances so require.

1.3 Terminology

The term 'Europeanisation' refers to the replacement of national legal provisions by those originating from the European Union.[26] Since the Treaty of Amsterdam the field of private international law is increasingly being Europeanised: Article 65 EC-Treaty (now: Article 81 TFEU) granted the Community institutions the competence to establish measures on private international law. The Europeanisation of private international law thus refers to the emergence and development at the European level of distinct instruments containing specific European private international law rules.

---

25 See e.g. Eyl 1965.

26 Another term is 'communitarisation', referring to the replacement of national legal provisions by Community law. However, the Treaty of Lisbon, which entered into force on 1 December 2009, has abolished the European Community. Using the term communitarisation is, therefore, currently less accurate. Cf., Von Hoffmann 1998, p. 15 and Pocar 2000, pp. 873–884.

The term 'international family law' has two meanings. It involves, on the one hand, the rules for cross-border family relations — the private international law rules — and, on the other hand, the body of international and European instruments and decisions of supranational courts which regulate family relationships.[27] In this study the former meaning of international family law has been taken as a basis; where the private international law rules in family matters are concerned.

As marriage and (registered) partnership are matters of national substantive law, this field is very diverse, that is to say, there are a number of types of family union that can be defined as such. In 2003 Siehr devoted an inquiry into the different types of family unions that nowadays exist, which revealed nine different types:

1. traditional marriage of opposite-sex partners,
2. "covenant marriage" according to the law of some States of the United States,
3. same-sex marriages such as those introduced in the Netherlands and Belgium,
4. registered partnerships of same-sex partners such as those introduced in the Scandinavian countries and in Germany,
5. registered partnerships of opposite-sex partners as introduced by the French PACS,
6. contractual partnerships of same-sex partners as introduced by the French PACS,
7. contractual partnerships of opposite-sex partners as introduced by the French PACS,
8. factual partnerships of opposite-sex partners such as those recognised in Slovenia and Croatia, as well as in South America as '*uniónes de hecho*'.
9. factual partnerships of same-sex partners such as those recognised in France as '*concubinage*' or in the United States.[28]

Although the last two types of family union defined (the factual partnerships) fall fully outside the scope of this study, this classification shows the broad range of types of family union. In this book, the term marriage refers to the union between two persons of a different sex or of the same sex that creates kinship. The term registered partnership refers to a registered, non-marital relationship between two persons (of a different or of the same sex) that is similar to marriage.

The comparison between the Dutch and the European choice of law rules in the field of family law concentrates on those on the dissolution of marriage and marriage-like registered partnerships.

Divorce is defined as the dissolution of the matrimonial bonds; hence, it refers to the legal method through which spouses change their legal (civil) status from married to single. This same definition applies to the termination of a registered partnership. In both cases the parties are free either to remarry or to re-enter into a registered partnership.

---

[27] Cf., Boele-Woelki 2008b, p. 4.

[28] Siehr 2003, p. 421. See equally Waaldijk 2005.

In July 2006, the Commission proposed to amend the Brussels II*bis*-Regulation *inter alia* by introducing common choice of law rules on divorce. The proposed amendment of the Brussels II*bis*-Regulation is often referred to as the Rome III-project.

However, Boele-Woelki rightly argued that this change of the name of the Brussels II*bis*-Regulation is striking in two respects.[29] Firstly, the introduction of choice of law rules within the scope of the instrument is seemingly of such great importance and significance as to justify the change of its name. Secondly, up until now, the designation 'Rome' has been used for instruments which only contained choice of law rules, whereas 'Brussels' indicated that only procedural issues were being addressed, such as jurisdiction, recognition and enforcement. Consequently, neither Rome III nor Brussels II*ter* would correctly indicate the Regulation's content.

Throughout this book the proposed amendment of the Brussels II*bis*-Regulation will be referred to as the Brussels II*ter*-Proposal.[30] Although the mentioned confusion that can arise considering the usual reference of 'Brussels' to procedural issues of private international is to be endorsed, this designation is the best reflection of the content of the regulation. The amendment concerns the Brussels II*bis*-Regulation: the common choice of law rules on divorce are proposed to be inserted into it.

1.4 Outline

This study can roughly be divided into three parts.

The first part, consisting of Chapters 2 and 3, contains a comprehensive overview and discussion of the national — i.e. the Dutch — dimension of the study. In Chapter 2 the Dutch choice of law rules on divorce will be discussed. In 1981 the Dutch Choice of Law Act on Divorce entered into force. Article 1 of this Act provides for an answer to the question of which law applies from Dutch perspective to an international divorce.

Subsequently, the Dutch choice of law rules on the termination of registered partnerships will be discussed in Chapter 3. These rules are included in the Dutch Choice of Law Act on Registered Partnerships. The choice of law rules on the termination of registered partnerships are of a more recent date than the ones on divorce. This logically follows from the fact that the concept of registered partnership is a relatively new institution, which was introduced in Dutch law in 1998. The Dutch Choice of Law Act on Registered Partnerships provides for the law applicable to the termination of registered partnerships in Articles 22 and 23.

---

29 Boele-Woelki 2008a, p. 783.

30 See equally De Boer 2008, p. 323.

The second part of this study, consisting of Chapters 4–6, is devoted to the European dimension of the research so far as it concerns the two chosen subfields divorce and termination of registered partnerships. Chapter 4 will elaborate on the evolution of international family law in the European Union: since the entry into force of the Treaty of Amsterdam in 1999 the development of European rules of international family law has moved rapidly. The EU legislature's competence to enact measures in the field of international family law in general and the question whether the European Union is specifically competent to enact common choice of law rules on divorce will be examined.

Chapter 5 will subsequently analyse the proposed European choice of law rules on divorce. In July 2006 the European Commission has proposed the introduction of common choice of law rules on divorce, the Brussels II*ter*-Proposal. The objectives and the content of this proposal will be analysed thoroughly.

The EU Member States have not exactly received the Brussels II*ter*-Proposal with open arms. On the contrary, some Member States have strongly opposed the introduction of a common choice of law on divorce. This opposition has ultimately led to the failure to reach an agreement on the issue. Chapter 6 will deal with the reasons behind this failure and possible alternatives will be reviewed. In March 2010, the Commission decided to move forward with one of the alternatives: a proposal implementing enhanced cooperation in the area of the choice of law on divorce was presented.[31]

Finally the third part, consisting of Chapters 7 and 8, provides for a (prelude to a) coordinating overview of European international family law.

Chapter 7 contains a comparative study of the two choice of law systems that have been analysed in the preceding chapters. The similarities and differences between the Dutch and the European system will be disclosed and explained as much as possible. This comparison pursues a dual aim: firstly it will be helpful to answer the question whether from the attempt to unify the European choice of law on divorce some more general directions can be deduced as regards the principles and methods of European international family law at large. Secondly, as the Netherlands was one of the opponents of the Brussels II*ter*-Proposal, the comparison will also attempt to answer the question whether the Dutch government has rightly opposed the introduction of the common choice of law on divorce.

In Chapter 8 the future of the Europeanisation of international family law will be discussed. From the analysis of the preceding chapters on the failure to reach a compromise on the Brussels II*ter*-Proposal lessons will be drawn for future projects. From these lessons some guidelines for the future unification of issues of international family law will be tried to be derived. Furthermore, the analysis will seek to instigate the development of a proper EU methodology of a coherent system of European international family law.

---

[31] Council Regulation (EU) No. 1259/2010 of 20 December 2010 implementing enhanced cooperation in the area of the law applicable to divorce and legal separation, OJ L343/10.

References

Regulations and Other Documentary Sources

Brussels I-Regulation. Council Regulation (EC) No. 44/2001 of 22 December 2000 on jurisdiction and the recognition and enforcement of judgments in civil and commercial matters, [2001] OJ L12/1

Brussels II*bis*-Regulation. Council Regulation (EC) No. 2201/2003 of 27 November 2003 on Jurisdiction and Enforcement of Judgments in Matrimonial Matters and Matters of Parental Responsibility, [2003] OJ L338/1

Brussels II*ter*-Proposal. Proposal for a Council Regulation amending Regulation (EC) No. 2201/2003 as regards jurisdiction and introducing rules concerning applicable law in matrimonial matters, COM(2006) 399 final

EU-Treaty. Treaty on the European Union of 7 February 1992, [1992] OJ C191/1 (original version), [2010] OJ C83/13 (consolidated version)

Hague Programme. The Hague Programme: Strengthening freedom, security and justice in the European Union, [2005] OJ C53/1

Maintenance Regulation. Council Regulation (EC) No. 4/2009 of 18 December 2008 on jurisdiction, applicable law, recognition and enforcement of decisions and cooperation in matters relating to maintenance obligations, [2009] OJ L7/1

Proposal on enhanced cooperation in the field of divorce. Council Regulation (EU) No. 1259/2010 of 20 December 2010 implementing enhanced cooperation in the area of the law applicable to divorce and legal separation, OJ L343/10

Rome I-Regulation. Regulation (EC) No. 593/2008 of the European Parliament and the Council on the law applicable to contractual obligations (Rome I), [2008] OJ L177/6

Rome II-Regulation. Regulation (EC) No. 864/2007 of the European Parliament and the Council on the law applicable to non-contractual obligations (Rome II), [2007] OJ L199/40

Books and Articles

Antokolskaia MV (2009) Family law and national culture. Arguing against the cultural constraints argument. In: Boele-Woelki K (ed) Debates in Family Law around the Globe at the Dawn of the 21st Century. Intersentia, Antwerpen, pp 37–51

Antokolskaia MV, De Hondt W, Steenhoff G (1999) Een zoektocht naar Europees familierecht. Kluwer, Deventer

Baratta B (2005) Verso la "comunitarizzazione" dei principi fondamentali del diritto di famiglia. Rivista di diritto internazionale privato e processuale 41:573–606

Boele-Woelki K (1997) The road towards a European family law. Electronic Journal of Comparative Law 1.1:1–12. Available at: www.ejcl.org/11/art11-1.html

Boele-Woelki K (2008a) To be or not to be: enhanced cooperation in international divorce law within the European Union. Victoria University of Wellington Law Review 39:779–792

Boele-Woelki K (2008b) What comparative family law should entail. Utrecht Law Review 4(2):1–24

Curry-Sumner I (2005) All's well that ends registered? Intersentia, Antwerpen

De Boer ThM (1993) De wisselwerking tussen materieel recht en conflictenrecht, Preadvies voor de Nederlandse Vereniging voor Rechtsvergelijking. Kluwer, Deventer

De Boer ThM (2008) The second revision of the Brussels II regulation: jurisdiction and applicable law. In: Boele-Woelki K, Sverdrup T (eds) European challenges in contemporary family law. Intersentia, Antwerpen, pp 321–341

De Oliviera G (2000) A European family law? (play it again, and again … Europe!). FJR 272–277

Dethloff N (2003) Arguments for and against unification and harmonisation of family law in Europe. In: Boele-Woelki K (ed) Perspectives for the harmonisation and unification of family law in Europe. Intersentia, Antwerpen, pp 37–64
Dethloff N (2004) Europäische Vereinheitlichung des Familienrechts. Archiv für die civilistische Praxis 204:544–568
De Vareilles-Sommières P (1998) Un droit international privé européen? In: De Vareilles-Sommières P (ed) Le droit privé européen. Economica, Paris, pp 136–147
Eyl HR (1965) Internationale echtscheiding in Nederland. Scheltema & Holkema N.V, Amsterdam
Fallon M (1998) Droit familial et droit des Communautés européennes. Revue Trimestrielle de Droit Familial 1998(3):361–400
Fallon M, Francq S (2004) La coopération judiciaire civile et le droit international privé. Vers un droit proprement communautaire des conflits de lois ou de juridiction. In: De Schutter O, Nihoul P (eds) Une Constitution pour l'Europe. Réflexions sur les transformations du droit de l'Union européenne. Larcier, Brussel, pp 239–301
Hesselink MW (ed) (2006) The politics of a European civil code. Kluwer Law International, The Hague
Jänterä-Jareborg M (2003) Unification of international family law in Europe—a critical perspective. In: Boele-Woelki K (ed) Perspectives for the unification and harmonisation of family law in Europe. Intersentia, Antwerpen, pp 194–216
Killerby M (1996) The council of Europe's contribution to family law (past, present and future). In: Lowe N, Douglas G (eds) Families across frontiers. Martinus Nijhoff Publishers, The Hague, pp 13–25
Koch H (1995) Private international law: a 'soft' alternative to the harmonisation of private law? European Review of Private Law 3:329–342
Kreuzer K (2001) La communautarisation du droit international privé: les acquis et les perspectives. Droit GLOBAL Law Unifier le droit: le rêve impossible?, no 2001/1, pp 97–137
Muir Watt H (2005) European integration, legal diversity and the conflict of law. Edinburgh Law Review 9:6–31
Pintens W (2003) Europeanisation of family law. In: Boele-Woelki K (ed) Perspectives for the unification and harmonisation of family law in Europe. Intersentia, Antwerpen
Pocar F (2000) La comunitarizzazione del DIPrivato: una European conflict of laws revolution. Rivista di diritto internazionale privato e processuale 36:873–884
Poillot-Peruzzetto S (2005) Les enjeux de la communautarisation. In: Fulchiron H, Nourissat C (eds) Le nouveau droit communautaire du divore et de la responsabilité parentale. Dalloz, Paris, pp 13–37
Reimann M (1995) Conflict of laws in Western Europe. A guide through the jungle. Transnational Publishers, Irvington
Remien O (2001) European private international law, the European community and its emerging area of freedom, security and justice. CMLR 38:53–86
Schulz A (2007) The state of development of uniform law in the field of European and international family and child law. The European Legal Forum 2006(6):278–289
Schwenzer I, Dimsey M (2006) Model family law code. From a global perspective. Intersentia, Antwerpen
Siehr K (1973) Wechselwirkungen zwischen Kollisionsrecht und Sachrecht. RabelsZ 37:466–484
Siehr K (2003) Family unions in private international law. NILR 50:419–435
Tenreiro M, Ekström M (2003) Unification of private international law in family law matters within the European Union. In: Boele-Woelki K (ed) Perspectives for the unification and harmonisation of family law in Europe. Intersentia, Antwerpen, pp 185–193
Thue HJ (2007) European private international law as the European solution, and the European economic area (EEA/EWR) problem. In: Reichelt G (ed) Europäisches Gemeinschaftsrecht und IPR. Ein Beitrag zur Kodifikation der Allgemeinen Grundsätze des Europäischen Kollisionsrechtes. Manzsche, Vienna

Von Bar C (2001) Le groupe d'études sur un Code civil européen. Revue international de droit comparé 53:127–139

Van Erp S (2002) European private international law as a transition stage? Electronic Journal of Comparative Law. Available at: www.ejcl.org/61/editor61.html

Von Hoffmann B (1998) European private international law. Ars Aequi Libri, Nijmegen

Waaldijk C (ed) (2005) More or less together: levels of legal consequences of marriage, cohabitation and registered partnerships for different-sex and same-sex partners. A comparative study of nine European countries, Paris: INED. Available at: www.ined.fr/fichier/t_publication/1034/publi_pdf1_document_de_travail_125.pdf

Chapter 2
The Dutch Choice of Law Rules on Divorce

2.1 Introduction

Despite the existence of the fundamental right to marry (Article 12 ECHR), there is no fundamental right to divorce. The European Court of Human Rights has held that such a right to divorce cannot be derived from the fundamental right to marry.[1] Therefore, each country can determine autonomously whether a marriage can be dissolved, and if so on what grounds.

Currently there are only a few legal systems in the world in which the concept of divorce is unknown.[2] In the vast majority of states the opportunity to dissolve a marriage is provided for. However, significant differences exist between the states' divorce laws concerning the grounds for divorce.

Arising from the growing number of cross-border relationships and the large number of foreigners residing in the Netherlands, Dutch courts are often faced with international divorce cases.

The term 'international divorce' refers to the situation in which the separating spouses are of different nationalities, live in different countries or live in a country of which they are not nationals.[3] The dissolution of a marriage of two foreigners, of a Dutch and a foreign party and of a Dutch party and a party with a double nationality falls within the scope of this definition. Moreover, the case of a Dutch couple residing abroad meets the criteria of this definition. If a Dutch court is faced with an international divorce, which law should it apply?

---

[1] ECtHR 18 December 1986, *Johnston and Others* v. *Ireland*, Application No. 9697/82.

[2] E.g. Malta, the Philippines and Vatican City.

[3] Definition of the European Commission; see Impact Assessment on Divorce, p. 4.

N.A. Baarsma, *The Europeanisation of International Family Law*,
DOI: 10.1007/978-90-6704-743-2_2,

The 1902 Hague Convention on Divorce was the first international instrument in this field.[4] However, this Convention is no longer in force.[5]

Currently there is no multilateral convention in force in the field of the applicable law to divorce. In the absence of an international convention in this field, each state can provide for its own rules on the law applicable to divorce.

This chapter concentrates on the current Dutch choice of law rules on the dissolution of a marriage. After a discussion on the foundation of the rules and the underlying rationale behind them (Section 2.2), the structure of the Dutch choice of law rules and their content will be considered at length (Sections 2.3–2.5). The chapter ends with a discussion of the bottlenecks of the current regulation and with a view to its amendment as it is proposed in the Dutch Proposal on Private International Law of September 2009 (Section 2.6). The proposed choice of law rules on divorce differ greatly from the current ones. In order to properly value the changes that are proposed, the current situation will firstly be set forth.

2.2 The Dutch Choice of Law Act on Divorce

2.2.1 Development of the Choice of Law on Divorce

For many years the application of foreign law to divorce in the Netherlands was taboo: divorce related to 'public policy and good morals'. Therefore, a Dutch court could only apply Dutch law to divorce.[6] In the 1970s, as a result of increasing opposition from lower courts and legal doctrine,[7] the Hoge Raad allowed for the application of foreign law to divorce. This new trend was inspired by the

[4] The Hague Convention of 12 June 1902 relating to the Settlement of the Conflict of Laws and Jurisdictions as regards to Divorce and Separation. According to this Convention the divorce could only be granted if the national law of the spouses and the law of the country where the divorce was petitioned would allow for divorce.

[5] The following countries were party to the 1902 Hague Divorce Convention: Belgium, France, Germany, Hungary, Italy, Luxembourg, the Netherlands, Poland, Portugal, Romania, Sweden, and Switzerland.

[6] HR 13 December 1907, *Boon* v. *Schmidt*, *W.* 8636. Moreover, the application of Dutch law to divorces of Dutch spouses was also based on Article 6 of the General Provisions Act (*Wet houdende algemeene bepalingen der wetgeving van het Koninkrijk*, Act of 15 May 1829, *Stcrt.* 1829, No. 28). This provision stipulates that the law concerning the rights, status and compentence of persons are binding on the Dutch, even when they are residing abroad. The Dutch courts also had to apply Dutch law to the divorce of a Dutch couple residing abroad, which had become completely estranged from the Dutch society. See further on this issue Wendels 1983, pp. 46–47.

[7] See Dubbink 1956, pp. 199–208, pointing out the changing attitude of lower courts towards the exclusive application of Dutch law. See also Wendels 1983, p. 47 ff.

Rivière-decision of the French *Cour de Cassation*, in which it provided for a three-folded cascade rule. According to this rule an international divorce is in principle governed by the law of the country of the parties' common nationality; in the absence of a common nationality, by the law of the parties' common place of residence; and in the absence of a common place of residence, by the *lex fori*.[8]

Initially, the Hoge Raad rather hesitatingly stated that the application of any other law than Dutch law was 'not excluded' and that the application of the common national law was 'possible'.[9] Subsequently, in 1977 the Hoge Raad adopted the *Rivière*-system.[10]

Article 1 of the Dutch Choice of Law Act on Divorce is the conclusion of this jurisprudential development. This Act is in force as of 10 April 1981.[11] The realisation of the CLAD was connected with the ratification of the Luxembourg Convention on the recognition of decisions concerning marriage and the Hague Convention on the recognition of divorce and legal separation.[12] The CLAD does not only provide choice of law rules, but also rules on the recognition of foreign decisions on divorces and of repudiation (Articles 2 and 3).

Article 1 of the Choice of Law Act on Divorce stipulates:

1. Whether dissolution of a marriage or judicial separation may be petitioned or demanded, and if so on what grounds, is determined:
   a. when the parties have a common national law, by that law;
   b. when there is no common national law, by the law of the country in which the parties have their habitual residence;
   c. when the parties have no common national law, and no habitual residence in the same country, by Dutch law.
2. For the purposes of the preceding paragraph, the parties shall be considered to have no common national law, if one of them manifestly lacks a real societal connection with the country of the common nationality. In that case the common national law shall nevertheless be applied if a choice for that law was made jointly by the parties or such a choice remains uncontested by one of the parties.
3. If a party possesses the nationality of more than one country, his or her national law shall be understood to be the law of that country of which he or she possesses the nationality and with which, taking into account all the circumstances, he or she has the closest connections.

---

[8] Cour de Cassation 17 April 1953, *RCDIP* 1953, p. 412.

[9] See HR 23 February 1973, *NJ* 1973, 366; and HR 28 November 1975, *NJ* 1976, 547.

[10] HR 27 May 1977, *NJ* 1977, 600. See also HR 4 May 1979, *NJ* 1979, 547. In 1979 the Hoge Raad introduced the 'authenticity test' in order to determine the existence of a real societal connection, see HR 9 February 1979, *NJ* 1979, 546. See further on the authenticity test *infra* Sect. 2.4.2.1.

[11] Act of 25 March 1981, *Stb.* 1981, No. 166, containing a regulation of the choice of law rules on the dissolution of the marriage and on legal separation and the recognition thereof, *Wet conflictenrecht echtscheiding*. Hereinafter abbreviated to 'CLAD'.

[12] Convention of 8 September 1967 on the Recognition of Decisions relating to the Marriage Bond, *Trb.* 1979, 130 ('Luxembourg Convention') and the Convention of 1 June 1970 on the Recognition of Divorces and Legal Separations, *Trb.* 1979, 131 ('Hague Convention').

4. Notwithstanding the preceding paragraphs, Dutch law shall be applied if the parties jointly chose such a law or such choice by one of the parties remains uncontested.[13]

Although placed in the final section of Article 1 CLAD, its principal rule is the *professio iuris* for Dutch law. Pursuant to Article 1(4), the spouses can choose for the application of Dutch law, even if they do not possess the Dutch nationality.

If the spouses have not made a *professio iuris*, there are various options. The connecting factors are hierarchical, meaning that if the court is unable to apply the first it will turn to the next. If the spouses have a common nationality, their common national law is applied. If, however, one of the spouses lacks any actual social ties to the country of common nationality, e.g. because he or she has already lived and worked abroad for a number of years, the common national law is not applied, as it does not reflect a close connection. In such a case, the parties are considered to have no common national law on the basis of Article 1(2) CLAD. If the spouses do not have a common nationality, the law of their common habitual residence is applied. If the spouses do not have a common nationality, and have no common habitual residence either, the divorce is governed by Dutch law.

2.2.2 Scope of Application: Same-Sex Marriages

Since 1 April 2001, Dutch law opened up the institution of civil marriage to same-sex couples: marriage is no longer restricted to persons of a different sex.[14] As the Choice of Law Act on Divorce had already entered into force in 1981, the dissolution of same-sex marriages has not been taken into consideration while drawing up the rules concerning the applicable law to divorce. Therefore, the question arises whether the term 'marriage' in the sense of Article 1 CLAD also includes the marriage of two persons of the same sex.

The Dutch Standing Committee on Private International Law has answered this question affirmatively. The Committee underlines that Dutch substantive law recognises only one type of marriage: that between two adult partners of which the relative sex is irrelevant. It would be contrary to the general principle that characterisation takes place according to the legal concepts of the law of the forum, if the new Dutch legal concept of marriage would be excluded from the CLAD, or if a distinction would be made within the CLAD between same-sex couples and couples of a different sex. Such treatment would probably also violate Article 1 of the Dutch Constitution and possibly Articles 8, 12 and 14 ECHR and Article 26 ICCPR.[15]

---

[13] Translation by Sumner and Warendorf 2003, p. 232.

[14] Act on the Opening of Marriage to same-sex couples of 21 December 2000, *Stb.* 2001, No. 9. Article 1:30 BW determines that two persons of a different or of the same sex can enter into a marriage.

[15] Staatscommissie 2001, para 8, p. 15.

In other words, a marriage between two persons of the same sex is characterised as a marriage in the sense of the CLAD. According to the Standing Committee on Private International Law Article 1 CLAD therefore applies likewise to the designation of the applicable law to the dissolution of same-sex marriages.

If Article 1 CLAD designates a foreign legal system as applicable, the application of this law to the dissolution of a same-sex marriage might encounter difficulties if this law does not know the same-sex marriage. The Standing Committee observes that, under certain circumstances, the court can set aside the foreign law and apply Dutch law either by means of the public policy exception (violation of the principle of equality),[16] or by considering the foreign law to be 'technically inapplicable' to the dissolution of same-sex marriages.[17]

It should be noted that the current situation, i.e. the absence of clear rules with respect to the dissolution of a same-sex marriage, is undesirable. The legislature is namely by no means bound to the advice of the Standing Committee and is fully free to draw up different rules on the private international law aspects of the dissolution of same-sex marriages. In all probability the legislature will follow the advice of the Standing Committee. The fact that according to Dutch substantive law only one type of marriage is recognised, i.e. the marriage open to couples regardless of their sex, seems to make any other position untenable. The legislature should interfere as soon as possible, as the absence of clear private international rules in this field leads to legal uncertainty for same-sex spouses.[18] Furthermore, the absence of such rules also leads to legal inequality for same-sex spouses *vis-à-vis* different-sex spouses, who can rely on Article 1 of the CLAD for the determination of the law applicable to divorce.

2.2.3 *Foundation of the CLAD:* Favor Divortii

The choice of law rules on divorce is a reasonably accurate reflection of the Dutch dominant position on the substantive divorce law. It is not very difficult for spouses to obtain a divorce, even against the wish of the other party.[19] If one of the spouses petitions for divorce, the sole Dutch ground for divorce of

---

[16] *Infra* Sect. 2.5.

[17] Staatscommissie 2001, para 8, p. 15: 'Mocht het buitenlands recht geslachtsgebonden, differentiërende bepalingen kennen zoals in het op de Islam georiënteerde recht doorgaans het geval zal zijn, kan met een beroep op strijd met het gelijkheidsbeginsel, dat in Nederland van openbare orde wordt beschouwd, dit buitenlandse recht opzij gezet worden en vervangen worden door het Nederlandse recht. Ook bestaat de mogelijkheid om zo'n buitenlands recht als technisch niet toepasbaar te beschouwen op huwelijken van partners van hetzelfde geslacht, en om deze reden uit te wijken naar het recht van de rechter.'

[18] Cf., the position of registered partners between 1 January 1998 and 1 January 2005 *infra* Sect. 3.3.2.

[19] See Struycken 1994, p. 102.

irretrievable breakdown of the marriage (Article 1:151 BW) is virtually automatically complied with.[20]

Dutch substantive divorce law is based on the so-called principle of *favor divortii*, i.e. the idea that the law should not preclude the wish of (at least one of) the parties to obtain a divorce.[21] This latter principle operates as the point of departure for the designation of the applicable law on divorce and has affected the construction of the choice of law rules of the CLAD. Three indications for this assumption can be found in the parliamentary proceedings: the possibility to choose Dutch law as the applicable law according to Article 1(4) CLAD,[22] the 'liberalisation' of the legislation in the field of divorce in the Netherlands and elsewhere,[23] and, finally, the lenient regulation on the recognition of foreign decisions on divorce as laid down in Articles 2 and 3 CLAD.[24]

The foundation of the CLAD on the *favor divortii* principle implies that the choice of law rule is not impartial to the substantive outcome of the dispute; on the contrary, it aims to favour the possibility to obtain a divorce in international cases.[25] Foreign law that does not permit divorce is contrary to the Dutch view of the law.

The most common device to facilitate a divorce and adhere to the *favor divortii* principle is to designate the *lex fori* as the sole or subsidiary applicable law or to allow a wide degree of party autonomy.[26] Both these instruments have to a certain extent been incorporated in the Dutch system.[27]

In the following it will be shown that the *favor divortii* principle is of great importance to the interpretation of Article 1 CLAD. If this provision leaves room for interpretation, it should be interpreted in such a way that it will designate a legal system that facilitates rather than obstructs the desired divorce.[28]

---

[20] See HR 6 December 1996, *NJ* 1997, 189, in which the Hoge Raad held that the fact that one of the spouses desires a divorce is a very serious indication that the marriage in question has broken down irretrievably.

[21] See Werkgroep IPR NVvR 1993, p. 137; Boele-Woelki 1994, pp. 173–174; Vlas 1996, p. 200; and Mostermans 2006, p. 41.

[22] See Memorandum of Amendment (NvW) *Kamerstukken II* 1980–1981, 16 004, No. 8, pp. 1–2. See *infra* Sect. 2.3.2.

[23] See Explanatory Memorandum (MvT), *Kamerstukken II* 1979–1980, 16 004, No. 3–4, pp. 1–2.

[24] See Werkgroep IPR NVvR 1993, p. 137.

[25] Cf., Curry-Sumner 2005, p. 446. See further also Struycken 1994, p. 102; and Van den Eeckhout 2004, p. 57.

[26] See Curry-Sumner 2005, p. 447, who refers to Siehr 1982, p. 50. See also Struycken 1994, p. 102. The *favor divortii* principle is furthermore supported if one examines the jurisdictional grounds under the Brussels II*bis*-Regulation: De Boer 1996; Boele-Woelki et al. 1998, pp. 218–220 and 223; Van den Eeckhout 2004, p. 58.

[27] *Infra* Sect. 2.3 for the party autonomy and Sect. 2.4.4 for the application of the *lex fori*.

[28] See Mostermans 2006, p. 43.

However, one must be careful not to overstretch the principle of *favor divortii*: it is not meant as a licence to allow any divorce.[29]

2.3 The Spouses' Choice as to the Applicable Law

2.3.1 General: Limited Choice

Parties requesting the dissolution of their marriage are granted the possibility to choose the applicable law. However, the parties are restricted in their choice by the requirement that the law chosen must correspond either to the *lex fori* (i.e. Dutch law) or to the law of their common nationality.[30]

Not all academics are convinced of this limitation of the possibility to choose the applicable law.[31] Van Maas de Bie wonders why couples of different nationalities do not have the opportunity to select the national law of either of the spouses.[32] Boele-Woelki also considers the possibility for the spouses to choose the application of the law of their common habitual residence as a valid choice.[33] Mostermans even goes another step further:

> what objection could there be against an extension of the parties' choice as to the law applicable to their divorce so as to include the law of the nationality of either spouse, and that of either spouse's former or future place of residence?[34]

The Dutch Standing Committee on Private International Law has considered these possibilities, but has reached the conclusion that the extension of the degree of party autonomy would produce a too complicated choice of law rule. Moreover, the Standing Committee does not notice any need in practice for such an extension of the legal systems out of which parties can choose.[35]

The limited degree of party autonomy in the field of divorce is rightly questioned. As becomes clear from the parliamentary proceedings, the goal of the CLAD is to facilitate the desired divorce.[36] Why, then, is there any limitation of

---

[29] See also Struycken 1994, p. 102 ff, who is a supporter of the *favor matrimonii*.

[30] Article 1(2), last sentence and 1(4) CLAD. The Hoge Raad has confirmed that parties can only select one of these two legal systems; see HR 21 December 2001, *NJ* 2002, 282.

[31] See generally Pontier 1997, pp. 300–302.

[32] Van Maas de Bie 1993, p. 664; and Van Maas de Bie 2002, p. 248 and p. 261.

[33] Boele-Woelki 1994, p. 181.

[34] Mostermans 1990, p. 138.

[35] Staatscommissie 1995, p. 5. However, it is not clear on which information the latter statement of the Standing Committee is based. See further *infra* Sect. 2.6 for a similar position of the Dutch legislator.

[36] See further *supra* Sect. 2.2.3.

the possible laws out of which the parties can choose? Why doesn't Article 1 CLAD grant the spouses the opportunity to choose any law that provides for divorce? It seems inconsistent with the *favor divortii* principle to restrict spouses in their possibility to choose the law applicable to their divorce in the way Article 1 CLAD does.

However, it is perfectly clear that there should be a connection between (one of) the spouses and the law to be applied to their divorce. Dutch private international law is theoretically based on the principle that the law applied should be the one that seems to be — due to its strong connections to the case — the most appropriate.[37] Party autonomy can deviate from this principle of closest connection insofar as that it may grant parties the possibility to choose the application of a certain law that might only be connected indirectly to their legal relationship. However, in family law matters it is common that parties are provided with a limited possibility to choose the applicable law: they can only choose the law with which they have a (close) connection based on alternative connecting factors such as nationality, common habitual residence and the *lex fori*.[38] This limitation of the party autonomy is usually intended to protect the private interests of the persons concerned or of those faced with the *professio iuris*.[39]

The possibilities that have been proposed by Boele-Woelki and Van Maas de Bie in order to extend the degree of the party autonomy in the field of international divorce fulfil the abovementioned condition. Both the nationality of either spouse and their common habitual residence provide for the necessary close connection between the spouses and the law to be applied to their divorce. Granting the parties the possibility of such an extended — yet still not unlimited — *professio iuris* even improves the probability that the law with which they are most closely connected is applied. Furthermore, the *favor divortii* principle would also benefit from such an extension: the spouses have more opportunities to influence the law applicable to their divorce and they are likely to choose the law most favourable to divorce in their case.

The abovementioned argument of the Dutch Standing Committee that an extension of the degree of party autonomy in the field of international divorce would produce a too complicated choice of law rule can be questioned: what exactly complicates the extension of the number of laws out of which parties can choose from two to four? In addition, a valid *professio iuris* of (one of) the spouses has the effect that the court is relieved of *ex officio* finding and applying any law other than the one chosen. This would produce a less complicated choice of law rule and even serve legal economy.

---

[37] Cf., Strikwerda 2008, pp. 35–36.

[38] Ibid., pp. 42–43.

[39] Cf., Pontier 1997, p. 337.

2.3.2 Choice for the Application of Dutch Law (Lex Fori)

It follows from Article 1(4) CLAD that the spouses, irrespective of their nationality or habitual residence, can opt for Dutch law as the law applicable to their divorce. This choice for Dutch law can be made in all circumstances, which means that the whole choice of law system of Article 1(1) to (3) CLAD can be disregarded. Consequently, the possibility to choose Dutch law as the applicable law to divorce is in fact the principal rule of Article 1 CLAD.[40] The spouses who opt for the application of Dutch law are not required to have any connection to the Netherlands or to Dutch law.[41]

This provision has been added to the regulation of the CLAD in a fairly late stage of the lawmaking process, in order to favour the application of the liberal, 'divorce-friendly' Dutch law:

> De mogelijkheid die de partijen in het vierde lid van artikel 1 wordt geboden om voor toepassing van het Nederlandse recht te kiezen, staat met name ten dienste aan die echtgenoten wier nationale of domiciliaire wet geen echtscheiding dan wel een beperkter echtscheidingsregeling dan de Nederlandse kent.[42]

Dutch substantive law can thus also apply to the divorce of foreign spouses. The only difference in comparison with Dutch spouses is that foreign spouses risk the arising of a so-called 'limping marriage'. This is the case if the Dutch decision on divorce is not recognised in their country of origin. The legislator's underlying consideration, however, is that this risk is outweighed by the undesirability of artificially upholding marriages that have in fact broken down.[43] Moreover, the spouses are obviously willing to take this risk.[44] Therefore, the goal of this provision is to favour divorce: the *favor divortii*.[45]

Same-sex couples can benefit from the possibility of Article 1(4) CLAD to choose Dutch law as the law applicable to their divorce. In such a case the risk of a limping legal relationship is less present; it is even more probable that the divorce would remedy an existing limping marriage.[46]

---

[40] See Van Rooij 1981, p. 424, who refers to the choice of law for Dutch law as the hidden principal rule of Article 1 CLAD. See also Strikwerda 2008, p. 97; and Ten Wolde 2009, p. 219.

[41] Cf., the conclusion of Advocate General Strikwerda at HR 4 June 1999, *NJ* 1999, 535 and HR 12 March 2004, *NIPR* 2004, 97.

[42] Memorandum of Amendment (NvW) *Kamerstukken II* 1980–1981, 16 004, No. 8, p. 2.

[43] Ibid.

[44] See equally Van Rooij and Polak 1987, pp. 216–217.

[45] See also Van Rooij 1981, p. 423; and Vonken 1981, p. 53.

[46] This presupposes that the same-sex marriage concerned has not been or cannot be recognised in the country of origin of (one of) the spouses.

2.3.3 *Choice for the Application of the Common National (Foreign) Law of the Spouses*

On the basis of Article 1(2), second sentence CLAD parties can opt for the application of foreign law; this choice is limited to the parties' common national law.[47] The meaning of this *professio iuris* is to give spouses having a common nationality the opportunity to block the application of the 'authenticity test' of Article 1(2), first sentence CLAD. If the parties have chosen the law of their common nationality, it is irrelevant under Dutch law that they have no actual societal connections with the country of their nationality, unlike the cases where the common national law is applied by operation of law.[48] If the spouses have chosen the law of their common nationality, the court has to apply this law even if the parties have no real societal connection with this country. The option to choose the application of the common national law thereby guarantees a predictable choice of law result.

Furthermore, a choice by the parties in favour of the law of the common nationality can prevent limping legal relationships. The option to choose the law of the common nationality provides the parties namely with the advantage that the application of their common national law to the divorce will increase the chance — in case of a possible return to the country of origin by (one of) the spouses — that the decision on divorce will be recognised in their country of origin.[49] In the framework of the recognition of a decision on divorce, it sometimes proves to be relevant to the authorities of the spouses' country of origin that the Dutch court has applied the law of this country to the divorce.[50]

2.3.4 *Formal Requirements of the* Professio Iuris

2.3.4.1 Choice Made Jointly or Remained Uncontested

The *professio iuris* is not bound by a certain procedure. It follows from Article 1(2) and (4) CLAD that the *professio iuris* on the law applicable to divorce must be made either jointly or by one party without being contested by the other.

If the choice has been made jointly there is — in principle — no doubt concerning the intention of the parties: both spouses desire the application of the chosen law.

---

47 See *inter alia* Rb.'s-Gravenhage 2 October 1990, *NIPR* 1991, 79; Rb.'s-Gravenhage 27 January 1992, *NIPR* 1992, 185; Rb.'s-Gravenhage 14 July 1992, *NIPR* 1992, 346; Hof Amsterdam 29 September 1994, *NIPR* 1995, 203; Rb.'s-Gravenhage 27 November 1996, *NIPR* 1997, 83; Rb.'s-Gravenhage 19 June 2002, *NIPR* 2002, 242; and Hof 's-Hertogenbosch 9 December 2004, *NIPR* 2005, 220.

48 See for the interpretation of the term 'societal connections' *infra* Sect. 2.4.2.1.

49 See Explanatory Memorandum (MvT), *Kamerstukken II* 1979–1980, 16 004, No. 3–4, p. 15.

50 See Hof Amsterdam 11 April 1996, *NIPR* 1997, 189.

Both the wording of Article 1(2), second sentence and Article 1(4) CLAD and the parliamentary history show that also a unilateral, but uncontested choice for the application of the common national law of the spouses or of Dutch law is valid. This condition 'uncontested' is not only fulfilled in case of reference by the defendant, but also in case of default of appearance:

> Ook in geval van referte lijkt er weinig tegen, het onweersproken blijven van een in de dagvaarding opgenomen rechtskeuze voor het Nederlandse recht, in deze zin op te vatten dat beide partijen er zich mee kunnen verenigen dat Nederlands recht op de vordering wordt toegepast. Het is echter de vraag, of eenzelfde overweging in verstekzaken mag worden aanvaard. Het niet verschijnen van de gedaagde behoeft niet te betekenen dat hij instemt met de toepassing van het Nederlandse recht, zo de dagvaarding een optie voor het Nederlandse recht bevat.
>
> [...] dat er aanleiding is, ook in verstekzaken een optie met betrekking tot toepassing van Nederlands recht, opgenomen in de dagvaarding, te honoreren.[51]

2.3.4.2 Implied Choice of the Spouses as to the Applicable Law?

In international divorce proceedings the dissolution of the marriage is often petitioned on the ground of 'irretrievable breakdown of the marriage' (Article 1:151 BW) and no specific considerations as to the applicable law are set.[52] The question that arises is whether the requesting party has intended an implied choice for the application of Dutch law according to Article 1(4) CLAD by setting this ground for divorce according to Dutch law. This question is particularly pressing if the parties have a common (foreign) nationality and the lack of a real societal connection of one of the parties with their country of origin has not been raised during the divorce proceedings; the court should in this case, strictly speaking, apply the common national law of the parties according to Article 1(1)(a) CLAD. If, however, the foreign law does not know this ground for divorce, the requesting party should be declared inadmissible, unless the court offers the parties the opportunity to comment on the applicable law. During the first few years after the entry into force of the CLAD, some Dutch courts have, in order to prevent such an unsatisfactory result, held Dutch law applicable on the basis of an implied choice of law whenever parties have referred to 'irretrievable breakdown of the marriage' as ground for divorce.[53]

---

51 Memorandum of Reply (MvA), *Kamerstukken II* 1980–1981, 16 004, No. 7, p. 3. In case law this position is followed: Hof 's-Gravenhage 10 March 2000, *NIPR* 2000, 173; and Rb. Alkmaar 7 July 2005, *NIPR* 2005, 314. See Vonken (Groene Serie Personen- en familierecht) Article 1 CLAD, n. 3.2 for a list of case law dating from before 2000.

52 See Vonken (Groene Serie Personen- en familierecht) Article 1 CLAD, n. 3.4.

53 See Rb.'s-Gravenhage 8 November 1983, *NIPR* 1985, 330; Rb. Amsterdam 23 May 1984, *NIPR* 1985, 110; Hof Arnhem 5 March 1985, *NIPR* 1986, 265; and Rb. Amsterdam 30 December 1987, to know from Hof Amsterdam 15 August 1988, *NIPR* 1988, 503.

However, Vonken has pointed out that such an implied choice as to the applicable law raises three – theoretical – objections.[54] Firstly, the court should not assume a *professio iuris* in cases in which parties did not intend it, as it presumes that parties have been aware of the possibility to choose the law applicable to their divorce. The fact that parties do not make any mention regarding the applicable law cannot be seised too fast in order to assume an implied choice for the application of Dutch law.[55] Furthermore, it is questionable whether parties intend to refer univocally to Dutch law by the single use of the ground 'irretrievable breakdown of the marriage'. This same ground can also be found in other legal systems.[56] Finally, it is not in the least certain that parties have been aware of the international character of their divorce. The possibility exists that one of the parties has not realised the possible implications of private international law and objects, in retrospect, to the application of Dutch law, for example for fear that a decision on divorce according to Dutch law will not be recognised in the country of origin of the parties.[57]

The Report of the Working Group on Private International Law of the Netherlands Association for the Administration of Justice seems to have put an end to the insecurity in this respect.[58] Nowadays no implied *professio iuris* for Dutch law can be derived from the single (uncontested) proposition that the marriage has irretrievably broken down. This implies that a *professio iuris* according to Article 1(4) CLAD requires an explicit reference to Dutch law.[59] Such an explicit reference includes a mention to Article 1:151 BW or the sole observation that Dutch law applies. If the defendant does not object, both parties seemingly desire the application of Dutch law.[60]

One should, however, distinguish the case in which the requesting party urges a foreign ground for divorce without explicitly referring to a *professio iuris* for the common national law pursuant to Article 1(2) CLAD. If the specified ground for divorce is part of the national divorce law of the parties, it goes without saying that the petitioner meant that the Dutch court should apply the foreign national law to the divorce. In such a case there is no need to fear that the requesting party has not been aware of possible implications of private international law. The respondent

---

[54] Vonken (Groene Serie Personen- en familierecht) Article 1 CLAD, n. 3.4.

[55] Cf., Mostermans 1996, p. 120.

[56] E.g. Belgium: Article 232 BW; Germany: Article 1565 BGB; UK: Sec. 1(1) Matrimonial Causes Act 1973; Austria: Article 49 Ehegesetz; Switzerland: Article 1422 ZGB; Turkey: Article 166 Turkish Civil Code.

[57] See Mostermans 1992, p. 159; Van Maas de Bie 2002, pp. 249–251; and Mostermans 2006, p. 44.

[58] Werkgroep IPR NVvR 1993, pp. 145 and 147–148.

[59] See Memorandum of Reply (MvA), *Kamerstukken II* 1980–1981, 16 004, No. 7, p. 4 ff.

[60] See Hof Amsterdam 15 February 1993, *NIPR* 1993, 403; Rb.'s-Gravenhage 29 November 1995, *NIPR* 1996, 197; and Hof 's-Gravenhage 6 March 1998, *NIPR* 1998, 273.

may also be expected to realise that the petition has been based on the common national law.[61]

2.3.4.3 Time of Choice

The choice for the application of Dutch law or of the common national law of the spouses has to be made during the divorce proceedings at the Dutch court. A choice of the spouses as to the law applicable to divorce made in a marriage contract has no legal consequences.[62]

In defended divorce proceedings a joint choice of law can be made not only at the beginning of the proceedings, but also at a later time during the proceedings, for example during the court session. Moreover, the *professio iuris* can still be lawfully agreed upon in appeal.[63]

As already mentioned above, a *professio iuris*, whether for Dutch law or for the common national law of the spouses, can also be honoured in case of default of appearance; such a choice is assumed to have remained uncontested as meant in Article 1(2) and (4) CLAD.[64] However, in case of default of appearance the *professio iuris* must in principle be made in the initiatory petition. If the requesting party makes a *professio iuris* after filing the petition, the respondent is not informed and cannot contest the choice.[65] Therefore, such a choice is not considered to be valid.

Once a party has opted for a certain legal system in accordance with Article 1(2) or (4) CLAD and the other party has followed this choice, the petitioner can only reconsider this choice later during the proceedings, provided that it would not unreasonably complicate the procedural position of the defendant.[66]

---

[61] Cf., Mostermans 1992, p. 158; Werkgroep IPR NVvR 1993, p. 148.

[62] See Memorandum of Reply (MvA), *Kamerstukken II* 1980–1981, 16 004, No. 7, pp. 3–4. Cf., HR 26 January 1996, *NIPR* 1996, 179; HR 21 December 2001, *NIPR* 2002, 77; and Hof 's-Hertogenbosch 9 December 2004, *NIPR* 2005, 220.

[63] *Professio iuris* in appeal: Memorandum of Amendment (NvW) *Kamerstukken II* 1980–1981, 16 004, No. 8, p. 2. See also Hof Amsterdam 5 October 1992, *NIPR* 1993, 76; Hof Amsterdam 21 February 2002, *NIPR* 2004, 207; and Hof Amsterdam 11 August 2005, *NIPR* 2006, 10.

[64] See Memorandum of Reply (MvA), *Kamerstukken II* 1980–1981, 16 004, No. 7, p. 3.

[65] See also Wendels 1983, pp. 70–71; Mostermans 2006, p. 43; Vonken (Groene Serie Personen- en familierecht) Article 1 CLAD, n. 3.3. Cf., Rb.'s-Gravenhage 17 September 1991, *NIPR* 1991, 356.

[66] See Hof 's-Gravenhage 28 July 1995, *NIPR* 1996, 58 and Rb.'s-Gravenhage 7 April 2000, *NIPR* 2000, 182. See for the case that a party revokes a former *professio iuris* with the consent of the other party: Hof Amsterdam 14 January 1999, *NIPR* 2000, 260; Hof 's-Hertogenbosch 26 January 2000, *NIPR* 2000, 97. See also HR 4 June 1999, *NJ* 1999, 535, in which the Hoge Raad considered that the legal remedy of appeal has not been created as opportunity to annul a divorce of a party whose petition to divorce has been granted in first instance, because the latter party gives — on further consideration — preference to the application of another law.

2.4 The Law Applicable to Divorce in the Absence of a *Professio Iuris*

Should the parties have made no *professio iuris* as explained above, the law applicable to their divorce is determined on the basis of the cascade rule of Article 1(1) to (3) CLAD.

The regulation of Article 1(1) to (3) CLAD entails the designation of the common national law of the spouses as the applicable law if they have a common nationality. However, as will be shown below, this provision is subject to some exceptions. If the spouses do not have a common nationality, the law of the country in which they have their common habitual residence is applied. If the spouses do not have a common nationality and have no shared habitual residence, Dutch law is applied.

The consequence of this system is that, if the common national law of the spouses does not provide for divorce, the Dutch court cannot pronounce the divorce. However, if parties do not possess the same nationality, the law of the common habitual residence will be applied and, if this law recognises the institution of divorce, the divorce can be granted, even if the respective national laws of the spouses do not provide for divorce. This consequence may seem surprising and even unfair, but the legislature has determined that it should be accepted in view of the advantage of the simplicity of the system.[67] Since Article 1(4) CLAD offers the spouses the opportunity to choose the application of Dutch law, the spouses always have the possibility to circumvent the application of their common national law. Therefore, the choice of law system provides for an escape clause.

The aim of the choice of law is to indicate in an international case — by means of one or more connecting factors — which legal system is to govern a particular question, by allocating it to one system or another. The choice of law rule should designate, in principle, the law of the country which is the most closely connected to the international relationship.[68] With regard to legal relationships in the field of family law, the nationality and the habitual residence of the persons involved are deemed to be the most suitable connecting factors as they refer to the personal law of the parties.[69]

2.4.1 Nationality or Domicile?

Traditionally the principle of nationality has been the leading principle in Dutch international family law.[70] Article 6 of the General Provisions Act stipulates:

67 Explanatory Memorandum (MvT), *Kamerstukken II* 1979–1980, 16 004, No. 3–4, p. 11.

68 Cf., Strikwerda 2008, p. 36.

69 Cf., Curry-Sumner 2005, p. 446.

70 See Strikwerda 2008, p. 72; and Ten Wolde 2009, p. 113.

> The laws concerning the rights, status and competence of persons are binding on the Dutch, even when they are residing abroad.[71]

Strictly speaking this provision, which is a product of the — at that time prevailing — theory of the statutists, is a unilateral choice of law rule and solely concerns Dutchmen and Dutch legislation. The General Provisions Act did not provide for the converse situation of foreigners residing in the Netherlands, but the Dutch courts held that in all matters of family law they too were governed by their national law. The Dutch courts have thereby extended the provision of Article 6 of the General Provisions Act — based on the nationality principle — to a multilateral choice of law rule.[72]

The principle of nationality, on which Article 6 of the General Provisions Act is based, assumes that an individual's national law best resolves questions concerning family relations and all matters linked — either directly or indirectly — to the individual's personal status.[73] One of the meanings of this principle, which is known in several legal systems, holds that the national law best responds to the expectations of a person who relies on this law in planning his or her family relations, even if this person lives in another country. In terms of this approach nationality is a constitutive element of one's identity.[74]

However, in the course of time the importance of the nationality principle has weakened. Nationality does not always seem to achieve the main criterion a connecting factor has to fulfil, i.e. the establishment of a 'social connection of an individual with a legal system'.[75] The introduction of both the principle of *favor* (e.g. as seen already for the CLAD the principle of *favor divortii*) and party autonomy into Dutch international family law have also played an important role in the weakened position of the nationality principle.[76]

Another way of solving issues of choice of law is to refer an international case to the parties' place of residence rather than to their nationality. Domicile as a connecting factor might better reflect the societal connection of a person with a certain legal system. In Dutch international family law this so-called principle of domicile has gained an ever stronger position.[77]

The notion of habitual residence has emerged as representing a compromise between domicile and nationality, or at least as a more acceptable connecting factor than domicile to be used as an alternative to nationality.

---

[71] *Wet houdende algemeene bepalingen der wetgeving van het Koninkrijk*, Act of 15 May 1829, *Stcrt.* 1829, No. 28.

[72] Cf., Kosters and Dubbink 1962, pp. 573–574; Strikwerda 2008, p. 72; and Ten Wolde 2009, p. 113.

[73] See Kosters and Dubbink 1962, pp. 580–581.

[74] Cf., Foblets 1997, p. 27.

[75] See Vischer 1999, p. 7; and Henrich 2001, p. 437.

[76] See Strikwerda 2008, p. 73.

[77] See Strikwerda 2008, pp. 80–81; Ten Wolde 2009, p. 113.

The three-part system of the choice of law rule of the CLAD gives certain priority to the nationality principle, but the principle of residence has obtained an important supplementary role joined to it.[78]

The introduction of the *professio iuris* in the field of divorce has made the classical controversy on the principles of nationality and domicile less important. The fact that nationality is the primary connecting factor is nothing more than an 'optical illusion'. Parties can rule out this effect by choosing Dutch law as the applicable law according to Article 1(4) CLAD.[79]

2.4.2 Common National Law of the Spouses

The law of the parties' common nationality is applied should the parties have made no *professio iuris* as explained above. The term common national law has to be taken literally: both parties should possess the same nationality.[80]

In determining whether the parties possess a common nationality, the parties' nationality is subject to an authenticity test (*realiteitstoets*, Section 2.4.2.1),[81] or an effectivity test (*effectiviteitstoets*, Section 2.4.2.2).[82]

Dutch courts regularly apply the common national law of the spouses, without (explicitly) verifying whether their nationality still has any practical significance.[83]

---

[78] See Explanatory Memorandum (MvT), *Kamerstukken II* 1979–1980, 16 004, No. 3–4, p. 9. See also Staatscommissie 1967, in: Frohn and Hennis 1995, p. 113: the rigid application of the principle of nationality does not lead to a solution if the spouses have different nationalities. Therefore, this principle should be abandoned in order to find a solution to such cases.

[79] See also Van Rooij 1981, p. 425.

[80] Explanatory Memorandum (MvT), *Kamerstukken II* 1979–1980, 16 004, No. 3–4, p. 11.

[81] In cases of a single nationality. The term '*authenticity test*' has been derived from Curry-Sumner 2005, p. 450. Other authors have referred to the mentioned test as the '*real social connection test*' (Van Rooij and Polak 1987, p. 179 and Frohn 1996, p. 50) or as the '*realitytest*' (Mostermans 1990, p. 135).

[82] In cases of multiple nationalities.

[83] See *inter alia*: Rb. Haarlem 30 October 2001, *NIPR* 2003, 87 (Turkish law); Rb.'s-Gravenhage 15 April 2002, *NIPR* 2002, 174 (Iranian law); Rb. Haarlem 20 January 2004, *NIPR* 2004, 125 (Turkish law); Rb.'s-Gravenhage 23 February 2004, *NIPR* 2004 (Turkish law); Rb.'s-Gravenhage 12 May 2004, *NIPR* 2004, 234 (Chinese law); Rb. 's-Gravenhage 20 September 2004, *NIPR* 2005, 16 (Spanish law); Rb.'s-Gravenhage 13 October 2004, *NIPR* 2005, 18 (Afghan law); Rb. Alkmaar 26 January 2006, *NIPR* 2006, 106 (Moroccan law); Rb.'s-Gravenhage 5 July 2006, *NIPR* 2006, 282 (Moroccan law); and Rb. Alkmaar 28 September 2006, *NIPR* 2006, 271 (Moroccan law). See Vonken (Groene Serie Personen- en familierecht) Article 1 CLAD, n. 4.2 for a list of case law dating from before 2000.

2.4.2.1 Authenticity Test

In order to determine whether the parties possess a common nationality, their nationality can be subject to an authenticity test (*realiteitstoets*). Article 1(2) CLAD states with respect to this test that no common nationality will be deemed to exist, if either of the parties manifestly lacks a 'real societal connection' with the country of their nationality. This implies that all the circumstances of the case will be taken into account, including the connections that tie a person to another country.[84] In case of a weakened nationality, i.e. a nationality that does not express a real societal connection of (one of) the spouses with the country of their nationality, the parties shall be considered to have no common national law. In such a case the common national law will not be applied, unless (one of) the parties have expressly chosen this law.[85] Parties can thus circumvent the application of the authenticity test by making a *professio iuris* for their common national law.

By means of the word 'manifestly' the Dutch legislator has indicated that the court cannot assume too quickly that a person lacks social ties to his or her country of nationality. The term has been added in order to prevent the principal rule of application of the national law from being undermined too much.[86]

The parliamentary history shows that the authenticity test fulfils two functions.[87] Firstly, it allows for the reference of a certain legal relationship to a legal system to which it is more closely connected. Secondly, the authenticity test may offer the possibility to dissolve the marriage of spouses whose national law would hamper or obstruct the divorce. In view of this latter function of the authenticity test, it can be argued that the connection to the country of common nationality can sooner be considered as considerably weakened if the divorce will be refused pursuant to the common national law than if it will be granted according to this law. Consequently, the authenticity test can also serve as an instrument to realise the *favor divortii*.[88]

The interpretation of the term 'real societal connection' has drawn quite some attention in Dutch literature.[89] The legislator resolutely chose for a criterion with certain indefiniteness; the court needs some margin of appreciation concerning the factors that are to be taken into account in the assessment of whether one of the

---

84 HR 9 June 1995, *NJ* 1995, 617; Hof 's-Gravenhage 18 October 2006, *NIPR* 2007, 5.

85 See *supra* Sect. 2.3.3.

86 Explanatory Memorandum (MvT), *Kamerstukken II* 1979–1980, 16 004, No. 3–4, p. 15. See also Rb.'s-Gravenhage, 26 January 2001, *NIPR* 2001, 100.

87 Explanatory Memorandum (MvT), *Kamerstukken II* 1979–1980, 16 004, No. 3–4, p. 14. See equally Werkgroep IPR NVvR 1993, pp. 142–143; and Vonken (Groene Serie Personen- en familierecht) Article 1 CLAD, n. 5.2.

88 See equally Strikwerda 1986, p. 6.

89 See *inter alia* De Boer 1991, p. 252 ff; Mostermans 2006, p. 48 ff; and Vonken (Groene Serie Personen- en familierecht) Article 1 CLAD, n. 5.5.

parties manifestly lacks a real societal connection with the country of his or her nationality.

In 1995 the Hoge Raad held that all the circumstances of the given case will be taken into account, including the connections that tie a person to another country.[90] In order to assume that either of the parties manifestly lacks a real societal connection to his or her country of origin, it is, however, not necessary that this party no longer has any connection to the country of his or her nationality.

De Boer has made an inventory of the factors that are of relevance to the manifest lack of a real societal connection and distinguished three types of factors:

1. *objective factors*, such as a more or less permanent stay outside the country of origin; a Dutch residence permit or a Dutch license to establish a business; employment in the Netherlands; a Dutch social security or disability insurance; maintenance obligations in the Netherlands; ability to understand, speak or write Dutch; possession of real estate in the Netherlands; being or having been in a Dutch school; membership of a Dutch association; a running request for naturalisation; stay in the country of origin for holiday or for visit to relatives; celebration of a marriage in the country of origin or in the Netherlands.
2. *subjective factors*, such as the intention to stay in the Netherlands or to return to the country of origin in due course; the (non-effectuated) wish to be naturalised to Dutchman; expectations for the future; instinctive connections; having become Dutch; (lack of) respect for the values of the country of origin; preservation of the prevailing religion of the country of origin.
3. *factors that tie others than the person in question* to the Netherlands, especially children who are born in the Netherlands, are in a Dutch school, are integrated in the Netherlands, speak Dutch, etc.; the parents and siblings of the person in question live in the Netherlands or in the country of origin; an extramarital partner of Dutch nationality.[91]

The word 'societal' in the term 'real societal connection' expresses that not primarily the subjective connections to the country of nationality are taken into consideration, but rather the economic and social connections. So the lack of a real societal connection cannot only be determined on the basis of subjective factors, especially not on the basis of statements of expectations of the future or of the extent to which parties feel connected to the country of residence or to the country of origin. Such statements are hard to verify and the other party can hardly challenge them. Therefore, mainly objective factors should in general be taken into account; these factors can be supplemented by subjective factors.[92] However, as the intentions of the parties do play a part, Kokkini-Iatridou has rightly pointed to

[90] HR 9 June 1995, *NJ* 1995, 617.

[91] De Boer 1991, p. 252 ff. The Working Group on PIL of the Dutch Association for the Administration of Justice also refers to these factors in its report; see Werkgroep IPR NVvR 1993, pp. 141–142.

[92] See also Werkgroep IPR NVvR 1993, pp. 141–142.

the fact that there is a certain manipulative element in the factors that are of relevance to the authenticity test.[93]

The answer to the question whether a real societal connection is manifestly lacking is determined by all circumstances of the case.[94] Therefore, it is not possible to give well-defined criteria or sets of criteria that should be met in order to assume the lack of a real societal connection. The court has to judge case by case whether a party possesses a real societal connection to his or her country of origin.

De Boer concludes that decisions concerning the lack or presence of a real societal connection are often based on arguments that differ from case to case and that, moreover, are appreciated differently.[95]

The authenticity test is an individual review: it is not required that *both* spouses have become estranged of the country of their nationality.[96] According to the formulation of Article 1(2) first sentence CLAD application of the national law of the parties will already be left aside, if either party manifestly lacks a real societal connection with the country of their nationality.[97]

Should the authenticity test also be applied to Dutch couples residing abroad? Strictly speaking Article 1(2), first sentence CLAD makes no distinction between spouses with a common foreign nationality and spouses with a common Dutch nationality. The provision has been formulated in general terms, which involves that the authenticity test should in principle also apply to Dutch couples residing abroad.[98]

However, one can wonder whether the application of the authenticity test to Dutch couples residing abroad is consistent with the rationale behind Article 1(2) CLAD. As is evident from the parliamentary history, the legislator has particularly had spouses with a common foreign nationality in mind. Thereby the leading principle has been to enable parties to obtain a desired divorce.[99] The Working Group on PIL of the Netherlands Association for the Administration of Justice argued that given this rationale it is perfectly justifiable not to consider too fast that the Dutch nationality of a Dutch couple residing abroad has diluted and, therefore, pleaded 'with some hesitation' for complete abolition of the authenticity test for Dutch couples residing abroad, if the divorce cannot be awarded according to the

---

93 Kokkini-Iatridou 1979, p. 581.

94 See HR 26 January 1996, *NIPR* 1997, 179.

95 De Boer 1991, p. 260.

96 Before the entry into force of the CLAD it was required that both parties lack a real societal connection with the country of their nationality. See Rb. Amsterdam 29 January 1970, *NJ* 1970, 188 and HR 9 February 1979, *NJ* 1979, 546 (annotated by J.C. Schultsz) and *Ars Aequi* 1979, p. 268 (annotated by H.U. Jessurun d'Oliviera).

97 Explanatory Memorandum (MvT), *Kamerstukken II* 1979–1980, 16 004, No. 3–4, p. 14.

98 Explanatory Memorandum (MvT), *Kamerstukken II* 1979–1980, 16 004, No. 3–4, pp. 15–16. In this sense also: Rb.'s-Gravenhage 22 October 1999, *NIPR* 2000, 15; Hof 's-Gravenhage 17 January 2001, *NIPR* 2003, 76.

99 Explanatory Memorandum (MvT), *Kamerstukken II* 1979–1980, 16 004, No. 3–4, p. 14.

law of the country of their habitual residence.[100] According to the Working Group the authenticity test can in this respect only be applied in very striking cases, in which it would be unreasonable towards the defendant to apply Dutch law as the common national law. The Working Group cites the example of a defending spouse who never had any connection to Dutch society and who has only obtained the Dutch nationality by marrying a Dutch partner. In such cases the defending spouse needs to argue explicitly that the real societal connection with the Netherlands is absent.[101]

Some authors rightly argue on the other hand that the omission of the authenticity test in case of Dutch spouses is an interpretation *contra legem* of Article 1(2) CLAD, as this provision has been formulated in general terms.[102] Particularly strong arguments should be raised to overrule such interpretation. However, the line of reasoning of the Working Group in regard to the omission of the authenticity test in the cases concerned does not show any of such arguments.[103] In addition, during the parliamentary proceedings explicit attention has been drawn to the fact that also in cases of Dutch couples residing abroad a lacking societal connection to the Netherlands can be found.[104] Therefore, the authenticity test should in principle also apply to Dutch couples residing abroad.

The question is whether the court has *ex officio* authority to apply the authenticity test of Article 1(2) CLAD, whenever the circumstances of the case justify the assumption that one of the parties lacks a real societal connection with the country of his or her nationality and such absence has not explicitly been stressed by one of the parties.

The court should, as much as possible, prevent effects of surprise for the parties by applying *ex officio* the choice of law. The requirements of due process imply that parties have a real chance to put forward the relevant facts for the determination of the applicable law.[105] This means that the court can confront the parties, by applying the authenticity test, with the application of a certain law (usually the law of the country of habitual residence or the *lex fori*) that may lead to a substantive result which parties may not have foreseen. Such a situation is unsatisfactory.

However, the opposite situation – omitting the authenticity test – encounters obstacles as well. In practice, it often occurs that parties with a common foreign nationality rely on the application of the Dutch ground for divorce 'irretrievable

---

[100] Werkgroep IPR NVvR 1993, pp. 142–143, 146–147, 149.

[101] Ibid., p. 149.

[102] See Boele-Woelki 1994, p. 175; and Van Maas de Bie 2002, p. 256. The Working Group on Private International Law was aware of the fact that the omission of the authenticity test in case of Dutch spouses residing abroad is at odds with the wording of Article 1(2) CLAD, see Werkgroep IPR NVvR 1993, p. 147.

[103] The Working Group pleaded 'with some hesitation' for the omission of the test.

[104] See Explanatory Memorandum (MvT), *Kamerstukken II* 1979–1980, 16 004, No. 3–4, pp. 15–16.

[105] See Mostermans 1996, pp. 131–132; and Staatscommissie 2002, p. 14 ff.

breakdown of the marriage'.[106] If these parties have already resided in the Netherlands for a long time, reasonable doubts can arise concerning their societal connection with their country of origin. The fact that parties reside durably in the Netherlands and, moreover, that they invoke a ground for divorce, which does not exist in their country of origin, justifies a closer review on the intensity of the societal connection of the parties with their country of origin. The omission of such a review could surprise parties with a substantive result, i.e. the petition will be declared inadmissible, that the petitioner in any case has not intended.[107]

Good practice requires therefore that the court has *ex officio* authority to raise the question of the societal connection and that parties will be offered the opportunity to express their opinion on the applicable law.[108] Parties can of course, as explained above, still make a *professio iuris* during the divorce proceedings.

2.4.2.2 Effectivity Test

If a person possesses the nationality of more than one country, the connection to the national law is faced with difficulties. In such cases it is not clear which of the nationalities concerned is considered the 'national law' according to Article 1(1)(a) CLAD. On the basis of Article 1(3) CLAD the national law of such a person shall be understood to be the law of that country of which he or she possesses the nationality and with which, taking all circumstances into account, he or she is most closely connected.

This so-called 'effectivity test' (*effectiviteitstoets*) was already applied before the entry into force of the CLAD.[109]

Application of the effectivity test takes place in the same way as the authenticity test, i.e. taking all circumstances of the case into account.[110] The effectivity test is an examination of the factual societal connections that the person in question has with both (or all) countries of his or her nationality. The effectivity

106 In Sect. 2.3.4.2 above it has been argued that such position should not be considered as a valid *professio iuris* for Dutch law pursuant to Article 1(4) CLAD.

107 See e.g. Rb. Alkmaar 20 June 1991, *NIPR* 1991, 322; Rb.'s-Gravenhage 14 July 1992, *NIPR* 1992, 347; Rb.'s-Gravenhage 17 September 1991, *NIPR* 1991, 356; Rb.'s-Gravenhage 27 October 1992, *NIPR* 1993, 89; Rb.'s-Gravenhage 23 March 1993, *NIPR* 1993, 242; Rb.'s-Gravenhage 11 May 1993, *NIPR* 1993, 246; Rb.'s-Gravenhage 1 December 1993, *NIPR* 1994, 97; Rb.'s-Gravenhage 29 December 1993, *NIPR* 1994, 102; Hof Amsterdam 6 October 1994, *NIPR* 1995, 204; Rb.'s-Gravenhage 25 September 1996, *NIPR* 1997, 78; Rb.'s-Gravenhage 20 March 1998, *NIPR* 1998, 187; Hof 's-Hertogenbosch 26 January 2000, *NIPR* 2000, 97; and Rb. Maastricht 28 March 2007, *NIPR* 2007, 118.

108 See Mostermans 1992, pp. 157–158; Werkgroep IPR NVvR 1993, pp. 140, 145, 148; HR 6 October 1995, *NJ* 1997, 257 (annotation Th.M. de Boer); Mostermans 2006, p. 52; Vonken (Groene Serie Personen- en familierecht) Article 1 CLAD, n. 5.6.

109 See HR 9 December 1965, *NJ* 1966, 378; and HR 27 May 1977, *NJ* 1977, 600.

110 See HR 6 October 1995, *NJ* 1997, 257 (annotation Th.M. de Boer); and HR 15 February 2002, *NIPR* 2002, 148.

test should be judged mainly in the light of objective factors, such as housing and working conditions, mastery of a language, the family situation of the person involved, etc. Subjective factors, such as hardly verifiable statements, can only be taken into account as support of the objective factors.[111] The court is not bound by statements of the parties, should they argue jointly that a certain nationality is the effective one.[112]

In cases in which it is difficult for the court to decide which of the nationalities of the party in question is the effective one, it is very well conceivable that the court will be influenced by the *favor divortii* principle underlying Article 1 CLAD.[113]

The nationality of the country of residence of the person involved will often be the effective nationality.[114]

The provision of Article 1(3) CLAD equally applies to Dutch people with more than one nationality. If the Dutch nationality is used as a connecting factor for the determination of the applicable law, the court should examine whether this nationality is the effective one.

Can the parties make a *professio iuris* for the application of the common national law on the basis of Article 1(2) CLAD and thereby block the application of the effectivity test of Article 1(3) CLAD?

A striking example in this respect is the case of spouses who both have the Moroccan nationality as well as Dutch nationality. Both reside for a long time in the Netherlands and, due partly to that reason, their Dutch nationality should be considered as their effective nationality. However, parties may have an interest in the application of Moroccan law to the dissolution of their marriage, as this might increase their chances on the recognition of their divorce in Morocco.[115] Strictly speaking, only Dutch law is considered as the national law of the persons in question according to Article 1(3) CLAD. So Moroccan law lacks as the common national law of the spouses in the sense of Article 1(2) CLAD and, consequently, the possibility to choose this law as the law applicable to the divorce lacks as well.[116] But given the rationale behind the *professio iuris* for the common national

---

[111] See *supra* Sect. 2.4.2.1.

[112] Cf., Mostermans 2006, p. 56.

[113] Ibid. At times the court even refrains from applying the effectivity test, e.g. Rb. Utrecht, 26 January 2005, *NIPR* 2005, 130.

[114] Cf., Mostermans 2006, p. 55. See also e.g. Rb.'s-Gravenhage 3 May 2006, *NIPR* 2007, 16; Rb.'s-Gravenhage 10 May 2006, *NIPR* 2007, 18; Rb.'s-Gravenhage 17 May 2006, *NIPR* 2007, 19; Hof 's-Gravenhage 25 March 2009, *NIPR* 2009, 260; Hof 's-Gravenhage 15 April 2009, *NIPR* 2009, 183.

[115] See concerning the difficulties with respect to the recognition of Dutch divorces in Morocco *inter alia*: Rutten 1997, p. 193 ff and Bouddount 2006.

[116] See Van Maas de Bie 2002, p. 257. See also: Hof Amsterdam 20 July 2000, *NIPR* 2002, 82. In the case of the Rechtbank Alkmaar of 15 November 2007 the described situation also arose, but the Rechtbank did not pay any attention to the fact that the wife possessed two nationalities; see Rb. Alkmaar 15 November 2007, *NIPR* 2008, 16.

law of the spouses (Article 1(2), second sentence CLAD), it is perfectly arguable that the court would accept the choice for the application of Moroccan law. The legislature intends to allow spouses possessing a common foreign nationality the opportunity to choose this common national law as the applicable law to their divorce in order to increase the chance of the recognition of the Dutch decision on divorce in their country of origin.[117] According to Article 1(2), second sentence CLAD such a *professio iuris* is lawful, irrespective of the actual societal connection that the parties may have with the country of their nationality.

Against this background it goes without saying not to require that the national law which the parties chose to be applied should be the law of the country of the effective nationality.[118] Furthermore, it does not follow imperatively from the system of Article 1 CLAD that the effectivity test takes precedence over the authenticity test. Consequently, the parties can choose the law of the non-effective nationality as the applicable law.[119]

Another question that arises is whether the authenticity test should be applied to the effective nationality. In other words, should the effective nationality of a person also be submitted to the authenticity test in order to determine whether or not the connection to the country of this nationality has considerably weakened?

It is possible that, although the court has determined on the basis of the effectivity test that a certain nationality of one of the spouses is the (most) effective one, this person has in fact no real societal connection to this country of origin either. The effective nationality should therefore be submitted to an authenticity test in order to determine whether the connection of the person concerned with this country represents a connection close enough to apply its law in a concrete case.[120] Should the authenticity test show that the person involved manifestly lacks a real societal connection to the country of the effective nationality too, application of the law of this country should be refrained from.[121]

2.4.2.3 Exceptional Cases

Two special categories of exceptional cases should be mentioned: on the one hand, stateless persons and persons whose nationality cannot be determined, and, on the

---

117 Cf., Explanatory Memorandum (MvT), *Kamerstukken II* 1979–1980, 16 004, No. 3–4, p. 15.

118 See equally Wendels 1983, p. 73; Staatscommissie 1995, p. 4; Mostermans 2006, p. 57; and Vonken (Groene Serie Personen- en familierecht) Article 1 CLAD, n. 6. See also: Rb. 's-Gravenhage 15 November 1988, *NIPR* 1989, 209; Rb.'s-Gravenhage 10 April 1996, *NIPR* 1996, 215a; and Hof Amsterdam 21 February 2002, *NIPR* 2003, 207.

119 Differently: Hof Amsterdam 20 July 2000, *NIPR* 2000, 266. According to the Hof Amsterdam, in determining whether a choice for the application of parties' common national law is valid, one must first apply the effectivity test in case either of the parties possesses a double nationality.

120 Cf., conclusion of Advocate General Strikwerda at HR 15 February 2002, *NJ* 2003, 371.

121 See with regard to choice of law of succession: Ten Wolde 1996, p. 32; and Knot 2008, p. 39.

other, refugees. In both these categories the application of the national law is not obvious.

It is possible that one (or both) of the spouses does not possess any nationality.[122] In such a case the connecting factor of nationality used by Article 1(1)(a) CLAD does not provide a solution as to which law applies to the divorce.

Since the connection to the national law of the spouses is not possible, the law applicable to divorce is determined by the next alternative connecting factor of Article 1 CLAD, i.e. the law of the country in which both spouses have their habitual residence.[123]

This also applies to persons whose nationality cannot reasonably be determined.[124]

Also in case one of the spouses (or both) is a refugee, the connection to the nationality is not obvious, even though this person may still possess this nationality. A refugee can hardly be submitted to the law of the country with which he wanted to or was forced to break off all ties.[125] The application of the national law of a refugee would then violate the principle of closest connection.[126]

The Treaty of Geneva concerning the Status of Refugees provides for a solution: Article 12(1) of the Treaty of Geneva determines that the personal status of a refugee is governed by the law of the country of domicile or, in the absence of a domicile, by the law of the country of residence.[127] Therefore, also in case of refugees the use of nationality as a connecting factor is not possible.

2.4.3 The Law of the Country in Which Both Parties Have Their Habitual Residence

In the absence of a common nationality, the habitual residence provides a secondary connection (Article 1(1)(b) CLAD). Accordingly, if the parties are habitually resident in the same country, the law of this country will be applied to their divorce. It is not required that the spouses share their habitual residence.

---

122 The cause of the absence of a nationality is usually a negative conflict between nationality laws. According to one law a certain fact, such as a marriage to a foreigner, leads to the loss of nationality, whereas this same fact might not lead to the acquisition of nationality according to the other law. See Strikwerda 2008, p. 76.

123 The application of the law of the common habitual residence of the spouses is also in conformity with Article 12(1) of the Treaty of New York concerning the Status of Stateless Persons (Treaty of 28 September 1954, *Trb.* 1957, No. 22), determining that the personal status of a stateless person is governed by the law of his country of domicile or, in the absence of a domicile, by the law of the country of his or her residence.

124 See Mostermans 2006, p. 57.

125 See Strikwerda 2008, p. 77.

126 See equally Ten Wolde 2009, p. 117.

127 Treaty of 28 July 1951, *Trb.* 1954, No. 88.

If the spouses no longer live together but do both have their residence within the same country, the law of this country is applied to their divorce.

'Habitual residence' is an autonomous concept, which forms part of the choice of law. The term 'habitual residence' originates from the Hague Conference. However, no definition of the term has ever been included in a Hague Convention; this has been a matter of deliberate policy.[128] The concept of habitual residence refers to the centre of someone's societal life or the place where the life of the person involved is actually taking place. It serves to provide a connection between the person concerned and the law of the county with which this person is in reality closely connected. All specific circumstances are taken into account in the determination of the place of habitual residence; the permanency of the actual residence and the intentions of the person in question are both important factors in this respect.[129] For choice of law purposes it can generally not be assumed that a person who resides for some time in the Netherlands for study purposes has established his habitual residence in the Netherlands. If a person immigrates to the Netherlands, however, the criterion will be complied with virtually directly at the actual establishment in the Netherlands.[130]

The term habitual residence is chosen to avoid possible problems of characterisation, which could arise with respect to the term 'domicile'. Habitual residence cannot be equated with the Dutch term 'domicile' ('*woonplaats*') as defined by the Dutch civil code (Article 1:10 BW). In this sense domicile is a purely internal law concept and is mainly meant to indicate the address at which the person concerned can be reached for judicial matters.[131]

It may very well occur that a person does not possess a domicile in the Netherlands in the sense of the Dutch civil code, but that this person has his habitual residence in the sense of choice of law in the Netherlands. Conversely, a person can have his domicile but no habitual residence in the Netherlands, because he is not socially integrated in the Dutch society.[132]

2.4.4 The **Lex Fori**

If the parties do not possess a common nationality nor have their habitual residence in the same country, Dutch law as the law of the court at which the petition on divorce has been filed (*lex fori*) should be applied according to Article 1(1)(c) CLAD. The *lex fori* is thus only used as a (last resort) subsidiary connecting factor.

---

[128] Cf., Dicey et al. 2006, p. 168.

[129] See Strikwerda 2008, pp. 80–81.

[130] Explanatory Memorandum (MvT), *Kamerstukken II* 1979–1980, 16 004, No. 3–4, pp. 11–12.

[131] HR 21 December 2001, *NJ* 2002, 282.

[132] See the annotation of J.C. Schultsz at HR 27 May 1977, *NJ* 1977, 600.

The Dutch Standing Committee on Private International Law acknowledged in 1967 that it would certainly be easy to submit all the divorces that are petitioned in the Netherlands to Dutch law. However, such a rule could entail serious objections for foreigners, whose marriage would be dissolved in the Netherlands according to Dutch law: they can experience in their country of origin, and possibly elsewhere, that the Dutch decision on divorce will not be recognised.[133]

In general and in principle it is not preferable to automatically give priority to the application of the *lex fori*, while this is contrary to the principles of private international law. This field of law is based on the recognition of an international legal order, which respects the existence of divergent legal systems and which gives, if necessary, priority to the application of the law of one of these systems.[134] The *lex fori* is, therefore, only applied subsidiarily in Dutch international divorce law.

2.4.5 Date of Reference

Whether the parties have a common nationality or whether they have their habitual residence in the same country should, in principle, be assessed according to the time of filing the petition. This date of reference has not been explicitly arranged for by the CLAD. According to the parliamentary proceedings the time of filing the petition is in principle decisive.[135] Thereby the parties cannot influence the designation of the applicable law by their own actions. However, in special cases it is conceivable that this principle is deviated from in favour of the time of the decision.[136]

The decision of the *Hoge Raad* of 6 October 1995 makes clear in which cases the date of reference concerned can be deviated from.[137] In this case the *Hoge Raad* held that the legislator clearly chose for the mentioned date of reference in order to prevent the parties from attempting to influence the designation of the applicable law during the divorce proceedings. Therefore, attention can be paid to an alteration of nationality after the divorce proceedings have commenced, if the person in question whose nationality is concerned did not intent to influence the designation of the applicable law and if the divorce can still be granted.

Considering the *favor divortii* principle it is defensible that, even if it seems that there has been a deliberate influencing of the designation of the applicable law, to take the alteration of nationality into account, provided that it would lead to the granting of the divorce, which would otherwise have been dismissed. Moreover,

133 Staatscommissie 1967, in Frohn and Hennis 1995, p. 113.

134 Staatscommissie 1995, p. 3.

135 Explanatory Memorandum (MvT), *Kamerstukken II* 1979–1980, 16 004, No. 3–4, p. 16.

136 Ibid., p. 16. In case law the same point of view is held: see *inter alia* Rb.'s-Gravenhage 22 October 1999, *NIPR* 2000, 15; Rb.'s-Gravenhage 7 March 2003, *NIPR* 2003, 246.

137 HR 6 October 1995, *NJ* 1997, 257.

this would serve legal economy: in a new procedure the alteration of nationality would be taken into account anyhow and the divorce would be granted.[138]

This line of reasoning with regard to the alteration of nationality also applies to the alteration of the habitual residence after the petition on divorce has been filed. Joppe draws special attention to the situation in which both spouses move their habitual residence to a new common country of residence or a new common country of residence is created because one of the spouses moves to the country of habitual residence of the other spouse. In these situations it is not obvious why the court should not take the alteration of the habitual residence into account, especially since there is no possibility to choose the law of this country with a view to the possible recognition of the Dutch decision on divorce.[139]

The question with respect to the date of reference also arises as part of the authenticity and effectivity test of Article 1(2) and (3) CLAD. Can the court, in the examination of the societal connection of the spouses with the country of their nationality, only pay attention to the circumstances of the case as they were at the beginning of the proceedings, or can it also take facts into consideration which have occurred afterwards?

As seen above, the time of filing the petition is in principle decisive. In special cases this principle can be deviated from in favour of the time of the decision. The *favor divortii* principle plays a role in this respect. Against the background of this principle the deviation from the date of reference concerned is conceivable in the determination of the societal connection, provided that it would lead to the allowance of the petition on divorce, which would otherwise have possibly been dismissed.[140]

2.5 Public Policy Exception

The public policy exception forms part of Dutch international divorce law, although the Choice of Law Act on Divorce does not specifically mention it.[141] Whenever the Dutch rules of the CLAD refer to foreign law, all kind of problems can arise. These problems mainly occur in relation to non-Western legal systems. Often the principle of equality of the sexes conflicts with certain non-egalitarian rules of Islamic law. Repudiation is the most significant example in this respect.

The willingness to apply foreign law can and must find its bounds if the application of this law threatens to have a disrupting effect on society. The

---

[138] See Mostermans 2006, p. 47. More reserved: Vonken (Groene Serie Personen- en familierecht) Article 1 CLAD, n. 4.5.

[139] Joppe 1982, p. 618.

[140] See also Joppe 1987, p. 53; and Vlas 1996, p. 201.

[141] The Dutch Proposal on Private International Law provides for a general public policy clause in Article 6, stipulating that the application of foreign law is to be left aside, if this would be manifestly incompatible with Dutch public policy. See on this provision more elaborately Staatscommissie 2002, p. 52 ff; and Explanatory Memorandum (MvT), *Kamerstukken II* 2009–2010, 32 137, No. 3, pp. 13–15.

so-called public policy exception takes effect if the principles and values that are considered to be fundamental to Dutch society are harmed.[142] The character of the public policy exception is current, i.e. its content is drawn from the fundamental social, political and moral perceptions prevailing in domestic public policy at any given time.[143] It is obvious that these perceptions are subject to the effects of time. Consequently, the court cannot merely ascertain whether in general a specific foreign provision is contrary to Dutch law, but it must also determine in particular whether the application of this provision would truly harm the fundamental moral and socio-economic values of the Dutch legal system.

It is evident that, while on the one hand such harm is not created by the fact that the grounds for divorce are not the same in the applicable foreign law as in Dutch law, there would on the other hand be a serious conflict with the principles of internal law and public morals if the court were to take into consideration a foreign provision on divorce which, for example, recognised the unilateral right of the husband to expel his wife from the matrimonial home. The institution of repudiation, which is recognised in many Islamic legal systems, whereby a husband may divorce his wife — even in her absence — by thrice saying '*ṭalāq*' (literally: 'I divorce you') in the presence of witnesses, will not be accepted by a Dutch court as the basis for a divorce, since this is something that is held as intolerable in Dutch society.[144] This is not because repudiation is unknown in Dutch law, but because it is, first and foremost, contrary to the principle of the equality of the sexes and, further, because repudiation is a private act without any security of a fair and impartial judgment.

As mentioned above, the public policy exception may also come into play in the event of the dissolution of a same-sex marriage.[145] If the designated foreign law differentiates according to sex, the principle of equality is violated and the court can apply the public policy exception. Thereby the foreign law can be set aside.

2.6 The Proposed Amendments of the Choice of Law on Divorce

In practice several problems on the interpretation and application of Article 1 CLAD have arisen.[146] An important point of criticism is the current — exceedingly confusing — formulation of Article 1 CLAD: its principal rule, i.e. the possibility to

[142] See on the public policy exception in general: Strikwerda 2008, p. 52 ff; and Ten Wolde 2009, p. 79 ff. The Hoge Raad held that the public policy exception can only be invoked against the application of foreign law and not against the application of Dutch law; see HR 12 May 2000, *NIPR* 2000, 172.

[143] See Blom 2003, p. 383 ff.

[144] HR 9 November 2001, *NIPR* 2002, 2 and Hof Amsterdam 25 January 2001, *NIPR* 2001, 91. Cf., also Van der Velden 2003, p. 1 ff.

[145] See *supra* Sect. 2.2.2.

[146] See for an enumeration of these problems: Werkgroep IPR NVvR 1993, p. 129 ff.

choose Dutch law as the applicable law, is to be found in the last section. Among other things the Working Group on PIL of the Netherlands Association for the Administration of Justice also points out that a thorough analysis of the case law by De Boer has shown that the regulation of Article 1 CLAD leads in practice in the majority of cases to the application of Dutch law (the *lex fori*).[147] In addition, the parties and their lawyers generally assume that Dutch law will be applicable.

On the basis of the results of its report the Working Group has recommended an adjustment of the regulation so that any international divorce filed before the Dutch courts is governed by Dutch law, unless (one of) the parties oppose to the application of Dutch law.[148] The Working Group proposes in fact the introduction of the so-called facultative choice of law in the field of international divorce law.[149]

In 1995 the Dutch Standing Committee on Private International Law, following the Working Group of the Netherlands Association for the Administration of Justice, advised the Dutch legislature to amend the choice of law on divorce.[150] The Standing Committee noted, however, that any such changes should only be introduced alongside a general codification of Dutch private international law.[151]

On 18 September 2009 the long-awaited proposal on the consolidation of Dutch private international law — to be included as Book 10 of the Dutch Civil Code — was published.[152] This proposal systematically and coherently

---

[147] De Boer 1991, p. 252 ff. In conjunction with the jurisdictional rules of the Brussels II*bis*-Regulation three of the four steps of the choice of law ladder of Article 1 CLAD lead to the designation of Dutch law as the applicable law. See also Boele-Woelki 1994, p. 179 ff; Van den Eeckhout 2000, p. 39 ff; Van Maas de Bie 2002, p. 258 ff.

[148] Werkgroep IPR NVvR 1993, pp. 150–151.

[149] See Van Maas de Bie 1993, p. 664; Boele-Woelki 1994, pp. 178–181; De Boer 1996, p. 227 ff.

[150] Staatscommissie 1995, p. 7.

[151] The majority of the Standing Committee had no such grave objection to the current regulation so that it would be necessary to promptly amend the Choice of Law Act on Divorce. It proposed therefore to wait with the amendment of Article 1 CLAD until the intended introduction of a General Private International Law Act, so that the new regulation of the applicable law to divorce can be tuned to the other content of the latter Act. See Staatscommissie 1995, p. 7.

Boele-Woelki 2008, p. 261 has urged the Dutch legislature to amend the choice of law on divorce within the foreseeable future, as the negotiations on the Brussels II*ter*-Proposal — introducing a common European choice of law on divorce — have failed in July 2008. The Dutch legislature has obeyed this call; see Explanatory Memorandum (MvT), *Kamerstukken II* 2009–2010, 32 137, No. 3, pp. 41–42: 'Overigens wordt momenteel onderhandeld over Europese regelgeving die strekt tot de invoering van regels inzake het toepasselijke recht in (echt)scheidingsprocedures. Indien deze regelgeving tot stand komt, zal zij op enig moment haar weerslag hebben op de in deze afdeling opgenomen bepalingen. Desalniettemin is besloten bij gelegenheid van deze consolidatie de Nederlandse regeling aan te passen, aangezien het moment van totstandkoming van Europese regelgeving nog hoogst onzeker is [...].'

[152] See *Kamerstukken II* 2009–2010, 32 137, No. 2. Hereinafter this Proposal will be referred to as the 'Dutch Proposal on Private International Law'. The Proposal is expected to enter into force either in the course of 2011 or in 2012.

brings together a considerable number of choice of law rules that currently apply.[153]

The proposed choice of law rule on divorce (Article 56) reads as follows:

1. Whether the dissolution of a marriage or legal separation may be pronounced and on what grounds, is determined by Dutch law.
2. In derogation from the provision of the preceding paragraph, the law of a common foreign nationality of the spouses will be applied if during the proceedings:
   a. a choice for that law has been made jointly by the parties or such a choice remains uncontested by one of the parties; or
   b. one of the spouses has made a choice for that law and both spouses have a real societal connection with the country of the common nationality.
3. A choice of law as meant in the preceding paragraph should be made expressly or be sufficiently clear from the terms used in the initiatory petition or the written defence.

Pursuant to this proposal, the principal rule on the law applicable to divorce is the application of the *lex fori*, Dutch law. This rule is regarded as a practical solution, which furthermore accords with the current practice in the majority of cases.[154]

By virtue of Article 8 of the Dutch Proposal on Private International Law, the application of the *lex fori* can be omitted should the case to a very limited degree be connected to Dutch law and should a much closer connection exist to another law.[155]

The *professio iuris* will be limited to the law of the common nationality of the spouses. Instead of acting as the primary choice of law rule in the field of divorce, the common nationality of the parties will thus only be applied should the parties have jointly chosen this law, or should such a choice of one of the parties remain uncontested.[156] The *professio iuris* will also be accepted in case of a unilateral choice, which has been contested by the other spouse, if both spouses have a real societal connection with their common country of origin. Currently Article 1 CLAD does not foresee this possibility. The Explanatory Memorandum clarifies the introduction of this possibility to apply the common national law of the spouses:

> Dit zal zich kunnen voordoen als de verweerder aan het nationale recht een verweer of aanspraak wil ontlenen, terwijl het Nederlandse recht zo'n verweer of aanspraak niet kent en de verzoeker juist daarom aan toepassing van het Nederlandse recht de voorkeur geeft. De realiteitstoets is hier positief geformuleerd omdat mag worden aangenomen dat

---

[153] See Explanatory Memorandum (MvT), *Kamerstukken II* 2009–2010, 32 137, No. 3, p. 1.

[154] According to the Explanatory Memorandum (MvT), *Kamerstukken II* 2009–2010, 32 137, No. 3, pp. 42–43.

[155] See Explanatory Memorandum (MvT), *Kamerstukken II* 2009–2010, 32 137, No. 3, pp. 17–18 expressly stating that also the *lex fori* can be set aside by this general provision of Article 8.

[156] See Staatscommissie 2001, p. 7. In support see also De Boer 1991, p. 260.

uitschakeling van het Nederlandse recht als *lex fori* vooral zal worden nagestreefd door verweerders die zich tegen de echtscheiding verzetten. Toepassing van gemeenschappelijk nationaal recht is dan gerechtvaardigd wanneer beide partijen een werkelijke maatschappelijke band met het land van de gemeenschappelijke nationaliteit hebben behouden.[157]

This explanation of the acceptance of a contested unilateral choice for the application of the common national law of the spouses is fairly complicated. What it comes down to is that the spouse requesting the application of the common national law may have an interest in the application of this law, from which he or she can derive a defence or a right which is not provided by Dutch law. The opposition of the other spouse to the application of the common national law can thus very well be connected to the fact that Dutch law does not provide for this defence or right and this spouse would, consequently, give priority to the application of Dutch law. According to the legislature this situation will mainly arise in case one of the spouses opposes the divorce. If the authenticity test shows that both spouses have retained a real societal connection with their common country of origin, the application of the law of this country is justified.

However, if either spouse has more than one nationality, should the court then apply the effectivity test in order to determine whether there is question of a common national law? The Standing Committee has determined on this issue that Article 56(2) is to be interpreted broadly. This means that also the nationality that cannot be regarded as the effective one can qualify for the national law that can be chosen pursuant to Article 56(2).[158] The text of Article 56(2) therefore expressly mentions the possibility to choose the law of 'a' common nationality. Although the Standing Committee has recommended the legislator to clarify this issue, the Explanatory Memorandum does not mention anything on this question.[159]

The formal requirements of the *professio iuris* on divorce will be expressed more clearly in this amended choice of law rule than Article 1 CLAD currently does: Article 56(3) makes clear that an implied choice of the applicable law is not possible, since the choice should be made expressly or be sufficiently clear from the terms used in the petition or the written defence.[160]

The Explanatory Memorandum to the Proposal on Private International Law contains the following statement on the time of the choice as to the applicable law:

Artikel 56 sluit echter niet uit dat echtgenoten al tijdens of zelfs vóór hun huwelijk een afspraak hebben gemaakt over het op een eventuele echtscheiding toe te passen recht.

---

[157] Explanatory Memorandum (MvT), *Kamerstukken II* 2009–2010, 32 137, No. 3, pp. 43–44.

[158] See Staatscommissie 1995, p. 7.

[159] Ibid., p. 7: 'Omdat de betekenis van het onbepaalde lidwoord wellicht niet voor iedere wetstoepasser aanstonds duidelijk is, verdient het naar het gevoelen van de Staatscommissie overweging hierop in de memorie van toelichting te wijzen.'.

[160] See also the general provision of Article 10 of the Dutch Proposal on Private International Law, stipulating that if a *professio iuris* is permitted, the choice should be made expressly or otherwise be sufficiently clear.

> Indien zij tevoren een (door artikel 56 toegestane) gezamenlijke keuze hebben gedaan en daarbij willen blijven, dienen zij die keuze in het verzoekschrift te bevestigen.[161]

This statement shows that the agreement between the spouses as to the law applicable to their divorce can already be made before or during the marriage. If the parties wish to persist in their choice they should subsequently confirm it in the initiatory petition. The Explanatory Memorandum points out that the previously chosen law will not be applied should one of the parties contest its application, as there is then no longer case of a joint choice.[162] This position can, however, be questioned: what purpose does a *professio iuris* in a marriage contract serve when it can be set aside at a later point of time? One of the primary goals of a *professio iuris* is to grant the spouses the certainty that the chosen law will be applied, which gives them the opportunity to rely on the substantive provisions of this law. The possibility to contest the choice in the petition for divorce contravenes this goal.

All references to the parties' habitual residence are removed from the choice of law on divorce. It is argued that if both parties are habitually resident abroad, the Dutch court will only be seized if both parties possess Dutch nationality.[163] The application of Dutch law in this case is fairly convincing, since Dutch law is in such cases not only the *lex fori* but also the common national law of the spouses.[164]

A transitional provision on the application of Article 56 will be added to the general transitional provisions relating to the Dutch Civil Code (Article 290). The amended choice of law rule on divorce will only apply to divorces and legal separations which have been requested after the entry into force of the latter Act.

Is the amendment of the choice of law to be welcomed? Foremost, Article 56 of the Dutch Proposal on Private International Law seems to be a better reflection of the current practice of the choice of law on divorce than Article 1 CLAD is. As seen above, Article 1 CLAD often leads to the designation of Dutch law as the applicable law. However, from its wording and structure Article 1 CLAD appears to be a neutral multilateral choice of law rule. Yet the employed exceptions and the *favor divortii* principle — and the occasional use of strange manoeuvres[165] — have eroded the seemingly neutral choice of law rule. Article 56 of the Dutch Proposal on Private International Law no longer gives the impression of a neutral choice of law rule and the application of Dutch law takes indeed first place. The provision of Article 56 will, therefore, lead to more legal certainty for the parties.

---

[161] See Explanatory Memorandum (MvT), *Kamerstukken II* 2009–2010, 32 137, No. 3, p. 43.

[162] Ibid. Cf., Staatscommissie 2008, pp. 6–7, which had requested the legislature to clarify this possibility: '[…] het tweede lid van het artikel betreffende de wet die van toepassing is op echtscheiding […] behoeft verduidelijking voor het geval waarin een aanvankelijk door echtgenoten overeengekomen rechtskeuze later wordt genegeerd door een eenzijdige rechtskeuze van een van hen.'.

[163] See Staatscommissie 1995, pp. 3–4.

[164] See equally Curry-Sumner 2005, pp. 453.

[165] See e.g. the omission of the authenticity test in case of a Dutch couple residing abroad, *supra* Sect. 2.4.2.1.

However, some critical thoughts are called for. Firstly, the restriction of the *professio iuris* to the common foreign national law of the spouses is not obvious.[166] The Standing Committee believed there to be insufficient grounds to grant parties the opportunity to choose the law of their common habitual residence at the cost of a too complicated choice of law rule.[167] Yet, would the principle of *favor divortii* not be better served if parties have a less limited degree of party autonomy?

Furthermore, the argument that, because in practice Dutch law is applied in the majority of international divorce cases, the choice of law rule should be amended in such a way that Dutch law applies in all cases, except in those which the parties choose the law of their common nationality, is not convincing.[168] Such argument does no justice to the particular function of the choice of law. In addition, the assertion that Dutch law is applied in the majority of international divorce cases may be doubted: the case law cited above shows that Dutch courts regularly apply foreign law.[169]

But more importantly: the question arises whether the principle of *favor divortii* actually extends that far that application of Dutch law in case of international divorce should be the principal rule?[170] Van Maas de Bie rightly argues that it is not desirable to favour the application of the *lex fori*, considering the thought of neutrality which underlies the field of private international law and by virtue of which all legal systems are equally eligible for application.[171] Strikingly, the Dutch Standing Committee observed exactly the same concerning granting categorical priority to the application of the *lex fori*, as this would ignore the principles of private international law, which are aimed at the recognition of an international legal order which respects the existence of divergent legal systems and which gives, if called for, priority to the application of a foreign legal system.[172] The Standing Committee therefore rightly stressed that a development in this direction should in general not be stimulated.[173] But why, then, will Article 1 CLAD be amended in such a way that the application of Dutch law (the *lex fori*) is the primary choice of law rule?

The Explanatory Memorandum to Proposal on Private International Law states on this issue that granting categorical priority to the *lex fori* would in the specific

---

[166] See also already *supra* Sect. 2.3.1.

[167] Staatscommissie 1995, p. 5.

[168] Cf., Werkgroep IPR NVvR 1993, p. 136; Explanatory Memorandum (MvT), *Kamerstukken II* 2009–2010, 32 137, No. 3, pp. 42–43.

[169] See *supra* note 83 of the current chapter. See also Vonken (Groene Serie Personen- en familierecht) Article 1 CLAD, n. 8.

[170] See also Boele-Woelki 1994, pp. 167–181; Vlas 1996, p. 202; Van Maas de Bie 2002, p. 261.

[171] Van Maas de Bie 2002, p. 261.

[172] Staatscommissie 1995, p. 3. See also Explanatory Memorandum (MvT), *Kamerstukken II* 2009–2010, 32 137, No. 3, p. 43.

[173] The Dutch legislature endorses to this position. See Explanatory Memorandum (MvT), *Kamerstukken II* 2009–2010, 32 137, No. 3, p. 43.

case of divorce meet the needs of legal practice.[174] However, in the absence of fundamental research it is not clear where the alleged needs of legal practice rest upon.

2.7 Conclusion

The Dutch choice of law on divorce is currently determined by Article 1 of the Choice of Law Act on Divorce. This Act is based on the *favor divortii* principle, implying that the choice of law rule often refers to the application of a legal system which does not preclude the wish of the parties to obtain a divorce.

The parties are offered the opportunity to choose the law applicable to their divorce. This choice, however, is limited to the law of the common nationality of the spouses (Article 1(2) CLAD) and Dutch law (the *lex fori*, Article 1(4) CLAD).

If the parties have not made a *professio iuris*, then their common national law is applied. In determining whether the spouses possess a common nationality, their nationality is subject to an authenticity test and to an effectivity test. The authenticity test applies in case of single nationality: no common national law is considered to exist if either of the parties lacks a real societal connection with the country of the common nationality. The effectivity test applies in case of double or multiple nationalities: the national law of a party with more than one nationality is the law of that country with which, taking into account all the circumstances, he or she has the closest connections. Both these tests imply that all the circumstances of the given case will be taken into account, including the connections that tie a person to another state.

In the absence of a common nationality, the law of the country in which both parties have their habitual residence will be applied. The habitual residence of the spouses does not need to be a common one. If the spouses do not have a common nationality and have no shared habitual residence, Dutch law (*lex fori*) will be applied.

Article 1 CLAD will be amended: Article 56 of the Dutch Proposal on Private International Law provides for the application of Dutch law (*lex fori*) in all cases, save for those in which the parties have made a *professio iuris*. The *professio iuris* is limited to the common national law of the parties.

[174] See Explanatory Memorandum (MvT), *Kamerstukken II* 2009–2010, 32 137, No. 3, p. 43: 'Het vooropstellen van het Nederlandse recht als toepasselijk recht komt voor dit specifieke onderwerp evenwel tegemoet aan de behoefte van de praktijk.'

References

Regulations, Conventions, Reports and Other Documentary Sources

Choice of Law Act on Divorce. Act of 25 March 1981, *Stb.* 1981, No. 166, containing a regulation of the choice of law rules on the dissolution of the marriage and on legal separation and the recognition thereof, *Wet conflictenrecht Echtscheiding*

Dutch Proposal on Private International Law. Vaststelling en invoering van Boek 10 (Internationaal privaatrecht) van het Burgerlijk Wetboek, *Kamerstukken II* 2009–2010, 32 137, No. 2

Impact Assessment on Divorce. Commission Staff Working Document—Annex to the proposal for a Council Regulation amending Regulation (EC) No. 2201/2003 as regards jurisdiction and introducing rules concerning applicable law in matrimonial matters, SEC(2006) 949

Staatscommissie (1967). Staatscommissie voor het Internationaal Privaatrecht, Advies met betrekking tot het conflictenrecht inzake de echtscheiding en de scheiding van tafel en bed, Report of 8 February 1967, in: Frohn/Hennis (1995)

Staatscommissie (1995). Staatscommissie voor het Internationaal Privaatrecht, Advies inzake Wet conflictenrecht echtscheiding, Report of 28 March 1995

Staatscommissie (2001). Staatscommissie voor het Internationaal Privaatrecht, Internationaal privaatrecht in verband met de openstelling van het huwelijk voor personen van hetzelfde geslacht, Report of 1 December 2001

Staatscommissie (2002). Staatscommissie voor het Internationaal Privaatrecht, Rapport Algemene Bepalingen IPR, Report of 1 June 2002

Staatscommissie (2008). Staatscommissie voor het Internationaal Privaatrecht, Advies van de Staatscommissie voor internationaal privaatrecht over Boek 10, Report of 2 July 2008.

The reports of the Dutch Standing Committee on Private International Law that have been drawn up as from 1995 are available at: http://www.justitie.nl/onderwerpen/wetgeving/over_wetgeving/privaatrecht/commissies-privaatrecht/staatscommissie-ipr.aspx

Werkgroep IPR NVvR (1993). Werkgroep Internationaal Privaatrecht van de Nederlandse Vereniging voor Rechtspraak, Knelpunten bij de toepassing van artikel 1 Wet Conflictenrecht Echtscheiding. Trema, 129–151

Books and Articles

Blom J (2003) Public policy in private international law and its evolution in time. NILR 50:373–399

Boele-Woelki K (1994) Der *favor divortii* im Niederländischen internationalen Scheidungsrecht. In: Boele-Woelki K (ed) Comparability and Evaluation, Liber Amicorum D. Kokkini-Iatridou. Nijhoff, Dordrecht, pp 167–181

Boele-Woelki K (2008) Europese unificatie conflictenrecht echtscheiding van de baan. FJR 30:261

Boele-Woelki K, Joustra C, Steenhoff G (1998) Dutch private international law at the end of the 20th century: pluralism of methods. In: Steenhoff G (ed) Netherlands reports to the 15th international congress of comparative law. Intersentia, Bristol, pp 203–227

Bouddount S (2006) Marokkaanse rechtspraktijk inzake de erkenning van in Nederland uitgesproken echtscheidingen. Migrantenrecht 21:362–365

Curry-Sumner I (2005) All's well that ends registered? Intersentia, Antwerpen

De Boer ThM (1991) Internationale echtscheiding: het kennelijk ontbreken van een maatschappelijke band. Ars Aequi 40:252–260

De Boer ThM (1996) Favor divortii en rechtsmacht Commentaar op artikel 2 van het voorstel voor een bevoegdheids- en executieverdrag inzake familie- en erfrecht. In: Kortmann SCJJ, Struycken AVM (eds) Op recht. Bundel opstellen aangeboden aan prof mr Struycken ter gelegenheid van zijn zilveren ambtsjubileum aan de Katholieke Universiteit Nijmegen. W.E.J. Tjeenk Willink, Zwolle, pp 19–31

Dicey AV, Collins LA, Morris JHC (eds) (2006) Dicey, Morris and Collins on the conflict of laws, 14th edn. Sweet & Maxwell, London

Dubbink CW (1956) Recente ontwikkelingen van het internationale echtscheidingsrecht. Nederlands Tijdschrift voor Internationaal Recht 3:199–208

Foblets MC (1997) Conflicts of law in cross-cultural family disputes in Europe today: who will reorient conflicts of law? Comparative and International Law Review South Africa 30:22–36

Frohn EN (1996) Netherlands judicial decision involving questions of private international law. NILR 43:41–55

Frohn EN, Hennis E (eds) (1995) Staatscommissie IPR: geselecteerde adviezen: Naar een afgewogen IPR. T.M.C. Asser Instituut, 's-Gravenhage

Henrich D (2001) Abschied vom Staatsangehörigkeitsprinzip? In: Hohloch G et al (eds) Festschrift für Hans Stoll. Mohr Siebeck, Tübingen, pp 437–449

Joppe IS (1982) De internationale echtscheiding en de bijkomende vorderingen tot alimentatie en scheiding en deling. NJB 57:617–624

Joppe IS (1987) Overgangsrecht in het internationaal privaatrecht en het fait accompli (diss. Leiden). Gouda Quint, Arnhem

Knot JG (2008) Internationale boedelafwikkeling Over het toepasselijke recht op de afwikkeling van nalatenschappen (diss. Groningen). Kluwer, Deventer

Kokkini-Iatridou D (1979) Mr. A. Wendels/Internationale echtscheidingen. RM Themis, pp 579–584

Kosters J, Dubbink CW (1962) Nederlands internationaal privaatrecht. De Erven F. Bohn, Haarlem

Mostermans PMM (1990) Party autonomy: why and when? In: De Boer ThM (ed) Forty years on: the evolution of postwar private international law in Europe. Kluwer, Deventer, pp 123–141

Mostermans PMM (1992) Enkele procesrechtelijke vragen bij toepassing van art. 1 WCE. FJR 14:156–160

Mostermans PMM (1996) De processuele behandeling van het conflictenrecht (diss. UvA). W.E.J. Tjeenk Willink, Zwolle

Mostermans PMM (2006) Echtscheiding, 3rd edn. Kluwer, Deventer

Pontier JA (1997) Conflictenrecht: grondslagen, methoden, beginselen en belangen (diss. Amsterdam). Ars Aequi Libri, Nijmegen

Rutten SWE (1997) Erven naar Marokkaans recht. Aspecten van Nederlands internationaal privaatrecht bij de toepasselijkheid van Marokkaans erfrecht. Intersentia, Antwerpen

Siehr K (1982) Domestic relations in Europe: European equivalents to American evolutions. The American Journal of Comparative Law 30:37–71

Strikwerda L (1986) Naar een gereduceerd conflictenrecht? Iets over bescherming, begunstiging en better law in het internationaal privaatrecht. Wolters-Noordhoff, Groningen

Strikwerda L (2008) Inleiding tot het Nederlandse Internationaal Privaatrecht, 9th edn. Kluwer, Deventer

Struycken AVM (1994) Favor matrimonii of favor divortii? FJR 16:102–106

Sumner I, Warendorf H (2003) Family law legislation of the Netherlands. Intersentia, Antwerpen

Ten Wolde MH (1996) Internationaal en interregionaal erfrecht in het Koninkrijk der Nederlanden (diss. Groningen). Kluwer, Deventer

Ten Wolde MH (2009) Inleiding Nederlands en Europees Internationaal Privaatrecht, Deel A. Algemeen deel en materieel IPR Personen-, familie- en erfrecht. Hephaestus, Groningen

Van der Velden FJA (2003) Talâq in de rechtszaal? Verstoting en openbare orde. Kluwer, Deventer

Van den Eeckhout V (2000) P.M.M. Mostermans, Echtscheiding. NIPR 38–41

Van den Eeckhout V (2004) Communitarization of private international law: tendencies to "liberalize" international family law. Tijdschrift@ipr.be 51–70. Article available at https://openaccess.leidenuniv.nl/bitstream/1887/16146/2/Microsoft+Word+-+engelsveerleiprtijdschrift definitief.doc%5B1%5D.pdf
Van Maas de Bie AR (1993) Artikelen 36-39 en 34 IPR-Schets: Echtscheiding, alimentatie en echtscheidingsgevolgen. WPNR 6106:663–667
Van Maas de Bie AR (2002) Internationale Scheidungen und Scheidungsfolgen in Deutschland und in den Niederlanden (diss. Leiden)
Van Rooij R (1981) Wetgeving internationale echtscheidingen. Ars Aequi 30:420–429
Van Rooij R, Polak MV (1987) Private international law in the Netherlands. Kluwer, Deventer
Vischer F (1999) Connecting factors. In: International Encyclopedia of Comparative Law—Volume III Private International Law. Mohr Siebeck, Tübingen, pp 3–33
Vlas P (1996) Echtscheiding in het IPR: de peildatum en het bijzondere geval. Ars Aequi 47:196–202
Vonken APMJ (1981) Het internationale echtscheidingsrecht. Het Personeel Statuut pp 50–54, 60–69
Vonken APMJ (Groene Serie Personen- en familierecht) Titel 9, Internationaal Privaatrecht. Internationale Echtscheidingen. Groene Serie Privaatrecht, Personen- en familierecht (Electronic database Plaza Kluwer Juridisch en Fiscaal, looseleaf)
Wendels A (1983) Internationale echtscheidingen. W.E.J. Tjeenk Willink, Zwolle

Chapter 3
The Dutch Choice of Law Rules on the Termination of Registered Partnerships

3.1 Introduction

On 1 January 1998 the Act introducing Registered Partnership entered into force in the Netherlands.[1] The parliamentary proceedings on this Act show that the institution of registered partnership has been introduced in order to pursue two objectives.[2] It was primarily created to guarantee equal treatment for same-sex couples wishing to have their relationship publicly recognised: registered partnership consequently provides for a status that is equal to marriage. Therefore, the rights and duties attached to registered partnership are practically the same as those attached to marriage.[3] The second objective of the Act introducing Registered Partnership was to provide an alternative for marriage to different-sex couples.

As well as a marriage, a registered partnership can break down. According to Dutch law a registered partnership shall end on the ground of 'irretrievable breakdown of the relationship' by reason of mutual consent of the partners, by dissolution at the request of one of the partners, or by conversion of a registered partnership into a marriage.[4]

---

[1] Act of 5 July 1997, *Stb.* 1997, No. 324 tot wijziging van Boek 1 van het Burgerlijk Wetboek en van het Wetboek van Burgerlijke Rechtsvordering in verband met opneming daarin van bepalingen voor het geregistreerd partnerschap. Shortly: Act introducing registered partnership.

[2] Memorandum in reply to the parliamentary report (NV), *Kamerstukken II* 1995–1996, 23 761, No. 7, p. 11. See also Boele-Woelki et al. 2007, p. 5 ff.

[3] One of the few differences is that no court-intervention is required in case of termination of a registered partnership by mutual consent.

[4] See Article 1:80c(1) BW, which determines that a registered partnership will also end due to death or a missing partner. This chapter only focuses on the termination of a registered partnership by mutual consent or by dissolution. See Sumner 2004b, pp. 231–237 and Mostermans 2006, pp. 64–65 on the choice of law rules on the termination of a registered partnership by conversion into a marriage.

N.A. Baarsma, *The Europeanisation of International Family Law*,
DOI: 10.1007/978-90-6704-743-2_3, © T.M.C. Asser press, The Hague,
The Netherlands, and the author 2011

Not all countries, however, know exactly this same ground for the termination of a registered partnership. In fact, the grounds for the termination of a registered partnership differ greatly.[5]

The breakdown of a registered partnership can very well involve an international element; e.g. on the basis of one or more of the following circumstances: the persons involved in a registered partnership are of different nationalities, or live in different countries, or live in a country other than the one in which their partnership has been registered, or live in a country of which they are not nationals.[6]

In such international cases the question can arise as to which legal system the Dutch court, notary or lawyer[7] has to apply to the termination of a registered partnership: Dutch law or foreign law? Therefore, choice of law rules is necessary in order to determine the law applicable to the termination of a registered partnership.

To date there is no international instrument in the field of registered partnerships.[8] Due to the fact that there are no international treaties, conventions or bilateral agreements applicable with regard to (the termination of) registered partnerships, each country can autonomously provide for choice of law rules in this field.

This chapter deals with the Dutch choice of law rules on the termination of registered partnerships. Firstly, the absence of a private international law treaty in the field of (the termination of) registered partnerships will be addressed (Section 3.2). After a brief overview of the realisation of the Dutch Choice of Law Act on Registered Partnerships and its foundation (Section 3.3), the choice of law rules on the termination of registered partnerships will be discussed (Section 3.4). Section 3.5 elaborates on the public policy exception. Finally, the question whether the Dutch Proposal on Private International Law will bring any changes as regards the law applicable to the termination of registered partnerships will be examined (Section 3.6).

---

[5] Cf., Sumner 2004a, p. 46, who concludes, after an overview of the various termination procedures available in five European countries, that '[…] *not only are the current registered partnerships in these five countries extremely divergent with respect to their entry requirements, but that the associated termination procedures provide yet another layer of complexity.*'

[6] Actually the same circumstances that give a divorce an international character determine whether the termination of a registered partnership bears such a character. Cf., *supra* Sect. 2.1.

[7] In accordance with Article 1:80c BW a registered partnership can be terminated either judicially or administratively. In case of an administrative termination the partners need to be assisted by one or more notaries or lawyers. See further *infra* Sect. 3.4.2.

[8] The International Commission for Civil Status has drawn up a Convention on the Recognition of Registered Partnerships (No. 32), opened for signature on 5 September 2007. See: http://www.ciec1.org/ListeConventions.htm. This Convention has not entered into force yet. The Convention focuses solely on the recognition of registered partnerships and does not establish any choice of law rules. Moreover, this Convention concentrates on the effects on civil status and is neutral as regards the effects concerning property or social effects, etc.

3.2 The Absence of a Treaty in the Field of Registered Partnerships

Save the Convention on the recognition of registered partnerships drawn up by the International Commission for Civil Status,[9] there is no international instrument in the field of registered partnerships.

The law applicable in respect of 'unmarried couples', a subject broader than registered partnerships, is on the Agenda of the Hague Conference on Private International Law. However, no priority has been given to the establishment of an instrument in this field of law.[10] The number of states that recognise the possibility of cohabitation outside marriage or of a registered partnership is too small.[11] Furthermore, a comparison of internal legal systems has shown that a wide range of solutions have evolved. Some systems regulate all the relationships arising from cohabitation, while others focus on certain aspects only, and still other systems leave the whole subject outside the law.[12]

Duncan has distinguished two difficulties that arise in achieving a uniform approach on this issue.[13] First, in those States which have introduced the institution of registered partnership, there will be a tendency, when developing private international law rules, to give preference to their own laws and procedures, or to

---

[9] Ibid.

[10] In April 2009 it was lastly confirmed that The Hague Conference leaves the issue without priority on the Agenda, see Conclusions and Recommendations adopted by the Council on General Affairs and Policy of the Conference of 31 March–2 April 2009. The Hague Conference does, however, recognise the need for a convention in this field; see Preliminary Document No. 9 of May 2000 for the attention of the Special Commission of May 2000 on General Affairs and Policy of the Conference, p. 5: '*The absence of clear private international law rules may inhibit free movement across borders by cohabitees where, for example, a status or legal right established in one jurisdiction is not recognised in another, or it may facilitate a partner who is intent on evading established obligations. On the other hand, there is an underlying issue of public policy and a perception in certain states that the recognition of legal consequences for cohabitation may undermine a policy of preference of marriage.*' See also Note on developments in internal law and private international law concerning cohabitation outside marriage, including registered partnership, Preliminary Document No. 11 of March 2008.

[11] See for a list of countries that recognise the concept of registered partnership Boele-Woelki et al. 2007, p. 103, footnote no. 1. Within the European Union currently fourteen Member States know some form of registered partnership, i.e. Austria, Belgium, Czech Republic, Denmark, France, Finland, Germany, Hungary, Luxembourg, the Netherlands, Portugal, Slovenia, Sweden and the United Kingdom. Cf., Curry-Sumner 2008, pp. 102–103.

[12] See Preliminary Document No. 5 of April 1992 for the attention of the Special Commission of June 1992 on General Affairs and Policy of the Conference. This point of view has been confirmed anew by the Special Commission in June 2000; see Preliminary Document No. 10 of June 2000 for the attention of the Nineteenth Session. See also Note on developments in internal law and private international law concerning cohabitation outside marriage, including registered partnership, Preliminary Document No. 11 of March 2008. See also Hausmann 2000, pp. 241–248; and Boele-Woelki et al. 2007, p. 267.

[13] Duncan 1999, pp. 3–4.

the laws and procedures of other States in which the institution exists. This is a natural tendency deriving from the practical need to avoid the vacuum that might otherwise arise.[14] Secondly the attitudes towards recognition of registered partnerships, in those States which do not provide for the registered partnership in their national laws, will vary.[15]

Doctrine is divided on the question whether the Hague Conference should give higher priority to the establishment of a convention in the field of-at least-registered partnerships.[16]

According to Duncan there are two reasons to develop a uniform approach to (some) private international law aspects of registered partnerships. In the first place, the legal vacuum that currently exists in many national legal systems needs to be filled: the status (if any) to be accorded to registered partners who move from one jurisdiction to another needs to be clarified. A solution might be found by establishing some generally accepted principles. Secondly, it would be desirable, at least in respect to those states which are willing to afford some level of recognition to foreign registered partnerships, to develop some uniformity in the approach to recognition in order to provide some continuity in the status of registered partners.[17]

Šarčević recognises the challenge for the Hague Conference on Private International Law of adopting uniform conflicts solutions for non-marital cohabitation.[18] The most difficult task would be to agree on a definition of the non-marital union to be regulated or to specify its main characteristics. By now one should be able to detect a minimum of common denominators, thus making it possible to identify the major characteristics of non-marital cohabitation most likely to be accepted by all States, including those where the institution is not (yet) regulated by substantive law. In his opinion, if these states had the option, it is more likely that they would join an international instrument with uniform choice of law rules rather than regulate the subject matter by national legislation.[19]

However, although Šarčević states that there is no doubt that it would be useful to unify the private international law aspects of registered partnerships in an international convention, he does not consider the time ripe yet to attempting to unify the choice of law rules for registered partnerships at the international level. New institutions require some 'digesting time' before acceptable uniform solutions can be found or before a large number of countries are even willing to discuss the subject matter at an international conference such as the Hague Conference.[20]

[14] As will be discussed below, the Dutch private international law rules are a good example of this approach. See further *infra* Sect. 3.3.3.

[15] See Duncan 1999, p. 4.

[16] See, in general, Goldstein 2006, p. 369 ff.

[17] See Duncan 1999, p. 3.

[18] Šarčević 1981, pp. 337–338; and Šarčević 1999, pp. 45–48.

[19] Šarčević 1999, p. 46.

[20] Ibid., pp. 47–48.

Joppe holds this same view on the unification of private international law issues of registered partnership. She argues that the large diversity of national regulations in this field makes it very hard to reach consensus on the international level. Moreover, a country will probably change its point of view with regard to the recognition of registered partnerships entered into abroad from the moment it introduces the institution of registered partnership in its own national legislation. Therefore, the establishment of an international convention should be postponed until the national developments in this field have more or less stabilised.[21]

Šarčević and Joppe rightly argue that, although the number of countries introducing the institution of registered partnership increases, it seems premature to try to reach an international consensus on the issue. This is very well reflected by the resistance that the Hague Conference experiences when it tries to give more priority to the establishment of an instrument on the issue of unmarried couples.[22]

3.3 The Dutch Choice of Law Act on Registered Partnerships

In the absence of an international convention that could be ratified, the Dutch legislator has introduced private international law provisions in respect to registered partnerships. As of 1 January 2005 the Dutch Choice of Law Act on Registered Partnerships is in force.[23] This Act does not only provide for rules concerning the termination of a registered partnership. The Act also includes choice of law rules on the entry into a registered partnership in the Netherlands and on the recognition of a registered partnership entered into abroad, on the legal personal ties between the partners, on the partnership property regime, and on maintenance obligations during the registered partnership as well as after termination of the registered partnership.

After some general remark (Section 3.3.1), Section 3.3.2 will elaborate on the characteristics of the CLARP. Subsequently, its substantive and temporal scope of application (Sections 3.3.3 and 3.3.4) will be discussed.

---

[21] Joppe (Groene Serie Personen- en familierecht), General remarks, n. 4.

[22] See Report of the Special Commission on General Affairs and Policy of the Conference of 31 March to 1 April 2005, Preliminary Document No. 32A of May 2005, pp. 28–29. The United States is one of the strongest opponents of any activity of the Hague Conference in this field.

[23] Act of 6 July 2004, *Stb.* 2004, Nos. 334 and 621, containing a regulation of the choice of law with regard to the registered partnership, *Wet conflictenrecht geregistreerd partnerschap*. Hereinafter abbreviated to 'CLARP'.

3.3.1 General

As mentioned above, the institution of registered partnership has been provided for in Dutch substantive law since 1 January 1998. Although the Dutch Standing Committee on Private International Law had already drawn up an advice concerning the choice of law on registered partnerships in May 1998, the legislator did not regulate this field of law until 1 January 2005.[24]

Why did the Choice of Law Act on Registered Partnerships only enter into force in January 2005? The legislator puts forward two reasons for this lapse of time:

> In verband met de ontwikkelingen rond het geregistreerd partnerschap en de openstelling van het huwelijk van personen van hetzelfde geslacht, die zich in de afgelopen drie jaar hebben voorgedaan, is enige tijd gewacht met de omzetting van het advies van de Staatscommissie in wetgeving. De openstelling van het huwelijk voor personen van hetzelfde geslacht heeft niet geleid tot afschaffing van het geregistreerd partnerschap. Hoewel het instituut van het geregistreerd partnerschap elders geleidelijk ingang vindt, is het niet waarschijnlijk dat binnen afzienbare tijd een verdragsregeling over internationaal privaatrechtelijke aspecten ter zake tot stand zal komen.[25]

Firstly, it was expected that the opening up of civil marriage to same-sex couples would lead to the abolition of the institution of registered partnership.[26] This has, however, not happened. When it became clear that the opening up of civil marriage would not lead to the abolition of the institution of registered partnership, the Minister of Justice declared that the private international law aspects of same-sex marriage should be regulated jointly with those of registered partnership.[27] But, as seen above in Section 2.2.2, the private international law aspects of same-sex marriage have been regulated separately from those of registered partnership.[28]

---

[24] Staatscommissie 1998; the advice dates from 8 May 1998 and has been published in *FJR* 1998, pp. 146–159.

[25] Explanatory Memorandum (MvT), *Kamerstukken II* 2002–2003, 28 924, No. 3, p. 2.

[26] See *NJB* 1999, p. 148 and 1295. As seen above, the institution of registered partnership was primarily created to ensure equal treatment for same-sex couples wishing to formalise their relationship. However, the abolition of the institution of registered partnership on the sole ground that the opening up of marriage to same-sex couples has led to fulfilment of the first objective of the Act introducing registered partnership would do no justice to the second objective of the latter Act, i.e. providing different-sex couples with an alternative for marriage.

[27] Letter of the Minister of Justice of mid 1999, to which is referred by Joppe 2000, p. 373 and by Jessurun d'Oliveira 2000, p. 300.

[28] Dutch substantive law recognises only one type of marriage, i.e. the marriage open to couples regardless of sex. Therefore, the same-sex marriage has been included in the already existing private international law rules on marriage.

Secondly, initially preference was given to the establishment of a multilateral convention on registered partnerships.[29] The Hague Conference on Private International Law would be the most obvious body to draw up such a convention.[30] However, despite the fact that this subject has been set on the Agenda of the Hague Conference, no priority has been given to the establishment of a convention in the field of the law applicable to unmarried couples.[31]

Also in the European context there is some development in the field of registered partnerships. Even though the European Commission has presented a Green Paper on Matrimonial Property of both marriage and extra-marital unions, this project is still in a preparatory stage. Moreover, the scope of application of this prospective Regulation will definitely be limited to the matrimonial property regime.

As it was unlikely that choice of law rules on registered partnerships would be drawn up in either European or international context within the foreseeable future, the Dutch legislature had to take action.[32]

Even though the advice of the Standing Committee of 1998 has been taken as a guideline in practice, legal certainty with regard to the law applicable to several questions of private international law regarding registered partnerships was at stake.[33] It must be stressed that the Standing Committee did not advocate this approach, as it urged the legislator to enact legal provisions on this issue.[34]

Jessurun d'Oliviera reproached the legislator with extreme carelessness in respect of all those registered partners who want to know, preferably in advance, under which circumstances the Dutch court has jurisdiction in international cases and which law will be applied to their partnership property regime, maintenance, and equalisation of pension rights, etc. Even if the institution of registered partnership would be abolished, there would still be a need for rules on private international law for the registered partnerships that have already been entered into and certainly for the recognition of the registered partnerships that have been entered into or terminated abroad.[35]

Ten Wolde has equally urged the legislator to quickly regulate the private international law issues on registered partnerships. His main concern was that legal

---

29 A conference discussing the possible establishment of a convention in this field has been organised by the Council of Europe in March 1999 in The Hague. See further Schrama 1999, p. 131 ff.

30 See equally Boele-Woelki 1999, p. 13.

31 See *supra* Sect. 3.2.

32 See Boele-Woelki 2003, p. 4848.

33 Certainly given the fact that the Choice of Law Act on Registered Partnerships solely applies to registered partnerships that have been concluded after the entry of this Act. See further *infra* Sect. 3.3.4.

34 See Staatscommissie 1998, para 2.

35 Jessurun d'Oliveira 1999, pp. 305–306. See also Joppe 2000, pp. 394–395.

practice was more or less adrift in this field, as certainty with regard to the choice of law is needed for legal practitioners so as to know how to advice their clients.[36] Although the Standing Committee has noticed in its advice that some anticipatory effect emanates from it,[37] this does not guarantee any certainty.[38] The legislator is namely by no means bound to the advice of the Standing Committee and is fully free to draw up different rules on the private international law aspects of registered partnerships. The absence of private international law rules in this field therefore led to legal uncertainty and thereby to legal inequality for registered partners.[39]

3.3.2 Characteristics of the CLARP

The Choice of Law Act on Registered Partnerships has a number of characteristics.[40] With regard to the termination of a registered partnership the following four characteristics are of particular importance.

In the first place, the underlying principle of the Act is that the equal treatment of marriage and registered partnership in substantive law should equally influence the choice of law rules on registered partnership. However, the relative rarity of the institution could necessitate deviations from the equal footing with marriage.

Secondly, the CLARP contains mostly unilateral choice of law rules. As opposed to multilateral choice of law rules that refer to foreign law as well as to national law, unilateral choice of law rules only indicate when the *lex fori* -Dutch law- applies.[41] The choice for unilateral choice of law rules in the CLARP is motivated by the fact that there are currently only a few countries that have incorporated the registered partnership, or a similar institution, in their legislation. Consequently, a multilateral choice of law rule might imply that the law of a foreign legal system that does not recognise the institution of registered partnership is designated as the applicable law. Such reference might lead to practical problems; the Dutch Standing Committee on Private International Law referred to this effect as the reference to a 'legal vacuum'[42]:

---

[36] Ten Wolde 2001, p. 141.

[37] See Staatscommissie 1998, para 2.

[38] Cf., Jessurun d'Oliveira 2000, p. 300 stating that '*the formal status of the Standing Committee's proposal is for the time being floating in limbo*'.

[39] See Ten Wolde 2001, p. 141.

[40] Boele-Woelki 2003 distinguishes six remarkable characteristics of the CLARP. Only four of the characteristics Boele-Woelki mentions are of importance with regard to the termination of a registered partnership. See also Joppe 2000, p. 374; Joppe (Groene Serie Personen- en familierecht), CLARP, n. 8; and Ten Wolde 2001, pp. 141–143.

[41] Cf., Strikwerda 2008, pp. 26–27; and Ten Wolde 2009, pp. 48–49.

[42] See Staatscommissie 1998, para 4: '*een juridisch luchtledig*'. See also Joppe 2000, p. 374; Ten Wolde 2001, p. 142; Explanatory Memorandum (MvT), *Kamerstukken II* 2002–2003, 28 924, No. 3, p. 3; and Frohn 2004, p. 290.

> Ten aanzien van een aantal onderwerpen bevat het voorstel geen alzijdige conflictregels, maar beperkt het zich tot het ontwikkelen van eenzijdige regels die aangeven in welke gevallen Nederlands intern recht toepasselijk is op geregistreerde partnerschappen die in Nederland zijn aangegaan. De keuze voor deze aanpak is uiteraard een gevolg van de overweging dat alzijdige verwijzingsregels op het terrein van het geregistreerd partnerschap in een *juridisch luchtledig* terecht zouden komen in al die gevallen dat zo'n conflictregel zou verwijzen naar een rechtsstelsel dat het geregistreerd partnerschap of verwante rechtsfiguren niet kent.[43]

The unilateral character of the choice of law rules of the CLARP has provoked some critique.[44] In order to prevent the situation in which the law of a country that does not recognise the institution of registered partnership is designated as the applicable law, the Dutch choice of law rules should be provided with connecting factors that lead to the applicability of a legal system that does recognise the registered partnership. Besides, a choice of law rule should designate the law to which the legal relationship is most closely connected.[45] From this point of view it is not entirely clear why the legislator chose for unilateral choice of law rules. The establishment of multilateral choice of law rules that are provided with connecting factors that designate the law of a country that recognises the institution of registered partnership would have been perfectly possible. The *locus celebrationis* could serve as an alternative connecting factor, instead of connecting to the nationality or the habitual residence of (one of) the partners. The use of the *locus celebrationis* as a connecting factor implies that only the law of a country that recognises the legal concept of registered partnership can be designated as the applicable law. The legislator has been aware of this connecting factor, since the *locus celebrationis* has been frequently used throughout the whole Act. However, one should be aware that the *locus celebrationis* does not *per se* reflect a close connection and is, therefore, not always a suitable connecting factor.[46]

The legislator has clearly indicated that, should in the future the number of countries that have introduced the institution of registered partnership in their legislation extend, it could be desirable to change the unilateral rules of the CLARP to multilateral choice of law rules.[47]

Although the use of multilateral choice of law rules as regards registered partnership should be stimulated, the current provisions seem to suffice at the moment. The unilateral choice of law rules of the CLARP do not only apply to

---

[43] Staatscommissie 1998, para 4 (emphasis added).

[44] See *inter alia* Ten Wolde 2001, p. 142; and Reinhartz 2004, p. 491.

[45] Cf., Strikwerda 2008, pp. 36–37.

[46] The connection that the *locus celebrationis* reflects depends on the criteria the *lex loci celebrationis* attaches to the entry into a registered partnership. E.g. in the Netherlands, a registered partnership can only be concluded if at least one of the persons involved has his/her residence in the Netherlands or possesses Dutch nationality (Article 80a(4) BW).

[47] Explanatory Memorandum (MvT), *Kamerstukken II* 2002–2003, 28 924, No. 3, p. 3:.'Ik [the Dutch Minister of Justice; NAB] ben mij overigens ten volle ervan bewust dat het te zijner tijd wenselijk kan blijken de regeling op dit punt bij te stellen.' The Standing Committee has equally advocated this point of view, see Staatscommissie 1998, para 4.

registered partnerships entered into in the Netherlands, but also to those entered into abroad. Consequently, there is no gap in the law as regards the law applicable to the termination of registered partnerships.[48]

The third characteristic of the CLARP is that if the choice of law rules refer to the law of the place of registration, it concerns a referral to this law in its entirety, i.e. the law including the private international law rules of that country (*Gesamtverweisung*). The Explanatory Memorandum to the CLARP explains this characteristic:

> Voor in het buitenland aangegane geregistreerde partnerschappen is gekozen voor aanknoping bij de «lex loci celebrationis», het recht van de staat waar de verbintenis is aangegaan, met inbegrip van het daar ontwikkelde internationaal privaatrecht. [...] In het algemeen worden de belangen van de partners in een elders geregistreerd partnerschap het beste gediend door bij het stelsel van de lex loci celebrationis aan te sluiten, onder meer omdat hun verwachtingen geacht mogen worden bij dat rechtsstelsel aan te sluiten.[49]

The legislator justifies the use of the *Gesamtverweisung* by stating that it is in the parties' interests to connect to the law of the state where the registered partnership has been concluded: generally their expectations can be considered to join this legal system. Ten Wolde has objected to this characteristic, notably from a practical point of view.[50] For it is too large a call on Dutch legal practice having to determine the content of the foreign private international law rules, in the event that such rules would already exist. In particular the legal certainty and the ease of use of the choice of law highly oppose a system in which the applicable law is to be determined according to non-existent or indefinite foreign private international law rules. Furthermore, this choice of law system is contrary to the general approach adopted with respect to *renvoi* in the Dutch choice of law.[51]

Finally, the CLARP makes a clear and systematic distinction between registered partnerships entered into in the Netherlands and those entered into abroad.[52] These two categories have found a separate regulation throughout the whole Act. Ten Wolde has opposed this distinction because it would violate the general principles of private international law as regards legal certainty and the ease of use of the choice of law. He argues that the same-multilateral-choice of law rules should apply to registered partnerships, regardless of the place they have been

---

48 In contrast to for example the Dutch - unilateral - choice of law rule on the winding up and distribution of estates, which only covers the situation in which the deceased had his habitual residence in the Netherlands. Dutch law does not provide any rule on the law applicable to the administration of estates when the deceased's last habitual residence had not been located in the Netherlands. See further on this issue Ten Wolde 1996, p. 298; and Knot 2008, p. 72 ff.

49 Explanatory Memorandum (MvT), *Kamerstukken II* 2002–2003, 28 924, No. 3, p. 3. The Standing Committee advocated the same point of view, see Staatscommissie 1998, para 4.

50 Ten Wolde 2001, p. 143.

51 See Article 5 of the Dutch Proposal on Private International Law, which determines that the choice of law rules refer solely to the substantive rules of the applicable law (*Sachnormverweisung*).

52 See Explanatory Memorandum (MvT), *Kamerstukken II* 2002–2003, 28 924, No. 3, p. 3.

entered into.[53] Although the application of the same choice of law rules to registered partnerships, irrespective of the *locus celebrationis*, is to be welcomed, the mentioned distinction in the CLARP does not seem to harm the general principles of private international law in question, as the distinction has been carried out systematically throughout the whole Act.

3.3.3 Scope of Application

Worldwide, the institution of registered partnership is still a relatively rare phenomenon. Besides, the countries that have regulated the institution of registered partnership have attached divergent legal consequences thereto.[54] The differences lie not only in the legal consequences attached to the registration of a partnership: in some countries the regulations merely create a simple contractual relationship, while in other legal systems the regulations determine personal status. The scope of the national regulations also differs: registered partnerships can be allowed for same-sex couples only (e.g., Scandinavian countries), or for both same-sex and different-sex couples (e.g., Belgium, the Netherlands), or even to asexual couples, such as brother-sister, or mother-daughter relationships (e.g., France, Spain).[55]

It is clear from the Dutch parliamentary proceedings that not all foreign forms of registered partnership can be recognised as such in the Netherlands.[56] Although the basic principle of the CLARP is that a registered partnership lawfully concluded abroad will be recognised as such in the Netherlands, the foreign institution does have to meet a set of criteria:

> Het wetsvoorstel beoogt regels te geven voor die samenlevingsvormen waaraan staatgevolg ('Standesfolge') is verbonden. Een typisch kenmerk is daarbij de registratie. Een ander kenmerk dat in deze van belang is, is dat het gaat om een rechtsinstituut dat exclusief is, dat wil zeggen een verbintenis die een huwelijk of ander partnerschap van een van de partners met een derde uitsluit en bestemd is voor de juridische bevestiging en bescherming van affectieve relaties. Van belang is verder dat het gaat om partnerschappen waarbij de partners, al dan niet van hetzelfde geslacht, op grond van de wet rechten en plichten hebben die gelijk zijn aan of in sterke mate georiënteerd zijn op die van het huwelijk. Te denken valt in het bijzonder aan de verplichting elkaar ter zijde te staan en elkaar het nodige te verschaffen. Voorts valt te denken aan de verplichting tot een

[53] Ten Wolde 2001, p. 143.

[54] Cf., Boele-Woelki 2000, p. 1054, concluding in 2000 that not one single national regulation was completely in conformity with another national regulation.

[55] See Joppe 2000, p. 372.

[56] The regulation of the CLARP differs in this respect from the advice of the Dutch Standing Committee on Private International Law, which proposed a more open-ended provision as regards characterisation by not posing the requirements mentioned in Article 2(5) CLARP. See Staatscommissie 1998, para 7 at Article 18.

evenredige bijdrage in de lasten van de samenleving, hoofdelijke aansprakelijkheid voor de schulden ten behoeve van de samenleving en dergelijke.[57]

These requirements have found a regulation in Article 2(5) CLARP, determining that:

> [...] a registered partnership entered into outside the Netherlands will only be recognised as such, if it forms a legally regulated form of cohabitation between two persons who maintain a close personal relationship, and the cohabitation, at least:
> a. was registered by an authority competent to do so in the place where it was entered into;
> b. excludes the existence of a marriage or other form of cohabitation with a third person regulated by law; and
> c. creates obligations between the partners which, in essence, correspond with those in connection with marriage.[58]

If a registered partnership concluded outside the Netherlands does not meet these criteria, it will not be recognised as such. Such partnership falls outside the scope of application of the choice of law rules of the CLARP.

The Standing Committee on Private International Law has suggested that the choice of law rules of the CLARP may be applied by analogy to other regulated forms of partnership.[59] Ten Wolde has strongly opposed this point of view: such analogical application would bring about an unnecessary complication, as it creates uncertainty. If it is deemed desirable that the choice of law rules apply to all regulated forms of partnership, then this should be stated expressly in the CLARP.[60] However, the Explanatory Memorandum to the CLARP remains silent on this question. Therefore, it should be assumed that the choice of law rules of the CLARP cannot be applied *per analogiam* to regulated forms of partnership that are not recognised as a registered partnership according to the criteria of Article 2(5) CLARP.[61]

3.3.4 Transitional Provision

Article 29 of the CLARP contains a transitional provision:

> 1. This Act shall not apply to registered partnerships concluded prior to the date of its entry into force.

[57] Explanatory Memorandum (MvT), *Kamerstukken II* 2002–2003, 28 924, No. 3, pp. 2–3.

[58] Translation by Sumner and Warendorf 2003, p. 245.

[59] Staatscommissie 1998, para 3.

[60] Ten Wolde 2001, pp. 141–142.

[61] It is highly uncertain which rules do determine the applicable law to those foreign partnerships that fall outside the scope of application of the CLARP. Arguably these partnerships can be considered as contracts. However, this is a matter of characterisation. See further on the characterisation of non-marital registered relationships, Jessurun d'Oliviera 2003, pp. 1–37. See also briefly Hausmann 2000, pp. 248–249.

2. Notwithstanding the provisions of paragraph (1), Article 21 of this Act applies to the equalisation of pension rights in case the registered partnership has been terminated or dissolved after the time of the entry into force of this Act.

According to this provision the rules provided for by the CLARP do not apply to registered partnerships concluded prior to the date of its entry into force. This means that the termination of registered partnerships is only governed by the CLARP if the partnership has been entered into on or after 1 January 2005. The law applicable to a registered partnership entered into before the CLARP took effect is determined on the basis of the general rules of private international law concerning registered partnerships, i.e. the proposal of the Dutch Standing Committee on Private International Law.[62] With regard to the law applicable to the termination of a registered partnership the proposal of the Standing Committee and the regulation of Articles 22 and 23 CLARP correspond.[63]

The provision of Article 29 CLARP is comprehensible, since the CLARP includes choice of law rules for all matters relating to registered partnerships. Although this is merely a theoretical question — the CLARP corresponds to the Standing Committee's proposal as regards the termination of registered partnerships — the provision of Article 29 CLARP is fairly strange with regard to the termination of a registered partnership. It is not logical that the time of the entry into a registered partnership is decisive for the applicable law to its termination. This date of reference does no justice to the principle of the closest connection. Quite some years can easily pass between the entry into the registered partnership and its termination. The date of reference in case of termination of a registered partnership could therefore have better been either the moment that the partners request at least one expert, be it a lawyer or a notary, to assist them in terminating their partnership, or the moment of filing the petition for dissolution of the registered partnership.[64] This date is a better reflection of the closest connection between the registered partnership and the law to be applied to its termination. Moreover, this date of reference is also used in international divorce cases, to which the choice of law rules on the termination of registered partnerships should conform as much as possible.[65]

The legislator should therefore have made an exception to the principal rule of Article 29(1) CLARP for the termination of a registered partnership similar to the exception of Article 29(2) with regard to the equalisation of pension rights.

---

[62] See for a case in which this situation was at issue Rb.'s-Gravenhage 22 September 2006, *NIPR* 2007, 109.

[63] See Staatscommissie 1998, para 7 at Articles 16 and 31.

[64] In case of termination sought on grounds of mutual consent and in case of dissolution sought on grounds of a sole petition, respectively.

[65] See *supra* Sect. 2.4.5.

3.4 The Law Applicable to the Termination of Registered Partnerships

The law applicable to the termination of registered partnerships is determined on the basis of Articles 22 and 23 of the CLARP.

Article 22

> Dutch law determines whether a registered partnership entered into in the Netherlands may be terminated by mutual consent or by dissolution and on which grounds.

Article 23

1. Dutch law determines whether a registered partnership entered into outside the Netherlands may be terminated by mutual consent or by dissolution and on which grounds.
2. In derogation from the provisions of paragraph (1), the law of the State where the registered partnership has been entered into will apply if the partners have jointly made a choice for that law in the contract made between them in respect of the termination by mutual consent of the registered partnership.
3. As regards the termination by dissolution and in derogation from the provisions of paragraph (1), the law of the State where the registered partnership has been entered into will be applied if, in the proceedings:
   a. the partners jointly chose this law or such a choice by one the partners remains uncontested[66]; or
   b. either partner chose such law and both partners have actual ties with the State where their registered partnership was entered into.
4. Dutch law governs the manner in which termination by mutual consent or the dissolution of a registered partnership entered into outside the Netherlands is made.[67]

3.4.1 *Foundation of the Choice of Law Rules on the Termination of Registered Partnerships:* **Favor Dissolutionis**

As mentioned above, the basic principle of the CLARP is that its rules should conform as much as possible to the equivalent rules on marriage.[68] But the fact that the registered partnership and similar legal institutions are relatively rare

[66] The translation of Sumner and Warendorf 2003 provides for another translation of this sentence: 'the partners jointly chose this law or such a choice made by one of the partners has not been revoked'. However, this translation is not entirely accurate, as revoking the choice implies that the other partner should act. Yet, an act of the other party is expressly not required, as the condition can also be fulfilled in case of default of appearance. See *infra* Sect. 3.4.5.2.

[67] Translation by Sumner and Warendorf 2003, p. 250.

[68] This is the result of the position taken in Dutch substantive law as described above, see *supra* Sect. 3.1.

concepts on the international level impedes full application *per analogiam* of the choice of law rules on marriage and divorce.[69]

With regard to the termination of a registered partnership, as with the dissolution of marriage, the underlying basic principle of substantive law is the undesirability of artificially upholding partnerships that have in fact broken down. Since the Dutch choice of law rules on divorce are based on the *favor divortii* principle[70] an equal stance has been adopted with respect to the termination of registered partnerships. In this respect reference has been made to the *favor dissolutionis* principle.[71]

The foundation of the CLARP on the principle of *favor dissolutionis* implies that it aims to favour the possibility to terminate a registered partnership in international cases. Although it might not exist, foreign law that does not allow for the termination of registered partnerships is contrary to the Dutch view of the law.

As with regard to divorce, the choice of law rules on the termination of registered partnerships lead in the majority of cases to the designation of Dutch law as the applicable law. In addition, the parties also have a limited opportunity to choose the law applicable to the termination of their registered partnership.

3.4.2 Structure of the Choice of Law on the Termination of Registered Partnerships

The choice of law on the termination of registered partnerships has been divided in two categories: the registered partnerships entered into in the Netherlands (Article 22) and those entered into outside the Netherlands (Article 23).

Article 23 CLARP makes a further distinction between termination by mutual consent and dissolution by the court. This structure can be traced back to Dutch procedural law. The Dutch legislator has created a two-track system for the termination of registered partnerships: the administrative procedure on the one hand and the judicial procedure on the other.[72] Registered partners wishing to terminate their partnership jointly (‘termination of the registered partnership by mutual consent’) are to make use of the administrative procedure. A registered partner wishing to terminate the relationship unilaterally (‘dissolution of the registered partnership’) is to make use of the judicial procedure.

The termination of a registered partnership by mutual consent is governed by Article 1:80d BW. The partnership is terminated by mutual consent of the partners

---

[69] See Staatscommissie 1998, para 4.

[70] See *supra* Sect. 2.2.3.

[71] See e.g. Curry-Sumner 2005, p. 447 ff.

[72] See Explanatory Memorandum (MvT), *Kamerstukken II* 1996–1997, 23 761, No. 3, p. 10. See further Curry-Sumner 2005, p. 149; and Boele-Woelki et al. 2007, p. 35 ff.

and does not require any judicial intervention. The termination is established by a mutual agreement signed by both partners and one or more lawyers or notaries. Article 1:80d(1) BW requires that both partners have agreed that the relationship has irretrievably broken down and that they wish to terminate their relationship.

If the termination is sought on grounds of a sole petition, a judicial procedure is required. It is worth noticing that, as opposed to the dissolution of a marriage, the judicial proceedings for the termination of a registered partnership may only be initiated upon a petition filed by one of the parties, thus excluding the possibility of a joint petition.[73]

This distinction made by Dutch procedural law is also found in Article 23 CLARP. Article 23(2) applies to the termination of a registered partnership by mutual consent, whereas Article 23(3) applies to the termination of a registered partnership on grounds of a sole petition.[74]

3.4.3 The Choice of Law Rules: General Remarks

The legislator has with regard to the choice of law rules on the termination of registered partnerships tried to join as much as possible the choice of law rules on divorce. However, two remarks must be made in this regard.

In the first place, full analogous application of the current choice of law rules on divorce could lead to the situation in which the law of a country that is devoid of provisions on the matter is designated as the applicable law.[75] It is perfectly possible that the common national law of the parties or the law of their common habitual residence do not provide for the possibility to enter into a registered partnership, let alone for rules on the termination of such a relationship. The application of the latter choice of law rules by analogy to the termination of registered partnerships could thus lead to the situation in which the registered partnership cannot be terminated.[76]

Secondly, the question arose as to which choice of law rules the legislator should join with respect to the choice of law on the termination of registered partnerships. For while the choice of law on divorce is currently determined in the Choice of Law Act on Divorce, the Dutch Standing Committee on Private

---

[73] Article 1:80c(1d) BW.

[74] See further *infra* Sect. 3.4.5 in which the law applicable to these two categories will be discussed more profoundly.

[75] See Explanatory Memorandum (MvT), *Kamerstukken II* 2002–2003, 28 924, No. 3, pp. 16–17.

[76] For exactly this reason the Dutch Standing Committee chose to draw up unilateral choice of law rules, because otherwise a 'legal vacuum' is designated. See Staatscommissie 1998, para 4. Moreover, as seen above, such a result would be contrary to the *favor dissolutionis* principle. See also Mostermans 2006, p. 66.

International Law proposed to amend these rules.[77] The proposed amendment of the choice of law rules on divorce entails that in principle Dutch law applies to an international divorce, unless the spouses choose for the application of their common national law. This *professio iuris* provides the spouses the opportunity to increase the chance that the Dutch decision on their divorce will be recognised in their country of origin. The legislator has settled the mentioned question in favour of the proposed amended choice of law rules on divorce.[78] However, the most important difference is that the possible recognition of the termination of a registered partnership by mutual consent or by dissolution in the country of origin of the partners is considered to be less important, notably if their national law is devoid of provisions on the matter.[79] Consequently, in case of a registered partnership entered into abroad the parties are provided the opportunity to make a *professio iuris* in favour of the law of the country where the partnership has been registered (*lex loci celebrationis*), which may or may not coincide with their common national law.

As already mentioned above, one of the characteristics of the CLARP is that it makes a clear and systematic distinction between registered partnerships entered into in the Netherlands and those entered into abroad.[80] With respect to the applicable law to the termination of a registered partnership this distinction has been equally upheld: Article 22 CLARP designates the law applicable to the former situation, whereas the applicable law to the latter situation is determined by Article 23 CLARP.

The principal rule regarding the applicable law to the termination of a registered partnership can be derived from Articles 22 and 23 CLARP: Dutch law will apply in all cases unless the partners have chosen the application of the *lex loci celebrationis*.[81] As a result, Curry-Sumner distinguished the following three categories:

a. registered partnerships entered into in the Netherlands;
b. registered partnerships entered into outside the Netherlands where termination is sought on grounds of mutual consent; and
c. registered partnerships entered into outside the Netherlands where dissolution is sought on grounds of a sole petition.[82]

Below these three categories will be discussed. The law applicable to the termination of registered partnerships of category a will be discussed in Section 3.4.4.

---

[77] In the Dutch Proposal on Private International Law this proposal has been copied; see further *supra* Sect. 2.6.

[78] See Explanatory Memorandum (MvT), *Kamerstukken II* 2002–2003, 28 924, No. 3, p. 17. See also Joppe 2000, p. 393 and Joppe (Groene Serie Personen- en Familierecht), Article 23 CLARP, n. 28.

[79] See Staatscommissie 1998, para 7 at Article 31; Explanatory Memorandum (MvT), *Kamerstukken II* 2002–2003, 28 924, No. 3, p. 17 and Mostermans 2006, p. 67.

[80] See *supra* Sect. 3.3.2.

[81] Curry-Sumner 2005, p. 457, stating that '*despite the apparent complexity of the Dutch choice of law rules* [...], *the ultimate scheme is based on a simple distinction.*'

[82] Curry-Sumner 2005, p. 457.

The choice of law on the termination of registered partnerships of categories b and c -those entered into abroad- will be discussed in Section 3.4.5.

3.4.4 Termination of Registered Partnerships Entered into in the Netherlands

Pursuant to Article 22 CLARP the termination of registered partnerships entered into in the Netherlands is governed by Dutch law, which determines whether these partnerships can be terminated by mutual consent or be dissolved and on which grounds.

The partners who have entered into a registered partnership in the Netherlands do not have the opportunity to make a *professio iuris* in favour of a foreign legal system.

Before the entry into force of the Choice of Law Act on Registered Partnerships, Dutch courts already applied this choice of law rule to the termination of registered partnerships entered into in the Netherlands.[83]

3.4.5 Termination of Registered Partnerships Entered into Abroad

In principle also the termination of registered partnerships entered into outside the Netherlands is governed by Dutch law (Article 23(1) CLARP):

> 1. Dutch law determines whether a registered partnership entered into outside the Netherlands may be terminated by mutual consent or by dissolution and on which grounds.

This provision gives the parties the certainty that their registered partnership can be terminated, even if this would not be possible according to the *lex loci celebrationis*. Article 23(1) CLARP thus favours the application of Dutch law and is based on the *favor dissolutionis* principle.[84]

The partners who have entered into a registered partnership outside the Netherlands do have the opportunity to choose the law applicable to the termination of their registered partnership pursuant to Article 23(2) and (3) CLARP. However, this *professio iuris* is limited to the law of the country where the partnership has been registered (*lex loci celebrationis*). The *professio iuris* according

[83] Dutch law was applied on the basis of the regulation as proposed by the Standing Committee in 1998. See Rb. Roermond 29 March 2001, *NIPR* 2001, 188; Rb.'s-Gravenhage 23 April 2003, *NIPR* 2003, 173; Rb.'s-Gravenhage 27 August 2003, *NIPR* 2003, 253; Rb.'s-Gravenhage 27 October 2003, *NIPR* 2004, 11; and Rb.'s-Gravenhage 10 December 2003, *NIPR* 2004, 119.

[84] See equally Reinhartz 2004, p. 495.

to Article 23(2) or (3) CLARP mostly aims at favouring the recognition of the termination of the registered partnership in the country where it has been concluded.[85]

The *professio iuris* on the termination of registered partnerships is at disposal of the partners both in case of the termination by mutual consent (Article 23(2) CLARP) and in case of the termination by dissolution (Article 23(3) CLARP):

2. In derogation from the provisions of paragraph (1), the law of the State where the registered partnership has been entered into will apply if they have jointly made a choice of that law in the contract made between the partners in respect of the termination by mutual consent of the registered partnership.
3. As regards the termination by dissolution and in derogation from the provisions of paragraph (1), the law of the State where the registered partnership has been entered into will be applied if, in the proceedings:
   a. the partners jointly chose this law or such a choice by one the partners remains uncontested; or
   b. either partner chose such law and both partners have actual ties with the State where their registered partnership was entered into.

According to these provisions the parties can deviate from the principal rule of Article 23(1) CLARP (i.e. application of Dutch law) by choosing the application of the *lex loci celebrationis*.

3.4.5.1 Limited *Professio Iuris*

The parties have a limited opportunity to choose the law applicable to the termination of their registered partnership: solely the *lex loci celebrationis* can be chosen.

The legislator has put forward the following arguments in support of this choice:

> De verwijzing naar het recht van de gemeenschappelijke nationaliteit of van de gewone verblijfplaats kan bij beëindiging van een geregistreerd partnerschap echter tot praktische problemen leiden, indien dat recht het instituut van het geregistreerd partnerschap niet kent. Voor de beëindiging van het geregistreerd partnerschap lijkt voor de partners veeleer een belang te zijn gelegen in het doen van een keuze voor het recht van het land waar het geregistreerd partnerschap is aangegaan. Voor hen zal met name van belang zijn of een beëindiging met wederzijds goedvinden of een rechterlijke beslissing over ontbinding kan worden erkend in het land waar het geregistreerd partnerschap is aangegaan.[86]

In the first place the legislator indicates that the referral to the law of the common nationality of the partners or to the law of their habitual residence may lead to practical problems in case of termination of a registered partnership, if this

[85] See Explanatory Memorandum (MvT), *Kamerstukken II* 2002–2003, 28 924, No. 3, pp. 16–17.

[86] Explanatory Memorandum (MvT), *Kamerstukken II* 2002–2003, 28 924, No. 3, pp. 16–17.

law does not know the institution of registered partnership. The legislator rightly stresses that the designation of the law of the common nationality of the partners or the law of their habitual residence may lead to practical problems. However, it is not obvious that such referral necessarily leads to problems. Moreover, in the absence of a *professio iuris*, the reference to a legal vacuum, i.e. a law which does not know the concept of registered partnership, is clearly undesirable. Yet this argument is not very convincing in case of a *professio iuris* by the parties: why protect the parties who deliberately chose the application of a law which does not allow for the termination of a registered partnership? Only considerations of legal economy come into mind.

Secondly, the legislature rightly argues that the partners have an interest in the possibility to choose the *lex loci celebrationis* as the applicable law. This interest is connected to the recognition of the termination of the registered partnership in the country in which it has been concluded.

The question remains why the parties are not granted with the possibility to choose any law allowing for the termination of a registered partnership. This would serve the *favor dissolutionis* principle. However, in comparison with the *professio iuris* in case of divorce, the situation is slightly more complicated in case of the termination of a registered partnership. The fact that a *professio iuris* would only serve the partners if the law chosen would allow for the termination of registered partnerships already limits the possible laws which the partners can choose. Yet is it necessary to ascertain already in advance that the laws out of which can be chosen allow for the termination of a registered partnership? Should a choice for, e.g., the law of the common habitual residence of the partners be excluded just because this law *might* not know the concept of registered partnership? Or is this law a valid option, provided that it allows for the termination of a registered partnership?

The danger of the referral to a 'legal vacuum' is less present in case of a *professio iuris* than in case of application of the choice of law rule of Article 23(1) CLARP. The parties wishing to terminate their registered partnership are, to begin with, not likely to opt for a law that does not provide for this opportunity. Furthermore, in two different ways Dutch law can still become applicable: either parties can revoke their *professio iuris*, or the provision on the *professio iuris* could be complemented with an 'auxiliary' rule which determines that if the law chosen does not provide for the termination of registered partnerships, the choice will not be effective and the law specified in the absence of a *professio iuris* will apply.[87] A third possibility is to allow the parties to make a new *professio iuris* for a law that does provide for the termination of the registered partnership.

[87] Cf., Article 6(2) of the Convention on the Law Applicable to Trusts and on their Recognition of 1 July 1985 ('Hague Trust Convention') for a similar 'auxiliary' rule. It is worth noticing that in the field of trusts the same problems occurred as in the field of registered partnerships. Just as the registered partnership, trust is a concept that is unknown in many legal systems. See Duncan 1999, p. 2; and Šarčević 1999, p. 46.

In light of the foregoing, the *professio iuris* on the termination of a registered partnership should be extended.[88] The possibility to choose the law applicable should, however, not be unlimited: there should be a connection between (one of) the partners and the law to be applied to the termination of their registered partnership. The extension of the degree of the party autonomy in this field to the law of the nationality of either partner or to the law of their common habitual residence fulfils this condition. The extended *professio iuris* should be complemented with the auxiliary rule that if the law chosen to the termination of the registered partnership does not know the concept of registered partnership, the choice is not effective and the law specified in the absence of a *professio iuris* applies.

3.4.5.2 Formal Requirements of the *Professio Iuris*

The formal requirements of the *professio iuris* on the termination of the registered partnership depend on whether the termination is sought on grounds of mutual consent (Article 23(2) CLARP) or on grounds of a sole petition (Article 23(3) CLARP).

When the registered partnership is terminated by mutual consent, Article 23(2) determines that the choice for the application of the *lex loci celebrationis* has to be made jointly by the partners in the contract terminating their registered partnership.

In case of termination on grounds of a sole petition, it is required that the partners have jointly chosen for the *lex loci celebrationis* or that this choice has been made by one partner and is not contested by the other (Article 23(3)(a) CLARP). This law will also be applied if one party has made a choice of law for the place where the partnership was registered and both parties have actual close ties with that country (Article 23(3)(b) CLARP).[89]

The legislature has emphasised that the *professio iuris* pursuant to Article 23(3) CLARP should in principle be made jointly.[90] However, it must be noted that this requirement is fairly strange, since the dissolution of a registered partnership can only be sought on grounds of a sole petition.[91]

Article 23 CLARP does not contain any provision on the time of choice.

In case of the termination of the registered partnership on grounds of mutual consent (Article 23(2) CLARP), the time of choice is obvious: the time of the conclusion of the contract between the partners on the termination of their registered partnership is decisive.

---

[88] Cf., *supra* Sect. 2.3.1 concerning the *professio iuris* on divorce.

[89] See for a detailed description of the authenticity test *supra* Sect. 2.4.2.1. The same test applies to the termination of a registered partnership. This implies that all circumstances of the case are taken into account in order to determine whether both parties have a real societal connection to the country where the partnership has been registered. This test enhances an individual review.

[90] See Explanatory Memorandum (MvT), *Kamerstukken II* 2002–2003, 28 924, No. 3, p. 17.

[91] Cf., *supra* Sect. 3.4.2.

If only one of the parties chooses the *lex loci celebrationis* according to Article 23(3) CLARP, this choice should in principle be made in the initiatory petition. If the requesting party makes a *professio iuris* after filing the petition in case of default of appearance, the respondent is not informed and has, consequently, no opportunity to contest the choice. Therefore, such a choice is not valid. In defended proceedings on the termination of a registered partnership a joint *professio iuris* can be made not only at the beginning of the proceedings, but also at a later time during the proceedings, for example during the court session. Moreover, the *professio iuris* can still be lawfully agreed upon in appeal.[92]

3.4.5.3 Formal Requirements of the Termination of Registered Partnerships Entered into Outside the Netherlands

The application of foreign law pursuant to a *professio iuris* according to Article 23(2) and (3) of the CLARP is restricted to the substantive requirements of the termination of a registered partnership. According to Article 23(4) CLARP Dutch law governs the formal requirements of the termination of the registered partnership entered into abroad, irrespective of the formal requirements posed by the law applicable by choice of the parties pursuant to Article 23(2) and (3) CLARP:

> 4. Dutch law governs the manner in which termination by mutual consent or the dissolution of a registered partnership entered into outside the Netherlands is made.

According to this provision Dutch law applies to the form and manner in which the termination of a registered partnership entered into abroad takes place.

The provision of Article 23(4) CLARP is based on the principle of protection.[93] The formal requirements to which the legislator refers are meant to guarantee the parties the protection provided for by Dutch law. This protection also extends to international cases of termination of registered partnerships in the Netherlands:

> Zo zou het denkbaar zijn dat naar het recht van het land waar het geregistreerd partnerschap is aangegaan, de beëindiging met wederzijds goedvinden kan plaatsvinden door middel van een onderhandse akte. In dergelijke gevallen dient rekening te worden gehouden met de beschermingsgedachte van het interne Nederlandse recht. Zo verlangt artikel 80c, onder c, van Boek 1 BW de betrokkenheid van deskundigen en in artikel 80d van Boek 1 BW, zij het niet op straffe van nietigheid, het regelen van een aantal onderwerpen. Ter bescherming van derden verlangt artikel 80e, tweede lid, van Boek 1 BW inschrijving in de registers van de burgerlijke stand. Om deze reden wordt in artikel 23, vierde lid, van het voorstel bepaald dat de wijze waarop het geregistreerd partnerschap dat in het buitenland is aangegaan, kan worden beëindigd met wederzijds goedvinden of ontbonden, door het Nederlandse recht wordt beheerst.[94]

---

92 Cf., the *professio iuris* on divorce, *supra* Sect. 2.3.4.3.

93 See Explanatory Memorandum (MvT), *Kamerstukken II* 2002–2003, 28 924, No. 3, p. 17.

94 Explanatory Memorandum (MvT), *Kamerstukken II* 2002–2003, 28 924, No. 3, p. 17.

The legislator has put forward two reasons for the application of Dutch law to the formal requirements of the termination of a registered partnership. One of the important cornerstones of Dutch law is third party protection. Dutch law therefore requires the registration of the termination of a registered partnership in the Registry of Births, Deaths, Marriages and Registered Partnerships. Furthermore, a minimum level of protection of the parties is guaranteed by the assistance of at least one expert.

What is meant by this provision? The Dutch Standing Committee on Private International Law formulated that the *professio iuris* of Article 23(2) and (3) of the CLARP is limited to the substantive requirements.[95] This means that the *lex loci celebrationis* solely determines the ground(s) for termination of the registered partnership.[96] Article 23(4) implies that the formal requirements as posed by Article 1:80c to 1:80e of the Dutch Civil Code should be complied with; this means *inter alia* that the termination has to be entered into the Dutch Registry of Births, Deaths, Marriages and Registered Partnerships.

If, however, the *professio iuris* only applies to the ground(s) for termination, it can be questioned whether the provision of Article 23(4) does not overleap the goal of the *professio iuris*, i.e. increasing the chance that the termination of the registered partnership will be recognised in the country in which it had been entered into. In other words, is the manner in which the termination has taken place decisive for recognition of the termination? Problems may arise with regard to the recognition of the administrative termination of a registered partnership.[97]

It should be pointed out that the partners are not strictly bound by the Dutch formal requirements of the termination of registered partnerships. The partners can have their registered partnership terminated in the country in which it has been entered into according to the local rules and, subsequently, have the termination of their registered partnership recognised in the Netherlands according to Article 24 CLARP.[98] The latter Article stipulates:

1. A registered partnership terminated outside the Netherlands by mutual consent will be recognised when it has been lawfully decreed.
2. Dissolution of a registered partnership obtained outside the Netherlands after a proper legal process will be recognised in the Netherlands, if pronounced by a court decision or a decision of another authority with jurisdiction in respect thereof.

---

95 See Staatscommissie 1998, para 7 at Article 31.

96 Cf., Frohn 2004, p. 293; Curry-Sumner 2005, p. 458; and De Groot 2007, p. 344. These authors mention that this provision concerns the form and manner of the termination.

97 See Curry-Sumner 2005, p. 480 concludes that '[*I*]*t is* [...] *unlikely that recognition of foreign administrative dissolutions of non-marital registered relationships will raise substantive problems in the countries studied* [i.e. *Belgium, France, the Netherlands, Switzerland and the United Kingdom; NAB*].' It is, however, not impossible that other jurisdictions refuse to recognise an administrative termination of a registered partnership.

98 Cf., Joppe 2000, p. 393. The rules on recognition and enforcement of the Brussels II*bis*-Regulation do not apply to the termination of registered partnerships, since the termination of non-marital relationships does not fall within the material scope of the Regulation (Article 1).

3. Dissolution of a registered partnership obtained outside the Netherlands which does not meet any of the terms laid down in the preceding paragraph, will nevertheless be recognised in the Netherlands when it is evident that the other party to the foreign proceedings agreed, explicitly or implicitly, either during or after such proceedings to have acquiesced to such a dissolution.[99]

As becomes clear from the wording of this provision, the termination of a registered partnership obtained abroad will quite easily be recognised in the Netherlands.[100]

3.5 Public Policy Exception

The Choice of Law Act on Registered Partnerships does not contain an explicit public policy exception concerning the termination of registered partnerships.[101] A specific public policy exception is provided for in Article 3:

> Notwithstanding Article 2, a registered partnership entered into outside the Netherlands will not be recognised, if such recognition would be irreconcilable with Dutch public policy.[102]

However, this exception only applies to the recognition of registered partnerships entered into outside the Netherlands. Even if the registered partnership meets all the requirements specified by Art 2(5) CLARP, it will not be recognised, if such recognition would be irreconcilable with Dutch public policy.

The provision of Article 3 CLARP does not apply to the termination of registered partnerships. Yet a general - implicit - public policy clause applies. The problems with regard to the application of foreign law in case of termination of registered partnerships are far less pressing than in case of divorce. Since the registered partnership is a concept that is (practically) solely known in Western legal systems,[103] the problems described above in Section 2.5 concerning divorce do not arise in case of the termination of a registered partnership. According to the choice of law rules of the CLARP only Dutch law and the *lex loci celebrationis*

---

[99] Translation by Sumner and Warendorf 2003, p. 251.

[100] See further Curry-Sumner 2005, p. 469 ff; and Mostermans 2006, pp. 110–111.

[101] The Dutch Choice of Law Acts rarely hold a public policy clause; if any, it only relates to recognition of foreign legal concepts, e.g. Article 3 of the CLARP. None of the Acts contains a public policy clause with regard to choice of law. The Dutch Proposal on Private International Law contains a public policy clause in Article 6 stipulating that the application of foreign law is to be left aside, if this would be manifestly incompatible with Dutch public policy. See on this provision more elaborately Staatscommissie 2002, p. 52 ff; Explanatory Memorandum (MvT), *Kamerstukken II* 2009–2010, 32 137, No. 3, p. 13–15.

[102] Translation by Sumner and Warendorf 2003, p. 245.

[103] This is shown by the list of countries that recognise registered partnership included in Boele-Woelki et al. 2007, p. 103 in footnote no. 1.

can be applied to the termination of a registered partnership; these legal systems recognise the concept of registered partnership.

Although it may only be a theoretical possibility, it might occur that a certain ground for the termination of a registered partnership pursuant to the *lex loci celebrationis* violates the fundamental principles and values of Dutch society. In such a case, the public policy exception guarantees that the court or the expert(s) involved in the establishment of the contract by which the registered partnership is terminated has the possibility to leave the application of the applicable foreign law aside and to apply Dutch law instead. It should be recalled, however, that public policy can only come into play in case of a manifest violation of the Dutch fundamental principles and values.[104]

3.6 Will the Dutch Proposal on Private International Law Bring any Changes?

As seen above, in September 2009 the Dutch Proposal on Private International Law was published.[105] This codification did not intend to bring about a fundamental amendment of the existing choice of law rules, save for those changes necessary to gear these existing rules to one another and to the general provisions.[106]

The applicable law to the termination of registered partnerships is provided for in Articles 86 and 87 of the Dutch Proposal on Private International Law. Article 86 determines the law applicable to the termination of registered partnerships that have been entered into in the Netherlands. This provision-setting out the application of Dutch law-has remained unchanged. Equally Article 87, determining the law applicable to the termination of registered partnerships that have been entered into abroad, has remained unchanged: its principal rule is the application of Dutch law. In deviation from the application of Dutch law, (one of) the partners can choose the application of the *lex loci celebrationis*. Article 87 did undergo some small textual changes.

The Dutch legislator has indicated not to adjust the unilateral character of the choice of law rules on registered partnerships.[107]

---

[104] See Strikwerda 2008, pp. 52–53; and Ten Wolde 2009, pp. 79–80.

[105] See *supra* Sect. 2.6.

[106] See Explanatory Memorandum (MvT), *Kamerstukken II* 2009–2010, 32 137, No. 3, p. 2: 'Met de codificatie is niet beoogd de reeds tot stand gekomen regelingen van conflictenrecht aan een fundamentele herziening te onderwerpen. Het gaat thans in hoofdzaak erom deze wetten op elkaar en op de algemene bepalingen af te stemmen.'

[107] See Explanatory Memorandum (MvT), *Kamerstukken II* 2009–2010, 32 137, No. 3, p. 46: 'Ten aanzien van de in Nederland aangegane geregistreerde partnerschappen is gekozen voor het opstellen van eenzijdige verwijzingsregels, die (alleen) aangeven wanneer het Nederlandse interne recht van toepassing is. Er is thans geen reden de regeling op dit punt aan te passen.'

The Explanatory Memorandum to the Dutch Proposal on Private International Law expresses more clearly the meaning of Article 87(4), determining that Dutch law governs the manner in which the termination of a registered partnership that has been entered into abroad is made.[108] The Explanatory Memorandum clarifies that this provision concerns the formal requirements of the termination.[109] Dutch law thus governs the form and manner of the termination of registered partnerships concluded abroad.

Unfortunately the Dutch legislature has not amended the transitional provision as regards the application of the choice of law rules on registered partnerships (Article 91 of the Dutch Proposal on Private International Law) so as to make an exception to the termination of registered partnerships entered into prior to the entry into force of the CLARP.[110] Consequently, the choice of law rules on the termination of registered partnerships remain only applicable to those registered partnerships which have been entered into after 1 January 2005.

3.7 Conclusion

Despite some activity in this field, to date there is no international treaty providing for a regulation of the private international law aspects of registered partnerships. Since 2005 Dutch law provides for the choice of law on registered partnerships. These rules have been laid down in the Choice of Law Act on Registered Partnerships.

As registered partnerships are placed as much as possible on an equal footing with marriage, the choice of law rules regarding the termination of registered partnerships sought connection to the choice of law rules on divorce.

The choice of law rules on the termination of registered partnerships are determined by Articles 22 and 23 CLARP. A distinction is made between registered partnerships entered into in the Netherlands and those entered into abroad. Article 22 applies to partnerships registered in the Netherlands; Dutch law applies to the termination of these partnerships. The parties are not granted a *professio iuris*. Article 23 determines the law applicable to the termination of registered partnerships concluded abroad. In principle Dutch law applies, unless the parties

---

[108] See *supra* Sect. 3.4.5.3.

[109] See Explanatory Memorandum (MvT), *Kamerstukken II* 2009–2010, 32 137, No. 3, p. 52: 'Het vierde lid betreft de formele vereisten: de wijze van beëindiging van het geregistreerd partnerschap dat in het buitenland is aangegaan, wordt beheerst door het Nederlandse recht. Bij ontbinding door de rechter is dus inschrijving van de rechterlijke uitspraak in de registers van de burgerlijke stand vereist.'

[110] The Dutch Proposal on Private International Law does contain a transitional provision on Article 56: the amended choice of law rule on divorce will only apply to divorces and legal separations which have been requested after the entry into force of the latter Act. This transitional provision will be added to the general transitional provisions relating to the Dutch Civil Code (Article 290). Cf., *supra* Sect. 2.6.

have chosen the application of the *lex loci celebrationis*. The application of the *lex loci celebrationis* is, however, restricted to the substantive requirements of the termination; Dutch law governs the formal requirements of the termination, i.e. to the form and manner in which the termination takes place (Article 23(4) CLARP). Consequently, the Dutch choice of law on the termination of a registered partnership is predominated by the *lex fori*.

The Dutch Proposal on Private International Law will not bring any changes to the choice of law on the termination of registered partnerships.

References

Regulations, Conventions, Reports and Other Documentary Sources

Choice of Law Act on Registered Partnerships. Act of 6 July 2004, *Stb.* 2004, Nos. 334 and 621, containing a regulation of the choice of law with regard to the registered partnership, *Wet Conflictenrecht Geregistreerd Partnerschap*

Dutch Proposal on Private International Law. Vaststelling en invoering van Boek 10 (Internationaal privaatrecht) van het Burgerlijk Wetboek, *Kamerstukken II* 2009–2010, 32 137, No. 2

Staatscommissie (1998). Staatscommissie voor het Internationaal Privaatrecht, Geregistreerd partnerschap, Report of 1 May 1998, available at: http://www.justitie.nl/onderwerpen/wetgeving/over_wetgeving/privaat-recht/commissies-privaatrecht/staatscommissie-ipr.aspx

Books and Articles

Boele-Woelki K (1999) De wenselijkheid van een IPR-verdrag inzake samenleving buiten huwelijk. FJR 21:11–13

Boele-Woelki K (2000) Private international law aspects of registered partnerships and other forms of non-marital cohabitation in Europe. Louisiana Law Review 60:1053–1059

Boele-Woelki K (2003) Internationaal privaatrecht wet(svoorstel) Conflictenrecht Geregistreerd Partnerschap. Ars Aequi 52:4848–4849

Boele-Woelki K, Curry-Sumner I, Jansen M, Schrama W (2007) Huwelijk of geregistreerd partnerschap? Kluwer, Deventer

Curry-Sumner I (2005) All's well that ends registered? Intersentia, Antwerpen

Curry-Sumner I (2008) European recognition of same-sex relationships: we need action now! IFL 12:102–109

De Groot G-R (2007) Private international law aspects relating to homosexual couples. In: Boele-Woelki I, Van Erp S (eds) General reports of the XVIIth congress of the international academy of comparative law. Bruylant, Brussel, pp 325–356

Duncan W (1999) Civil law aspects of emerging forms of registered partnerships. private international law issues, presentation fifth European conference on family law 15–16 March 1999

Frohn EN (2004) De wet conflictenrecht geregistreerd partnerschap. FJR 123:290–294

Goldstein G (2006) La cohabitation hors mariage en droit international privé. Recueil des Cours 320:9–390

Hausmann R (2000) Überlegungen zum Kollisionsrecht registrierter Partnerschaften. In: Gottwald P et al (eds) Festschrift für Dieter Henrich. Verlag Ernst und Werner Gieseking, Bielefeld, pp 241–265

Jessurun d'Oliveira HU (1999) Het geregistreerd partnerschap, het 'homohuwelijk' en het IPR. NJB 74:305–306

Jessurun d'Oliveira HU (2000) Registered partnerships, PACSES and private international law. Some reflections. Rivista di diritto internazionale privato e processuale 36:293–322

Jessurun d'Oliviera HU (2003) Autonome kwalificatie in het internationaal privaatrecht: geregistreerde niet-huwelijkse relaties. In: Boele-Woelki K et al (eds) Het plezier van de rechtsvergelijking. Opstellen over unificatie en harmonisatie van het recht in Europa, aangeboden aan prof.mr. E.H. Hondius. Kluwer, Deventer

Joppe IS (2000) Het geregistreerd partnerschap in het Nederlandse IPR. WPNR 6403:371–375, 6404:391–395

Joppe IS (Groene Serie personen- en Familierecht) Titel 5A, Internationaal privaatrecht. Wet conflictenrecht geregistreerd partnerschap Groene Serie Privaatrecht, Personen- en familierecht (Electronic database Plaza Kluwer Juridisch en Fiscaal, looseleaf)

Knot JG (2008) Internationale boedelafwikkeling Over het toepasselijke recht op de afwikkeling van nalatenschappen (diss. Groningen). Kluwer, Deventer

Mostermans PMM (2006) Echtscheiding, 3rd edn. Kluwer, Deventer

Reinhartz BE (2004) Het wetsvoorstel Wet conflictenrecht geregistreerd partnerschap. WPNR 6583:491–498

Šarčević P (1981) Cohabitation without marriage: the Yugoslavian experience. The American Journal of Comparative Law 29:315–338

Šarčević P (1999) Private international law aspects of legally regulated forms of non-marital cohabitation and registered partnerships. Yearbook of Private International Law 1:37–48

Schrama W (1999) Niet-huwelijkse leefvormen en het IPR. FJR 21:131–133

Strikwerda L (2008) Inleiding tot het Nederlandse Internationaal Privaatrecht, 9th edn. Kluwer, Deventer

Sumner I, Warendorf H (2003) Family law legislation of the Netherlands. Intersentia, Antwerpen

Sumner I (2004a) Happy ever after? The problems of terminating registered partnerships. In: Digoix M, Festy P (eds) Same-sex couples, same-sex partnerships, and homosexual marriages: a focus on cross-national differentials. Documents de travail n° 124. INED, Paris, pp 35–46

Sumner I (2004b) Dissolution of registered partnerships: excursion in conversion. IFL, pp 231–237

Ten Wolde MH (2001) De uitgangspunten van het Voorstel voor een aantal IPR-bepalingen over het geregistreerd partnerschap nader beschouwd. EchtscheidingsBull, pp 141–143

Ten Wolde MH (2009) Inleiding Nederlands en Europees Internationaal Privaatrecht, Deel A Algemeen deel en materieel IPR Personen-, familie- en erfrecht. Hephaestus, Groningen

Chapter 4
The Europeanisation of International Family Law: The EU Legislature's Competence

4.1 Introduction

The preceding chapters have set forth the Dutch choice of law rules on divorce and on the termination of registered partnerships. However, as private international law is being 'Europeanised', national choice of law rules of the EU-Member States are more and more displaced by common European rules. The European Union is gaining more and more ground in the field of private international law. The need of unified private international law rules on issues of family law stems from the free movement of persons, one of the fundamental freedoms of the EU.[1] With the increasing mobility of Union citizens within the EU, the number of cross-border family relationships has grown as well. Private international law is the most qualified instrument to deal with questions of law arising from such international family relations.[2]

The choice of law in the field of divorce is subject to this European unification process as well. In July 2006 the European Commission has proposed the introduction of common choice of law rules on divorce in the already existing Brussels II*bis*-Regulation; this proposal is referred to as the Brussels II*ter*-Proposal.

The idea of a uniform European system of private international law is not new.[3] Due to the international nature of the situations and the legal problems involved, international cooperation is of great importance to private international law. Therefore, for a long time such cooperation has already taken place. The two most important actors in the field of private international law are the Hague Conference on Private International Law and the Council of Europe.

---

[1] Article 45 *et seq* TFEU.

[2] Cf., Meeusen 2007a, p. 341.

[3] See Fernandez Rozas and Sanchez Lorenzo 1991, p. 218: In 1889 a Spanish Minister, Manuel Silvela, has proposed the creation of a 'Código del derecho internacional privado' for the European States. See also Frankenstein 1950 and Jessurun d'Oliveira 2002, p. 265.

N.A. Baarsma, *The Europeanisation of International Family Law*,
DOI: 10.1007/978-90-6704-743-2_4, © T.M.C. Asser press, The Hague,
The Netherlands, and the author 2011

The involvement of private international law in the European integration process is of a much more recent date. Only since 1999 has the European Union been a serious player in the field: the Treaty of Amsterdam transferred competence to the European Community to enact measures of private international law. Ever since, the European legislature pursues a true policy of unifying issues of private international law. Until recently the field has only been Europeanised as regards the rules on jurisdiction and recognition and enforcement of foreign judgments. The development of uniform European choice of law rules is currently being pursued.[4]

This chapter concentrates on the Europeanisation of the Union's competence in the field of international family law. Firstly, the development of this competence will be set forth (Section 4.2). Subsequently, the question why the European Union actually develops a unified system of international family law will be elaborated upon (Section 4.3). Thirdly, the scope and limits of the competence of the European legislature to enact measures in this field of law will be discussed (Section 4.4). In Section 4.5 the role of the European Court of Justice in international family law will be set forth. Since three EU-Member States — Denmark, Ireland and the United Kingdom — do not fully participate in the field of private international law a '*Europe à deux vitesses*' has emerged, which will be dealt with in Section 4.6. This chapter will conclude with an assessment of whether the European Union is competent to unify the choice of law on divorce (Section 4.7).

4.2 The Transfer of Competence in the Field of International Family Law to the EU

Although the EU has primarily focused on the establishment of common rules in the field of trade law, in 1998 the European Council in Vienna emphasised that the aim of a common judicial area is to make life simpler for citizens, in particular in cases affecting the everyday life of the citizens, such as divorce.[5] Since the entry into force of the Treaty of Amsterdam in May 1999, judicial cooperation within the field of family law has become an important element in the construction of an area of freedom, security and justice within the European Union.

In the last decade the European doctrine on private international law has largely concentrated on the effects of the Treaty of Amsterdam on the development of

---

[4] E.g. the Rome I-Regulation containing choice of law rules on contractual obligations and the Rome II-Regulation containing choice of law rules on non-contractual obligations. The applicable law to maintenance obligations is determined by the Hague Protocol on the Law Applicable to Maintenance Obligations of 23 November 2007, which has not entered into force yet.

[5] Vienna Action Plan, para 39.

private international law.[6] However, in order to properly value the changes brought by the Treaty of Amsterdam in this field, the situation before its entry into force on 1 May 1999 should be recalled.[7] The evolution of private international law can roughly be divided into three periods: the situation prior to the Treaty of Amsterdam (Section 4.2.1), the situation brought about by the Treaty of Amsterdam (Section 4.2.2) and, finally, the situation after 1999 (Section 4.2.3).

4.2.1 Prior to the Treaty of Amsterdam

In the period prior to the entry into force of the Treaty of Amsterdam matters of private international law were unified by means of intergovernmental cooperation: no competence was transferred to the European institutions.

Two aspects of the development of private international law in the European legal order prior to the Treaty of Amsterdam are of importance.[8] Firstly, Article 220 of the EEC-Treaty (Section 4.2.1.1) and, secondly, the provisions of Title VI of the Treaty of Maastricht as regards private international law (Section 4.2.1.2).

4.2.1.1 Article 220 EEC-Treaty

In the beginning European Community law barely affected private international law. The general feeling was that the Community legal order concerned administrative law and regulations.[9] The only provision to be mentioned is Article 220 of the 1958 EEC-Treaty, which incited Member States 'so far as is necessary' to enter into negotiation with each other with a view to securing for the benefit of their nationals, *inter alia*, the simplification of formalities governing the reciprocal recognition and enforcement of judgments of courts or tribunals and of arbitration awards.[10] The establishment of common private international law rules took place

---

[6] See *inter alia* Von Hoffmann 1998; Kohler 1999; Drappatz 2002; Dohrn 2004. Little consideration was given to the impact of European integration on private international law prior to the Treaty of Amsterdam. Remien 2001, p. 80 describes this as '*astonishing*'; Fletcher 1982, p. 46 already complained that '*insufficient attention*' had been paid to the significance of private international law in the European legal order.

[7] See Fiorini 2008c and Fallon and Francq 2004, p. 256 ff for a thorough analysis of the evolution of European private international law.

[8] A third aspect of the development of private international law in the European legal order is that in the period prior to the Treaty of Amsterdam several Community Directives contained choice of law rules. However, this aspect will be left out of account. See on this issue further: Von Hoffmann 1995, Reich 1996 and Joustra 1999.

[9] Cf., Jessurun d'Oliveira 2002, p. 120; and Bogdan 2006, p. 6.

[10] With the entry into force of the Treaty on the Functioning of the European Union on 1 December 2009 this provision has disappeared.

through intergovernmental cooperation. Strictly speaking Member States did not of course need Article 220 to conclude treaties of public international law, but it provided for a framework.[11]

Three important private international law conventions have been developed on the basis of Article 220 EEC-Treaty: the Brussels I-Convention, the parallel Lugano Convention[12] and the Rome Convention.

Article 220 EEC-Treaty was interpreted extensively, enabling cooperation beyond the original mandate: the Brussels I-Convention dealt not only with the recognition and enforcement of foreign judgments, but also with jurisdiction.[13] The latter Convention is restricted to civil and commercial matters and excludes, among other things: 'the status and legal capacity of natural persons, rights in property arising out of a matrimonial relationship, wills, or successions', i.e. the core of family law.[14] Family law was excluded from the scope of the Convention, as the substantive laws of the Member States in that field diverge extremely and would, therefore, lead to 'abuse of the notion of public policy, using it to refuse recognition to foreign judgments'.[15]

4.2.1.2 Title VI of the Treaty of Maastricht

The Treaty of Maastricht marked a first turning point in the development of private international law in the European Union. The provision of Article 220 EEC-Treaty has been maintained, but new provisions have been added. Title VI of the Treaty of Maastricht contains provisions on the cooperation in the field of Justice and Home Affairs. Article K.1 determined that judicial cooperation in civil matters was an area of common interest for the purposes of achieving the objectives of the Union and in particular the free movement of persons.[16] Judicial cooperation in civil matters became an element of European

---

[11] Cf., Hellner 2002, p. 9.

[12] The Lugano Convention on Jurisdiction and the Enforcement of Judgments in Civil and Commercial Matters of 16 September 1988, [1988] OJ L319/9.

[13] The Brussels I-Convention contains rules on international jurisdiction, as the negotiators of the Convention realised that unification of the effects of judgments would be useless without the unification of jurisdictional rules. See Hellner 2002, p. 9; and Kessedijan 2004, p. 188.

[14] See Article 1(2(1)) of the Brussels Convention.

[15] See P. Jenard, Report on the Convention of 27 September 1968 on jurisdiction and the enforcement of judgments in civil and commercial matters, [1979] OJ C59/1, spec. at p. 10. See further Kohler 1992, pp. 221–240.

[16] See in general Bieber and Monar 1995.

cooperation and was placed under the 'third pillar' (Article K.1(6) Treaty of Maastricht).[17]

Compared to Article 220 EEC-Treaty, the Treaty of Maastricht constituted a widening of the judicial cooperation in civil matters in two respects.[18] Firstly, the area covered was wider: not only recognition and enforcement, but also jurisdiction and choice of law were included. Secondly, Article K.4(2) Treaty of Maastricht granted the Commission the right of initiative parallel to that of the Member States.

Although the Treaty of Maastricht did constitute a more specific legal basis for judicial cooperation in civil matters, no competence to enact measures in the field of private international law was transferred to the European Community.[19] This was made clear by the European Court of Justice in the *Johannes*-case:

> [N]either the national provisions of private international law determining the substantive national law applicable to the effects of a divorce nor the national provisions of civil law substantively regulating those effects fall within the scope of the Treaty.[20]

Yet in another field the Treaty of Maastricht did mean a step forward: it introduced the concept of EU citizenship (now Article 20 *et seq* TFEU), entailing a rethink about the economic nature of the principle of free movement.[21] The Treaty of Maastricht attempted to convert 'market citizenship', i.e. the individual is purely a holder of economic freedoms, into a broader idea of 'Union citizenship'.[22] The introduction of the concept of Union citizenship represents a key moment in the history of the political integration in the EU: on the basis of Article 21(1) TFEU every Union citizen is awarded the right to move and reside freely within the territory of the Member States. Up until the Treaty of Maastricht this right was exclusively reserved for workers and their family members.[23] Consequently, the free movement of persons has been detached from its purely economical meaning and may concern any European citizen.

---

[17] The Treaty of Maastricht introduced three pillars, forming the structure of the European Union. The first pillar, the Community pillar, corresponds to the three Communities: the European Community, the European Atomic Energy Community and the former European Coal and Steel Community. The second pillar consists of the common foreign and security policy of Title V of the Treaty of Maastricht. The third pillar, finally, was dedicated to police and judicial cooperation in civil and criminal matters of Title VI of the Treaty of Maastricht. The cooperation in the second and third pillar is intergovernmental, whereas the cooperation in the first pillar is supranational. See further Dittrich 1996, p. 105 ff.

[18] See also Hellner 2002, pp. 10.

[19] See further Müller-Graff 1994.

[20] ECJ Case C-430/97 *Johannes* [1999] ECR I-3475, para 27.

[21] See Carrera 2005, p. 700. Equally Poillot-Peruzzetto and Marmisse 2001, p. 460.

[22] See on European citizenship generally: Marias 1994, p. 1 ff.

[23] According to Fallon the introduction of citizenship thereby actually meant the insertion of a 'fifth' freedom, added to the four original fundamental freedoms. See Fallon 2007, pp. 151–152.

The European Court of Justice has attached great importance to the concept of European citizenship, repeatedly stating that it was destined to be the fundamental status of nationals of the Member States.[24]

4.2.2 The Treaty of Amsterdam

The Treaty of Amsterdam marked a true turning point in the development of European private international law: it entrusted the European Community with competence in matters of judicial cooperation in order to progressively establish an area of freedom, security and justice.[25] The Treaty of Amsterdam transferred judicial cooperation in civil matters from the 'third' to the 'first' pillar of European integration.[26] With this Treaty the European Community has entered a new phase of integration, namely the phase of political integration.

The relevant provisions on private international law are placed in Title IV of the third part of the EC-Treaty on 'Visas, asylum, immigration and other policies related to the free movement of persons'. Article 61(c) stipulates that, in order to establish an 'area of freedom, security and justice', the Council shall adopt measures in the field of judicial cooperation in civil matters as provided for in Article 65. The latter Article stipulates, in turn, the following:

> Measures in the field of judicial cooperation in civil matters having cross-border implications, to be taken in accordance with Article 67 and insofar as necessary for the proper functioning of the internal market, shall include:
> a. improving and simplifying:
>   – the system for cross-border service of judicial and extrajudicial documents;
>   – cooperation in the taking of evidence;
>   – the recognition and enforcement of decisions in civil and commercial cases, including decisions in extrajudicial cases;
> b. promoting the compatibility of the rules applicable in the Member States concerning the conflict of laws and of jurisdiction;
> c. eliminating obstacles to the good functioning of civil proceedings, if necessary by promoting the compatibility of the rules on civil procedure applicable in the Member States.

Measures based on Article 65 EC-Treaty needed to fulfil three specific requirements: they must concern 'judicial cooperation in civil matters', secondly 'have

---

[24] See, e.g., ECJ Case C-413/99 *Baumbast and R.* v. *Secretary for the Home Department* [2002] ECR I-7091; and ECJ Case C-184/99 *Grzelczyk* [2001] ECR I-6139. See further *infra* Sect. 4.3.2.1.

[25] Cf., Fiorini 2008a, p. 7: *'on 1 May 1999 the private international law landscape changed dramatically within Europe with the entry into force of the Treaty of Amsterdam'*.

[26] Jayme and Kohler 1997, p. 385, referred in this respect to '*Saulenwechsel*'.

cross border implications' and, 'be necessary for the proper functioning of the internal market'.

On the basis of this provision all three questions of private international law can be Europeanised, since the enumeration of lit. (a)–(c) covers jurisdiction, applicable law and recognition and enforcement of foreign judgments.

The European Commission has interpreted the provision of Article 65 EC-Treaty extensively, producing an impressive number of regulations in the area of mutual recognition and enforcement of judgments, cooperation between Member States, and more recently attempting to unify choice of law rules in a number of fields.[27]

The first Community instrument in the field of international family law was the Brussels II-Regulation, which entered into force in the Member States on 1 March 2001.[28] This regulation replaced the Convention on jurisdiction and the recognition and enforcement of matrimonial matters (the Brussels II-Convention), which had never come into force. The Brussels II-Regulation was subsequently replaced by the Brussels II*bis*-Regulation, which widened its scope of application to matters of parental responsibility.[29]

Several difficulties can be distinguished surrounding the interpretation of Article 65 EC-Treaty. Below some general difficulties will be discussed (Section 4.2.2.1), followed by a number of the specific difficulties concerning the internal market requirement (Section 4.2.2.2).

4.2.2.1 General Difficulties Surrounding the Interpretation of Article 65 EC

Legal doctrine has accentuated that the formulation of Article 65 EC-Treaty is, to say the least, not very definite. Gaudemet-Tallon has remarked wryly on this lack of clarity:

> [O]r le texte de l'article 65 est loin d'être un modèle de clarté.[30]

As a consequence of the indistinct formulation of Article 65 EC-Treaty the scope of the Europeanisation of private international law pursuant to Title IV of the EC-Treaty was far from being the subject of a generally accepted interpretation.[31] It was argued that the ambiguity and broad nature of the expressions

---

[27] See Staudinger 2007, p. 260: '[…] *the legislative machinery is working unceasingly at supranational level*'; and Fiorini 2008a, p. 7.

[28] Denmark is, however, excluded. See further *infra* Sect. 4.6.2.

[29] This Regulation entered into force on 1 March 2005.

[30] Gaudemet-Tallon 2001, p. 326. See equally Kohler 1999, p. 8 ('[…] *la coopération judiciaire en matière civile est, sur le plan institutionnel, hésitante et incomplète et, sure le plan matériel, de portée incertaine.*'); Leible and Staudinger 2000, p. 225; Spamann 2001, p. 21; Partsch 2003, p. 293 ff; Borrás 2005, p. 432 ff; Pataut 2005, p. 668.

[31] The most disputed part of Article 65 EC was the question whether certain measures are necessary for the proper functioning of the internal market. See further *infra* Sect. 4.2.2.2.

used in Article 65 EC implied a full transfer of power to the Community in order to establish uniform rules in the field of private international law:

> Bien que le texte de l'article 65 puisse susciter quelques doutes quant à l'ampleur de la compétence conférée à la Communauté européenne [...] la *ratio conventionis* est claire. Un espace [de liberté, de sécurité et] de justice (art. 61 TCE) en vue de la garantie de la libre circulation des personnes (titre IV TCE) implique une identification facile de la juridiction compétente, une indication claire du droit applicable, l'existence de jugements rapides et équitables et des procédures efficaces d'exécution.[32]

The restrictions, moreover, contained in Article 65 EC were vague enough to leave considerable discretion to the Community legislature, which indeed seemed to interpret Articles 61(c) and 65 EC as conferring upon the Community an unlimited competence to unify private international law.[33]

Another difficulty of the interpretation of Article 65 EC-Treaty was its placement in Title IV of the third part of the EC-Treaty, entitled 'Visas, asylum, immigration and other policies related to the free movement of persons'. For this reason Article 65 EC had been said to be limited to the free movement of persons.[34]

The historical explanation for the connection to the free movement of persons can be found in the origins of Title IV of the EC-Treaty.[35] Before the entry into force of the EC-Treaty in 1999, the Treaty of Maastricht placed judicial cooperation in civil law matters under the third pillar on justice and home affairs, which at that time was considered as providing for additional measures in order to achieve the free movement of persons.[36]

For two reasons, however, Article 65 EC was not limited to the free movement of persons. In the first place, Article 61 EC only referred to the free movement of persons in lit. (a) and not in lit. (c), on which Article 65 is based.[37] Furthermore, Article 65 EC explicitly referred to 'measures necessary for the proper functioning of the internal market'. The internal market does not only contain the free movement of persons, but also free movement of goods, services and capital

---

[32] Kreuzer 2001, p. 128. See equally *inter alia* Hess 2000, p. 23; Struycken 2000, pp. 736–737; Leible and Staudinger 2000, p. 229; Pocar 2005, p. 148; Rüberg 2005, p. 84.

[33] Cf., Meeusen 2007b, p. 290. See also Pintens 2005, p. 1222.

[34] See *inter alia* Basedow 1997, p. 609; Basedow 2000, p. 697; Israël 2000, p. 96 ff; Kreuzer 2001, p. 128. Basedow regarded Article 95 EC as proper legal basis for measures with regard to private international law in the field of the other three fundamental freedoms.

[35] See Drappatz 2002, p. 107 ff; Gonzalez Beilfuss 2004, p. 121.

[36] Article K.1 of the Treaty of Maastricht read: 'For the purposes of achieving the objectives of the Union, in particular the free movement of persons, [...] Member States shall regard the following matters of common interest: [...] 6. judicial cooperation in civil matters.'

[37] See Drappatz 2002, p. 107; Mansel 2002, p. 1.

(Article 14(2) EC-Treaty).[38] Consequently, a measure taken on the basis of Article 65 could be linked to one of these four freedoms.[39]

4.2.2.2 The Internal Market Requirement

The internal market requirement, i.e. measures should be necessary for the proper functioning of the internal market, was by far the most highly disputed requirement of Article 65 EC and its meaning heavily divided doctrine.[40]

A first point of discussion is the degree of 'necessity' which is required.[41] The unification of private international law may be considered necessary 'to eliminate the inconveniences arising from the diversity of the rules of conflict'.[42] A slightly stronger position is expressed in the preamble to the Brussels I-Regulation, stating that 'certain differences between national rules governing jurisdiction and recognition of judgments hamper the sound operation of the internal market.'[43] Others have expressed more strongly the view that diversity in private international law is entirely incompatible with the internal market.[44]

A second of a subject of discussion surrounding the internal market requirement is whether or not Article 65 EC allowed for the enactment of universal choice of law rules, meaning that the choice of law rule can designate the law of a Member State of the European Union or the law of a third country. In general, no doubt existed as to whether the competence of the Community on the basis of Article 61(c) in conjunction with 65(b) EC extended to cases concerning the relation between two or more EU-Member States (intra-European cases).[45] However, it is

---

[38] See Van Houtte 2001, p. 2; Duintjer Tebbens 2002, pp. 173–174; Bogdan 2006, p. 9; Rossi 2007, p. 937 Note 1.

[39] Cf., Opinion of the Legal Service of the European Council of 5 February 1999 concerning the legal consequences of the Treaty of Amsterdam on the revision of the Brussels Convention, Doc. 5290/99; and Freudenthal 2007, pp. 39–40.

[40] See Dickinson 2005, p. 209 ff; and Knot 2008, p. 171, referring for an overview of the different opinions to Traest 2003, p. 87, 88. With respect to the Europeanisation of issues of international family law the president of the European Union Committee of the British House of Lords posed the cynical question 'what has it got to do necessarily with the European Union?' See House of Lords, European Union Committee, 10th Report of Session 2004–2005, The Hague Programme: a five year agenda for EU justice and home affairs, report on the examination of witness Baroness of Upholland, Q71.

[41] Cf, Mills 2009, p. 178 ff.

[42] See the Rome Convention, p. 4.

[43] Recital No. 2 of the Preamble to the Brussels I-Regulation.

[44] E.g. Remien 2001, p. 64.

[45] It must be stressed that the question of the scope of application of choice of law rules is also often being regarded from the point of view of the limits of the Community competence under Article 5 EC. This Article stipulates that the Community must act within the limits of the powers conferred upon it and of the objectives assigned to it therein. E.g. Rüberg 2005, p. 99 ff; and Knot 2008, p. 177 ff.

not clear whether this competence extended equally to cases concerning the relation between a Member State and a third country (extra-European cases).[46]

According to some no such territorial limitation can be ensued from the concept 'internal market', that Article 65 EC only allowed for the enactment of intra-European choice of law rules.[47] The proper functioning of the internal market is not prejudiced by the application of a third country's law, if that law is designated by universal choice of law rules which are in conformity with the internal market.[48] Such choice of law rules prevent unnecessary complications, as whenever an extra-European case is connected to more than one Member State, the choice of law rules of these Member States may very well refer to the application of divergent national systems. This would not contribute to the functioning of the internal market: as far as the internal market is concerned, there is no difference between a purely intra-European case and a case which involves two Member States and a third country. Therefore, the existence of diverging choice of law rules for extra-European cases within the territory of the European Community precludes the establishment of the European judicial area: the same risk of divergent solutions and the same need for unification at the European Community level exists in these cases as in intra-European cases. Such situation would still lead to forum shopping and would equally endanger the legal security within the internal market.[49] Therefore, the purpose of Article 65 allowed for an interpretation of this provision so as to include the competence for the adoption of universal choice of law rules by the Community.

Evidently, this point of view is not fully supported. Some point out that it is impossible to prove the necessity, for the proper functioning of the internal market, of choice of law rules referring to the laws of a third State under certain circumstances.[50] The Community is awarded competence to enact measures of private international law in order to establish an area of freedom, security and justice, in which a European judicial area is to be created. Legal relationships between

---

[46] Cf., the external competence of the Community. The case law of the European Court of Justice has well-established that the existence of an internal Community competence implies a corresponding external competence for negotiations with third countries insofar as such negotiations are necessary for attaining one of the targets of the Community. See ECJ Case 22/70 *Commission* v. *Council* [1971] ECR 263 (ERTA-doctrine). The Court of Justice has repeated this statement in *inter alia* ECJ Opinion 1/94 of 15 November 1994, *WTO* [1994] ECR 5267; and ECJ Opinion 1/03 of 7 February 2006, *Lugano* [2006] ECR I-1145. See elaborately on the external competence of the EU: Tridimas and Eeckhout 1984; Kotuby 2001; Wilderspin and Rouchaud-Joët 2004; and Boele-Woelki and Van Ooik 2006.

[47] See *inter alia* Leible and Staudinger 2000, p. 230; Struycken 2001, p. 470; Wagner 2004, p. 147; Pataut 2005, pp. 667–674; Knot 2008, pp. 177–180.

[48] See Meeusen 2006, p. 31.

[49] See also Basedow 2000, p. 703; Kotuby 2001, p. 3; Basedow 2002, p. 41; Dohrn 2004, p. 123 ff.

[50] See *inter alia* Remien 2001, p. 76; Grundmann 2002, p. 335; Wilderspin 2001, p. 236; Gaudemet-Tallon 2004, p. 769; Lequette 2008, p. 509 ff.

Member States and third countries do not have any connection the latter judicial area and should, therefore, be excluded.

The difficulty, or maybe even the impossibility, to differentiate between intra- and extra-European cases, is generally regarded as necessitating the wide interpretation of Article 65 EC as to encompass the competence to enact universal choice of law rules.[51]

Finally, directly after the entry into force of the EC-Treaty, the question arose whether or not Article 65 EC related to matters of international family law. One may wonder which areas of private international law can be qualified as being necessary for the proper functioning of the internal market. It has been argued that because of this restriction, the scope of Article 65 EC does not cover matters of international family law.[52] However, as will be shown below, this discussion has been superseded by the Treaty of Nice, which inserted an explicit reference to international family law in Article 67(5) EC.

4.2.3 After the Treaty of Amsterdam

The Treaty of Amsterdam has been succeeded by two new treaties: the Treaty of Nice and the Treaty of Lisbon. Whereas the Treaty of Nice has only brought small changes, the changes brought by the Treaty of Lisbon in the field of private international law are anything but small.

4.2.3.1 The Treaty of Nice

The Treaty of Nice entered into force on 1 February 2003. It brought some technical changes in the sphere of decision-making in the field of judicial cooperation in civil matters. Up until the Treaty of Nice, the European Council could only adopt measures in the field of judicial cooperation in civil matters by unanimity. This voting requirement has been replaced by qualified majority voting. However, the abolishment of the requirement of unanimity does not apply unlimited: Article 67(5) EC-Treaty determines that the co-decision procedure applies to measures provided in Article 65 *with the exception of aspects relating to family law*. Accordingly, matters of international family law still remain within reach of the 'quasi'-intergovernmental cooperation.[53]

---

[51] See equally Basedow 2000, p. 704; Basedow 2002, p. 41; Mansel 2003, pp. 145–147; Wagner 2004, p. 142; Pataut 2005, pp. 667–674; Meeusen 2007a, p. 345; Vonken 2006, pp. 49–50; and Knot 2008, p. 180. See further *infra* Sects. 5.4.1.1 and 8.4.2.1.

[52] Schack 1999, pp. 805–808; Beaumont 1999, pp. 223–229; Sonnenberger 2001, p. 121; Linke 2002, pp. 545–546.

[53] Cf., Kohler 2003, p. 404.

Maintaining the requirement of unanimity for matters of international family law did make clear that matters of international family law definitely fall within the scope of Articles 61 and 65 EC-Treaty.

4.2.3.2 The Treaty of Lisbon

On 1 December 2009 the long awaited reform of the EC-Treaty has entered into force. This treaty amends the Treaty on the European Union (EU-Treaty) and the Treaty establishing the European Community (EC-Treaty). The need to review the Union's constitutional framework, particularly in light of the accession of ten new Member States in 2004, was already highlighted in a declaration annexed to the Treaty of Nice in 2001. The Laeken Declaration of December 2001 committed the EU to improving democracy, transparency and efficiency, and set out the process by which a constitution aiming to achieve these goals could be created.[54] Subsequently, the European Constitution was established.[55] However, in 2005 the adoption of the Constitution failed after negative results of referenda held in France and in the Netherlands.

In June 2007, two years after the failure of the European Constitution, the European Council decided to move on: the Treaty on the Functioning of the European Union has been drafted.[56]

Also for quite some time the faith of the Treaty of Lisbon remained unclear following the negative referendum in Ireland in June 2008. Full ratification by all 27 Member States was of course needed before the Treaty could enter into force. A second Irish referendum on the Treaty of Lisbon was held on 2 October 2009. In this second referendum the Treaty got overwhelming support in Ireland.[57] After the Irish referendum both Poland and the Czech Republic — the last two Member States left to do so — also ratified the Treaty of Lisbon.[58]

---

[54] See: http://european-convention.eu.int/pdf/LKNEN.pdf.

[55] Treaty Establishing a Constitution for Europe, agreed on 18 June 2004, [2004] OJ C310/1. This Treaty is hereinafter referred to as the 'European Constitution'.

[56] Hereinafter abbreviated to: TFEU. This Treaty is equally referred to as the 'Reform Treaty' and 'the Treaty of Lisbon'.

[57] See: http://news.bbc.co.uk/2/hi/europe/6901353.stm.

[58] The Czech Constitutional court has reviewed the Treaty of Lisbon twice. In 2008 the Czech Constitutional Court has held that the Treaty of Lisbon is not as such in contravention of the constitutional order of the Czech Republic. In 2009 the Constitutional Court has reviewed a further submission of the Treaty, yet this time of the 'Lisbon Amendments to the Rules of Procedure'. Also this second review has led the Constitutional Court to the conclusion that the Treaty of Lisbon does not contravene the Czech constitutional order. In order to ensure the ratification of the Treaty of Lisbon by the Czech Republic, the European Council agreed that the Czech Republic will be granted the opt-out from the Charter of Fundamental Rights of the European Union, which will be formalized following the adoption of the next European Union Treaty.

Even though it is a new instrument, the Treaty on the Functioning of the European Union has kept for a large part the structure and substance of the proposed European Constitution. As a result, the preparatory documents for the European Constitution remain of importance.

The modification of the provisions of the Union's competence in the field of private international law was strongly desired. Closing a review of the impact of the Treaty of Amsterdam, Drobnig remarked:

> A great step forward – private international law recognised as Community task – has been achieved but at a high price on the technical level. Thus on the balance it has been a mixed success. One hopes that the next Revision Conference will rectify this major mistake.[59]

As mentioned above, the modification of the treaty provisions on EU competence in the field of judicial cooperation in civil matters was originally foreseen in the European Constitution. The draft EU Constitutional Treaty, as initially agreed by the EU's constitutional Convention in July 2003, contained in Article III-170 a specific provision on civil law cooperation.[60] In this provision the internal market requirement of Article 65 EC-Treaty had been completely abolished:

> The Praesidium felt that there was no longer any justification for keeping the current reference to "the proper functioning of the internal market" (Article 65 TEC) in the new provision. The phrase is included in existing Article 65 TEC partly because this provision is an element of Community policies and is linked to the free movement of persons in the context of the internal market.
>
> Once the new Treaty contains a separate title on the area of freedom, security and justice, the reference to "the proper functioning of the internal market" can be considered redundant. Moreover, the most important aspect to be to emphasised in this context is that the envisaged measures under judicial cooperation in civil matters have a "cross-border impact", reference to which is included in the proposed provision.[61]

This provision was subsequently amended by the Inter-Governmental Conference of 17–18 June 2004 which negotiated the final text of the proposed Constitutional Treaty. During this conference the final text of Article III-269 was adopted and the internal market requirement had reappeared, be it in a weakened form.[62]

The Treaty of Lisbon copied Article III-269 of the European Constitution. In addition, it introduced a special passerelle clause in the provision on the EU's competence in judicial cooperation in civil matters.[63]

---

[59] Drobnig 2000, p. 201. See also Bodénès-Constantin 2005, p. 94 ff, spec. pp. 104–120, stating that 'the limits of the Community competence of Article 65 EC-Treaty were quite uncertain (*ratione materiae, ratione personae* and *ratione loci*).'

[60] See Draft EU Constitutional Treaty, [2003] OJ C169/1, CONV 850/03.

[61] CONV 614/03, p. 20.

[62] However, the 'reappearance' of this internal market requirement was not explained. Cf., Knot 2008, p. 175. See on Article III-269 and its implications for (international) family law: Pintens 2005, pp. 1222–1223.

[63] See Presidency Conclusions of the Brussels European Council of 21–22 June 2007, DOC 11177/1/07 REV 1, p. 28. See further *infra* Sect. 4.4.5.

The Treaty on the Functioning of the European Union replaced Title IV of the third part of the EC-Treaty on 'Visas, asylum, immigration and other policies related to the free movement of persons' by Title V bearing the heading 'area of freedom, security and justice'.[64] This Title belongs to the third part — on Union Policies and Internal Actions — of the Treaty on the Functioning of the European Union. The Treaty on the Functioning of the European Union bundled together all measures concerning the area of freedom, security and justice in one title, as a result of which the question whether or not the EU's competence solely concerns measures related to the free movement of persons belongs to the past.[65]

The Reform Treaty inserted a separate chapter on judicial cooperation in civil matters (Chapter 3), containing one provision. This provision, Article 81, determines:

1. The Union shall develop judicial cooperation in civil matters having cross-border implications, based on the principle of mutual recognition of judgments and of decisions in extrajudicial cases. Such cooperation may include the adoption of measures for the approximation of the laws and regulations of the Member States.
2. For the purposes of paragraph 1, the European Parliament and the Council, acting in accordance with the ordinary legislative procedure, shall adopt measures, particularly when necessary for the proper functioning of the internal market, aimed at ensuring:
   (a) the mutual recognition and enforcement between Member States of judgments and of decisions in extrajudicial cases;
   (b) the cross-border service of judicial and extrajudicial documents;
   (c) the compatibility of the rules applicable in the Member States concerning conflict of laws and of jurisdiction;
   (d) cooperation in the taking of evidence;
   (e) effective access to justice;
   (f) the elimination of obstacles to the proper functioning of civil proceedings, if necessary by promoting the compatibility of the rules on civil procedure applicable in the Member States;
   (g) the development of alternative methods of dispute settlement;
   (h) support for the training of the judiciary and judicial staff.
3. Notwithstanding paragraph 2, measures concerning family law with cross-border implications shall be established by the Council, acting in accordance with a special legislative procedure. The Council shall act unanimously after consulting the European Parliament.

   The Council, on a proposal from the Commission, may adopt a decision determining those aspects of family law with cross-border implications which may be the subject of acts adopted by the ordinary legislative procedure. The Council shall act unanimously after consulting the European Parliament.

   The proposal referred to in the second subparagraph shall be notified to the national Parliaments. If a national Parliament makes known its opposition within six months of the date of such notification, the decision shall not be adopted. In the absence of opposition, the Council may adopt the decision.

[64] See in general on the (necessary) reform of the area of freedom, security and justice: Labayle 2005; Müller-Graff 2005; Reestman and Goudappel 2008; and Poillot-Peruzzetto 2008.

[65] Cf., *supra* Sect. 4.2.2.1.

The most important change in comparison with Article 65 EC-Treaty is made with regard to the internal market requirement. The substitution of words — 'particularly when' (Article 81 TFEU) instead of 'insofar as' (Article 65 EC) — dilutes the internal market requirement by removing its imperative character. The legal basis of Union action in the field of judicial cooperation in civil matters is thus formally expanded.[66]

This expansion joins the wish to dissociate the common European rules in the area of private international law from their dependence on the internal market expressed in Article 65 EC and to allocate to these rules a clear place as an essential element of the area of freedom, security and justice that the EU is aspiring to be. Meeusen has strongly argued in favour of the conferral of powers to the European Union that are not exclusively associated with the internal market.[67] Detaching the competence to enact measures in the field of private international law from the internal market is congruent with the idea that the development of European legislation to facilitate cross-border activities is also important outside the strict market sphere.[68]

The removal of the necessary link with the internal market has the advantage of clarifying the existence of legal basis for the Union competence, particularly as regards to the adoption of measures in the field of international family law and the question of external competence.[69]

Section 4.4 below will discuss the requirements of Article 81 TFEU.

4.3 Why is the EU Developing a Unified System of International Family Law?

When discussing the establishment of a unified European system of international family law, the question arises why the EU is actually developing such a system. A unification of the choice of law in family issues would fulfil several general objectives (Section 4.3.1). These objectives can, however, be fulfilled by any unification and not specifically at the European level.

Subsequently, one may wonder why the European Union has a specific interest in the unification of international family law. The growing attention for issues of

---

[66] See also Dickinson 2005, pp. 217–218; Kreuzer 2006, p. 27; Fiorini 2008c, p. 976; Gaertner 2008, pp. 293–294; De Groot and Kuipers 2008, pp. 110–111; and Knot 2008, p. 176.

[67] See Meeusen 2006, p. 20 ff.

[68] Cf., Dethloff 2003, p. 58.

[69] See also Fiorini 2008c, p. 977.

international family law results from the increasingly important place that the citizen occupies in the EU.[70] Are there any specific aims and objectives to be achieved by the European private international law rules, as compared to those of e.g. the Hague Conference? This question can be answered with a definite 'yes'. European law and the development of the choice of law rules resting thereupon are not solely directed at, say, the prevention of forum shopping, but equally at the furthering of the aims and objectives of the European Union and to effectively enforce EU law to this end.[71] Besides the classical aims of private international law the European choice of law thus pursues its own goals, which will be discussed in Section 4.3.2.

The specific objectives and methods that are characteristic of private international law were once universally shared: in the nineteenth century uniformity of decisions (*Entscheidungseinklang*) was the ultimate goal. This consensus was greatly influenced by Von Savigny.[72] Yet this consensus has dissolved over time.[73] The challenge for the European Union now is to again find such consensus on the objectives and methods of private international law.

4.3.1 General Objectives Fulfilled by a Choice of Law Unification

The establishment of a unified system of choice of law offers a number of advantages over the situation in which every national state has its own system. If every state autonomously provides for the choice of law, logically these national systems may differ from one legal system to another. E.g. whereas in certain states the choice of law issues concerning personal status are governed by the national law of the person involved, yet other legal systems refer these issues to the law of the person's habitual residence.

Basedow has distinguished three objectives that would be fulfilled by unifying the choice of law: such unification would increase legal certainty, provide for more decisional harmony and grant better protection to the legitimate expectations of the parties.[74] In addition to these objectives, one could envisage two more objectives that would be fulfilled by the unification of the choice of law rules: the prevention of limping relationships and the achievement of justice. As these objectives are closely interconnected, it is not always possible to separate one from another.

---

[70] A 'citizen's Europe' is strived for. See Communication from the Commission to the European Parliament and the Council, An area of freedom, security and justice serving the citizen, COM(2009) 262 final, p. 5.

[71] Cf., Schilling 2006, pp. 46–47. See also already Badiali 1985, pp. 40–41.

[72] See Von Savigny 1849. See more elaborately *infra* Sect. 4.3.1.

[73] Cf., Fentiman 2008, p. 2021.

[74] Basedow 2000, p. 703.

The unification of the choice of law rules would, firstly, increase legal certainty. This objective has equally been endorsed by the European institutions.[75] The increase of legal certainty with regard to international family law would as such contribute to the free movement of persons: it is argued that European citizens will be less reluctant to move and reside within the EU if the effects on their family status and rights are clear.[76] It must be stressed that the free movement of persons may not be affected by the choice of law process as such. According to De Boer mobility can only be impeded by a refusal to recognise legal relationships that have been validly created in another Member State, under its own substantive law in national cases or in accordance with its private international law rules in cross-border cases.[77] However, Meeusen rightly emphasised that the free movement of persons can also be impeded if the choice of law rule itself or the substantive law designated by it is discriminatory *vis-à-vis* the citizens of other Member States.[78]

Secondly, the unification of the choice of law rules would contribute to more decisional harmony (*Entscheidungseinklang*), the achievement of which is considered as a (theoretical) goal of private international law. Von Savigny already argued:

> [...] daß auch die Rechtsverhältnisse, in Fällen einer Collision der Gesetze, dieselbe Beurtheilung zu erwarten haben, ohne Unterschied, ob in diesem oder jenem Staate das Urtheil gesprochen werde.
>
> Der Standpunkt, auf den wir durch diese Erwägung geführt werden, is der einer völkerrechtlichen Gemeinschaft der mit einander verkehrenden Nationen [...].[79]

According to Von Savigny decisional harmony would ultimately mean that each court in the world would decide the same case according to the same legal system.[80] However, many national choices of law rules have currently been formulated from the perspective of national values and standards. Therefore, the unification of the choice of law would contribute to the principle of decisional harmony. It must nevertheless be stressed that decisional harmony within the territory of the EU entails more than the sole unification of the choice of law rules:

---

[75] See The Hague Programme. See also Council and Commission Action Plan implementing the Hague Programme on strengthening freedom, security and justice in the European Union, [2005] OJ C198/1.

[76] Tenreiro and Ekström 2003, p. 187. See equally Dohrn 2004, p. 9 ff. Not all authors agree with this point of view; according to Nott 2002, p. 10 the EU is using the principle of free movement of persons '*in order to make even greater inroads into the traditional territory of conflict of laws*'.

[77] De Boer 2008b, p. 329.

[78] See Meeusen 2008, p. 335.

[79] Von Savigny 1849, para 348, p. 27. Vonken 2006, p. 119 concludes that in the beginning of the 21st century decisional harmony is still one of the '*Leitmotive*' of private international law.

[80] Von Savigny 1849, para 360, p. 114: '*Wird diese bereits angefangene Entwicklung des Rechts nicht durch unvorhergesehene äußere Umstände gestört, so läßt sich erwarten, daß sie zuletzt zu einer völlig übereinstimmenden Behandlung unserer Lehre in allen Staaten führen wird.*'

a systematic application of these common rules is needed.[81] In this respect the European Court of Justice can and must play an important role.[82]

Unified choice of law rules ensure that the same law will be applied to a certain situation, irrespective of the competent court seised. An important aspect of the fulfillment of this objective is that it will lead to the prevention of 'forum shopping'.[83] The prevailing view is, however, that only few people do calculate in this sense, unless a great deal of money is involved.[84] Therefore, in matters of international family law the prevention of forum shopping is not often a compelling reason for unification.[85]

Moreover, unification of the choice of law would grant better protection to the legitimate expectations of the parties. When a person moves to another country he does not primarily do so in order to change his status or personal law. That this is one of the consequences of moving may come to many people as an unwanted and unexpected surprise.[86] This objective is closely connected to the two

---

[81] In this respect Bogdan 2006, p. 12 rightly argues that full decisional harmony would require more than a unification of the choice of law rules of the Member States as such, namely equally a unified approach to a number of general doctrines of private international law. See *infra* Sect. 8.4.4.2 for a more detailed discussion on the need of a unified approach to these general doctrines.

[82] The role of the ECJ in this respect is, however, dependent on the preliminary references that will be requested. See further *infra* Sect. 4.5.

[83] According to Rüberg 2005, p. 64, two distinct forms of forum shopping can be distinguished. The first type of forum shopping is one on formal/procedural grounds, in which factors such as the easy accessibility of the court, the quality and speed of the procedure, the costs and the rules on evidence are taken into account. See on this type of forum shopping D. Henrich, Attachment No. 1 to the Protocol of the Meeting of the 'Deutscher Rat für Internationales Privatrecht' of 12 April 2002 in Würzburg, p. 35. By the second — dominant — type of forum shopping a specific court is seised on the basis of substantive law considerations, namely the law applied to the case *and* to ancillary claims. This second form of forum shopping is also referred to as 'law shopping' or 'system shopping'. See as regards system shopping also Kreuzer 1991, p. 230; and Meeusen 2007c, p. 266 ff.

[84] See McEleavy 2004, p. 627, 628 who states with regard to divorce: '*[T]he real motive in striking first to gain or preserve a jurisdictional advantage will not of course be the manner or facility with which a marriage may be ended, but the desire to secure as advantageous a financial settlement as possible.*' See equally De Boer 2008a, p. 340. The Commission did acknowledge that the rules of financial provision ancillary to divorce (in particular maintenance and the division of matrimonial property) may play an important role in determining a party's choice of forum. These issues are the subjects of other Green Papers. See Commission Staff Working Document – Annex to the Green Paper on applicable law and jurisdiction in divorce matters, SEC(2005)331 of 14 March 2005, p. 3.

[85] In other fields of law, such as non-contractual obligations, the Commission considered the prevention of forum shopping as the *raison d'être* of common choice of law rules. See Lagarde 2004, p. 230: '[…] *la crainte du forum shopping est à l'origine de la conclusion de la convention de Rome du 19 juin 1980 sur la loi applicable aux obligations contractuelles et de l'adoption prochaine du règlement Rome II sur la loi applicable aux obligations extra contractuelles.*'.

[86] See, however, De Boer 2008a, pp. 321–322 on the '*justified expectations of the parties*'. Most parties do have expectations, but these are connected with notions of material justice and not with the law to be applied. It is in general questionable to what extent people who deliberately move abroad should be protected against 'unwanted and unexpected surprises'.

aforementioned objectives: more legal certainty will lead to better predictability of the outcome of a case, which in turn contributes to the protection expectations of the citizens.

Fourthly, common choice of law rules would minimise the risk of limping relationships.[87] If the law applicable to a legal relationship differs from Member State to Member State, this could imply that the legal status of a person equally differs from one Member State to another. In family law certainty as to status is crucial. People live in reliance of the continued existence of the familial relationships they enter into.[88] In this respect Meeusen has rightly stressed that, given the current status of European integration, there is no doubt that anyone carrying out cross-border activities is entitled to expect that these activities take place within a 'legal area', where the legal instruments of the Member States are coordinated in a satisfactory way, providing legal certainty and effective means of law enforcement.[89]

Finally, uniform choice of law rules would enable the achievement of justice, that is to say so-called 'conflicts justice'.[90] The absence of common choice of law rules could lead to the application of, e.g., a legal system to a divorce with which the marriage in question has (virtually) no connection. The task of a choice of law rule is not only to determine the law applicable, but also to refer the case to the 'right' legal order, i.e. the applicable law should be the law of that legal system that is, due to its connections to the case, most appropriate to its resolution. Von Savigny already advocated

> daß bei jedem Rechtsverhältniß dasjenige Rechtsgebiet aufgesucht werde, welchem Rechtsverhältniß seiner eigenthümlichen Natur nach angeört oder unterworfen ist.[91]

Von Savigny expected that there would be a worldwide consensus on the connecting factor to be chosen for every legal relationship, which would lead each court in the world to the application of the same national legal system. However, to date such worldwide consensus has never emerged.

As mentioned above, these five objectives can be fulfilled by any unification of the choice of law and not specifically in the European context. In this regard a more global approach — which could potentially be reached by a convention of the Hague Conference on Private International Law — is to be preferred over a regional European unification, as it obviously ensures that the indicated objectives are fulfilled in a better way: the more states applying uniform rules, the better the objectives are fulfilled.[92]

---

87 See equally Dohrn 2004, p. 14 ff.

88 Cf., Dethloff 2003, p. 50; Curry-Sumner 2005, p. 522.

89 Meeusen 2006, p. 23.

90 See also briefly Wagner 2007, p. 105.

91 Von Savigny 1849, para 348, p. 28.

92 See more elaborate on the relationship between the European Union and the Hague Conference *infra* Sect. 8.4.4.3.

4.3.2 Specific European Aims and Objectives

In areas where the EU regulates issues of private international law proper 'European' policy objectives will play a role. This logically follows from the fact that the unification of private international law in the EU is not considered as an objective in itself, but it is rather used as an instrument to achieve other European goals.[93] In other words, international family law is being Europeanised as part of a package of measures, *inter alia* to promote integration, to enhance judicial cooperation, to give substance to the concept of European citizenship and to ensure the sound functioning of the internal market. As will be shown below, one can clearly notice that the development of the European Union as such has brought about new objectives to be strived for by the European rules of private international law.[94]

The principal objective of the establishment of a common European private international law is the creation of the internal market (Section 4.3.2.1). The Treaty of Amsterdam explicitly placed the development of a European private international law in the light of the establishment of an area of freedom, security and justice (Article 61 EC, now Article 81 TFEU). This area is, therefore, of crucial importance to the development of European international family law (Section 4.3.2.2). Thirdly, the Council has declared the principle of mutual recognition as the cornerstone of the development of private international law rules. Therefore, the impact of this principle as regards the arrangement of the choice of law cannot be left undiscussed (Section 4.3.2.3). Fourthly, the protection of stability interests will be discussed (Section 4.3.2.4). As will become clear, also these objectives are strongly interrelated. Finally, in the European founding treaties a number of aims and objectives can be found, which will be addressed in Section 4.3.2.5.

4.3.2.1 The Internal Market: the Free Movement of Persons

One of the principal objectives of the European Union as a whole is the creation of an internal market: a unified economic area (Article 3(3) EU-Treaty). Within the framework of this internal market — defined as an area without internal frontiers — European law aims at the abolishment of all obstacles between the Member States to the free movement of goods, persons, services and capital (Article 26 TFEU). The connection to the internal market in the field of international family law will — by its nature — mostly be established through the free movement of persons.

The very creation and existence of an internal market within the EU is likely to increase typical private international law situations: e.g. more international marriages will be contracted, as more people live abroad. The creation of an internal market is, moreover, only conceivable if private parties carry it into effect by

[93] Cf., Traest 2002, p. 1830.

[94] Cf., Borrás 2005, p. 369.

entering into cross-border legal relationships. In the absence of unified European substantive private law rules, private international law holds an important function in this respect since it guarantees the coordination of the diverging national legal systems. Therefore, the interest of the European Union in private international law is obvious.[95]

Indeed, private international law exists for the purpose of the establishment and functioning of the internal market.[96]

The legislative activities in the field of international family law aim to stimulate the free movement of Union citizens throughout the EU: it is argued that the pursuit of an internal market with the free movement of economically active people (Article 45 *et seq* TFEU) as well as of the unobstructed mobility of Union citizens in general (Article 21 TFEU) cannot be fully realised without the development of a unified system of international family law.[97] It is presumed that the existing differences in (international) family law among the EU-Member States are an obstacle to the free movement of persons.[98] The unification of private international law rules regarding cross-border family relations is considered as the proper way to overcome this obstacle. Recently the European Commission's Vice-President Barrot stated on this issue:

> in a European area without internal borders, any legal barriers that could undermine the freedom of movement of individuals must be eliminated. The main objective of Community instruments in this domain [i.e. international family law; NAB] is to simplify things for those 'living as Europeans' by providing solutions to the problems encountered by people who live, get married, work, retire or inherit in a different Member State.[99]

Initially there was discussion whether or not international family law was excluded from European law. Since the EU is a supranational organisation that has traditionally acted almost entirely for economic reasons and with economic motives, the link with family law is not obvious at first sight.[100] A confrontation with the difficulties of (international) family law did exist, but the European

---

95 See equally Israël 2001, p. 135; Nott 2002, p. 3; Meeusen 2007b, p. 287.

96 Ex Article 65 EC-Treaty limited the competence of the European legislature to enact measures of private international law to those 'necessary for the proper functioning of the internal market'. The current provision (Article 81 TFEU) has abandoned this imperative character, but does still refer to the internal market ('particularly when necessary for the proper functioning of the internal market').

97 According to Mr. Vogelaar, a former Director-General of the Internal Market of the Commission 'the differences between national legal systems and the lack of unified rules of conflict definitely impede the free movement of persons [...] among Member States'; see [1980] OJ C282/1.

98 Cf., Basedow 1994, spec. at p. 198; De Groot 2001, p. 619; Tenreiro and Ekström 2003, p. 187.

99 See Press Release No. IP/09/445 of 20 March 2009, 'EU's commitment to making everyday life easier for European families'.

100 Cf., Poillot-Peruzzetto and Marmisse 2001, p. 460; Borrás 2005, p. 347 ff; McNamara and Martin 2006, p. 9; Meeusen 2007a, pp. 330–331.

authorities have always taken a restrictive stance.[101] There is legal terminology in European law as regards family, but the existing case law of the European Court of Justice and the Court of First Instance shows that they have traditionally been rather reserved in any interference in the field of (international) family law of the Member States.[102]

However, nowadays this question is no longer under discussion: international family law falls within the scope of European law. Over the last few years the areas in which the EU has interfered have gradually changed and, even if they relate to an economic goal, the interests of the European citizens have become more and more important.[103] Cross-border questions of family law have become part of the everyday life of an increasing number of European citizens. One of the priorities of the Luxembourg Presidency of 2005 therefore recognised:

> [C]ivil law, and more particularly the cross-border aspects of the rights of the family, is of major importance.[104]

The increasing interest in the Europeanisation of international family law is connected to the change of the free movement of persons, which has gradually lost its purely economic connotation.[105] This change is very well illustrated by the introduction of the concept of Union citizenship (Article 20 *et seq* TFEU).[106] This concept made the rights to enter, reside and stay in the territory of another Member State an integral part of the 'legal heritage' of every Union citizen.[107] The citizenship of the European Union, integrating the national citizenship without

---

[101] See Roth 1991, pp. 634–636; Struycken 1992, pp. 307–308, pp. 351–358; (briefly) Siehr 2003, p. 419 ff; Van den Eeckhout 2004, p. 52.

[102] See for an in-depth study in this field Kohler 1996, spec. p. 79. Some examples of the European case law in this field: ECJ Case 24/71 *Meinhardt* v. *Commission* [1972] ECR 269; ECJ Case 267/83 *Diatta* v. *Land Berlin* [1985] ECR 567; ECJ Case 59/85 *State of the Netherlands* v. *Reed* [1986] ECR 1283; CFI Case T-43/90 *José Miguel Diaz Garcia* v. *European Parliament* [1992] ECR II-2619; and CFI Case T-85/91 *Khouri* v. *Commission* [1992] ECR II-2637.

[103] See Borrás Report, para 1: '[…] *integration is now no longer purely economic and is coming to have an increasingly profound effect on the life of the European citizen* […]. *The issue offamily lawtherefore has to be faced as part of the phenomenon of European integration.*' Already in 1966 Zweigert predicted that the European Union would deal with matters of international family law, since to his opinion divergent choice of law rules for personal matters would, in the long term, have disintegrative effects within the European Union. See Zweigert 1966, p. 558: '*In der Tat erweisen sich im Bereich des Personalsstatuts die kollisionsrechtlichen Divergenzen als so beträchtlich, dass auf die Länge desintegrierende Effekte nicht ausbleiben werden.*' See equally *inter alia* Kreuzer 1991, p. 230; Gaudemet-Tallon 2000, p. 238; Müller-Graff and Kainer 2000, p. 351; Dethloff 2003, p. 58; Borrás 2005, p. 348.

[104] See: http://www.eu2005.lu/en/presidence/priorites_et_pgm/priorites/index.html#justice.

[105] See Poillot-Peruzzetto and Marmisse 2001, p. 460; and Carrera 2005, p. 700.

[106] See also *supra* Sect. 4.2.1.2.

[107] See Communication of the Commission to the Council and to the European Parliament on the follow-up to the recommendations of the High-Level Panel on the Free Movement of Persons, COM(1998) 403 final, pp. 1–2.

replacing it, is characterised by a set of rights and duties aiming 'to strengthen and enhance the European identity and enable European citizens to participate in the Community integration process in a more intense way.'[108]

The European Court of Justice attaches great importance to European citizenship: it has systematically described Union citizenship as being destined to be the fundamental status of nationals of the Member States.[109] Furthermore, in a considerable number of judgments the ECJ has accordingly decided in favour of the mobility of Union citizens: they are granted maximum mobility throughout the Union, independently of any economic activity.[110]

In his Opinion in the *Boukhalfa*-case Advocate General Léger has explored the limits of the concept of the Union citizenship:

> If all the conclusions inherent in that concept are drawn, every citizen of the Union must, whatever his nationality, enjoy exactly the same rights and be subject to the same obligations. Taken to its ultimate conclusion, the concept should lead to citizens of the Union being treated absolutely equally, irrespective of their nationality. Such equal treatment should be manifested in the same way as among nationals of one and the same State.[111]

With respect to international family law, the case law of the ECJ on the interpretation of the concept of Union citizenship has led to two important decisions: *Garcia Avello*[112] and *Grunkin-Paul*.[113] These cases connect to a number of previous cases on the interpretation of Article 18 EC-Treaty (now: Article 21 TFEU), in which the Court held that national legislation which places certain nationals of the Member States concerned at a disadvantage simply because they have exercised their freedom to move and reside freely in another Member State is a restriction of this right.[114] In the two cases mentioned above, in which the ECJ intervened to amend a limping legal relationship, the Court held that

---

[108] See: http://ec.europa.eu/public_opinion/flash/fl_213_sum_en.pdf. See also Wollenschläger 2009. The integrative policy pursued by the concept of Union citizenship is reflected by the rights that are attached to it (Articles 21–24 TFEU).

[109] See *inter alia* ECJ Case C-184/99 *Grzelczyk* [2001] ECR I-6193, para 31; Case C-413/99 *Baumbast and R.* v. *Secretary for the Home Department* [2002] ECR I-9919, para 82; Case C-224/02 *Pusa* [2004] ECR I-5763, para 16; and Case C-135/08 *Rottmann* v. *Freistaat Bayern* [2010] ECR (not yet reported), para 43.

[110] See the ECJ judgments on the interpretation of the ex Articles 12, 17 and/or 18 EC-Treaty (now: Articles 18, 20 and 21 TFEU) starting with the judgment in Case C-85/96 *Martínez Sala* [1998] ECR I-2691.

[111] See para 63 of the Opinion of Advocate General Léger in ECJ Case C-214/94 *Ingrid Boukhalfa* v. *Bundesrepublik Deutschland* [1996] ECR I-2253.

[112] ECJ Case C-148/02 *Garcia Avello* [2003] ECR I-11613.

[113] ECJ Case C-353/06 *Grunkin-Paul* [2008] ECR I-07639.

[114] See equally ECJ Case C-224/02 *Pusa* [2004] ECR I-5763, para 19; Case C-406/04 *De Cuyper* [2006] ECR I-6947, para 39; and Case C-499/06 *Nerkowska* [2008] ECR I-03993, para 32.

> although, as Community law stands at present, the rules governing a person's surname are matters coming within the competence of the Member States, the latter must none the less, when exercising that competence, comply with Community law.[115]

However, a link with European law should exist. In *Garcia Avello* this link existed because the children involved had dual nationalities (Belgian and Spanish). The refusal of the Belgian authorities to recognise a name given by the Spanish authorities therefore constituted a violation of the principle of non-discrimination.[116]

Yet in *Grunkin-Paul* the persons involved had only one nationality (the German); the refusal to recognise a validly registered name under the law of a Member State (Denmark), the country in which the child was born, could therefore not constitute discrimination on grounds of nationality. However, the ECJ held that even where a person has only one nationality, his country of origin may not refuse to recognise a name which is changed in the Member State in which he is born and resides:

> having to use a surname, in the Member State of which the person concerned is a national, that is different from that conferred and registered in the Member State of birth and residence is liable to hamper the exercise of the right, established in Article 18 EC, to move and reside freely within the territory of the Member States.[117]

This case law makes clear that the principle of free movement of persons is detached from its purely economic connotation: both cases concerned children. Instead a more generalised concept of this principle is employed, which is equally at the centre of the European policy plans in the framework of the judicial cooperation in civil matters: the cooperation is not only aimed at the promotion of intra-European mobility of economically active persons.[118]

4.3.2.2 The Establishment of an Area of Freedom, Security and Justice: a Common European Judicial Area

With the progression towards the completion of the internal market, the Treaty of Amsterdam has enshrined a new Union objective in Article 2 of the EU-Treaty:

> to maintain and develop the Union as an area of freedom, security and justice in which the free movement of persons is assured in conjunction with appropriate measures with respect to external border controls, asylum, immigration [...].

The Council regards the development of an area of freedom, security and justice as a logical follow-up to its earlier objectives:

---

115 ECJ Case *Garcia Avello*, paras 25 and 26; and ECJ Case *Grunkin-Paul*, para 16.

116 ECJ Case *Garcia Avello*, paras 27 *et seq.*

117 ECJ Case *Grunkin-Paul*, para 22.

118 Cf., Wagner 2004, p. 138; Meeusen 2006, p. 21.

> [T]he European Council has already put in place for its citizens the major ingredient of a shared area of prosperity and peace: single market, economic and monetary union, and the capacity to take on global political and economic challenges. The challenge of the Amsterdam Treaty is now to ensure that freedom, which includes the right to move freely throughout the Union, can be enjoyed in conditions of security and justice accessible to all. It is a project which responds to the frequently expressed concerns of citizens and has a direct bearing on their daily lives.[119]

The Treaty of Lisbon led to a more determined wording: instead of the objective of the Treaty of Amsterdam to 'maintain and develop' an area of freedom, security and justice, the Treaty on the Functioning of the European Union specifies that the Union 'shall offer its citizens an area of freedom, security and justice without internal borders' (Article 3(2) EU-Treaty). This reflects that the EU now seemingly considers itself beyond the development phase of the establishment of the area of freedom, security and justice.

The pursuit of this area with regard to judicial cooperation in civil matters is allocated to Title V of the third part of the Treaty on the Functioning of the European Union (Article 81 TFEU). What is to be understood by the area of freedom, security and justice? No definition can be found in the Treaties. However, these notions are considered to be of fundamental importance, since the Commission emphasised that 'freedom, security and justice are key values that form an integral part of the European model of society: they are a cornerstone of European integration.'[120] It is thus clear that the area of freedom, security and justice plays an important part in the process of European integration. Within the framework of European integration the cooperation in the area of justice is significant:

> for reasons deeply embedded in history and tradition, judicial systems differ substantially between Member States. The ambition is to give citizens a common sense of justice throughout the Union. Justice must be seen as facilitating the day-to-day life of people.
>
> Reinforcement of judicial cooperation in civil matters [...] represents a fundamental stage in the creation of a European judicial area which will bring tangible benefits for every Union citizen. Law-abiding citizens have a right to look to the Union to simplify and facilitate the judicial environment in which they live in the European Union context. Here principles such as legal certainty and equal access to justice should be a main objective, implying identification of the competent jurisdiction, clear designation of the applicable law, availability of speedy and fair proceedings and effective enforcement procedures.[121]

Accordingly, the aim of judicial cooperation in civil matters is to make life simpler for European citizens, in particular in cases affecting their everyday life.[122]

---

119 Tampere Presidency Conclusions, para 2.

120 Communication from the Commission to the European Parliament and the Council, An area of freedom, security and justice serving the citizen, COM(2009) 262 final, p. 2. This document relates to the Stockholm Programme.

121 Vienna Action Plan, paras 15–16.

122 See the Hague Programme, p. 11 and 13.

This aim should be accomplished *inter alia* by 'promoting the compatibility' of choice of law rules in a European judicial area (Article 81(2)(c) TFEU).[123]

The European Council attaches great importance to the establishment of the area of freedom, security and justice. During the European Council meeting in Tampere in 1999, the establishment of this area has been designated as one of the most important objectives: it has been placed *at the very top* of the political agenda.[124] The European Council subsequently posed that 'the enjoyment of freedom requires a genuine area of justice'.[125] The following statement shows that the development of unified private international law rules should mainly be seen from the premise of an 'area of justice':

> [I]n a genuine European Area of Justice individuals and businesses should not be prevented or discouraged from exercising their rights by the incompatibility or complexity of legal and administrative systems in the Member States.[126]

In this European judicial area international family law occupies a prominent position: it has even been referred to as its '*vecteur essentiel*'.[127] In January 2007 the Informal Justice and Home Affairs Council recognised the 'importance of family law issues for the creation of a true area of justice.'[128]

The question that arises is what the relation of the area of freedom, security and justice to the internal market is. The area of freedom, security and justice seems to rest upon a much broader approach than the internal market, which may cause a certain tension between these notions.[129] From the European policy plans regarding the area of freedom, security and justice it is clear that the area is aimed at the furthering of the functioning of the internal market: the promotion intra-European mobility resulting from the principle of the free movement is the focal point in these plans.[130] In this context the internal market no longer seems to play a definite part, which is confirmed by the entry into force of the Treaty on the Functioning of the European Union removing the imperative character of the internal market requirement.[131]

---

[123] Vienna Action Plan, para 39. See further on the requirement 'promoting the compatibility of the rules applicable in the Member States concerning conflict of laws' *infra* Sect. 4.4.1.

[124] Tampere Presidency Conclusions, Recital 3 of the Preamble.

[125] Ibid., para 5.

[126] Ibid., para 28.

[127] Hubert 2000, p. 71. See equally Poillot-Peruzzetto 2005, p. 331; and, less pronounced, Martiny 2007, p. 72.

[128] Informal Justice and Home Affairs Council Meeting in Dresden of 14–16 January 2007, see: http://www.eu2007.de/en/News/Press_Releases/January/0115BMJFamilienrecht.html. This position was restated in Press Release 8364/07 (Presse 77) of the 2794th Justice and Home Affairs Council Meeting in Luxembourg of 19–20 April 2007, p. 12, available at: http://www.consilium.europa.eu/ueDocs/cms_Data/docs/pressData/en/jha/93741.pdf.

[129] Cf., Israël 2001, p. 149; Borrás 2005, p. 368; Knot 2008, p. 173.

[130] See *inter alia* Vienna Action Plan, paras 15, 16 and 39.

[131] See *supra* Sect. 4.2.3.2.

The successor to the expired Hague Programme, the Stockholm Programme, continues the direction in which the European Union is heading in the field of judicial cooperation in civil matters: the promotion of mobility of citizens throughout the Union remains a focal point. The Stockholm Programme indicates that an important priority for the coming years will be to focus on the interests and needs of citizens.[132]

4.3.2.3 The Principle of Mutual Recognition

In a reasonably short time, the principle of mutual recognition has developed into an important principle of European law. This principle was initially developed in the framework of the internal market and was used for purposes of European integration. In the *Cassis de Dijon* case the principle of mutual recognition appeared for the first time in the scope of the free movement of goods.[133] Subsequently, the ECJ has gradually extended the principle of mutual recognition to the other freedoms protected by the EC-Treaty.[134] From the traditional economic freedoms, the principle of mutual recognition has now spread through many other fields of Union law, including private international law.[135]

The principle of mutual recognition was not used in the field of European private international law until the Treaty of Amsterdam of 1997. Especially the conclusions of the Tampere European Council of 1999 placed the principle of mutual recognition of judgments at the heart of European integration in the field of

[132] See the Stockholm Programme, p. 3. See equally Communication from the Commission to the European Parliament and the Council, An area of freedom, security and justice serving the citizen, COM(2009) 262 final, p. 10: 'In an area of increasing mobility, the priority should be to develop and promote a European judicial area for citizens by removing the remaining restrictions on the exercise of their rights. Judgments, for example, must be recognised and easily enforced from one Member State to another.' See more elaborately on the Stockholm Programme: Wagner 2010, pp. 97–100.

[133] ECJ Case 120/78, *Rewe-Zentral AG* v. *Bundesmonopolverwaltung für Branntwein* [1979] ECR 649. The ECJ truly introduced the criterion of equivalence in Case 272/80 *Criminal proceedings* v. *Frans-Nederlandse Maatschappij voor Biologische Producten BV* [1981] ECR 3277, paras 14–16.

[134] ECJ Case 205/84 *Commission* v. *Germany* (*German Insurance*) [1986] ECR 3755 (freedom of establishment); ECJ Case C-76/90 *Säger* [1991] ECR I-42221 (freedom to provide services); ECJ Case C-55/94 *Gebhard* [1995] ECR I-4165 (free movement of persons). See for an extensive analysis of the development of the principle of mutual recognition: Mansel 2006, p. 664 ff.

[135] One can wonder, however, whether this principle is suitable to be directly transposed to the field of private international law. Cf., Kohler 2003, p. 407: '*Die Übertragung des gemeinschaftsrechtlichen Anerkennungsprinzips auf die Urteilsanerkennung ist jedoch fragwürdig. Jenes Prinzip ist für die Marktfreiheiten des EG-Vertrags entwickelt worden.*' Less strong also Fallon and Meeusen 2002, p. 46.

private international law.[136] The principle of mutual recognition is an important objective in the development of a genuine European judicial area.[137] This principle is now expressed in Article 81(1) TFEU.

When discussing the principle of mutual recognition, the main question that arises is what this principle actually involves. The Commission states that

> [m]utual recognition is a principle that is widely understood as being based on the thought that while another state may not deal with a certain matter in the same or even a similar way as one's own state, the results will be such that they are accepted as equivalent to decisions by one's own state. Mutual trust is an important element, not only trust in the adequacy of one's partners rules, but also trust that these rules are correctly applied.[138]

Two important notions follow from this definition: equivalence and mutual trust. However, any further interpretation by the European legislature of these notions or the principle of mutual recognition is lacking. This is probably a matter of deliberate policy so as to keep the principle flexible and apply it differently depending on the area concerned. The European Court of Justice did emphasise in *Gözütok and Brügge* that the main contribution of the principle of mutual recognition is to bridge existing differences in the laws of the Member States.[139]

For some time, it seemed as if the principle of mutual recognition in the European judicial area would give full priority to the establishment of common rules on recognition and enforcement of foreign judgments.[140,141] The European

---

[136] Tampere Presidency Conclusions, paras 33–37. See also the Hague Programme, p. 11, in which the Council noted that in order for the principle of mutual recognition to become effective, mutual trust needed to be strengthened by progressively developing a European judicial culture based on the diversity of legal systems and unity through European law. See further *infra* Sects. 8.4.2.2 and 8.4.2.3.

[137] See Decision No 1149/2007/EC of the European Parliament and of the Council establishing for the period 2007–2013 the Specific Programme 'Civil Justice' as part of the General Programme 'Fundamental Rights and Justice', [2007] OJ L257/16. In Article 2(1)(a) of this Decision is determined that the one of the general objectives of the Programme is 'to promote judicial cooperation with the aim of contributing to the creation of a genuine European area of justice in civil matters based on mutual recognition and mutual confidence.'.

[138] See Communication from the Commission to the Council and the European Parliament, Mutual Recognition of Final Decisions in Criminal Matters, COM(2000) 495 final, p. 4.

[139] ECJ joined Cases C-187/01 and C-385/01 *Gözütok and Brügge* [2003] ECR I-1345, para 33.

[140] Until 2008 all measures enacted by the Union on the basis of Article 65 EC namely focused on rules of jurisdiction and recognition and enforcement, e.g. the Brussels I-Regulation and Brussels II*bis*-Regulation. See also Jayme and Kohler 2001, p. 501; Jessurun d'Oliveira 2002, pp. 130–131.

[141] However, it is not only a matter of priority that the European legislature primarily established common rules on recognition and enforcement. See Meeusen 2007c, p. 270 pointing out that the unification of the choice of law is '*by far more difficult than obtaining European consensus on common rules for recognition and enforcement. For that reason, it seems that the choice of the Community legislator to give priority to procedural mutual recognition shouldn't really be explained by strategic considerations (in particular by the idea of a strong stimulus given to the harmonisation of the choice-of-law rules) but rather appears to be inspired more by practical arguments.*'.

Council of Tampere namely endorsed the principle of mutual recognition to become 'the cornerstone of judicial cooperation' in civil matters.[142] Subsequently, the Council adopted a programme of measures for the implementation of the principle of mutual recognition of decisions in civil and commercial matters, the Mutual Recognition Programme.

This emphasis on the recognition of judicial decisions in civil matters could mean that the choice of law is taken to the background or is at least approached in a very functional and auxiliary way.[143] This conclusion is all the more confirmed by the Mutual Recognition Programme, in which the Council solely marginally dealt with choice of law issues and pointed out that

> the implementation of the mutual recognition principle may be facilitated through harmonisation of conflict-of-law rules.[144]

Without any reservation, the annex of the Mutual Recognition Programme mentions measures in the field of choice of law among the 'ancillary measures'.[145] From this perspective, the principle of mutual recognition leads to the question of the necessity of European choice of law rules.[146] For what is the purpose of the choice of law if a judicial decision rendered by a court in one of the Member States can be recognised throughout the European Union after all?

Although it cannot be denied that the impact and importance of common choice of law rules is greatly reduced by the abolition of exequatur,[147] the choice of law does pursue more aims than the sole facilitation of the recognition of judicial decisions. No justice is done to the doctrine of the choice of law if it is solely regarded as facilitating the recognition of foreign judgments. Especially in terms of the achievement of justice, legal certainty and predictability for the parties concerned the choice of law plays an important part. The position of the Council as

---

[142] Tampere Presidency Conclusion, para 33.

[143] See Meeusen 2004, p. 58 ff. According to Coester-Waltjen the mutual recognition of judicial decisions entails that the establishment of common European choice of law rules can even be completely abandoned. See Coester-Waltjen 2006, p. 400.

[144] Mutual Recognition Programme, p. 6. Very critical as regards this facilitating function of the choice of law, however, Meeusen 2007c, pp. 265–266; and De Boer 2009, pp. 305–308.

[145] Mutual Recognition Programme, p. 9.

[146] Cf., Lagarde 2005, p. 15: '*Vielleicht ist nun der Moment gekommen, an dem man sich fragen sollte, ob dieser Grundsatz der gegenseitigen Anerkennung nicht die Grenzen zwischen Kollisionsnormen im Internationalen Privatrecht und Anerkennungsnormen im international Verfahrensrecht zugunsten der letzteren ein wenig verschiebt?*'; Gaertner 2006, p. 99; Dethloff 2007, p. 997: '*Auch wenn das Primärrecht keinen Wechsel vom klassischen Verweisungssystem des Internationalen Privatrechts zum Anerkennungsprinzip erzwingt, wirft der Einzug vom Anerkennungsregeln in das künftige Personen-, Familien- und Erbrecht grundlegende Methodenfragen auf.*'

[147] See, with regard to the Brussels II*bis*-Regulation, Meeusen 2007c, p. 266.

regards the functional role of the choice of law thus fully disregards that it actually serves a proper function. For this reason the *Anerkennung statt IPR*-approach of the Union legislature has been severely criticised by legal doctrine.[148]

Consequently, it must be concluded that the influence of the principle of mutual recognition does in this regard not seem to be very advantageous as regards the establishment of a common choice of law. However, the Union legislature seems to change its approach, as it increasingly concentrates on the unification of issues of the choice of law.[149]

The principle of mutual recognition has two distinctive characteristics that affect the development of European rules on international family law.[150] The first characteristic of the principle of mutual recognition in this respect is that the legal traditions and systems of the Member States should be respected, implying that the European area of justice does not aim to question the substantive legal systems of the Member States.[151] The European integration in the field of justice is to be built on respect for the diversity of national systems.[152] This approach is connected to the European motto 'united in diversity'. Secondly, as seen above, EU law assumes by virtue of the principle of mutual recognition an equivalence of the legal norms of the Member States, which is implied by the concept of mutual trust that underlies the principle of mutual recognition.[153]

4.3.2.4 Protection of 'Stability Interests'

The specific European objectives show that the European Union strives for the protection of two specific interests.[154] On the one hand, the EU aims to protect specific interests that are directed at the integration of European citizens residing

---

148 See further *infra* Sects. 4.4.4.2 and 6.5.

149 All the legislative activities in the field of international family law concern jurisdiction, applicable law and recognition and enforcement. See also Jayme and Kohler 2002, pp. 461–462.

150 A third characteristic is the debate on the question whether the principle of mutual recognition incorporates a hidden choice of law rule referring to the law of the Member State of origin of a person or a product. However, this aspect will be left out of account; see for a survey of the relevant literature De Schutter and Francq 2005, p. 644. The country of origin principle is currently almost unanimously rejected; see Ballarino and Ubertazzi 2004, p. 118; and Wilderspin 2007, No. 6, pp. 26–28.

151 Communication from the Commission to the Council and the European Parliament, Area of Freedom, Security and Justice: Assessment of the Tampere Programme and future orientations, COM(2004) 401 final, p. 10 ff. See equally Mattera 1998, pp. 5–17; Mansel 2006, p. 661.

152 See The Hague Programme, p. 11; and Communication from the Commission to the European Parliament and the Council, An area of freedom, security and justice serving the citizen, COM(2009) 262 final, p. 11.

153 Cf., Israël 2001, p. 141; and Meeusen 2007c, p. 273.

154 See equally Dutta 2009, pp. 565, 571–572.

outside their home country.[155] On the other hand, the European Union strives for the protection of 'stability interests', i.e. interests connected to striving for the stability of the legal positions of persons who have made use of their freedom of movement.

The European Court of Justice has started off the process of the protection of stability interests in its case law concerning the determination of surnames.[156] This jurisprudential development is visible in the cases *Konstantinidis*,[157] *Garcia Avello* and *Grunkin-Paul*. In these last two cases the ECJ clearly highlighted the interest of stability:

> a discrepancy in surnames is liable to cause serious inconveniences for those concerned at both professional and private levels resulting from, *inter alia*, difficulties in benefiting, in the Member State of which they are nationals, from the legal effects of diplomas or documents drawn up in the surname recognised in another Member State of which they [i.e. the persons involved; NAB] are also nationals.[158]

The protection of stability interests is especially important for the realisation of the internal market, as the fundamental freedoms can solely be ensured if the exercise of those freedoms does not involve the loss of legal positions that have already been acquired in another Member State. In this respect the principle of mutual recognition comes into play. Naturally, in the whole area of international family law the protection of stability interests is significant.[159] People live in reliance of the continued existence of the familial relationships they live in. The protection of stability interests is, consequently, closely connected to the abovementioned objective of minimising the risk of limping relationships.[160]

---

155 A good example of the result of this integrative policy of the European Union is the use of the connecting factor of habitual residence, see *infra* Sect. 5.5.3.1. Also the prohibition of discrimination on grounds of nationality pursuant to Article 18 TFEU is a consequence of the latter policy.

156 It is to be noted that a very similar approach is visible in the field of international company law; see *inter alia* ECJ Case C-212/97 *Centros* [1999] ECR I-1459; ECJ Case C-208/00 *Überseering* [2002] ECR I-09919; ECJ Case C-167/01 *Inspire Art* [2003] ECR I-10155; and ECJ Case C-411/03 *Sevic* [2005] ECR I-10805.

157 ECJ Case C-168/91 *Konstantinidis* [1993] ECR I-1191, paras 15 *et seq*, in which the court held that the freedom of establishment is obstructed if the true pronunciation of a surname according to the language of the home state is distorted by the official transliteration of that name according to the law of the present state of residence.

158 ECJ Case *Garcia Avello*, para 36. See for an equal stance ECJ Case *Grunkin-Paul*, paras 23–28.

159 However, see Funken 2009, p. 178 stating that it is not obvious that the decisions *Garcia Avello* and *Grunkin-Paul* have broader implications for a person's civil status, as: '*der Name bildet wegen seiner Identifizierungsfunktion eine besondere Materie im Bereich des Personalstatuts, die sich von sonstigen Statusfragen unterscheidet.*'

160 See *supra* Sect. 4.3.1. See equally Dohrn 2004, p. 14 ff.

4.3.2.5 Other Aims and Objectives Ensuing from European Law

The founding treaties of the European Union require a number of interests to be respected by the European legislature in all its activities. Therefore, these interests are also to be taken into account in common European rules on international family law. Without having the intention to enumerate exhaustively these interests, the following three are of particular importance to the field of international family law:

- the principle of non-discrimination on grounds of nationality (Article 18 *et seq* TFEU);
- the respect for human rights (Article 6 EU-Treaty in conjunction with Article 67 TFEU); and
- the respect for the national identities of the Member States (Article 4(2) EU-Treaty).

Both the principle of non-discrimination and the requirement to respect the national identities of the Member States will be discussed below, where will become clear what the precise effects of these interests on the European choice of law in family issues are.[161]

4.4 EU Competence to Enact Measures of International Family Law: Scope and Limits of Article 81 TFEU

The establishment of common choice of law rules in the field of family law ultimately leads to the question whether the EU actually has competence to unify the choice of law on family law issues.

Every Union action requires a legal basis: the European legislature has only the powers expressly or impliedly conferred on it by the Treaties.[162] The question of Union competence is crucial, because a lack of competence might result in the measure being annulled by the European Court of Justice.[163] Article 4(2)(j) TFEU confers on the Union a shared competence with the Member States in the field of the area of freedom, security and justice. Moreover, Article 81 TFEU provides for the competence of the Union in the field of judicial cooperation in civil matters, which determines that

---

[161] See *infra* Sects. 5.5.3.2 and 8.4.2.2 respectively. See for the influence of the requirement to respect human rights on European private international law further Van den Eeckhout 2008. The duty to respect human rights particularly influences the doctrine of the public policy; see further Rutten 1998.

[162] See Article 5(1) EU-Treaty stipulating that '[T]he limits of Union competences are governed by the principle of conferral'. Article 5(2) determines that under the principle of conferral, the Union shall act only within the limits of the competences conferred upon it by the Member States in the Treaties to attain the objectives set out therein. See on this issue Hellner 2002, p. 19.

[163] See for example ECJ Case 294/83 *Les Verts* v. *European Parliament* [1986] ECR 1339.

1. [T]he Union shall develop judicial cooperation in civil matters having cross-border implications, based on the principle of mutual recognition of judgments and of decisions in extrajudicial cases. [...]
2. For the purposes of para 1, the European Parliament and the Council [...] shall adopt measures, particularly when necessary for the proper functioning of the internal market [...].

Two general requirements can be deducted from this provision: measures based on Article 81 TFEU must firstly concern 'judicial cooperation in civil matters' and secondly 'have cross border implications'. Furthermore, the measures can be adopted 'particularly when necessary for the proper functioning of the internal market'. In addition, every legislative act should respect the principles of proportionality and subsidiarity.[164]

In the following these requirements will be discussed.

4.4.1 Judicial Cooperation in Civil Matters

Article 81(2) TFEU contains in lit. (a)–(h) a list of areas which are considered as falling within the field of judicial cooperation in civil matters:

(a) the mutual recognition and enforcement between Member States of judgments and of decisions in extrajudicial cases;
(b) the cross-border service of judicial and extrajudicial documents;
(c) the compatibility of the rules applicable in the Member States concerning conflict of laws and of jurisdiction;
(d) cooperation in the taking of evidence;
(e) effective access to justice;
(f) the elimination of obstacles to the proper functioning of civil proceedings, if necessary by promoting the compatibility of the rules on civil procedure applicable in the Member States;
(g) the development of alternative methods of dispute settlement;
(h) support for the training of the judiciary and judicial staff.

In contrast with Article 65 EC-Treaty, this (extended) list of areas for potential action contained Article 81(2) TFEU is exhaustive.[165]

Rules unifying the choice of law rules in family matters come under the area listed in lit. (c) and should consequently fulfil the requirement of 'ensuring the compatibility of the rules applicable in the Member States concerning conflict of laws'.

Does this requirement include a unification of the choice of law? Article 81(2)(c) TFEU aims at ensuring the *compatibility* of the choice of law rules, which

---

[164] See Article 5(1) EU-Treaty: 'The use of Union competences is governed by the principles of subsidiarity and proportionality.'

[165] See Fiorini 2008c, p. 977. Less strong, however, Mansel et al. 2010, p. 25. Contra Hess 2010, p. 76: '*Art. 81* [...] *führt verschiedene Handlungsfelder der ziviljustiziellen Zusammenarbeit exemplarisch auf.*'

seems more favourable to the harmonisation of the choice of law rules.[166] However, the experiences so far indicate that the usual ambition of the European institutions is rather to achieve a total uniformity of these rules in the Member States.[167] Does such ambition then fall outside the scope of the Union competence according to Article 81 TFEU?

There are two arguments that argue in favour of Article 81 TFEU allowing for the unification of the choice of law.[168] In the first place, the fields enumerated in Article 81 TFEU should not be seen in isolation: e.g. pursuant to the Brussels II*bis*-Regulation decisions on divorce have to be recognised within the EU regardless of the law applied.[169] Ideally such liberal rules of recognition would require unified choice of law rules. Accordingly, when unified choice of law rules are the proper basis for the current rules on recognition, the interpretation of Article 81(2)(c) TFEU should not preclude such unification.[170] Secondly, the unification of the choice of law rules promotes the compatibility of these rules better than harmonisation, since harmonisation of choice of law rules does not exclude the risk of diverging decisions. In other words, the compatibility of the national choice of law rules can be promoted as long as it is possible that, due to diverging national choice of law rules, one and the same legal relationship will be judged differently in the courts of different Member States.[171]

---

[166] Cf., as regards the identical wording of Article 65 EC-Treaty Von Hoffmann 1998, p. 31; Kohler 1999, p. 20; Partsch 2003, p. 310; Gaudemet-Tallon 2005, p. 166; Mansel 2006, p. 659.

[167] Bogdan 2006, p. 12. All Regulations concerning choice of law enacted and proposed so far involve the unification of the choice of law rules at issue.

[168] See Basedow 2000, p. 706, who brought up a third reason as well: the enumeration of Article 65 EC-Treaty of areas falling within the field of judicial cooperation in civil matters was not exhaustive, as it stipulated that the measures adopted 'shall include' those listed in lit. (a)–(c) of that Article. However, this argument is no longer valid under the Treaty on the Functioning of the European Union, as Article 81(2) TFEU does contain an exhaustive list of areas of potential action.

See equally in favour of Article 65 EC allowing for the unification of the choice of law Leible and Staudinger 2000, p. 228; Basedow 2002, p. 40; Kohler 2003, p. 408; Wagner 2004, p. 128. According to De Vareilles-Sommières 1998, pp. 136–137 the Union's approach aimed at the unification of issues of private international law can be explained by the nature of Community law: '[...] *le droit communautaire est au contraire, par sa nature un droit commun aux différents Etats composant la communauté européenne, et le principe de son action est moins la coordination que l'uniformisation.*'

[169] See Article 21(1) in conjunction with Article 25 of the Brussels II*bis*-Regulation.

[170] Cf., Wagner 2004, pp. 128–129.

[171] This same consideration led Kreuzer 1991, p. 231 to the conclusion that the choice of law should be unified: '*L'intégration du droit des conflits de lois dans le cadre de la C.E. doit prendre la forme d'une unification de ces règles.* [...] *Le simple rapprochement des droits ne présente pourtant guère d'utilité dans la sphère du droit international privé. La maigre intégration réalisée* via *le rapprochement des normes de conflits de lois s'avère inapte à justifier l'effort considérable à fournir en vue d'aboutir à l'harmonisation du droit international privé effectuée par le biais de législations nationales.* [...] *La devise à cet égard doit s'énoncer comme suit: «Du droit international privé national au droit international privé unifié (et pas seulement harmonisé)».*'

4.4.2 *Cross-Border Implications*

Measures to be taken under Article 81 TFEU are limited to those having 'cross-border implications'.

There is an important analogy between private international law and European law in this respect. Both fields of law require '*éléments d'extranéité*' to come into play: both European law and private international law are by their nature destined to regulate situations which are connected to more than one national legal order.[172]

The requirement at hand entails that Article 81 TFEU cannot serve as legal basis for measures regulating purely internal situations. Accordingly, the European Union has no competence to enact legislation on substantive (family) law matters.[173] European interference in the field of family law can therefore only concern its private international law aspects.

In relation to the objective described in Article 81(2)(c) TFEU, i.e. the compatibility of the rules applicable in the Member States concerning the conflict of laws, the requirement that the measure to be taken must concern civil matters having cross-border implications probably has no independent value. Measures unifying the choice of law have by their very nature a cross-border character.[174]

4.4.3 *'Particularly when Necessary for the Proper Functioning of the Internal Market'*

Although the internal market requirement is no longer an investitive requirement — which it was under Article 65 EC-Treaty — it does still play a role. Yet the reference to the internal market is now merely an illustration of the type of measures that the Union may take.[175]

Already under the EC-Treaty the majority of doctrine appeared to support the treatment of the internal market requirement of Article 65 EC as having little or no significance:

> Die Erforderlichkeit [...] kollisionsrechtlicher Regelungen für das reibungslose Funktionieren des Binnenmarktes dürfte sich daher in der Regel leicht begründen lassen: Sobald die privaten Angelegenheiten einer Person über eine nationale Grenze hinwegreichen,

[172] See also Israël 2001, p. 235 ff; Jessurun d'Oliveira 2002, pp. 268–269; Borrás 2005, p. 347 ff; Pataut 2005, p. 670; Pontier 2005, p. 15.

[173] See Pintens 2003; Martiny 2006, p. 123; Basedow 2009, p. 457.

[174] See also Labayle 1997, p. 856; Remien 2001, p. 74; Traest 2003, p. 85; Dohrn 2004, p. 62; Rossi 2004, p. 65.

[175] Cf., Fiorini 2008c, p. 976.

> unterliegen sie potentiell verschiedenen Privatrechtsordnungen und es können daher binnenmarktschädliche Reibungen auftreten.[176]

The Treaty on the Functioning of the European Union has formalised this point of view in Article 81 TFEU. However, given the broad interpretation that had already been given to Article 65 EC-Treaty in this respect, it is questionable whether the amendment will 'add much impetus to any further expansion in practice'.[177]

The dilution of the internal market requirement equally involves that the question whether or not the European Union's competence with regard to judicial cooperation in civil matters extends to the regulation of extra-European cases does no longer arise.[178] The Union's competence pursuant to Article 81 TFEU does not depend on the necessity of the measure for the proper functioning of the internal market and does consequently not restrict this competence to intra-European cases. Article 81 TFEU thus grants the EU the competence to enact universal choice of law rules, i.e. choice of law rules that can designate the law of a Member State or the law of a third country.

The competence of the Union to regulate extra-European cases pursuant to Article 81 TFEU raises the question to what extent the European Union is competent to conclude international conventions with third countries in the field of private international law.

Until the Treaty of Lisbon, the question of the external competence of the EU in the field of private international law was governed by the ERTA-doctrine.[179] Pursuant to this doctrine the existence of internal Union competence also has consequences for the external competence: if and to the extent that internal EU law for a certain subject-matter exists, the EU also acquires external competence for international instruments covering the same scope, which might affect these internal rules. A case-by-case assessment was necessary to find out whether the EU was competent to conclude an international instrument and if so, whether that competence was exclusive.

---

176 Wiedmann 2007, p. 877, Note 10. See equally Kohler 1999, p. 16, footnote 26; Basedow 2000, p. 703 (treating Article 65(b) as an '*implicit recognition* [...] *that the compatibility of conflict rules is necessary for the proper functioning of the internal market*'); Leible and Staudinger 2000, p. 228 ff; Hellner 2002, p. 21 ff; Schmahl 2003, p. 1868, Note 4 ('*Das reibungslose Funktionieren des Binnenmarktes ist immer dann betroffen, wenn Beziehungen bezüglich Personen oder Sachen bestehen, welche sich in den anderen Mitgliedstaaten aufhalten oder befinden.*'); Mansel 2006, p. 658 ('*Das Merkmal des reibungslosen Funktionierens des Binnenmarkts ist im Sinne des Art. 65 EG ist weit zu verstehen.*'); Herzog (looseleaf), para 65.02. Contra *inter alia* Gaudemet-Tallon 2001, p. 328; Lequette 2008, p. 509 ff.

177 Fiorini 2008c, pp. 976–977.

178 Cf., *supra* Sect. 4.2.2.2.

179 See *supra* note 46 of the current chapter.

The Treaty on the Functioning of the European Union partly codified the ERTA-doctrine and the subsequent ECJ opinions on external competence. Article 216 TFEU stipulates that the Union is competent to conclude international agreements in three situations:

1. if the Treaties so provide;
2. if the conclusion of an agreement is necessary in order to achieve an objective (either referred to in the Treaties or provided for in a legally binding Union act); or,
3. if the conclusion of an agreement is likely to affect common rules or alter their scope.

Article 216 TFEU does not determine whether the external competence is exclusive or shared.[180] The provision is, however, to be read in conjunction with Article 3(2) TFEU, which determines that the Union has exclusive competence

> for the conclusion of international agreements when its conclusion is provided for in a legislative act of the Union or is necessary to enable the Union to exercise its internal competence, or in so far as its conclusion may affect common rules or alter their scope.

Although these provisions still involve quite some uncertainty,[181] they do provide for a legal basis, clarifying that the Union is exclusively competent to conclude international agreements in many areas of private international law.

4.4.4 The Principles of Subsidiarity and Proportionality

The use of Union competences is in general governed by the principles of subsidiarity and proportionality (Article 5(1) EU-Treaty). The application of these principles has been specified in the Protocol on the principles of subsidiarity and proportionality annexed to the EU-Treaty and the Treaty on the Functioning of the European Union.[182] This Protocol determines in Article 5 that any draft legislative act should contain a detailed statement making it possible to appraise compliance with the principles of subsidiarity and proportionality.

The European Court of Justice has confirmed that the limitations of subsidiarity and proportionality, particularly the former, are primarily political, and that the

---

[180] Cf., Fiorini 2008c, p. 982; Mansel et al. 2010, p. 26.

[181] See on the complex difficulties that may arise in the combined effect of Articles 3(2) and 216 TFEU Fiorini 2008c, pp. 982–983.

[182] Protocol No. 2 on the application of the principles of subsidiarity and proportionality [2008] OJ C115/206.

European legislature has a broad discretion in these matters. A measure will only be reviewed on these grounds if it is manifestly inappropriate.[183]

Some have argued that the European unification of the private international law rules of the Member States respects, by its very nature, the principles of subsidiarity and proportionality, as it does not require any changes of national substantive law.[184] However, it is to be doubted whether this position holds true, as the following will show that the principles of subsidiarity and proportionality are to be taken into account in establishing common European choice of law rules.[185]

4.4.4.1 The Principle of Subsidiarity

Since the European Union has no exclusive competence in the field of judicial cooperation in civil matters (pursuant to Article 4(2)(j) TFEU), it must respect the principle of subsidiarity pursuant to Article 5 EU-Treaty.[186]

Two requirements are connected to this principle. In the first place, the Union can only act within the limits of the powers conferred to it (principle of conferral). Secondly, by virtue of the principle of subsidiarity the Union can regulate only those matters where the proposed action cannot satisfactorily be achieved by the Member States on the national level and can be more effectively accomplished at Union level.

The principle of subsidiarity imposes to the institutions, particularly to the Commission, to state for any proposed measure the reasons on which it is based; the reasons for concluding that a Union objective can be better achieved by the European Union must be substantiated by qualitative or, wherever possible, quantitative indicators.[187]

The Protocol on the principles of subsidiarity and proportionality underlines the importance of the compliance with the principle of subsidiarity, as it assigns a right of complaint to each national Parliament (Article 6 *et seq* of the Protocol). Any national Parliament or any chamber of a national Parliament may, within a specific time limit, send a reasoned opinion stating why it considers that the draft in question does not comply with the principle of subsidiarity.

---

183 The ECJ has not often annulled European legislation on grounds of violation of the principles of subsidiarity and proportionality. See e.g. ECJ Case C-491/01 *R* v. *Secretary of State for Health, ex parte British American Tobacco (Investment) Ltd.* [2002] ECR I-11453; ECJ Case C-154/04 *R (Alliance for Natural Health)* v. *Secretary of State for Health* [2005] ECR I-6451.

184 E.g. De Groot and Kuipers 2008, p. 110.

185 Cf., Hellner 2002, p. 19.

186 Article 5(3) EU-Treaty: 'Under the principle of subsidiarity, in areas which do not fall within its exclusive competence, the Union shall act only if and in so far as the objectives of the proposed action cannot be sufficiently achieved by the Member States, either at central level or at regional and local level, but can rather, by reason of the scale or effects of the proposed action, be better achieved at Union level.'

187 See Article 5 of the Protocol on Subsidiarity and Proportionality.

4.4.4.2 The *Anerkennung statt IPR*-Approach

In European context several regulations have established unified rules on jurisdiction and on recognition and enforcement, *inter alia* the Brussels I-, Brussels II*bis*- and Maintenance-Regulations. Consequently, several authors posed the question as to what room these regulations leave for unified choice of law rules.[188] This movement is indicated as the *Anerkennung statt IPR*-approach, implying that European private international law is based on recognition rules and the choice of law is no longer of importance within the EU. The question concerning the applicable law can namely be said to be of secondary importance, as long as the judicial decision or judgment is recognised in the other Member States. The *Anerkennung statt IPR*-approach is said to bring about a change of basic principles of private international law (*Prinzipienwechsel* or *Systemwechsel*): the traditional system of the referral of a certain case to a legal system by means of the choice of law is replaced by a system in which the personal or family situation is recognised as such.[189]

As seen above, the emphasis on the establishment of common rules on the recognition of judicial decisions stems from the principle of mutual recognition. The European Council of Tampere namely endorsed the principle of mutual recognition to become 'the cornerstone of judicial cooperation in both civil and criminal matters'.[190]

However, as has already been noticed in literature, the *Anerkennung statt IPR*-approach seems to neglect some important aspects of private international law:

> Die Koordinierung der Privatrechtsordnungen der Mitgleidstaaten allein mit den Mitteln des Verfahrensrechts und einer unkritischen Übertragung des gemeinschaftsrechtlichen Prinzips der gegenseitigen Anerkennung ist jedoch ein *Irrweg*. Er verdrängt das internationale Privatrecht und ignoriert damit die Wechselbezüglichkeit zwischen dieser Materie und dem internationalen Verfahrensrecht.[191]

In particular three important private international law aspects are neglected.

In the first place, unified rules on jurisdiction and recognition and enforcement cannot be seen independently from unified choice of law rules, since unified choice of law rules most certainly contribute to the functioning of the former rules.[192] Common choice of law rules would give a more stable basis to the duty of mutual recognition of judgments. The unification of the choice of law rules would even

---

[188] See *inter alia* Jayme and Kohler 2001, pp. 501–514; Gaudemet-Tallon 2002, p. 185; Coester-Waltjen 2004, pp. 121–129; Henrich 2005, pp. 422–423; Vigand 2005, p. 95 ff; Coester-Waltjen 2006, pp. 392–400; Gaertner 2006, p. 101 ff; and Mansel 2006, pp. 651–731.

[189] See Kohler 2002, pp. 147–163; Baratta 2007, pp. 4–11.

[190] Tampere Presidency Conclusion, para 33. See further on the principle of mutual recognition and *supra* Sect. 4.3.2.3.

[191] Kohler 2003, p. 412 [emphasis added]. See equally Gaertner 2006, p. 102 ff.

[192] See *inter alia* Von Savigny 1849, p. 77; Kohler 2003, p. 406 ff; Lagarde 2004, p. 227 ff; Wagner 2004, p. 128; Weber 2004, p. 3; Meeusen 2007c, p. 272.

facilitate the mutual recognition of judgments.[193] Currently the significant differences between the choice of law rules of the EU-Member States and their even more diverging substantive law rules imply that the results of proceedings depend heavily on which court that has decided the case. The fact that courts of the Member States would apply the same choice of law rules to determine the law applicable to a given situation reinforces the mutual trust in judicial decisions given in other Member States.[194]

Moreover, as Gaertner has pointed out, the choice of law contributes to the realisation of justice.[195] In this regard reference is made to so-called 'conflicts justice'[196]: the choice of law rules does not only determine the law applicable, but they also refer the case to the 'right' legal order.[197] Consequently, the aim is to secure justice already at the level of the choice of law, so that not only the recognition of the respective judgment or decision is decisive, but also the application of the 'appropriate' law itself.

Thirdly, the choice of law fulfils a significant function in terms of legal certainty: for the parties involved in a cross-border family dispute the predictability of the applicable law is very important. Although the knowledge that a judicial decision is to be recognised throughout the EU grants the parties the certainty that their situation will not lead to a limping relationship, it does not provide them with any certainty as regards the law to be applied to their situation.[198]

4.4.4.3 The Principle of Proportionality

In addition to the principle of subsidiarity the Union has to respect the principle of proportionality, implying that the content and the form of the Union action is only justified if it does not exceed what is necessary to achieve the objectives of the Treaties (Article 5(4) EU-Treaty).

The principle of proportionality relates to the legal nature of the means used to achieve the objective, i.e. the type of instrument used.[199] Article 81(1) TFEU

---

193 Cf., the Mutual Recognition Programme, p. 6.

194 See also Explanatory Memorandum to the Brussels II*ter*-Proposal, p. 1.

195 Gaertner 2006, pp. 102–103. See equally Jayme and Kohler 2001, p. 502; Lagarde 2004, p. 232 ff.

196 See on conflicts justice further *infra* Sect. 8.4.3.

197 Cf., the theory of Von Savigny 1849, para 348, p. 27. See further *supra* Sect. 4.3.1.

198 Moreover, in a considerable number of areas of family law there is no instrument yet providing for the automatic recognition of judicial decisions from the EU-Member States.

199 See Kapteyn and VerLoren van Themaat 1998, p. 145. The Protocol on the principles of subsidiarity and proportionality which was annexed to the EC-Treaty contained the following on the principle of proportionality: 'The form of Community action shall be as simple as possible, consistent with satisfactory achievement of the objective of the measure and the need for effective enforcement. The Community shall legislate only to the extent necessary. Other things being equal, directives should be preferred to regulations and framework directives to detailed measures.' However, the current Protocol does not contain any such provision.

refers to the general concept of 'measures'. This term must be considered as including all the legal instruments as provided for by Article 288 TFEU.[200] Article 288 determines:

> To exercise the Union's competences, the institutions shall adopt regulations, directives, decisions, recommendations and opinions.
>
> A regulation shall have general application. It shall be binding in its entirety and directly applicable in all Member States.
>
> A directive shall be binding, as to the result to be achieved, upon each Member State to which it is addressed, but shall leave to the national authorities the choice of form and methods. [...]

This provision leaves the legislative institutions a wide margin of discretion to choose the legal instrument best suited to regulate a certain subject-matter.[201] In the area of private international law, practice has shown that there is a clear preference for the regulation.[202]

The choice of regulations over directives and treaties[203] offers clear advantages.[204] The primary advantage of regulations is that they are directly applicable and have primacy over national law. In contrast to directives, regulations do not need to be transposed into national law. As a result of the need to transpose directives into national law, directives do not ensure uniform law, since the Member States are free as to the means and wording of transposition.[205] Since the Europeanisation of private international law precisely aims at uniformity, the directive is a less appropriate measure, as 'obstacles' such as lack of legal certainty and forum shopping, which underlie the need for unification, will not be removed.

In addition, a major advantage of regulations is that they, once concluded, take direct effect within the Member States. There will be no delays. As a consequence, the assumption is that regulations will necessarily lead to more legal consistency within the internal market.[206] In matters private international law legal consistency is vital, for it ensures legal certainty.

---

[200] Cf., with regard to Article 65 EC-Treaty, Basedow 2000, p. 706; Leible and Staudinger 2000, p. 233; Van Houtte 2001, p. 4; Traest 2003, p. 93 ff; Boele-Woelki and Van Ooik 2004, p. 370; Calvo Caravaca 2006, p. 26; Freudenthal 2007, p. 40.

[201] Cf., with regard to Article 65 EC-Treaty: Boele-Woelki and Van Ooik 2004, p. 370.

[202] Since the EC-Treaty has entered into force, only regulations have been proposed and adopted in the field of private international law.

[203] A treaty can, however, not be concluded on the basis of Article 81 TFEU in conjunction with Article 288 TFEU.

[204] See for an enumeration of these advantages Kreuzer 1991, pp. 241–242.

[205] This disadvantage of directives is clearly illustrated by the abundant amount of case law of the ECJ in case of non-transposition, incomplete or tardy transposition of directives. See for an overview: Borchardt (looseleaf).

[206] Cf., Boele-Woelki and Van Ooik 2004, p. 370.

Other advantages of the regulation that are raised are: the possibility of interpretations by the European Court of Justice, the impossibility to make reservations,[207] and the impossibility of unilateral resignation.

The Commission's Proposal for a Maintenance Regulation contains a clear statement as to justify the choice of instrument, including all abovementioned advantages:

> The proposal contains indeed uniform rules on applicable law, which are detailed, precise and unconditional and require no implementation in national law. If Member States had, on the contrary, margin of appreciation for the implementation of these rules, one would reintroduce the legal uncertainty that this proposal specifically intended to eliminate. [...] In a more general way, transparency is a vital objective in this context; the rules applicable in the Community should be easily and uniformly understood without the need to seek the provisions of national law that transpose the content of the Community instrument, bearing in mind that national law will very often be foreign to the plaintiff. Opting for a Regulation enables the Court of Justice to ensure that it is applied uniformly throughout the Member States.[208]

Finally, a clear advantage of a regulation is its effect towards newly acceding Member States: regulations form part of the *acquis communautaire*, i.e. the body of common rights and obligations which bind all the Member States together within the European Union. Applicant countries are obliged to accept the European Union's *acquis* before they can join the Union.[209]

In view of all these advantages of a regulation, it can be stated that a regulation is in the interest of legal certainty and predictability.[210]

Although the regulation is considered to be the most 'invasive' legal instrument, most authors agree that it is the instrument *par excellence* to create uniform European rules.[211] Consequently, the unification of the choice of law rules in family matters in the form of a regulation complies with the principle of proportionality.

---

[207] See Kapteyn and VerLoren van Themaat 1998, p. 324: '*The general application of a regulation concerns the impersonal, non-individualized character of the situation to which it applies as well as legal effects it entails for the legal subjects to whom it is addressed.*'

[208] Proposal for a Maintenance Regulation, COM(2005) 649 final, p. 9.

[209] See Leible and Staudinger 2000, pp. 233–234.

[210] See also Lazic 2008, p. 77.

[211] See *inter alia* De Vareilles-Sommières 1998, p. 146; Basedow 2000, p. 20; Compte rendu des séances de travail du Groupe européen de droit international privé, Dixième réunion à Rome de 15–17 septembre 2000, p. 5, available at: www.gedip-egpil.eu; Kreuzer 2001, p. 129 ff ('*Conventions et règlements unifient le droit international privé, les directives l'harmonisent.*'); Leible and Staudinger 2000, p. 233; Gaudemet-Tallon 2002, p. 166; Boele-Woelki and Van Ooik 2004, p. 370; Calvo Caravaca 2006, pp. 26–27; Fallon 2006, p. 509; Pocar 2008, p. 7. However, contra Fallon and Francq 2004, pp. 271–272.

4.4.5 Legislative Procedure: Article 81(3) TFEU

The legislative procedure to be followed in order to adopt EU measures on private international law is provided for by Article 81(2) and (3) TFEU:

> 2. [...] the European Parliament and the Council, acting in accordance with the ordinary legislative procedure [...]
> 3. Notwithstanding paragraph 2, measures concerning family law with cross-border implications shall be established by the Council, acting in accordance with a special legislative procedure. The Council shall act unanimously after consulting the European Parliament.
>
> The Council, on a proposal from the Commission, may adopt a decision determining those aspects of family law with cross-border implications which may be the subject of acts adopted by the ordinary legislative procedure. The Council shall act unanimously after consulting the European Parliament.
>
> This proposal shall be notified to the national Parliaments. If a national Parliament makes known its opposition within six months of the date of such notification, the decision shall not be adopted. In the absence of opposition, the Council may adopt the decision.

According to the general rule provided for in Article 81(2) TFEU, the Council enacts measures 'in accordance with the ordinary procedure', i.e. by following the co-decision procedure for measures relating to judicial cooperation in civil matters (Article 289 in conjunction with Article 294 TFEU).

However, Article 81(3) TFEU excludes family law from this legislative procedure and the Council can only act by unanimity in matters of family law. As a result, the exercise of the legislative competence of the EU in the field of international family law is restricted by a 'right of veto' conferred to each Member State.[212] The reason of this strict legislative procedure for matters of international family law is because family law is a highly sensitive issue of law, particularly since it touches upon the very socio-political, cultural and religious heart of a nation. Family law is an area in which the Member States wish to retain a certain amount of control, not only as regards the substantive (national) law but also as regards the private international law rules. In each legal system the latter rules are usually well-coordinated with the substantive family law rules.[213] To date the EU-Member States did not prove to be willing to 'give up' their national sovereignty in this field of law. Therefore, the ultimate EU decision-making power in the field of

---

[212] Possibly with the exception of the United Kingdom, Ireland and Denmark, which hold a special position in the cooperation in civil and commercial matters. See further *infra* Sect. 4.6.

[213] See also Baratta 2007, pp. 4–11.

international family law rests with the national governments of the Member States, which are all represented in the European Council.

The Treaty on the Functioning of the European Union does introduce a special passerelle clause in Article 81(3). The Council may, on a proposal from the Commission, decide by unanimity and after consulting the European Parliament that certain aspects of family law may be the subject of acts adopted by the ordinary legislative procedure. The EC-Treaty already provided for such a clause in Article 67(2),[214] but the passerelle clause of Article 81(3) TFEU also requires that national parliaments be notified of the Commission proposal. The Treaty on the Functioning of the European Union thus gives the national parliaments, in accordance with the objective to strengthen the 'democratic legitimacy of the Union', the power to veto this passerelle. It thereby introduces a better safeguard for the Member States' interests in this sensitive field.[215] The question is, accordingly, whether the passerelle of Article 81(3) is ever likely to see the light of day given the highly charged and political, moral, cultural and religious sensitivities surrounding questions of family law.

4.5 The Role of the European Court of Justice

Prior to the Treaty of Lisbon, the European Court of Justice enjoyed only a limited jurisdiction in matters of private international law under Article 68(1) EC-Treaty. Solely the courts against whose decisions there was no judicial remedy under national law had the ability to request the European Court of Justice for a preliminary ruling.[216] This procedure deviated from the general procedure of Article 234 EC-Treaty allowing every national court to request the ECJ for a preliminary ruling.

---

[214] In 2005 the Commission attempted to apply the passerelle clause of Article 67(2) EC-Treaty with regard to maintenance obligations. See Communication from the Commission to the Council calling on the Council to provide for measures relating to maintenance obligations taken under Article 65 of the Treaty establishing the European Community to be governed by the procedure laid down in Article 251 of the Treaty, COM(2005) 648 final. However, a great majority of the Member States was reluctant to accept this 'transition' from unanimity to the co-decision procedure. Consequently, the consultation procedure was applied to the adoption of the Maintenance Regulation. See Borrás 2007, pp. 56–57.

[215] See Fiorini 2008c, p. 976.

[216] Cf., order of the ECJ in Case C-278/09 *Olivier Martinez and Robert Martinez* v. *MGN Ltd.* [2009] ECR I-11099.

The system of Article 68(1) EC-Treaty was not very likely to contribute to the uniform interpretation and application of EU private international law.[217] Although Article 67(2) second indent EC-Treaty did require the Council, after May 2004, to take a decision with a view to adapting the jurisdiction of the Court, the Council has not taken any initiative on this basis. As a result the Commission proposed to adapt the jurisdiction of the ECJ in the fields covered by Title IV of the EC-Treaty in such a way that the ECJ's jurisdiction would align on the general scheme of the Treaty. Such alignment would fulfil several objectives:

> In particular, alignment of the rules concerning the jurisdiction of the Court in Title IV on the ordinary law will:
> - ensure the uniform application and interpretation of Community law in this area as in all others;
> - make it possible to strengthen judicial protection, in fields that are particularly sensitive in terms of fundamental rights;
> - remedy a paradoxical retrograde step in judicial protection as a result of the Amsterdam Treaty in civil matters covered by Article 65 of the EC Treaty; and
> - enable the Community judicial system to perform normally without any fear of operating problems in this area.[218]

The Treaty on the Functioning of the European Union provides for this desired alignment: the whole area of freedom, security and justice falls within the scope of application of the ECJ pursuant to Article 267 TFEU.[219] The limitation of the ECJ's jurisdiction is thus abolished. Preliminary references may, consequently, be requested by every national court, even one of first instance, if a ruling is necessary to enable the judgment to be given, with courts of final appeal being obliged to bring the matter before the ECJ.

This is a significant change that will definitely improve the consistency of the application and interpretation of European private international law rules without

---

[217] The European Court of Justice itself held the same view, warning that limiting 'access to the Court would have the effect of jeopardising the uniform application and interpretation of Community law throughout the Union, and could deprive individuals of effective judicial protection and undermine the unity of the case-law. […] The preliminary ruling system is the veritable cornerstone of the operation of the internal market, since it plays a fundamental role in ensuring that the law established by the Treaties retains its Community character with a view to guaranteeing that that law has the same effect in all circumstances in all the Member States of the European Union. […] One of the Court's essential tasks is to ensure just such a uniform interpretation, and it discharges that duty by answering the questions put to it by the national courts and tribunals.' See Report of the Court of Justice on certain aspects of the application of the Treaty on European Union (Luxembourg, May 1995), pp. 5–6. This Report is available at: http://www.ena.lu/report_court_justice_european_communities_luxembourg_1995-020004416.html. See also the Hague Programme, p. 27.

[218] See Communication from the Commission on the Adaptation of the provisions of Title IV of the Treaty establishing the European Community relating to the jurisdiction of the Court of Justice with a view to ensuring more effective judicial protection, COM(2006) 346 final, pp. 3–9.

[219] See Kapteyn 2008, pp. 47–48.

forcing litigants to 'exhaust' domestic remedies.[220] This consistency is promoted even further by the new rules of procedure of the European Court of Justice, which provide for an urgent procedure for preliminary references relating to the area of freedom, security and justice (Article 23a of Protocol No. 3 on the Statute of the ECJ).[221]

4.6 Territorial Limits to European Private International Law: *'Europe à Deux Vitesses'*

The Treaty of Amsterdam has led to what is called a '*Europe à deux vitesses*': a 'two-speed' cooperation has emerged since three EU-Member States — Denmark, Ireland and the United Kingdom — did in principle not take part in the adoption of measures under Title IV of the EC-Treaty and were consequently not bound by them.

Article 69 EC-Treaty granted a special status to the United Kingdom, Ireland and Denmark in the field of judicial cooperation in civil matters:

> The application of this Title [Title IV of the third part of the EC-Treaty; NAB] shall be subject to the provisions of the Protocol of the position of the United Kingdom and Ireland and to the Protocol on the position of Denmark [...].

As a result, Articles 61 *et seq* EC-Treaty did not apply to these three Member States, since they were afraid they would lose control over immigration and asylum after a transfer of legislative power to the European Community. Although the same fear was not expressed with regard to the judicial cooperation in civil matters, the two protocols excluded the participation of the three Member States in measures pursuant to Title IV of the EC-Treaty in general.[222]

Although the Treaty of Lisbon has brought some changes to this situation, in essence the positions of the three mentioned Member States have not altered. There are still two protocols that exclude the participation of the United Kingdom and Ireland on the one hand and Denmark on the other in the adoption of measures pursuant to Title V of the third Part of the Treaty on the Functioning of the European Union. However, both protocols contain escape clauses which may enable the three countries to be included in future legislation in the field of private international law. On a case-by-case basis, the three Member States mentioned can decide whether or not they want to take part in a certain action of the Community under Title IV of the EC-Treaty. This system has been referred to as participation '*à la carte*'.[223]

---

[220] See equally Fiorini 2008c, p. 978; De Groot and Kuipers 2008, p. 114.

[221] Article 23a has not been inserted in the Protocol on the Statute of the European Court of Justice by the Treaty of Lisbon, but it results from Decision 2008/79/EC, [2008] OJ L24/42.

[222] See Basedow 2000, p. 695; Drappatz 2002, pp. 144–145.

[223] Pocar 2008, p. 6. See also Basedow 2009, p. 459.

The two mentioned protocols have a different mechanism of participation, which will be discussed in Sections 4.6.1 and 4.6.2, respectively.

4.6.1 United Kingdom and Ireland

The Protocol on the Position of the United Kingdom and Ireland, annexed to the EU-Treaty and the Treaty on the Functioning of the European Union, provides that these Member States in principle do not take part in the adoption by the Council of proposed measures pursuant to Title V of Part Three of the Treaty on the Functioning of the European Union.[224] Both the United Kingdom and Ireland may, however, notify the Council that they wish to take part in the adoption and application of any proposed measure under this Title, by means of the so-called 'opt-in' mechanism (Article 3 of the Protocol). Even if the United Kingdom and Ireland have not decided to participate in the adoption of a measure, they may notify the Council that they wish to accept the measure after the adoption (Article 4 of the Protocol).

During the meeting of the Justice and Home Affairs Council of 12 March 1999, both the United Kingdom and Ireland declared their firm intention to fully participate in judicial cooperation in civil matters.[225]

In the legislative procedure on the adoption of the Brussels II*ter*-Proposal — initiated under the regime of the EC-Treaty — the question arose whether the opt-in mechanism still applied to a measure amending an instrument to which the United Kingdom and Ireland had previously opted in. The Brussels II*ter*-Proposal namely foresaw an amendment of an existing instrument. According to Fiorini it cannot reasonably be argued that the acceptance of one instrument should oblige the country opting in to accept all future amendments to that instrument that would be introduced by another, separate, instrument.[226] The whole protocol could otherwise be very easily circumvented, which would contradict its ratio.[227]

The new Protocol provides for clarity in this respect: the Protocol on the position of the United Kingdom and Ireland determines that the provisions of the Protocol do equally apply to measures amending an existing measure by which the United Kingdom and Ireland are bound (Article 4a of the Protocol). Consequently, the United Kingdom and Ireland keep the right to decide not to opt-in to such an

---

[224] Protocol No. 21 on the position of the United Kingdom and Ireland in respect of the Area of freedom, security and justice, [2008] OJ C115/295.

[225] See Press Release No. 6545/99 (Presse 70) of the 2166th Council Meeting of Justice and Home Affairs held in Brussels 12 March 1999, p. 12.

[226] Fiorini 2008b, p. 187.

[227] Moreover, it would not be too hard to settle the choice of law issues on divorce by means of a separate instrument, as is the case with the common choice of law rules on contractual obligations (Rome I) and non-contractual obligations (Rome II).

amending measure. The Council 'may urge them to make a notification' that they wish to take part in the adoption and application of the proposed measure.[228]

4.6.2 Denmark

The Protocol on the position of Denmark has been shaped somewhat differently from the one on the position of the UK and Ireland. Under the EC-Treaty Denmark has effectively stated in a protocol that it will not be bound by any Union measure, *inter alia* in the field of judicial cooperation in civil matters.[229] Unlike the United Kingdom and Ireland, Denmark cannot (partially) opt-in. The concluded Community measures in the field of private international law could only be extended to Denmark by means of individual conventions pursuant to Article 293 EC-Treaty.[230] Consequently, Denmark truly stayed behind in the process of Europeanisation of private international law.

The Protocol on the position of Denmark as annexed to the EU-Treaty and the Treaty on the Functioning of the European Union maintains the status quo, but a separate annex is added to the protocol, which essentially reproduces the terms of the Protocol on the position of the United Kingdom and Ireland.[231] The Treaty of Lisbon has opened the possibility that Denmark's opt-out regarding the judicial cooperation in civil matters in the EU can be changed, subject to approval by referendum.[232] Whereas the annex will not be applicable until and unless Denmark decides to substitute it for a part in the original Protocol, it is the State's declared intention to avail itself of the option to participate in the adoption of Title V of Part

---

[228] Article 4a(2) of Protocol No. 21 on the position of the United Kingdom and Ireland in respect of the Area of Freedom, Security and Justice, annexed to the EU-Treaty and the Treaty on the Functioning of the European Union.

[229] See 5th Protocol to the EC-Treaty on the position of Denmark, [1997] OJ C340/101.

[230] Very critical on the position of Denmark: Barents 1997, p. 332 ff, spec. p. 343: '*In view of this situation one may ask if Denmark does not already have one leg outside the Union.*' Equally Hailbronner and Thierry 1998, p. 601 ff; Basedow 2000, p. 696; and Leible and Staudinger 2000, p. 226.

[231] Protocol No. 22 on the position of Denmark, annexed to the EU-Treaty and the Treaty on the Functioning of the European Union, [2008] OJ C115/299.

[232] See Article 8 of the Protocol on the position of Denmark referring to the constitutional require-ments. Fiorini 2008c, p. 981 has pointed out that the Danish 'blanket opt-out' may soon come to an end: the Danish Minister of Foreign Affairs announced that a referendum on whether to keep the opt-outs should be organised before the next Danish parliamentary election, i.e. before 2011 (see: http://politiken.dk/newsinenglish/article710274.ece). The Danish Prime Minister has confirmed this intention. This referendum could lead not only to the substitution of the annex to Part I of the protocol, but also to the complete abolition of the current status in freedom, security and justice matters, as Article 7 of the protocol provides. A poll of October 2009 shows that a majority favour such complete abolition (see: http://img.borsen.dk/img/cms/cmsmedia/857_content_2_3900.pdf).

Three of the Treaty on the Functioning of the European Union.[233] If approved, Denmark will be able to cooperate in justice and home affairs on a case-by-case basis. Consequently, in the future the position of Denmark as 'stay-behind' in the area of European private international law may (soon) come to an end.

4.7 Synthesis: Is the European Union Competent to Enact a Common Choice of Law on Divorce?

The analysis of the competence of the European Union with regard to the choice of law rules on divorce has been considered as superfluous, since the competence to enact unified rules on private international law in the field of divorce had already been given by the existence of the Brussels II-Regulation: the choice of law rules on divorce are merely inserted in the latter regulation.[234] However, as some Member States — *inter alia* Sweden, the United Kingdom and the Netherlands — hold the view that the European Union is not competent to enact common choice of law rules on divorce, the assessment of the Union's competence in this field is of importance.

The European Commission has published the Brussels II*ter*-Proposal in July 2006, which means that the Union's competence is to be based on Article 65 EC-Treaty.

The development of a unified choice of law on divorce will be set forth below (Section 4.7.1). Subsequently, the European Union's competence to unify the choice of law on divorce will firstly be discussed on the basis of Article 65 EC-Treaty (Section 4.7.2) and then on the basis of Article 81 TFEU (Section 4.7.3).

4.7.1 The Development of a Unified Choice of Law on Divorce

Free movement of persons does not only provide opportunities for employment, but it also facilitates personal relationships with cross-border dimensions. The existence of 'international' marriages is thus an indirect consequence of the fundamental right of free movement. The increase in 'international' marriages within the European Union has led, in consequence, to a rise in the number of 'international' divorces.[235] According to EU figures, about 170,000 international divorce proceedings take place each year in the European Union, representing

233 See the Recital of the Protocol No. 22.

234 Cf., Kohler 2008, p. 1674.

235 See for the definition of an 'international' divorce, *supra* Sect. 2.1.

approximately 16% of all divorces.[236] This high number of individuals affected by divorce in international context explains the interest of the European Union to unify the choice of law in this field.[237]

Against this background the adoption of the Brussels II-Regulation was already considered a necessary measure in the sense of Article 65 EC-Treaty, since differences in the national rules on jurisdiction and enforcement hampered the free movement of persons and the sound operation of the internal market.[238] This Regulation provides for rules on jurisdiction and recognition and enforcement in matrimonial matters and in matters of parental responsibility, but does not contain any choice of law rules.

In the EU, an international couple wishing to get divorced is subject to the competence rules laid down in the Brussels II*bis*-Regulation, which provides a multitude of alternative grounds for jurisdiction (Article 3). Once a divorce proceeding is brought before the court of a Member State, the applicable law is determined pursuant to the national choice of law rules of that Member State. Yet, the choice of law rules on divorce differ greatly from one Member State to another: a scale of possibilities arises, varying from a systematic application of the *lex fori* to the determination of the applicable law on the basis of a scale of connecting factors, which are to be interpreted flexibly or inflexibly, referring to the national law or the law of the habitual residence of either or both spouses.[239] The choice of law rules on divorce are often strongly connected to the substantive law approach, which differs between more liberal States (such as Sweden and the Netherlands) and more conservative States (such as Ireland).[240] This means that the consequences for the parties concerned can vary depending on which law is applicable to their divorce; it may thus be of great relevance to the spouses in which country the divorce proceedings are initiated.

---

[236] Impact Assessment on Divorce, p. 11 ff, spec. at p. 13. These figures are, however, challenged by the British House of Lords, which expressed serious doubts as to the reliability of these statistical surveys. See House of Lords Rome III Report, pp. 8–9. Moreover, in the course of time the Commission seemed to be juggling with these figures: whereas in the impact assessment the estimated 170,000 international divorces represent about 16% of the total number of divorces (see Impact Assessment on Divorce, p. 13), later on the same 170,000 divorces suddenly represent 19% of all divorces (see the letter of the Vice-President of the European Commission of 7 December 2006, *Kamerstukken I/II*, 2006–2007, 30 671, F and No. 6). See further *infra* Sect. 6.3.1.

[237] The European Commission makes moreover an appeal to a 2006 survey that revealed that 60% of the EU population expected the European Union to facilitate cross-border divorce legislation. This Flash Eurobarometer No. 188 on Family Law was performed by the Gallup Organization and can be found at: http://ec.europa.eu/public_opinion/flash/fl188b_en.pdf.

[238] Cf., recital No. 4 of the Preamble to the Brussels II-Regulation.

[239] See further *infra* Sect. 5.2.2.

[240] It is to be noted that Malta is even more conservative than Ireland, as it does not provide for divorce in its substantive law at all. Maltese law does, however, not provide for any choice of law rules on this issue either. See for an overview of the differences in both the substantive and choice of law approaches in divorce of the Member States further *infra* Sect. 5.2.

Already before the entry into force of the EC-Treaty, the Council adopted the Vienna Action Plan, which assigned the Commission to

> examine the possibilities to draw up a legal instrument on the law applicable to divorce (Rome III): After the first step on divorce matters taken with Brussels II in the field of jurisdiction and the recognition and enforcement of judgments, the possibilities to agree on rules determining the law applicable in order to prevent forum shopping need to be explored on the basis of an in depth study.[241]

Accordingly, the Member States were asked to reply to a questionnaire on the law applicable to divorce.[242] Moreover, the Commission charged the Asser Instituut (The Hague) with a preparatory study on the choice of law on divorce.[243]

The Hague Programme, successor of the 'expired' Vienna Action Plan, invited the Commission to submit a Green Paper on 'the conflict-of-law rules in matters relating to divorce (Rome III)'.[244] The Green Paper on Applicable Law and Jurisdiction in Divorce Matters was accordingly presented on 14 June 2005, inviting interested governments, organisations and individuals to contribute their views and information on the law applicable to divorce. The Green Paper described a number of problems that may arise in the absence of a unified choice of law on divorce. These shortcomings are: the lack of legal certainty and predictability for the spouses, insufficient party autonomy, the risk of results that do not correspond to the legitimate expectations of the citizens, the risk of difficulties for EU citizens living in a third States and the risk of rush to court.[245] The Commission, accordingly, proposed a number of possible solutions: maintaining the status quo, harmonising the choice of law rules, providing the spouses the possibility to choose the law applicable to their divorce, revising the grounds of jurisdiction listed in Article 3 of the Brussels II*bis*-Regulation, revising the rule on residual jurisdiction of Article 7 of the latter Regulation, providing spouses the possibility to choose the competent court, introducing the possibility to transfer a case, and combining different solutions.[246]

---

241 Vienna Action Plan, para 41.

242 See Council Document No. 8838/00 JUSTCIV 66 of 31 May 2000, containing an overview of the replies to this questionnaire; and Council Document No. 8839/00 JUSTCIV 67 of 5 June 2000 for a compilation of these replies.

243 This Study, which is called 'Practical Problems Resulting from the Non-Harmonization of Choice of Law Rules in Divorce Matters', dates from December 2002 and can be found at: http://ec.europa.eu/justice_home/doc_centre/civil/studies/doc/divorce_matters_en.pdf.

244 The Hague Programme, p. 13. See equally Communication from the Commission to the Council and the European Parliament — The Hague Programme: Ten priorities for the next five years. The Partnership for European renewal in the field of Freedom, Security and Justice, COM(2005) 184 final.

245 See Green Paper on Divorce, pp. 3–6.

246 Ibid., pp. 6–11.

This public consultation has yielded at least 70 responses.[247]

In July 2006 the European Commission published the Brussels II*ter*-Proposal, *inter alia* introducing a common choice of law on divorce. On the basis of an impact assessment, the Commission proposed a revision of the Brussels II*bis*-Regulation.[248] Because 'none of the individual policy options completely address the problems or fully achieve the policy objectives', the proposal combines 'different aspects of the policy options' so that 'a higher degree of effectiveness could be achieved.'[249] The revision includes the unification of the choice of law on divorce offering the spouses a limited possibility to choose the law applicable to their divorce.[250]

4.7.2 Competence Pursuant to Article 65 EC-Treaty

In Section 4.2.2.1 above, it became clear that Article 65 EC-Treaty required four investitive requirements be met. The unification of the choice of law on divorce should concern a measure on judicial cooperation in civil matters, have cross-border implications, be necessary for the proper functioning of the internal market and fulfil the principles of subsidiarity and proportionality.

The requirement that the unification of the choice of law should be a measure in the field of judicial cooperation in civil matters does not pose any problem. Article 65 EC contained in lit. (a)–(c) a list of areas which are considered as falling within the field of judicial cooperation in civil matters. Rules unifying the choice of law on divorce come under the area listed in lit. (b) and should thus promote the compatibility of the rules applicable in the Member States concerning the conflict of laws and of jurisdiction. The unification of the choice of law complies with this requirement.[251]

Secondly, the unification of the choice of law on divorce should have cross-border implications. Measures on private international law have by their very nature cross-border implications. This requirement is thus fulfilled in case of the unification of the choice of law on divorce.

Thirdly, the unification of the choice of law must be necessary for the proper functioning of the internal market. According to some this is by no means a matter

[247] The responses to the Green Paper — at least those which are not requested to remain private — are published at: https://ec.europa.eu/justice_home/consulting_public/news_consulting_public_en.htm. The Commission declared, strangely enough, to have received '*approximately* 65 submissions in response to the Green Paper' [emphasis added], see the Explanatory Memorandum to the Brussels II*ter*-Proposal, p. 5. For an analysis of the responses to the Green Paper see Oderkerk 2006, pp. 119–128.

[248] The impact assessment on divorce has been made on the basis of a study drawn up by EPEC.

[249] Impact Assessment on Divorce, p. 23.

[250] See for an elaborate discussion of the proposed choice of law rules on divorce *infra* Chap. 5.

[251] Cf., *supra* Sect. 4.4.1.

of course.[252] It is acknowledged that the European legislature has a certain margin of appreciation in ascertaining whether a measure is necessary for the proper functioning of the internal market.[253] The European institutions often refer to this margin of appreciation, equally in case of the Brussels II*ter*-Proposal:

> The present proposal facilitates the proper functioning of the internal market since it will eliminate any obstacles to the free movement of persons who are currently faced with problems due to the remaining differences between the national laws with regard to applicable law and jurisdiction in matrimonial matters.[254]

The internal market requirement should not be interpreted too narrowly.[255] Such interpretation is in line with the goal set by Article 61 EC-Treaty, i.e. a progressive establishment of an area of freedom, security and justice. This goal seems hard to reconcile with a very strict internal market requirement. The wide interpretation of the internal market requirement of Article 65 EC also allows for the unification of choice of law rules, which are not as such necessary for the internal market, but which do have an important supportive function for the exercise of the fundamental freedoms and, hence, for the functioning of the internal market. The choice of law rules can then be considered as necessary for the *proper* functioning of the internal market, which is a condition for an already functioning market.[256] From this perspective the unification of the choice of law on divorce is necessary for the proper functioning of the internal market, since the establishment of such rules will have a stimulating effect towards the internal market. The question whether the internal market requires a common choice of law on divorce should be considered in the context of the free movement of persons. The shortcomings resulting from the absence of a unified choice of law on divorce indicated by the Commission hamper the free movement of persons, and thus require the adoption of European measures in this field. Furthermore, without EU action in the area of divorce, the problems identified will not be resolved and the policy objective of a common judicial area that makes life for the EU citizens easier will not be achieved.[257]

The unification of the choice of law rules on divorce will thus remove an obstacle to the free movement of persons and will, hence, contribute to the proper functioning of the internal market.[258]

Finally, the principles of subsidiarity and proportionality must be fulfilled. According to the Explanatory Memorandum of the Brussels II*ter*-Proposal the principles of subsidiarity and proportionality are met.[259] The objectives of the

252 See Rauscher 2002, p. 889.

253 Cf., Kohler 2001, p. 43; Hellner 2002, p. 18; Wagner 2004, p. 138; Rüberg 2005, p. 80.

254 Brussels II*ter*-Proposal, p. 6.

255 See equally Hess 2000, p. 23; Meeusen 2007a, pp. 342–343; and Knot 2008, pp. 173–174.

256 Cf., Leible and Staudinger 2000, p. 229; Leible 2003, p. 17; Rüberg 2005, p. 81.

257 See Impact Assessment on Divorce, p. 28.

258 Some Member States do not agree with this point of view, see *infra* Sect. 6.3.1.

259 Brussels II*ter*-Proposal, p. 7.

Brussels II*ter*-Proposal cannot be accomplished by the Member States and the instrument of the regulation does not go beyond what is necessary to achieve the objectives.[260]

The European legislature was, in accordance with Article 65 EC-Treaty, competent to enact measures unifying the choice of law on divorce.

Pursuant to Article 67(5) EC-Treaty the Brussels II*ter*-Proposal resorted under the consultation procedure, signifying that the Commission has to submit the proposal to the Council, which is in turn obliged to seek the opinion of the European Parliament.[261] The ultimate decision on the proposal is made by the Council and, as the Brussels II*ter*-Proposal concerns a measure in the field of international family law, a unanimous decision from the Council is required.

As to attain the required unanimity on the Brussels II*ter*-Proposal, the Council has made several attempts to reach a result acceptable to all Member States. However, at its meeting of 5 and 6 June 2008 the Council concluded that there was no unanimity on taking the Brussels II*ter*-Regulation forward and that insurmountable difficulties precluded such unanimity in the foreseeable future.[262]

The European Parliament's Committee on Civil Liberties, Justice and Home Affairs produced its report on the Brussels II*ter*-Proposal on 19 September 2008, which contains a draft legislative resolution.[263] On 21 October 2008 — over four months after the Council's decision not to take the proposal forward — the European Parliament has adopted this legislative resolution by an overwhelming majority approving, subject to amendments, the Brussels II*ter*-Proposal.[264] The European Parliament probably adopted the legislative resolution on the Brussels

---

[260] See also Wagner 2004, p. 149 ff. However, not all Member States agreed with this point of view; see further *infra* Sect. 6.3.2.

[261] See ECJ Case 138/79 *SA Roquette Frères* v. *Council* [1980] ECR 3333; and ECJ Case 139/79 *Maizena GmbH* v. *Council* [1980] ECR 3393. In these so-called Isoglucose Cases, the ECJ held that the Council could not act legally in disposing of a proposal of the Commission without receiving the opinion of the European Parliament. The duty to consult includes the requirement to reconsult whenever the text finally adopted, viewed as a whole, differs substantially from the text on which the European Parliament has already been consulted, except where the amendments essentially correspond to the Parliament's wishes. However, the Council is not obliged to follow the opinion of the European Parliament. See further Kapteyn and VerLoren van Themaat 1998, p. 419 ff.

[262] See EU Council Factsheet on decisions in civil law matters, p. 2, available at: http://www.consilium.europa.eu/ueDocs/cms_Data/docs/pressData/en/jha/101000.pdf. In Chap. 6 the failure to reach a compromise on the Brussels II*ter*-Proposal will be analysed.

[263] Report of the European Parliament of 19 September 2008, A6-0361/2008. Earlier versions of the Report of the European Parliament are also available. See Working Document on the law applicable in matrimonial matters of 21 June 2007, DT\673609EN.doc, and the Draft Report of the European Parliament of 9 January 2008, 2006/0135(CNS).

[264] The Resolution was adopted by 522 votes to 89 with 35 abstentions. See: http://www.europarl.europa.eu/oeil/file.jsp?id=5372262. This Resolution has been annexed to this study as Appendix 3.

II*ter*-Proposal in order to exert some political pressure on the Member States and the Council into reconsidering and approving the Proposal.[265]

4.7.3 Competence Pursuant to Article 81 TFEU

As seen above, the Treaty on the Functioning of the European Union has liberalised the competence of the European Union as regards the judicial cooperation in civil matters, notably by diluting the internal market requirement.[266]

Since the European Union was already competent to unify the choice of law on divorce according to Article 65 EC-Treaty, its competence pursuant to Article 81 TFEU is easily established. On the basis of Article 81 TFEU the internal market requirement is no longer investitive. As some Member States have questioned whether a unified choice of law on divorce would be necessary for the proper functioning of the internal market,[267] the amended provision on the Union's competence of Article 81 TFEU may offer a solution to this issue.

4.8 Conclusion

This chapter examined the Europeanisation of the Union's competence to enact measures in the field of international family law. International family law is brought more and more under the influence of the European Union. Mainly after the entry into force of the Treaty of Amsterdam in 1999, the Europeanisation of the whole domain of private international law has developed rapidly. The EC-Treaty has granted the European Union the competence to enact measures in the field of private international law (ex Article 61(c) in conjunction with Article 65 EC-Treaty) in order to progressively establish an area of freedom, security and justice. The Treaty on the Functioning of the European Union has taken the integration a step further: it no longer requires Union measures in the field of private international law to be necessary for the proper functioning of the internal market.

Common rules for matters of international family law would be of avail to the establishment of the area of freedom, security and justice. Such rules will contribute to the creation of a European judicial area, which is to bring tangible benefits for every Union citizen. Unified choice of law rules on issues of international family law will, moreover, serve a number of specific objectives: they will

[265] Cf., the statement of Mr. Panayiotis Demetriou, Member of the European Parliament ('*This report is a strong political signal to the Council to push the Member States to adopt an EU instrument on the matter.*'), available at: http://www.epp-ed.eu/Press/showpr.asp?PRControlDocTypeID=1&PRControlID=7913&PRContentID=13771&PRContentLG=en.

[266] See *supra* Sect. 4.2.3.2.

[267] See further *infra* Sect. 6.3.1.

ensure more legal certainty, prevent forum shopping, provide for more decisional harmony, grant better protection to the legitimate expectations of the parties and contribute to the achievement of justice.

The competence of the EU pursuant to Article 81 TFEU to provide for unified choice of law rules is bound to certain limits. It must concern rules in the field of judicial cooperation in civil matters and ensure the compatibility of the rules applicable in the Member States on conflict of laws. The EU can enact such measures particularly when necessary for the proper functioning of the internal market. In addition, the principles of subsidiarity and proportionality must be fulfilled. Article 81(3) TFEU requires a unanimous Council decision for the adoption of a measure in the field of international family law, meaning that every Member State holds a power of veto.

The assessment of the competence of the EU as regards the unification of the choice of law on divorce shows that the requirements of both Article 65 EC and Article 81 TFEU are fulfilled. However, not all Member States agreed with this point of view, as a result of which no unanimity could be reached on the establishment of a common European choice of law on divorce.

References

Regulations, Conventions, Reports and Other Documentary Sources

Brussels I-Convention. The Brussels Convention on Jurisdiction and the Enforcement of Judgments in Civil and Commercial Matters of 27 September 1968, [1972] OJ C299/32

Brussels I-Regulation. Council Regulation (EC) No 44/2001 of 22 December 2000 on jurisdiction and the recognition and enforcement of judgments in civil and commercial matters, [2001] OJ L12/1

Brussels II*bis*-Regulation. Council Regulation (EC) No. 2201/2003 of 27 November 2003 on Jurisdiction and Enforcement of Judgments in Matrimonial Matters and Matters of Parental Responsibility, [2003] OJ L338/1

Brussels II*ter*-Proposal. Proposal for a Council Regulation amending Regulation (EC) No. 2201/2003 as regards jurisdiction and introducing rules concerning applicable law in matrimonial matters, COM(2006) 399 final

COSAC Report. Report of the subsidiarity and proportionality check on the Brussels II*ter*-Proposal organised in November 2006 by COSAC, Report No. 1/2006. The COSAC-Report and the Annex thereto are available at: http://www.cosac.eu/en/info/earlywarning/doc/results/

EEC-Treaty. Treaty of 25 March 1957, *Trb.* 1957, 91

EC-Treaty. Treaty Establishing the European Community, Amsterdam 2 October 1997, [1997] OJ C340/1

EU-Treaty. Treaty on the European Union of 7 February 1992, [1992] OJ C191/1 (original version), [2010] OJ C83/13 (consolidated version)

EU-Treaty (Nice version). Treaty on the European Union of 7 February 1992, [2006] OJ C321E/1

Green Paper on Divorce. Green Paper on applicable law and jurisdiction in divorce maters, COM(2005) 82 final

Hague Programme. The Hague Programme: Strengthening freedom, security and justice in the European Union, [2005] OJ C53/1

Hague Protocol on the Law Applicable to Maintenance Obligations. Protocol on the Law Applicable to Maintenance Obligations of 23 November 2007. Protocol to the Hague Convention of 23 November 2007 on the International Recovery of Child Support and Other Forms of Family Maintenance

Impact Assessment on Divorce. Commission Staff Working Document – Annex to the proposal for a Council Regulation amending Regulation (EC) No. 2201/2003 as regards jurisdiction and introducing rules concerning applicable law in matrimonial matters, SEC(2006) 949

Mutual Recognition Programme. Council draft Programme of measures for implementation of the principle of mutual recognition of decisions in civil and commercial matters of 30 November 2000, [2001] OJ C12/1

Rome I-Regulation. Regulation (EC) No. 593/2008 of the European Parliament and the Council on the law applicable to contractual obligations (Rome I), [2008] OJ L177/6

Rome II-Regulation. Regulation (EC) No. 864/2007 of the European Parliament and the Council on the law applicable to non-contractual obligations (Rome II), [2007] OJ L199/40

Rome III-Proposal. See Brussels II*ter*-Proposal

Stockholm Programme. The Stockholm Programme – An open and secure Europe serving and protecting the citizens of 2 December 2009, available at: http://ec.europa.eu/justice_home/news/intro/doc/stockholm_program_en.pdf

Tampere Presidency Conclusions. Presidency Conclusions of the Tampere European Council of 15–16 October 1999, available at: http://www.consilium.europa.eu/ueDocs/cms_Data/docs/pressData/en/ec/00200-r1.en9.htm

Treaty of Amsterdam. Treaty Establishing the European Community, Amsterdam 2 October 1997, [1997] OJ C340/1

Treaty on the Functioning of the European Union. Treaty on the Functioning of the European Union of 13 December 2007, [2010] OJ C83/46 (consolidated version)

Treaty of Lisbon. Treaty of Lisbon amending the Treaty on European Union and the Treaty establishing the European Community, 13 December 2007, [2007] OJ C306/1

Treaty of Maastricht. Treaty on the European Union of 7 February 1992, [1992] OJ C191/1

Vienna Action Plan. Justice and Home Affairs Council meeting of 3 December 1998, Action Plan of the Council and the Commission on how best to Implement the Provisions of the Treaty of Amsterdam on an Area of Freedom, Security and Justice, [1999] OJ C19/1

Books and Articles

Badiali G (1985) Le droit international privé des Communautés européennes. Recueil des Cours 191:1–182

Ballarino T, Ubertazzi B (2004) On *Avello* and other judgments: a new point of departure in the conflict of laws? Yearbook of Private International Law 6:85–128

Baratta R (2007) Problematic elements of an implicit rule providing for mutual recognition of personal and family status in the EC. IPRax 27:4–11

Barents R (1997) Some observation on the treaty of Amsterdam. MJ 4:332–345

Basedow J (1994) Konstantinidis v. Bangemann oder die Familie im europäischen Gemeinschaftsrecht. ZEuP 5:197–199

Basedow J (1997) Die Harmonisierung des Kollisionsrecht nach dem Vertrag von Amsterdam. EuZW 8:609

Basedow J (2000) The communautarization of the conflict of laws under the Treaty of Amsterdam. CMLR 37:687–708

Basedow J (2002) Die Vergemeinschaftung des Kollisionsrecht nach dem Vertrag von Amsterdam. In: Baur JF, Mansel HP (eds) Systemwechsel im europäischen Kollisionsrecht. Verlag C.H. Beck, München, pp 19–46

Basedow J (2009) The communitarisation of private international law. RabelsZ 73:455–460
Beaumont PR (1999) Treaty of Amsterdam-community competence in private international law. ICLQ 48:225–229
Bieber R, Monar J (eds) (1995) Justice and home affairs in the European union: the development of the third pillar. European Interuniversity Press, Brussels
Bodénès-Constantin A (2005) La codification du droit international privé français. Editions Defrénois, Paris
Boele-Woelki K, van Ooik RH (2004) The communitarization of private international law. In: Grosheide FW, Hondius E (eds) Molengrafica international contract law 2003. Intersentia, Antwerpen, pp 343–383
Boele-Woelki K, Van Ooik RH (2006) Exclusieve externe bevoegdheden van de EG inzake het Internationaal Privaatrecht. Gevolgen voor de toetreding van de EG tot de Haagse Conferentie. NTER 194–201
Bogdan M (2006) Concise introduction to EU private international law. Europa Law Publishing, Groningen
Borchardt KD (looseleaf) Section P.I. Direckte Klagen. In: Dauses MA (ed) Handbuch des EU-Wirtschaftsrechts. Beck, München
Borrás A (2005) Le droit international privé communautaire: réalités, problèmes et perspectives d'avenir. Recueil des Cours 317:313–536
Borrás A (2007) Prinzipien des Internationalen Familienrechts. In: Reichelt G (ed) Europäisches Gemeinschaftsrecht und IPR. Manzsche, Wien, pp 55–67
Calvo Caravaca AL (2006) The private international law of the European Community. In: Pereznieto Castro L et al (eds) Tradition and innovation of private international law at the beginning of the third millennium. Liber in memoriam of professor Friedrich K. Juenger. Juris Publishing, New York, pp 23–44
Carrera S (2005) What does free movement mean in theory and practice in an Enlarged EU? European Law Journal 11:699–721
Coester-Waltjen D (2004) Das Anerkennungsprinzip im Dornröschenschlaf? In: Mansel HP et al (eds) Festschrift für Erik Jayme. Sellier, München, pp 121–129
Coester-Waltjen D (2006) Anerkennung im Internationalen Personen-, Familien- und Erbrecht und das Europäische Kollisionsrecht. IPRax 26:392–400
Curry-Sumner I (2005) All's well that ends registered? Intersentia, Antwerpen
De Boer ThM (2008a) The second revision of the Brussels II regulation: jurisdiction and applicable law. In: Boele-Woelki K, Sverdrup T (eds) European challenges in contemporary family law. Intersentia, Antwerpen, pp 321–341
De Boer ThM (2008b) Unwelcome foreign law: public policy and other means to protect the fundamental values and public interests of the European Community. In: Malatesta A et al (eds) The external dimention of EC private international law in family and succession matters. CEDAM, Milan, pp 295–330
De Boer ThM (2009) The purpose of uniform choice-of-law rules: the Rome II regulation. NILR 56:295–332
De Groot G-R (2001) Auf dem Wege zu einem europäischen (internationalen) Familienrecht. ZEuP 9:617–627
De Groot G-R, Kuipers J-J (2008) The new provisions on private international law in the Treaty of Lisbon. MJ 15:109–114
De Schutter O, Francq S (2005) La proposition de directive relative aux services dans le marché intérieur: reconnaissance mutuelle, harmonisation et conflits de lois dans l'Europe élargie. Cahiers de Droit Européen 41:603–660
Dethloff N (2003) Arguments for and against unification and harmonisation of family law in Europe. In: Boele-Woelki K (ed) Perspectives for the harmonisation and unification of family law in Europe. Intersentia, Antwerpen, pp 37–34
Dethloff N (2007) Familien- und Erbrecht zwischen nationaler Rechtskultur, Vergemeinschaftung und Internationalität. Perspektiven für die Forschung. ZEuP 15:992–1005

De Vareilles-Sommières P (1998) Un droit international privé européen? In: De Vareilles-Sommières P (ed) Le droit privé européen. Economica, Paris, pp 136–147

Dickinson A (2005) European private international law: embracing new horizons or mourning the past? Journal of Private International Law 1:197–236

Dittrich A (1996) Der Schütz der Unionsbürger durch die justitielle Zusammenarbeit. In: Müller-Graff PC (ed) Europäische Zusammenarbeit in den Bereichen Justiz und Inneres. Nomos, Baden-Baden

Dohrn H (2004) Die Kompetenzen der Europäischen Gemeinschaft im Internationalen Privatrecht (diss. Bielefeld). Mohr Siebeck, Tübingen

Drappatz T (2002) Die Überführung des internationalen Zivilverfahrensrechts in eine Gemeinschaftskompetenz nach Art. 65 EGV. J.C.B. Mohr (Paul Siebeck), Tübingen

Drobnig U (2000) European private international law after the Treaty of Amsterdam: perspectives for the next decade. King's College Law Journal 11:190–201

Duintjer Tebbens H (2002) Ein Ziviljustizraum in der Europäischen Union - auf Kosten einer Aushölung der internationalen Zusammenarbeit? In: Baur JF, Mansel HP (eds) Systemwechsel im europäischen Kollisionsrecht. Verlag C.H. Beck, München, pp 171–192

Dutta A (2009) Succession and wills in the conflict of laws on the eve of europeanisation. RabelsZ 73:547–606

Fallon M (2006) Les projets européens en matière de conflits de lois: une mise en contexte. Revue de la Faculté de droit de l'Université de Liège 51:503–547

Fallon M (2007) Constraints of internal market law on family law. In: Meeusen J et al (eds) International family law for the European Union. Intersentia, Antwerpen, pp 149–181

Fallon M, Meeusen J (2002) Private international law in the European Union and the exception of mutual recognition. Yearbook of Private International Law 4:37–66

Fallon M, Francq S (2004) La coopération judiciaire civile et le droit international privé. Vers un droit proprement communautaire des conflits de lois ou de juridiction. In: De Schutter O, Nihoul P (eds) Une Constitution pour l'Europe. Réflexions sur les transformations du droit de l'Union européenne. Larcier, Brussel, pp 239–301

Fentiman R (2008) Choice of law in Europe: uniformity and integration. Tulane Law Review 82:2021–2051

Fernandez Rozas JC, Sanchez Lorenzo SA (1991) Curso de derecho internacional privado. Editorial Civitas, Madrid

Fiorini A (2008a) The codification of private international law in Europe: could the community learn from the experience of mixed jurisdictions? Electronic Journal of Comparative Law 12:1–16

Fiorini A (2008b) Rome III—choice of law in divorce: is the Europeanization of family law going too far? International Journal of Law, Policy and the Family 22:178–205

Fiorini A (2008c) The evolution of European private international law. ICLQ 57:969–984

Fletcher IF (1982) Conflict of laws and European community law. North-Holland Publishing Company, Amsterdam

Frankenstein E (1950) Projet d'un code européen de droit international privé. E.J. Brill, Leiden

Freudenthal M (2007) Schets van het Europees civiel procesrecht Europees burgerlijk procesrecht voor de Nederlandse rechtspraktijk. Kluwer, Deventer

Funken F (2009) Das Anerkennungsprinzip im internationalen Privatrecht: Perspektiven eines europäischen Anerkennungskollisionsrecht für Statusfragen (diss. Hamburg). Mohr Siebeck, Tübingen

Gaertner V (2006) European choice of law rules in divorce (Rome III): An examination of the possible connecting factors in divorce matters against the background of private international law developments. Journal of Private International Law 2:99–136

Gaertner V (2008) Die Privatscheidung im deutschen und gemeinschaftsrechtlichen Internationalen Privat- und Verfahrensrecht (diss. Heidelberg). Mohr Siebeck, Tübingen

Gaudemet-Tallon H (2000) Le droit privé et droit communautaire: quelques réflexions. Revue du Marché commun et de l'Union européenne, pp 228–242

Gaudemet-Tallon H (2001) Quel droit international privé pour l'union européenne? In: Borchers PJ, Zekoll J (eds) International Conflicts of Laws for the Third Millennium, Essays in honor of Friedrich K. Juenger. Transnational Publishers, Ardsley, pp 317–338

Gaudemet-Tallon H (2002) De l'utilité d'une unification du droit international privé de la famille dans l'union européenne? In: de Moura Ramos RM et al (eds) Estudos em homenagem à Professora Doutora Isabel de Magalhães Collaço. Livraria Almedina, Coimbra, pp 159–185

Gaudemet-Tallon H (2004) Droit international privé et Code civil. In: Lequette Y, Leveneur L (eds) 1804–2004 Le Code civil, un passé, un présent, un avenir. Dalloz, Paris

Gaudemet-Tallon H (2005) Le pluralisme en droit international privé: richesses et faiblesses (Le funambule et l'arc-en-ciel). Recueil des Cours 312:9–488

Gonzalez Beilfuss C (2004) Relaciones e interacciones entre derecho comunitario, derecho internacional privado y derecho de familia europeo en la construcción de un espacio judicial común. Anuario español de derecho internacional privado 4:117–187

Grundmann S (2002) Internationales Privatrecht als Verfassungsordnung. RIW 48:329–343

Hailbronner K, Thierry C (1998) Amsterdam—Vergemeinschaftung der Sachbereiche Freier Personenverkehr, Asylrecht und Einwanderung sowie Überführung des Schengen-Besitzstands auf EU-Ebene. EuR 5:583-615

Hellner M (2002) The limits to judicial cooperation in civil matters: taking legality seriously. In: Hohloch G (ed) Wege zum Europäischen Recht. Nomos, Baden-Baden, pp 9–22

Henrich D (2005) Anerkennung statt IPR: Eine Grundsatzfrage. IPRax 25:422–423

Herzog PE (looseleaf) Commentary on Art. 65. In: Campbell D, Cotter S (eds) The law of the European Community: a commentary on the EC Treaty. Matthew Bender, New York, paragraph 65.02

Hess B (2000) Die "Europäisierung" des internationalen Zivilprozessrechts durch den Amsterdamer Vertrag - Chancen und Gefahren. NJW 53:23–32

Hess B (2010) Europäisches Zivilprozessrecht. C.F. Müller, Heidelberg

Hubert P (2000) Quels avenirs pour l'Europe de la justice et de la police? Rapport du groupe "Coopération dans les domaines de la justice et des affaires intérieurs". La Documentation Française, Paris

Israël J (2000) Conflicts of law and the EC after Amsterdam a change for worse? MJ 7:81–99

Israël J (2001) Europees internationaal privaatrecht. De EG, een *comitas Europaea* en 'vrijheid, veiligheid en rechtvaardigheid'. NIPR 19:135–149

Jayme E, Kohler C (1997) Europäisches Kollisionsrecht 1997: Vergemeinschaftung durch "Säulenwechsel"? IPRax 17:385–401

Jayme E, Kohler C (2001) Europäisches Kollisionsrecht 2001: Anerkennungsprinzip statt IPR? IPRax 21:501–514

Jayme E, Kohler C (2002) Europäisches Kollisionsrecht 2002: Zur Wiederkehr des Internationalen Privatrechts. IPRax 22:461–471

Jessurun d'Oliveira HU (2002) The EU and a metamorphosis of private international law. In: Fawcett J (ed) Reform an developments of private international law, essays in honour of sir Peter North. Oxford University Press, New York, pp 111–136

Joustra CA (1999) Europese richtlijnen en internationaal privaatrecht. WPNR 6370:664–670

Kapteyn PJG (2008) Rechtsbescherming in de hervormde Europese Unie. In: Meeusen J et al (eds) Het Verdrag van Lissabon: de Europese impasse doorbroken (?). Intersentia, Antwerpen, pp 47–48

Kapteyn PJG, VerLoren van Themaat P (1998) Introduction to the law of the European Communities, 3rd edn. edited and further revised by L.W. Gormley. Kluwer Law International, London

Kessedijan C (2004) Le droit international privé et l'intégration juridique européenne. In: Einhorn T, Siehr K (eds) Intercontinental Cooperation Through Private International Law Liber Amicorum P.E. Nygh. T.M.C. Asser Press, Den Haag, pp 187–196

Knot JG (2008) Internationale boedelafwikkeling Over het toepasselijke recht op de afwikkeling van nalatenschappen (diss. Groningen). Kluwer, Deventer

Kohler C (1992) L'article 220 du Traité CEE et les conflits de juridictions en matière de relations familiales: premières reflections. Rivista di diritto internazionale privato e processuale 28:221–240

Kohler C (1996) La Cour de Justice des Communautés européennes et le droit international privé. In: Comité français de droit international privé, Travaux de l'année 1993–1994, 1994–1995. Editions Pédone, Paris, pp 71–95

Kohler C (1999) Interrogations sur les sources du droit international privé européen après le traité d'Amsterdam. RCDIP 88:1–30

Kohler C (2001) Status als Ware: Bemerkungen zur europäischen Verordnung über das internationale Verfahrensrecht für Ehesachen. In: Mansel HP (ed) Vergemeinschaftung des Europäischen Kollisionsrecht. Carl Heymanns Verlag, Köln, pp 41–53

Kohler C (2002) Systemwechsel im europäischen Anerkennungsrecht: von der EuGVVO zur Abschaffung des Exequaturs. In: Baur JF, Mansel HP (eds) Systemwechsel im europäischen Kollisionsrecht. C.H. Beck Verlag, München, pp 147–163

Kohler C (2003) Der europäische Justizraum für Zivilsachen und das Gemeinschaftskollisionsrecht. IPRax 23:401–412

Kohler C (2008a) Zur Gestaltung des europäischen Kollisionsrecht für Ehesachen: Der steinige Weg zu einheitlichen Vorschriften über das anwendbare Recht für Scheidung und Trennung. Zeitschrift für das gesamte Familienrecht 55:1673–1681

Kotuby CT (2001) External Competence of the European Community in the Hague Conference on Private International Law: Community Harmonization and Worldwide Unification. NILR 48:1–30

Kreuzer K (1991) *Lex communis europaea de collisione legum*: Utopie ou nécessité? In: España y la codificación internacional del Derecho internacional privado. Eurolex, Madrid, pp 225–246

Kreuzer K (2001) La communautarisation du droit international privé: les acquis et les perspectives. Droit GLOBAL Law Unifier le droit: le rêve impossible?, no 2001/1, pp 97–137

Kreuzer K (2006) Zu Stand und Perspektiven des Europäischen Internationalen Privatrechts. RabelsZ 70:1–88

Labayle H (1997) Un espace de liberté, de sécurité et de justice. Revue Trimestrielle de Droit européen 33:813–881

Labayle H (2005) 'L'Espace de liberté, sécurité et justice dans la Constitution pour l'Europe. Revue Trimestrielle de Droit Européen 42:1–46

Lagarde P (2004) Développements futurs du droit international privé dans une Europe en voie d'unification: quelques conjectures. RabelsZ 68:225–243

Lagarde P (2005) Internationales Privatrecht und Europarecht. In: Kieniger EM (ed) Denationalisierung des Privatrechts?. Mohr Siebeck, Tübingen

Lazic V (2008) Recent Developments in Harmonizing 'European Private International Law' in Family Matters. European Journal of Law Reform 10:75–96

Leible S (2003) Die Europäisierung des internationalen Privat- und Prozessrechts: Kompetenzen, Stand der Rechtsvereinheitlichung und Perspektiven. In: Sánchez Lorenzo S, Moya Escudero M (eds) La cooperación judicial en materia civil y la unificación del derecho privado en Europa. Dykinson, Madrid, pp 13–38

Leible S, Staudinger A (2000) Art. 65 EGV im System der EG-Kompetenzen. The European Legal Forum 1:225–235

Lequette Y (2008) De Bruxelles à La Haye (*Acte II*) Réflexions critiques sur la compétence communautaire en matière de droit international privé. In: Azzi T (ed) Vers de nouveaux équilibres entre ordres juridiques. Liber amicorum Hélène Gaudemet-Tallon. Dalloz, Paris, pp 503–544

Linke H (2002) Die Europäisierung des Internationalen Privat- und Verfahrensrechts. Traum oder Trauma? In: Schütze RA (ed) Einheit und Vielfalt des Rechts, Festschrift für Reinhold Geimer zum 65. Geburtstag. C.H. Beck Verlag, München, pp 529–554

Mansel HP (2002) Zum Systemwechsel im europäischen Kollisionsrecht nach Amsterdam und Nizza. In: Baur JF, Mansel HP (eds) Systemwechsel im europäischen Kollisionsrecht. C.H. Beck Verlag, München, pp 1–15

Mansel HP (2003) Das Staatsangehörigkeitsprinzip im deutschen und gemeinschafts-rechtlichen Internationalen Privatrecht: Schutz der kulturellen Identität oder Diskriminierung der Person? In: Jayme E (ed) Kulturelle Identität und Internationales Privatrecht. C.F. Müller Verlag, Heidelberg, pp 119–154

Mansel HP (2006) Anerkennung als Grundprinzip des Europäischen Rechtsraums. Zur Herausbildung eines europäischen Anerkennungs-Kollisionsrechts: Anerkennung statt Verweisung als neues Strukturprinzip des Europäischen internationalen Privatrechts? RabelsZ 70:651–731

Mansel HP, Thorn K, Wagner R (2010) Europäisches Kollisionsrecht 2009: Hoffnungen durch den Vertrag von Lissabon. IPRax 30:1–27

Marias EA (1994) From market citizen to union citizen. In: Marias EA (ed) European citizenship. European Institute of Public Administration, Maastricht

Martiny D (2006) Ein Internationales Scheidungsrecht für Europa. In: Freitag R et al (eds) Internationales Familienrecht für das 21. Jahrhundert. Sellier. European Law Publishers, München, pp 119–135

Martiny D (2007) Objectives and values of (private) international law in family law. In: Meeusen J et al (eds) International family law for the European Union. Intersentia, Antwerpen, pp 69–99

Mattera A (1998) Le principe de reconnaissance mutuelle: instrument de préservation des traditions et des diversités nationales, régionales et locales. Revue du Marché Unique Européen 2:5–17

McEleavy P (2004) The communitarization of divorce rules: what impact for English and Scottish law? ICLQ 53:605–642

McNamara R, Martin F (2006) Brussels calling: the unstoppable Europeanisation of Irish family law. Irish Journal of Family Law 9:8–21

Meeusen J (2004) Fifteen theses on Brussels I, Rome I and the European Union's institutional framework. In: Meeusen J et al (eds) Enforcement of international contracts in the European Union, Convergence and divergence between Brussels I and Rome I. Antwerpen, Intersentia, pp 43–67

Meeusen J (2006) Op weg naar een communautair internationaal familie(vermogens)recht? Enkele Europeesrechtelijke beschouwingen. In: Mededelingen van de Nederlandse Vereniging voor Internationaal Recht Europees internationaal familierecht. T.M.C. Asser Press, Den Haag, pp 1–70

Meeusen J (2007a) What has it got to do necessarily with the European Union?: international family law and European (economic) integration. The Cambridge Yearbook of European Legal Studies 2006–2007, pp 329–355

Meeusen J (2007b) Instrumentalisation of private international law in the European Union: towards a European conflicts revolution? European Journal of Migration and Law 9:287–305

Meeusen J (2007c) System shopping in European private international law in family matters. In: Meeusen J et al (eds) International family law for the European Union. Intersentia, Antwerpen, pp 239–278

Meeusen J (2008) Public policy in European private international law: In response to the contribution of professor Th.M. de Boer on "Unwelcome foreign law". In: Malatesta A et al (eds) The external dimension of EC private international law in family and succession matters. CEDAM, Milan

Mills A (2009) The Confluence of public and private international law. Cambridge University Press, Cambridge

Müller-Graff PC (1994) The legal basis of the third pillar and its position in the framework of the European Union Treaty. CMLR 31:493–510

Müller-Graff PC (2005) Der "Raum der Freiheit, der Sicherheit und des Rechts" im neuen Verfassungsvertrag für Europa-Neuerungen und Notwendigkeit seiner Rekonstruktion. In: Gaitanides C et al (eds) Europa und seine Verfassung. Baden-Baden, Nomos

Müller-Graff PC, Kainer F (2000) Die justizielle Zusammenarbeit in Zivilsachen in der Europäischen Union. Deutsche Richterzeitung 78:350–354

Nott SM (2002) For better or worse? The Europeanisation of the conflict of laws. Liverpool Law Review 24:3–17
Oderkerk AE (2006) Het Groenboek inzake het toepasselijke recht en de rechterlijke bevoegheid in echtscheidingszaken. NIPR 24:119–128
Partsch PE (2003) Le droit international privé européen. De Rome à Nice (diss. Liège). Larcier, Brussels
Pataut E (2005) De Bruxelles à La Haye. Droit international privé communautaire et droit international privé conventionnel. In: Jobard-Bachellier MN, Lagarde P (eds) Le droit international privé: esprit et méthodes. Mélanges en l'honneur de Paul Lagarde. Dalloz, Paris, pp 661–695
Pintens W (2003) Grundgedanken und Perspektiven einer Europäisierung des Familien- und Erbrechts [Teil 1-3]. Zeitschrift für das gesamte Familienrecht 50:329–336, 417–425, 499–505
Pintens W (2005) Familie und Familienrecht in der europäischen Verfassung. In: Hofer S et al (eds) Perspektiven des Familienrechts, Festschrift für Dieter Schwab. Gieseking, Bielefeld
Pocar F (2005) The EU as actor in private international law. In: Brand RA, Walter M (eds) 2 CILE Studies, Private Law, Private International Law & Judicial Cooperation in the EU-US Relationship. Thomson/West, Eagan, pp 143–151
Pocar F (2008) The "communitarization" of private international law and its impact on the external relations of the European Union. In: Malatesta A et al (eds) The External dimension of EC private international law in family and succession matters. CEDAM, Milan, pp 1–15
Poillot-Peruzzetto S, Marmisse A (2001) Le droit international privé communautaire de la famille. Revue des Affaires Européennes, pp 460–468
Poillot-Peruzzetto S (2005) Les enjeux de la communautarisation. In: Fulchiron H, Nourissat C (eds) Le nouveau droit communautaire du divore et de la responsabilité parentale. Dalloz, Paris, pp 13–37
Poillot-Peruzzetto S (2008) Le défi de la construction de l'espace de liberté, de sécurité et de justice. In: Azzi T (ed) Vers de nouveaux équilibres entre ordres juridiques. Liber amicorum Hélène Gaudemet-Tallon. Dalloz, Paris
Pontier JA (2005) Europees conflictenrecht. Een complexe geschiedenis in vogelvlucht. Vossiuspers UvA, Amsterdam
Rauscher Th (2002) Leidet der Schutz der Ehescheidungsfreiheit unter der VO Brüssel II?. In: Schütze RA (ed) Einheit und Vielfalt des Rechts. Festschrift für Reinhold Geimer zum 65. Geburtstag. C.H. Beck, München, pp 883–901
Reich N (1996) EG-Richtlinien und Internationales Privatrecht. In: Lagarde P, von Hoffmann B (eds) L'européanisation du droit international privé. Bundesanzeiger, Cologne, pp 109–128
Reestman JH, Goudappel FANJ (2008) Het Verdrag van Lissabon en de Ruimte van Vrijheid, Veiligheid en Recht. SEW 56:441–445
Remien O (2001) European private international law, the European Community and its emerging area of freedom, security and justice. CMLR 38:53–86
Rossi LS (2004) 'L'incidenza dei principi del diritto comunitario sul diritto internazionale privato: dalla "comunitarizzazione" alla "constitutionalizzazione". Rivista di diritto internazionale privato e processuale 40:63–84
Rossi M (2007) Art. 65 EGV. In: Calliess C, Ruffert M (eds) EUV/EGV Das Verfassungsrecht der Europäischen Union mit Europäischer Grundrechtecharta. C.H. Beck, München
Roth WH (1991) Der Einfluß des Europäischen Gemeinschaftsrechts auf das Internationale Privatrecht. RabelsZ 55:623–673
Rüberg S (2005) Auf dem Weg zu einem europäischen Scheidungskollisionsrecht (diss. Konstanz). Available at: http://www.ub.uni-konstanz.de/kops/volltexte/2005/1694/pdf/Rueberg.pdf
Rutten SWE (1998) Mensenrechten en het IPR: scheiden of trouwen? NJCM-Bulletin: Nederlands Tijdschrift voor de Mensenrechten 23:797–811
Schack H (1999) Die EG-Kommission auf dem Holzweg von Amsterdam. ZEuP 7:805–808
Schilling K (2006) Binnenmarktkollisionsrecht. De Gruyter Recht, Berlin

Schmahl S (2003) Artikel 65 EGV. In: Bardenhewer-Rating A, Grill G, Jakob T, Wölker U (eds) Kommentar zum Vertrag über die Europäische Union und zur Gründung der Europäischen Gemeinschaft. Nomos, Baden-Baden

Siehr K (2003) Family unions in private international law. NILR 50:419–435

Sonnenberger HJ (2001) Das Internationale Privatrecht im dritten Jahrtausend—Rückblick und Ausblick. Zeitschrift für vergleichende Rechtswissenschaft 100:107–136

Spamann H (2001) Choice of law in a federal system and an internal market. Jean Monnet Working Paper 8/2001

Staudinger A (2007) From international conventions to the Treaty of Amsterdam and beyond: What has changed in judicial cooperation in civil matters? The European Legal Forum 6:257–265

Struycken AVM (1992) Les conséquences de l'intégration européenne sur le développement du droit international privé. Recueil des Cours 232:256–383

Struycken AVM (2000) Het Verdrag van Amsterdam en de Haagse Conferentie voor internationaal privaatrecht. WPNR 6421:735–745

Struycken AVM (2001) Le droit international privé d'origine communautaire et les États tiers. Revue des Affaires Européennes 2001–2002(4):469–479

Tenreiro M, Ekström M (2003) Unification of private international law in family law matters within the European Union. In: Boele-Woelki K (ed) Perspectives for the unification and harmonisation of family law in Europe. Intersentia, Antwerpen, pp 185–193

Traest M (2002) Eenmaking van internationaal privaatrecht: een begripsomschrijving. Tijdschrift voor Privaatrecht 39:1737–1837

Traest M (2003) De Europese Gemeenschap en de Haagse Conferentie voor het Internationaal Privaatrecht. Maklu, Antwerpen

Tridimas T, Eeckhout P (1984) The External Competence of the Community and the Case-Law of the Court of Justice: Principle versus Pragmatism. Yearbook of European Law 14:143–177

Van den Eeckhout V (2008) Promoting human rights within the union: the role of European private international law. European Law Journal 14:105–127

Van den Eeckhout V (2004) Communitarization of private international law: tendencies to "liberalize" international family law. Tijdschrift@ipr.be 51–70. Article available at https://openaccess.leidenuniv.nl/bitstream/1887/16146/2/Microsoft+Word+-+engelsveerleiprtijdschrift-definitief.doc%5B1%5D.pdf

Van Houtte H (2001) De gewijzigde bevoegdheid van de Europese Unie inzake IPR. In: van Houtte H, Pertegás Sender M (eds) Het nieuwe Europese IPR: van verdrag naar verordening. Intersentia, Antwerpen, pp 1–10

Vigand S (2005) La construction de l'espace de liberté, de securité et de justice: vers un droit international privé communautaire de la famille (diss. Panthéon-Assas, Paris II)

Vonken APMJ (2006) De internationale beslissingsharmonie nader beschouwd. Tijdschrift voor Privaatrecht 43:9–125

Von Hoffmann B (1995) Richtlinien der Europäischen Gemeinschaft und Internationales Privatrecht. Zeitschrift fur Rechtsvergleichung, Internationales Privatrecht und Europarecht 36:45–54

Von Hoffmann B (1998) The relevance of European community law. In: von Hoffmann B (ed) European private international law. Ars Aequi Libri, Nijmegen, pp 19–37

Von Savigny FK (1849) System des heutigen römischen Rechts, Band VIII, 2. Neudruck der Ausgabe Berlin (Scientia Verlag, Aalen 1981)

Wagner R (2004) EG-Kompetenz für das Internationale Privatrecht in Ehesachen? RabelsZ 68:119–153

Wagner R (2007) Zu den Chancen der Rechtsvereinheitlichung im internationalen Familienrecht. Das Standesamt 60:101–107

Wagner R (2010) Die politischen Leitlinien zur justitiellen Zusammenarbeit in Zivilsachen im Stockholmer Programm. IPRax 30:97–100

Weber A (2004) Die Vergemeinschaftung des internationalen Privatrechts (diss. Frankfurt am Oder). TENEA, Berlin

Wiedmann T (2007) Artikel 65 EGV. In: Schwarze J (ed) EU-Kommentar. Nomos, Baden-Baden

Wilderspin M (2001) Le droit international privé des contrats (autres que les contrats conclus par les consommateurs). Revue des affaires européennes 2001–2002:424–439

Wilderspin W (2007) Que reste-t-il du principe du pays d'origine? Le regard des internationalistes. Europe - Actualités du droit communautaire 6:26–28

Wilderspin M, Rouchaud-Joët AM (2004) La compétence externe de la Communauté européenne en droit international privé. RCDIP 93:1–48

Wollenschläger F (2009) Die Unionsbürgerschaft und ihre Dynamik für den Integrationsprozess jenseits des Marktes. Zeitschrift für Europarechtliche Studien 12:1–52

Zweigert K (1966) Einige Auswirkungen des Gemeinsamen Marktes auf das Internationale Privatrecht der Mitgliedstaaten. In: Von Caemmerer E et al (eds) Probleme des europäischen Rechts Festschrift für Walter Hallstein zu seinem 65. Geburtstag. Vittorio Klostermann, Frankfurt am Main, pp 555–569

Chapter 5
The Proposed European Choice of Law Rules on Divorce

5.1 Introduction

As mentioned in Section 2.1 above, there is no multilateral convention or Regulation between the EU-Member States on the law applicable to divorce. Therefore, each Member State currently provides autonomously for rules on this issue.[1] However, according to the European Commission this situation has the following shortcomings: it leads to lack of legal certainty and predictability for the spouses, insufficient party autonomy, risk of results that do not correspond to the legitimate expectations of the citizens, risk of difficulties for Community citizens living in a third State, and risk of a rush to court.[2]

The Commission has accordingly proposed the introduction of common choice of law rules on divorce in the Brussels II*bis*-Regulation, which contains common rules on jurisdiction and the recognition and enforcement of judgments in matrimonial matters and in matters of parental responsibility (Brussels II*ter*-Proposal).[3] The introduction of common choice of law rules on divorce is regarded as a means to removing the mentioned shortcomings resulting from the lack of such rules.

[1] Within the framework of the Hague Conference on Private International Law a convention with regard to the choice of law on divorce did exist. However, this 1902 Hague Convention is no longer in force. According to Beyer the absence of such a convention is already a strong indication for the difficulty to find a consensus on this subject matter; see Beyer 2007, p. 21.

[2] See Green Paper on divorce, pp. 3–6.

[3] Since July 2006 on the basis of meetings of the Committee on Civil Law Matters (Rome III) and of the comments of the delegations, five more drafts have been published: Document No. 5274/07 JUSTCIV 4, 12 January 2007; Document No. 7144/07 JUSTCIV 47, 9 March 2007; Document No. 11295/07 JUSTCIV 183, 28 June 2007; Document No. 13445/07 JUSTCIV 250, 3 October 2007; and Document No. 9712/08 JUSTCIV 106, 23 May 2008. The Brussels II*ter*-Proposal and the last mentioned Council draft have been annexed to this study as Appendices Nos. 1 and 2, respectively.

N.A. Baarsma, *The Europeanisation of International Family Law*,
DOI: 10.1007/978-90-6704-743-2_5, © T.M.C. ASSER PRESS, The Hague,
The Netherlands, and the author 2011

Besides the introduction of common choice of law rules, the Brussels II*ter*-Proposal also provides spouses the possibility to choose the competent court in divorce cases.[4]

This chapter closely examines the proposed common choice of law rules on divorce. Currently the EU-Member States have very different approaches with regard to divorce, both as regards substantive law and as regards the choice of law. These approaches will be discussed in Section 5.2. Subsequently, the choice of law rules of the Brussels II*ter*-Proposal will be analysed: their objectives (Section 5.3), scope of application (Section 5.4) and content (Section 5.5) will be inquired into. Further the application of foreign law (Section 5.6) and the public policy exception (Section 5.7) will be elaborated upon. Finally, the question whether the Brussels II*ter*-Proposal actually attains the objectives as set out in its Explanatory Memorandum will be discussed (Section 5.8).

5.2 Divorce in Substantive and Private International Law of the Member States

The core of the problems indicated by the Commission in the Green Paper on divorce is that the EU-Member States are far from united in their approach on divorce.

Substantive law and private international law are to a certain extent interrelated: if the substantive law supports a certain policy, this policy is often reflected in the choice of law rules as well.[5] This interrelationship is very well illustrated by divorce. If the aim of the internal law is not to preclude divorces (the principle of *favor divortii*), this will certainly influence the arrangement of the choice of law rules: these rules are very likely to favour the dissolution of the marriage as the outcome of the case. In contrast to this approach, the substantive divorce laws of some other Member States support a completely opposite policy, one that favours

---

[4] The proposed Art. 3a(1) states that 'the spouses may agree that a court or courts of a Member State are to have jurisdiction in a proceeding between them relating to divorce or legal separation provided that they have a substantial connection with that Member State by virtue of the fact that

(a) any of the grounds of jurisdiction listed in Article 3 applies, or
(b) it is the place of the spouses' last common habitual residence for a minimum period of 3 years, or
(c) one of the spouses is a national of that Member State or, in the case of the United Kingdom and Ireland, has his or her "domicile" in the territory of one of the latter Member States.'

This provision falls outside the scope of this study and will not be further dealt with, see for a more detailed discussion e.g. Lazic 2008, p. 80 ff.

[5] Cf., De Boer 2008a, p. 331 ff.

the preservation of the marriage (the principle of *favor matrimonii*). This policy implies that also in international cases a divorce will not easily be granted.[6]

Consequently, the values of the internal law may influence the outcome of cross-border cases and, hence, the policy to be propagated by the choice of law rules. With regard to the European unification of the choice of law on divorce one can already notice the tension in this respect. The profound differences in approach between the Member States constitute a serious obstacle to the establishment of unified choice of law rules.[7]

In order to properly value the choice of law rules of the Member States, a brief outline of their substantive divorce laws will be given. Subsequently, the different approaches of the Member States with regard to their choice of law on divorce will be set forth.

5.2.1 The Substantive Divorce Laws of the Member States

With the exception of Malta, all Member States provide for divorce in their national law. Nevertheless, large differences exist between these national systems in terms of both the grounds for divorce and the difficulty and length of time it takes to acquire a divorce.[8]

From the studies and questionnaires performed as part of the preparation of the Brussels II*ter*-Proposal, it is clear that the ground of irretrievable breakdown of the marriage prevails overall, yet also fault as ground for divorce still holds quite a prominent position.[9] However, none of the Member States provides for fault-based divorce as the sole ground for divorce.

The largest differences between the divorce laws of the Member States are not in the grounds for divorce, but in the conditions for divorce. Within the EU the two most extreme examples are, on the one hand, Ireland where divorce can only be obtained after a waiting period of 4 years and upon court approval of a number of cumulative conditions and, on the other hand, Sweden where there is no inquiry into the reasons for wanting a divorce and a waiting period of 6 months is only required in cases where there is no mutual consent between spouses and if they have any children younger than 16.

---

[6] See in general De Boer 1993; Brilmayer 1995, pp. 9–112.

[7] See also De Boer 2008a, p. 334 ff. See further *infra* Sect. 6.5 for a discussion on the methodological problems underlying the European unification of the choice of law rules on divorce.

[8] See for an overview of the substantive divorce laws of all Member States the European Judicial Network website: http://ec.europa.eu/civiljustice/divorce/divorce_gen_en.htm.

[9] See e.g. Council Document No. 8839/00 JUSTCIV 67, Inventory of delegations' replies to the questionnaire on the law applicable to divorce (Rome III), p. 3 ff; EPEC Study on divorce, p. 36 ff; and Annex 1 to the Impact Assessment on Divorce, pp. 33–34.

These differing conditions for divorce in the Member States have their roots in the achievement of different compromises between two competing poles: in all Member States tensions exist between conservative and liberal family values. Moreover, in the divorce process a balance between the state and the autonomy of the spouses needs to be found.[10] Because the substantive divorce laws have been liberalised to a different extent in the Member States, currently five historical grounds for obtaining a divorce are present in the European Union, which can broadly be categorised as follows:

- fault-based divorce (divorce as sanction);
- divorce based on the irretrievable breakdown of the marriage (divorce as remedy or failure);
- divorce on the ground of separation for a declared period of time;
- divorce by mutual consent (divorce as an autonomous decision by the spouses themselves); and
- divorce on demand (divorce as a right).[11]

Rather than comparing the details of the different autonomous grounds on divorce of the Member States, a comparison is drawn on whether the Member State in question holds comparatively liberal or rather restrictive grounds for divorce. The table below shows this classification of the divorce laws of the Member States.[12] The most liberal category of states, where divorce is 'on demand', does not require any divorce ground. The category of states with comparatively strict divorce grounds do not provide for divorce upon mutual consent grounds, whereas in the category of states with comparatively liberal divorce grounds the possibility to divorce upon mutual consent grounds exists.

[10] See Antokolskaia 2006, pp. 33–58.

[11] Ibid., p. 34.

[12] This table is a copy from Table 6.3 of the EPEC Study on divorce, p. 39, to which Bulgaria and Romania, the two Member States that have acceded to the EU after the publication of this study, have been added.

Classification of the substantive divorce laws of the Member States			
Divorce on demand	Comparatively liberal grounds for divorce	Comparatively strict grounds for divorce	Divorce is not permitted
Finland	Austria	Cyprus	Malta
Sweden	Belgium	Ireland	
	Bulgaria	Italy	
	Czech Republic	Poland	
	Estonia	Slovak Republic	
	France	Slovenia	
	Germany	Spain[13]	
	Greece		
	Hungary		
	Latvia		
	Lithuania		
	Luxembourg		
	the Netherlands[14]		
	Portugal		
	Romania		
	United Kingdom		

5.2.2 The Choice of Law Rules on Divorce of the Member States

The previous paragraph shows that there are significant differences between the substantive divorce laws of the Member States. Furthermore, the respective choice of law rules on divorce differs as well. According to the nature of the choice of law rules, the Member States can be broadly divided into two categories.[15]

In the first category, the States exclusively apply their own national law (*lex fori*) to international divorce proceedings. Seven Member States belong to this

[13] By the entry into force of the new Spanish divorce law (Law 15/2005 of 8 July 2005, Boletín Oficial del Estado, No. 163, de 09-07-2005, pp. 24458–24461) Spain would change from the category of states with comparatively strict divorce grounds to the category of states where divorce is on demand.

[14] It is to be noted that, although EPEC has placed the Netherlands in the category of states with comparatively liberal grounds for divorce, it would have been more appropriate to place the Netherlands in the category of states where divorce is on demand. As seen in Sect. 2.2.3, the Dutch ground for divorce of irretrievable breakdown of the marriage (Article 1:151 BW) is virtually automatically complied with.

[15] See the EPEC Study on divorce, pp. 42–43. See equally Commission Staff Working Document, Annex to the Green Paper on applicable law and jurisdiction in divorce matters, SEC(2005) 331, p. 7 ff; Rüberg 2005, p. 16 ff; Martiny 2006, 123 ff; and Oderkerk 2006, pp. 119–128.

category.[16] The desire to apply solely the *lex fori* can either originate from a very strict or a very lenient internal law approach towards divorce.[17]

In the second category, the Member States determine the applicable law on the basis of a (hierarchical) scale of connecting factors that seek to ensure the application of the law with which the spouses are most closely connected. The majority of the Member States belong to this category.[18] The connecting factors employed in the Member States vary, but in most cases they include criteria based on the nationality or habitual residence of (either of) the spouses. In some Member States the choice of law rules on divorce include the reference to the *lex fori* as the applicable law. The provisions that are based on the approach of the closest connection attempt to determine a 'community' between the spouses, such as their common place of residence, their common place of habitual residence or their common nationality. Generally both spouses are decisive and reference is made to the law, which has lastly governed the personal relations of the spouses.[19]

France is the only Member State that does not belong to either of these categories, since it applies a unilateral choice of law rule to divorce, which solely specifies under which conditions French law applies. According to Article 309 of the French Code Civil, French law applies if both spouses have French nationality or if both spouses have their domicile in France or if no other court but the French court is competent to rule on an application on divorce.[20]

The following table shows the broad classification of the choice of law rules on divorce of the Member States.

---

[16] I.e. Cyprus, Denmark, Finland, Ireland, Latvia, Sweden and the United Kingdom.

[17] E.g. the internal law approach of Ireland is based on the principle of *favor matrimonii*, whereas the internal law approach of Finland is based on the principle of *favor divortii*. Both Member States apply exclusively the *lex fori* to any divorce.

[18] Eighteen Member States belong to this category: Austria, Belgium, Bulgaria, Estonia, Germany, Greece, Hungary, Italy, Lithuania, Luxembourg, the Netherlands, Spain, the Czech Republic, Poland, Portugal, Romania, Slovakia and Slovenia.

[19] Cf., Rüberg 2005, p. 107.

[20] See on this provision of French law Carbonneau 1978, pp. 446–460. As of 1 July 2006 Article 310 has been renumbered to 309 Code Civil (Ordonnance No. 2005-759 du 4 juillet 2005).

Classification of the choice of law rules on divorce of the Member States				
Lex fori applied exclusively	First connecting factor based on the limited *professio iuris* of the spouses	First connecting factor based on nationality	First connecting factor based on residence/domicile	Unilateral choice of law approach
Cyprus Denmark Finland Ireland Latvia Sweden United Kingdom	Belgium the Netherlands	Austria Bulgaria Czech Republic Germany Greece Hungary Luxembourg Portugal Romania Italy Poland Slovakia Slovenia Spain	Estonia Lithuania	France

According to Ruberg the overview of the autonomous rules on divorce of the Member States (both the substantive rules and the choice of law rules) leads to two conclusions.[21] In the first place, neighbouring countries do not necessarily share the same substantive law approach on divorce, despite possible common cultural convictions. Secondly, the various choice of law approaches of the Member States even enhance the existing differences in their substantive law approaches, as the different choice of law approaches show that there seemingly is quite some discretion as to which legal system applies to the dissolution of a marriage.

These differences in both the substantive law and the choice of law approaches of the Member States and the resulting problems have inclined the European Commission to search for a solution: because of these differences, it may be of great relevance to the spouses in which country the divorce proceedings are initiated.[22] One of the solutions would, according to the Commission, be the

[21] Rüberg 2005, pp. 19–20: '[…] *zum einem, dass sich benachbarte Länder in Bezug auf ihre Rechtsordnung trotz ihrer gemeinsamen kulturellen Überzeugungen, ihrer daraus resultierenden gemeinsamen praktischen Bedürfnisse oder ihrer gemeinsamen Sprache in Scheidungsrecht nicht unbedingt einander anlehnen.* […] *Zum zweiten lassen die verschiedenen Kollisionsrechte erahnen, wie viel Willkür bestimmt, welche Rechtsordnung über die Scheidung oder gerichtliche Trennung entscheidet.* […] *Die Unterschiede im materiellen Recht werden damit durch das autonome Kollisionsrecht in Europa noch verstärkt*'.

[22] See for the problems resulting from the absence of common choice of law rules on divorce *supra* Sect. 5.1.

introduction of common choice of law rules based on a set of uniform connecting factors.[23] The Brussels II*ter*-Proposal gave shape to this solution.

5.3 The Objectives of the Brussels II*ter*-Proposal

The Brussels II*ter*-Proposal aims to attain the following five objectives:

- *Providing for a Clear and Comprehensive Legal Framework*

The overall objective of the Brussels II*ter*-Proposal is to provide a clear and comprehensive legal framework in matrimonial matters in the European Union and to ensure adequate solutions to the citizens in terms of legal certainty, predictability, flexibility and access to court.[24]

- *Strengthening Legal Certainty and Predictability*

The Explanatory Memorandum to the Brussels II*ter*-Proposal states:

> [T]he great differences between and complexity of the national conflict-of-law rules make it very difficult for international couples to predict which law will apply in matrimonial proceedings.[25]

Because of the differences between the substantive divorce laws of the Member States, the conditions for divorce and the consequences for the parties concerned can differ drastically, depending on which Member State's law is applicable. It may, moreover, also have significant implications for ancillary matters, such as the division of matrimonial property or maintenance obligations. Accordingly, the large differences between the national choice of law rules of the Member States lead to legal uncertainty, as spouses are virtually unable to predict the law applicable to their divorce.

The Commission holds that by introducing common choice of law rules, spouses are enabled to easily predict which law will apply to their divorce, which will in turn lead to more legal certainty: spouses know where they stand.[26]

---

[23] Green Paper on Divorce, pp. 6–7. The Commission introduces 8 policy options in the Green Paper ranging from leaving the situation unchanged (status quo) to a combination of the different solutions envisaged, see Green Paper on Divorce, pp. 6–11. The Brussels II*ter*-Proposal contains a combination of these policy options, as none of the individual policy options completely addresses the problems or fully achieves the policy objectives. By combining different aspects of the policy options, a higher degree of effectiveness could be achieved. See Impact Assessment on Divorce, p. 23.

[24] See Recital No. 5 of the Preamble to the Brussels II*ter*-Proposal and the Explanatory Memorandum, p. 3.

[25] Explanatory Memorandum to the Brussels II*ter*-Proposal, p. 3.

[26] Ibid., p. 3.

- *Increasing Flexibility and Party Autonomy*

The majority of the choice of law rules of the Member States foresees only one solution in a given situation, e.g. the application of the common national law of the spouses or of the *lex fori*. This may not always allow for sufficient flexibility.

In this regard, the Commission cites the example of a couple that may feel closely connected with a state where they have lived for a long time although they do not possess the nationality of that state.[27] On the other hand, in some cases spouses may live in another country than their country of origin for a number of years and still feel more closely connected to their country of origin. As a result, citizens are not always able to get divorced according to the law of a state with which they feel the closest connection. This may lead to results that do not correspond to the 'legitimate expectations' of the spouses, as they are unlikely to be aware that the conditions for divorce may change when they move to another Member State.[28]

The introduction of a limited degree of party autonomy in the Brussels II*ter*-Proposal could render the rules more flexible. Party autonomy in the field of divorce could be particularly useful in cases of divorce by mutual consent.

- *Ensuring Access to Court*

The Brussels II*ter*-Proposal equally seeks to improve access to court in divorce proceedings, mainly by introducing the possibility to choose the competent court in the latter proceedings. The possibility to choose the competent court in divorce cases will enhance access to court for spouses who are of different nationalities. The possibility of choice of court (Article 3a Brussels II*ter*-Proposal) applies regardless of whether the couple lives in one of the Member States or in a third State. The choice of court is, however, limited to the court or courts of a Member State with which the spouses have a substantial connection.

In addition, the Brussels II*ter*-Proposal specifically addresses the need to ensure access to court for spouses of different nationalities who live in a third State. The proposal introduces furthermore a uniform and exhaustive rule on residual jurisdiction in order to enhance legal certainty and ensure access to court in matrimonial matters for spouses who live in a third State but who would like to bring proceedings in a Member State with which they have a close connection (Article 7 Brussels II*ter*-Proposal).

- *Preventing a 'Rush to Court'*

From the beginning the Brussels II(*bis*)-Regulation has been criticised not only for including far too many jurisdiction grounds, but also for not ranking them in any hierarchy.[29] This is claimed to encourage forum shopping.

Under the Brussels II*bis*-Regulation the competent court which is seised firstly has exclusive jurisdiction according to the *lis pendens*-rule of Article 19(1). As a result,

---

[27] Green Paper on Divorce, p. 4.

[28] Impact Assessment on Divorce, pp. 5–6.

[29] See McEleavy 2004, pp. 618–620; and Boele-Woelki and González Beilfuss 2007, p. 33.

both spouses may rush to court in order to be the first to initiate the proceedings to ensure that the divorce is governed by a particular law so as to safeguard his or her interests. This gives an advantage to the economically stronger party, who can more easily afford in-depth legal advice regarding the choice of law rules and the substantive laws of the available fora, as well as the additional costs of a legal dispute abroad.

The unification of the choice of law rules on divorce will prevent a rush to court: calculations on where to start divorce proceedings are useless as regards the applicable law to divorce if the courts of all Member States are to apply the same law to the divorce. Irrespective of the Member State in which the divorce proceedings are initiated, the same law is applied.

Should the abovementioned objectives be attained on the Union level?[30] It is clear that both strengthening legal certainty and predictability and preventing a 'rush to court' can only be achieved by Union action. No Member State acting alone is able to attain these objectives. While the Member States acting alone could theoretically improve the objectives of increasing flexibility and party autonomy and ensuring access to court, also for these objectives the appropriate level of action is probably the Union one.[31] For example, if increasing flexibility by introducing limited party autonomy in the field of both jurisdiction and the choice of law on divorce is a European goal which the Member States can work towards, the Union objective cannot be fully achieved unless all Member States introduce the same options.

Therefore, the objectives set by the Commission in the Brussels II*ter*-Proposal can best be attained on the Union level.

5.3.1 *Exclusion of* Renvoi

One means to attain the objectives of the Brussels II*ter*-Proposal, mainly the objective of strengthening legal certainty and predictability,[32] is the exclusion of *renvoi*. Article 20d determines:

> The application of a law designated under this Regulation means the application of the rules of that law other than its rules of private international law.

The Brussels II*ter*-Proposal contains so-called *Sachnormverweisungen*, i.e. choice of law rules that refer solely to the substantive rules of the applicable law.[33] It is clear that there is no place for *renvoi* if the parties have chosen the law to be applied to their divorce. If they have made such a choice, it is clearly the intention

---

[30] As far as this question entails issues of subsidiarity and proportionality, see *supra* Sect. 4.4.4.

[31] Cf., Fiorini 2008, p. 185.

[32] See Explanatory Memorandum to the Brussels II*ter*-Proposal, p. 10.

[33] Article 20d of the Brussels II*ter*-Proposal thus precludes a so-called *Gesamtverweisung*, i.e. a choice of law rule that refers to a certain legal system including the choice of law rules of that law. Kropholler 2000, p. 393 points to the fact that the fundamental exclusion of *renvoi* is part of a particularly firmly-rooted tradition of the Hague Conventions, which has been taken up by other international instruments as well. See on *renvoi* in general: Sauveplanne 1990.

that the substantive law provisions of the chosen law be applicable; their choice accordingly excludes any possibility of *renvoi* to another law.[34]

With regard to the question whether *renvoi* should be allowed if the parties have not chosen the applicable law, it is clear that in cases in which the law of a Member State is designated as the applicable law the issue of *renvoi* does not arise. If the choice of law rules on divorce are unified within the European Union, all Member States apply the same choice of law rules, which means that every reference to the law of a Member State will automatically be accepted.[35]

However, with regard to cases in which the law of a third country is designated as the applicable law the exclusion of *renvoi* is not obvious. The issue of *renvoi* arises where the common choice of law rules refer an issue to the law of another country which, under its choice of law rules in turn refers the issue back to the law of the forum (*Rückverweisung*) or to the law of yet another country (*Weiterverweisung*). Kohler has questioned the exclusion of both these forms of *renvoi* in extra-European cases:

> Es geht um die Rückverweisung. Dass diese im Verhältnis zwischen Mitgliedstaaten ausgeschlossen ist, folgt aus der Vereinheitlichung der Verweisungsnormen. Art. 20d des Vorschlags schließt aber die Rück- und Weiterverweisung generell aus, also auch dann, wenn auf das Recht eines Drittstaates verwiesen wird. Dies sollte überdacht und eine Lösung angestrebt werden, nach der zumindest die Rückverweisung auf das Recht des Gerichtsstaates (eventuell auch eine Weiterverweisung auf das Recht eines anderen Mitgliedstaats) angenommen wird.[36]

According to this opinion, *renvoi* should, at least in cases of *Rückverweisung*, be accepted. Although the acceptance of a *Rückverweisung* is certainly tempting — it allows the competent court to apply its own law — it should be rejected from a methodological point of view.[37] The choice of law rules of the Brussels II*ter*-Proposal are based on the principle of the closest connection. These rules have been constructed in such a way that they refer — in the view of the European legislature — to the most closely connected law. From this perspective, accepting *renvoi* would be contrary to the principle of the closest connection.[38] Furthermore,

---

[34] Cf., Report on the Convention on the law applicable to contractual obligations (Giuliano-Lagarde Report), [1980] OJ C 282/1, at Article 15.

[35] Cf., with regard to the European choice of law on succession, Knot 2008, pp. 200–201.

[36] Kohler 2008a, pp. 1679–1680. See also generally Martiny 2007, p. 96; and Siehr 2008, pp. 90–91.

[37] Incidentally accepting *renvoi* would involve a strict European definition of the concept. Cf., Kropholler 2006, p. 178 stating that countries can take: '*eine verschiedene Haltung zu den einzelnen Renvoi-Fällen (Rückverweisung im engeren Sinne, Weiterverweisung, Zirkelverweisung etc.)*' See Knot 2008, p. 126 for an overview of the different positions taken with respect to *renvoi*.

[38] See also Report on the Convention on the law applicable to contractual obligations (Giuliano-Lagarde Report), [1980] OJ C 282/1, at Article 15: '*the exclusion of renvoi is justified in international conventions regarding conflict of laws. If the Convention attempts as far as possible to localize the legal situation and to determine the country with which it is most closely connected, the law specified by the conflicts rule in the Convention should not be allowed to question this determination of place*'. Cf., with regard to Dutch private international law, Ten Wolde 2009, p. 66.

Kropholler rightly points to the fact that the aim of the regulation is the development of a new, uniform choice of law, which refers directly to the applicable substantive law, and not the development of a '*Superkollisionsrecht*', which refers to the existing choice of law systems.[39] Finally, accepting *renvoi* could endanger decisional harmony between the Member States, unless the use of *renvoi* is strictly defined. Therefore, the uniform European choice of law system requires the exclusion of *renvoi*.[40]

In Section 5.8 below the question whether the Brussels II*ter*-Proposal actually succeeds in attaining the objectives at issue will be discussed on the basis of the following analysis of the scope of application and the content of the proposed choice of law rules.

5.4 The Scope of Application of the Proposed Choice of Law Rules

In the following, the scope of application of the Brussels II*ter*-Proposal is divided into three distinct aspects: its territorial scope of application, its substantive scope of application and, finally, its temporal scope of application.

5.4.1 Territorial Scope of Application

5.4.1.1 Universal Application

Although no special mention is made in the original Brussels II*ter*-Proposal, the proposed choice of law rules are to apply universally.[41] Consequently, the choice of law rules can designate the law of a Member State or the law of a third State.

[39] Kropholler 2000, pp. 393–394. See also Rüberg 2005, pp. 104–105.

[40] It is to be noted that the exclusion of *renvoi* has more substantial advantages: it has the merit of simplicity and it has favourable effects towards strengthening legal certainty and predictability. Moreover, allowing *renvoi* would only detract from the clarity and ease of use that the uniform choice of law on divorce aims to realise, as it implies a considerable burden on legal practitioners and courts.

[41] Athough the universal nature of the choice of law rules is expressly mentioned in the Explanatory Memorandum to the Brussels II*ter*-Proposal (p. 10), strangely enough the actual Proposal does not make any mention of it. Cf., Meeusen 2007a, p. 345. According to Jayme and Kohler the lack of an explicit mention of the universality of the choice of law rules can be attributed to the fact that it has apparently been generally accepted ('*Allgemeingut geworden*'). See Jayme and Kohler 2007, p. 494.

In the Council-draft of 12 January 2007 a provision has been inserted on the universal character of the choice of law rules. The latter provision stipulates that

> [T]he law designated by this Regulation shall be applied whether or not it is the law of a Member State.[42]

Choice of law rules with a universal scope of application have several advantages.[43]

The application of the same law to a particular legal relationship by the courts of the Member States is one of the ultimate aims of the European unification of private international law. This holds true not only for intra-European legal relationships, but also for those involving extra-European aspects. While Union measures taken under Article 81 TFEU cannot influence the choice of law rules applied by third States, they can bring the choice of law provisions of Member States into line, which would at least reduce the risk of diverging judgments given within the Union.

Secondly, universal choice of law rules have the advantage that the Union and its Member States make a uniform appearance *vis-à-vis* third States.[44] In all Member States of the European Union the same choice of law rules are applied to a certain case regardless of the nature of the case, i.e. whether it concerns the relation among Member States or between a Member State and a third State.

In the third place, the universal scope of application is preferable from a practical point of view: it would provide for clarity and ease of use of the choice of law rules, and would thereby enhance legal certainty.[45] Without universally applicable choice of law rules the practical use of the regulation would be undermined: limiting the scope of application to intra-European cases would result in further fragmentation of the choice of law rules. For if only intra-European cases are regulated, this would lead to 'double-track' choice of law rules: rules at a national level rules for cases with relation to third countries, and rules at a European level for intra-European cases. This does offer the possibility to establish a European system of private *interregional* law, which might allow for a closer cooperation between the Member States on the basis of mutual trust.[46] The European Union could thereby also promote and advance specific European objectives, such as the principle of mutual recognition and the creation of an area of freedom, security and justice.[47]

---

[42] See Council Document No. 5247/07 JUSTCIV 4 of 12 January 2007, p. 8.

[43] In general opposed to universally applicable European choice of law rules Ten Wolde 2004; and Calvo Caravaca 2006, pp. 38–40.

[44] See Basedow 2000, p. 702.

[45] Cf., Knot 2008, p. 178.

[46] Ibid., p. 179. See Ten Wolde 2004, pp. 504–506 for the advantages of a private interregional law system.

[47] Cf., Vonken 2006, p. 48. See further *infra* Sect. 8.4.2.1 on the question whether the character of the European Union requires an intra-European choice of law system.

However, Remien rightly stressed that it may be doubted whether such differentiation between intra- and extra-European cases is to be recommended, as there will most certainly be cases in which it is very hard to decide whether a certain situation concerns an intra- or an extra-European case.[48] Does the possession of common property of two French spouses in, e.g., Tunisia imply that the divorce should be considered as an extra-European case? And what about the divorce of an Indian couple, which has lived together in Slovenia for 5 years, the husband still resides there and the wife has already returned to India 3 years earlier? In the latter case the competence of the Slovenian court can be established according to the Brussels II*bis*-Regulation (Article 3(1)(a)(fifth indent)). Yet this case is only connected to one Member State: does this imply that it is an extra-European case?

Consequently, the establishment of universally applicable choice of law rules circumvents the need to make the intricate differentiation between intra- and extra-European relationships, as the same choice of law rules can be applied regardless of the nature of the case. The establishment of universally applicable choice of law rules on divorce is thus to be welcomed.

5.4.1.2 Denmark, Ireland and the United Kingdom

In Chapter 4, the respective positions of the United Kingdom, Ireland and Denmark with regard to judicial cooperation in civil matters pursuant to Title V of the Third Part of the Treaty on the Functioning of the European Union have been set forth.[49]

Denmark does not in principle participate at all in the European unification of matters of private international law. Therefore, if the Brussels II*ter*-Regulation enters into force, Denmark will not be bound by it. The only way Denmark can be bound to the common choice of law rules is by means of a convention to this end between Denmark and the other EU-Member States. It is, however, questionable if such a convention will be drawn up considering the fact that there is no convention similar to the Brussels II*bis*-Regulation yet. This situation may change if Denmark changes its position with respect to the judicial cooperation in civil matters in the EU.[50]

In accordance with Article 3 of the Protocol on the position of the United Kingdom and Ireland, these Member States have the opportunity to opt-into the adoption and application of any proposed measure under Title V TFEU. With regard to the proposed Brussels II*ter*-Regulation the United Kingdom and Ireland

---

48 Remien 2001, p. 75. Stone argues that an '*entirely perverse complexity*' would arise from any attempt to distinguish between intra- and extra-European disputes; see Stone 2004, p. 213. See also Struycken 2000, p. 739; Bergé 2003, p. 231; Kohler 2003, p. 411; Borrás 2005, p. 525; and Vonken 2006, p. 49.

49 See *supra* Sect. 4.6.

50 Cf., *supra* Sect. 4.6.2.

had until 26 October 2006 to opt-in, which they have each decided not to do.[51] The UK's opposition is based on the assumption that the proposed imposition of foreign law would carry with it fundamental changes in the form of increased costs, delays and difficulties in settling cases.[52] Such changes are, to the opinion of the House of Lords, not in conformity with the principles of subsidiarity and proportionality and also exceed the legal basis by the Treaty.[53] The Brussels II*ter*-Regulation will therefore not apply in the United Kingdom and Ireland.

5.4.2 *Substantive Scope of Application*

The Brussels II*ter*-Proposal applies to divorce and to legal separation. It expressly excludes marriage annulment from its scope of application (Section 5.4.2.1). The question is whether the Brussels II*ter*-Proposal determines the applicable law to the dissolution of same-sex marriages and to the termination of registered partnerships (Sections 5.4.2.2 and 5.4.2.3, respectively).

5.4.2.1 Marriage Annulment

The Brussels II*ter*-Proposal expressly states in its Preamble that the proposed choice of law rules apply only to divorce and legal separation. These rules do not extend to marriage annulment, as this issue is considered to be too closely linked to the conditions for the validity of the marriage.[54] According to the Commission annulment of a marriage is to be regarded as

> a reaction to defects in the contracting of a marriage. Member States' annulment arrangements primarily pursue public-order objectives (e.g. preventing bigamy). The validity of the marriage is therefore better determined according to the conditions of the law which provided for the prerequisites of entering into the marriage, or by the national law of the person concerned.[55]

The issue of marriage annulment is, furthermore, considered inappropriate for party autonomy.[56] Hence, the choice of law issues concerning marriage annulment are left to the national laws of the Member States.

---

[51] See Hodson 2007, pp. 32–34.

[52] See www.publications.parliament.uk/pa/ld200506/ldselect/ldeucom/272/27202.htm.

[53] House of Lords Rome III Report, pp. 10–11. See further *infra* Sect. 6.3.2.

[54] See recital No. 6 of the Preamble to the Brussels II*ter*-Proposal. See equally Explanatory Memorandum to the Brussels II*ter*-Proposal, pp. 7, 9.

[55] Impact Assessment on Divorce, p. 25.

[56] Cf., the Impact Assessment on Divorce, p. 25: '*issues related to the validity of the marriage do not belong to the autonomy of the spouses, since they are related to the protection of the public interest*'.

5.4.2.2 Dissolution of Same-Sex Marriages?

A pressing question concerns the status of same-sex marriages: does the dissolution of these marriages fall within the scope of the proposed choice of law rules of the Brussels II*ter*-Regulation? This is a highly controversial issue.[57]

Recital No. 5 of the Preamble of the Brussels II*ter*-Proposal stipulates that

> [t]his Regulation should provide a clear and *comprehensive* legal framework in matrimonial matters in the European Union [...]. [emphasis added]

From this wording one could conclude that the proposed rules apply to *all* international divorce cases within the European Union, irrespective of the nature of the marriage at hand.

However, witness the following statement in a press release of the Council, the issue has probably been subject of debate:

> the proposal does not determine the law applicable to a marriage. The definition of marriage and the conditions of the validity of a marriage are matters of substantive law and are therefore left to national law. Consequently, the court of a Member State which has jurisdiction as regards divorce or legal separation may assess the existence of a marriage according to its own law.[58]

On the one hand, it would be odd if the Brussels II*ter*-Proposal obliged the authorities of a Member State to dissolve a marriage, if it does not recognise the type of marriage in question. On the other hand, the exclusion of a certain type of marriage in advance seems to contradict the aim of the Brussels II*ter*-Proposal to provide for a comprehensive legal framework in matrimonial matters.

In the Council draft on the Brussels II*ter*-Proposal of 23 May 2008 this discussion has been put into the following provision:

> Nothing in this Regulation shall oblige the courts of a Member State whose law does not provide for divorce or does not recognise the marriage in question for the purposes of divorce proceedings to pronounce a divorce by virtue of the application of this Regulation.[59]

This provision leaves the question whether the Brussels II*ter*-Proposal equally covers the dissolution of same-sex marriages to the discretion of each individual Member State, which may apply the proposed choice of law rules to the dissolution of any type of marriage it recognises. Considering the position of many Member States as regards the institution of same-sex marriage, it is likely that the majority of the Member States will not apply the choice of law rules of the

---

[57] Cf., the question whether the dissolution of same-sex marriage currently falls within the scope of the Brussels II*bis*-Regulation. This issue is highly disputed, see the national reports of the Member States in: Boele-Woelki and González Beilfuss 2007. See also Gaudemet-Tallon 2007, p. 156 ff.

[58] See Press Release No. 8364/07 (Presse 77) of the 2794th Council Meeting of Justice and Home Affairs held in Luxembourg 19–20 April 2007, p. 11.

[59] Council Document No. 9712/08 JUSTCIV 106 of 23 May 2008, Article 20e-1, p. 16.

Brussels II*ter*-Proposal to the dissolution of the latter type of marriage: most Member States do not recognise the same-sex marriage at all. As far as the same-sex marriage is recognised, it is generally not recognised as a marriage but as a registered partnership.[60]

The susceptibility of the issue of same-sex marriages makes it hardly surprising that the Brussels II*ter*-Proposal does not automatically apply to the dissolution of same-sex marriages. However, the solution to leave the issue to the discretion of the Member States does not seem to be the most suitable one.[61] It might have been better to follow a clear approach: either to not sear one's wings and to leave the whole subject matter aside or to reconcile oneself to reality — in which same-sex marriages simply exist — by autonomously defining the concept of marriage and to determine that the choice of law rules of the Brussels II*ter*-Proposal apply to the dissolution of *any* marriage as defined by the Proposal.

It is most unfortunate that the Brussels II*ter*-Proposal fails to provide for a clear and concise regulation as regards the dissolution of same-sex marriages. The choice of law rules of the Brussels II*ter*-Proposal is therefore, not very conducive to legal certainty for same-sex spouses.[62]

5.4.2.3 Termination of Registered Partnerships?

Does the unified choice of law rules of the Brussels II*ter*-Proposal equally extend to the termination of registered partnerships? The Brussels II*ter*-Proposal is limited to the dissolution of marriages. Therefore, the proposed choice of law rules cannot be considered to include other similar formal relationships, such as registered partnerships, which are currently recognised in many European countries.[63]

Member States are of course free to decide to apply by analogy the common choice of law rules on divorce to the termination of registered partnerships. Yet not all national concepts of registered partnership might be suitable for the application *per analogiam* of the unified choice of law rules on divorce, as in some Member States the concept of registered partnership verges more on a contractual agreement between the partners than on a marriage.

---

[60] See for the analysis of the recognition of the Dutch same-sex marriage in a number of EU-Member States: Boele-Woelki et al. 2007, p. 190.

[61] See also Heinze 2008, p. 113 ff, spec. pp. 114–115 as regards the issue of the preliminary question.

[62] It must be noted that the Brussels II*ter*-Proposal does introduce a *forum necessitatis* for cases in which the courts that have jurisdiction are situated in Member States whose law does not recognise the marriage in question for the purposes of pronouncing divorce. Same-sex spouses may apply for divorce in another Member State: either the Member State of the nationality of either spouse or the Member State of the *locus celebrationis*. See Article 7a of the Brussels II*ter*-Proposal, introduced in Council Document No. 13445/07 JUSTCIV 250 of 3 October 2007, p. 6.

[63] See Curry-Sumner 2005, p. 428 and Mostermans 2006, p. 10, both concluding this with regard to the current Brussels II*bis*-Regulation. The Brussels II*ter*-Proposal does not bring any changes in this respect.

5.4.3 Temporal Scope of Application

The Brussels II*ter*-Proposal does not contain any explicit transitional provision with regard to the choice of law on divorce. In the absence of a specific transitional provision, the general provision of Article 64(1) of the Brussels II*bis*-Regulation will most probably apply, which stipulates:

> [T]he provisions of this Regulation shall apply only to legal proceedings instituted, to documents formally drawn up or registered as authentic instruments and to agreements concluded between the parties after its date of application in accordance with Article 72.

The temporal scope of application implies that the national choice of law rules on divorce of the Member States will continue to apply until the Brussels II*ter*-Regulation has entered into force. The common European choice of law rules on divorce will only apply to divorce proceedings that have been commenced after the entry into force of the Brussels II*ter*-Regulation.

5.5 The Proposed Choice of Law on Divorce

The proposed choice of law on divorce firstly offers the parties a limited opportunity to choose the law which is applicable to their divorce. In the absence of a choice by the parties, the applicable law is determined on the basis of a cascade rule.

In the following, the proposed choice of law rules will be discussed taking into consideration both the original Brussels II*ter*-Proposal and the proposed amendments that have subsequently been made by both the European Parliament and several Presidencies of the European Council.[64] The legislative procedure requires the Commission to submit the proposal to the Council, which in turn is obliged to seek the opinion of the European Parliament. The ultimate decision on the proposal is made by the Council and, as the Brussels II*ter*-Proposal concerns a measure in the field of international family law, a unanimous Council decision is required.[65]

5.5.1 The Spouses' Choice as to the Applicable Law

As a principal rule the Brussels II*ter*-Proposal introduces the possibility for the spouses to choose the law applicable to their divorce in Article 20a. This

---

[64] The last Council-draft on the Brussels II*ter*-Proposal of 23 May 2008 and the Legislative Resolution of the European Parliament have both been included as Appendices to this book. The earlier Council-drafts and other Council documents on the Brussels II*ter*-Proposal are available at http://register.consilium.europa.eu.

[65] Cf., *supra* Sect. 4.4.5.

possibility is part of a general trend towards liberalisation in private international law which more and more frequently recognises that it is the individual, and not the state, who can best weigh the relevant choice of law interests.[66] In European private international law party autonomy is becoming a fundamental principle.[67]

Currently only a few Member States allow the spouses to choose the law applicable to their divorce. This possibility exists at the moment in Belgium,[68] Germany,[69] and the Netherlands.[70] Consequently, for many Member States the introduction of the *professio iuris* on divorce would constitute a true novelty.

Consensus exists between the Member States as regards the possibility in itself to choose the law applicable to divorce.[71] However, there has been some discussion on the alternatives out of which the parties can choose and the formal requirements surrounding the *professio iuris*.

The possibility to choose the law applicable to divorce is provided for in Article 20a(1) of the Brussels II*ter*-Proposal:

> 1. The spouses may agree to designate the law applicable to divorce and legal separation. The spouses may agree to designate one of the following laws:
>   a. the law of the State of the last common habitual residence of the spouses insofar as one of them still resides there.
>   b. the law of the State of the nationality of either spouse, or, in the case of United Kingdom and Ireland, the "domicile" of either spouse.
>   c. the law of the State where the spouses have resided for at least 5 years;
>   d. the law of the Member State in which the application is lodged.

One of the objectives of the Brussels II*ter*-Proposal is to increase flexibility. Article 20a puts this objective into effect, as it allows the parties to choose the law applicable to their divorce. But in order to ensure the application of a law with which the spouses have a close connection and to avoid the application of 'exotic' laws, the choice is limited.[72] The alternatives out of which the spouses can choose have been subject of amendment in both the Council drafts and the resolution of the European Parliament.

---

66 See Hohloch 2007, p. 263; Basedow 2008, p. 14 ff.

67 See *inter alia* Martiny 2007, pp. 90–91; Hohloch 2007, p. 262; Pertegás 2007, p. 329 ff; and Rühl 2008, p. 209.

68 Article 55(2) of the General Private International Law Act of 16 July 2004. The parties can choose either their common national law or the *lex fori*.

69 Article 14(3) EGBGB.

70 Article 1(2, second sentence) and (4) CLAD. See for the rationale behind the *professio iuris* on divorce in Dutch law *supra* Sect. 2.3.

71 See Press Release No. 8364/07 (Presse 77) of the 2794th meeting of the Council on Justice and Home Affairs, held in Luxembourg 19–20 April 2007, p. 8. See equally Boele-Woelki 2008a, p. 261; Boele-Woelki 2008b, p. 784; and Jänterä-Jareborg 2008, p. 337.

72 See Explanatory Memorandum to the Brussels II*ter*-Proposal, p. 9. See equally Green Paper on Divorce, p. 7.

The third possibility — the law of the State where the spouses have resided for at least 5 years — met with resistance by some Member States and its necessity was questioned. In the Council draft of 9 March 2007 the option to choose for the law of the State where the spouses have resided for at least 5 years had made its exit.[73] By contrast, the European Parliament proposed to maintain this possibility, but to amend it in such a way as to allow spouses the opportunity to choose the law of the state where they have resided for at least 3 years.[74] The European Parliament thereby proposed to bring in line all the time criteria posed by the Brussels II*ter*-Proposal to 3 years.[75]

The Council has proposed the introduction of another possibility. Already in the first draft of January 2007, the Council added the possibility to choose the law of the current habitual residence of the spouses.[76] This possibility seems a good extension, as it certainly is a law with which the spouses have a close connection.

The European Parliament has proposed the insertion of a fifth alternative out of which the spouses can choose: the law of the State in which the marriage took place (the *lex loci celebrationis*).[77] According to the rapporteur it 'makes sense' to allow the spouses the possibility to choose the law of the State in which the marriage took place.[78] Moreover, in the justification to the Report of the European Parliament it is stated that

> [I]t seems rational that his criterion should be included with the others for the purpose of choosing the applicable law.[79]

Yet why would the inclusion of the possibility to choose for the *lex loci celebrationis* be 'rational' or 'make sense'? The close connection between the marriage and the *locus celebrationis* is not obvious.[80] According to the European Parliament the choice by the parties of a country to celebrate their marriage should be reasonably presumed as implying possible acceptance of the law of that country

---

[73] See Council Document No. 7144/07 JUSTCIV 47 of 9 March 2007 and Council Document No. 9714/07 JUSTCIV 106 of 23 May 2008.

[74] See the Legislative Resolution of the European Parliament of 21 October 2008, A6-0361/2008, Amendment 21.

[75] The Brussels II*ter*-Proposal also contains time criteria in Articles 3a(1)(b) and 7(a). Both these time criteria have been set to 3 years.

[76] See Council Document No. 5247/07 JUSTCIV 4 of 12 January 2007, p. 5. The addition of this possibility has been equally proposed by the European Parliament: Legislative Resolution of the European Parliament of 21 October 2008, A6-0361/2008, Amendment 18 and the Explanatory Statement to the Report of the European Parliament of 19 September 2008, A6-0361/2008, p. 19.

[77] See Legislative Resolution of the European Parliament of 21 October 2008, A6-0361/2008, Amendments 22 and 23.

[78] Explanatory Statement to the Report of the European Parliament of 19 September 2008, A6-0361/2008, p. 19.

[79] See the justification to Amendments 22 and 23 of the Report of the European Parliament of 19 September 2008, A6-0361/2008, p. 13.

[80] The connection that the *locus celebrationis* reflects depends on the criteria the *lex loci celebrationis* attaches to the entry into a marriage.

as well.[81] However, given the existing wedding tourism — couples marrying at an exotic location with which they do not have any connection, such as Las Vegas, Hawaii or the Seychelles — the *locus celebrationis* cannot be considered as automatically implying a close connection. Furthermore, the assumption made by the European Parliament that the choice by the parties of a country to celebrate their marriage should be reasonably presumed as implying possible acceptance of the law of that country can be strongly opposed. This view can — to a large extent — be subscribed to with regard to the matrimonial law, yet not with regard to the divorce law.

5.5.2 Formal Requirements of the Professio Iuris

For a *professio iuris* to be valid, it must comply with certain formalities. The *professio iuris* of Article 20a of the Brussels II*ter*-Proposal is bound to some specific formal requirements. Article 20a(2) stipulates with regard to these formal requirements:

> 2. An agreement designating the applicable law shall be expressed in writing and be signed by both spouses at the latest at the time the court is seised.

Pursuant to Article 20a(2) two formal requirements must be met. The first one relates to the form of the *professio iuris*: it has to be determined by a written agreement and signed by both spouses. The second formal requirement concerns the time of the conclusion of the agreement: it needs to be made at the time the court is seised at the latest. In the following both these formal requirements will be discussed.

5.5.2.1 Form of the Agreement on the *Professio Iuris*

Article 20a(2) of the Brussels II*ter*-Proposal contains two requirements on the form of the *professio iuris*: it should be determined by a written agreement and signed by both spouses. These requirements make clear that the *professio iuris* on divorce can only be realised by a joint choice of the spouses. A unilateral choice by one of the spouses cannot meet these requirements and is therefore not valid.

This formal requirement shows that the parties who wish to initiate divorce proceedings on the basis of mutual consent will benefit the most from the possibility to choose the applicable law.[82]

---

[81] See the justification to Amendment 23 of the Report of the European Parliament of 19 September 2008, A6-0361/2008, p. 13.

[82] See also Lazic 2008, p. 91; Calvo Caravaca and Carrascosa González 2009, p. 52.

There has been quite some debate on this formal requirement in the Council.[83] Apparently, some Member States could not agree with the requirements on the form of the agreement on the *professio iuris*.[84] Consequently, several proposals for additional formal requirements were passed in review.

The last Council draft added firstly the additional requirement that the agreement must also be dated by both spouses.[85] Moreover, it equally poses another formal requirement in addition to Article 20a(2) Brussels II*ter*-Proposal:

> [...] If the law of the Member State where both spouses have their habitual residence at the time the agreement is concluded provides for additional formal requirements, those requirements have to be satisfied. If the spouses are habitually resident in different Member States and the laws of those states provide for different formal requirements, the agreement is formally valid if it satisfies the requirements of either of those laws.[86]

Finally, the Council added the following sentence to the provision as regard the form of the agreement:

> Any communication by electronic means which provides a durable record of the agreement shall be equivalent to 'writing'.[87]

With regard to a *professio iuris* made in a marriage contract, the European Parliament has proposed in its resolution to supplement Article 20a(2) with the following:

> If the agreement forms part of a marriage contract, the formal requirements of that contract must be met.[88]

All in all, one can conclude that the Council and the European Parliament proposed to sharpen up the formal requirements of Article 20a of the Brussels II*ter*-Proposal.

---

[83] See *inter alia* Paulino Pereira 2007, p. 392; De Boer 2008a, pp. 329–331.

[84] As the comments of the delegations of the Member States on the Brussels II*ter*-Proposal as part of the negotiations in the Council are not available, the reasons of the opposition of the Member States in this respect are obscured.

[85] See Council Document No. 9712/08 JUSTCIV 106 of 23 May 2008, Article 20a(3), p. 13: 'Such agreement [i.e. agreement designating the applicable law; NAB] shall be expressed in writing, dated and signed by both spouses'.

[86] See Council Document No. 9712/08 JUSTCIV 106 of 23 May 2008, p. 13. The resolution of the European Parliament contains more or less the same amendments, see the Legislative Resolution of the European Parliament of 21 October 2008, A6-0361/2008, Amendment 24.

[87] See Council Document No. 9712/08 JUSTCIV 106 of 23 May 2008, p. 13. See for similar provisions *inter alia*: Article 23(2) of the Brussels I-Regulation and Article 4(2) of the Maintenance Regulation.

[88] Legislative Resolution of the European Parliament of 21 October 2008, A6-0361/2008, Amendment 24.

5.5.2.2 Implied Choice of The Spouses as to the Applicable Law?

Pursuant to the requirement of Article 20a(2) as regards the form of the agreement on the *professio iuris* on divorce, Article 20a of the Brussels II*ter*-Proposal seems to exclude an implied *professio iuris*. Such choice as to the applicable law is, on the face of it, not valid considering the requirements that the agreement must be expressed 'in writing and signed by both spouses'.

But what about a covenant on divorce regulating the divorce and its consequences such as parental responsibility and matrimonial property that has been fully geared to a specific legal system, yet without any specific consideration as to the applicable law to divorce? The question that presents itself is whether the spouses have intended an implied choice for the application of the given law to divorce by fully gearing their covenant on divorce to the specific legal system. Such a covenant does comply with the formal requirement of Article 20a(2), as it is an agreement that has been expressed in writing and signed by both spouses.

However, as a *professio iuris* presumes that the parties have been aware of the possibility of the option to choose the law applicable to divorce, the assumption of such a choice in cases in which parties did not expressly intend it, does not seem very sensible. In addition, it is not in the least certain that the parties have been aware of the international character of their divorce.[89]

5.5.2.3 Time of Choice

With regard to the time factor, Article 20a of the Brussels II*ter*-Proposal allows the spouses to choose the applicable law at any time before the court is seised. In order to clarify this matter, the Council proposed two additions to Article 20a:

1. Without prejudice to paragraph 4 an agreement designating the applicable law may be concluded and modified at any time, but at the latest at the time the court is seised.
2. [...]
3. If the law of the forum so provides, the spouses may also designate the applicable law before the court in the course of the proceedings. In such a case, it is sufficient that such designation is recorded in court in accordance with the law of the forum.[90]

A *professio iuris* can thus be agreed upon either before the divorce proceedings have commenced or even during the proceedings, if the law of the forum so provides. The proposal of the Council concerning the extension of the time to choose the applicable law in the course of the proceedings can be endorsed, as there does not seem to be any reason why a *professio iuris* should not be permitted after the court has been seised.[91] The rationale of allowing the parties to choose the applicable law is to increase flexibility; this objective is attained even more by

---

[89] Cf., the objections raised against the assumption of an implied choice as to the applicable law to divorce according to Dutch choice of law, *supra* Sect. 2.3.4.2.

[90] Council Document No. 9712/08 JUSTCIV 106 of 23 May 2008, pp. 13–14.

[91] See equally Ibili 2006, p. 744.

extending the time-limit within which the agreement must be concluded. Moreover, the extension of the time-limit would equally be in the interest of the judiciary, as a *professio iuris* enables the competent court to simply apply the chosen law. Any determination of the applicable law on the basis of Article 20b of the Brussels II*ter*-Proposal can then be omitted.

The dependence on the law of the forum for the validity of a *professio iuris* during the divorce proceedings cannot be considered as a factor that contributes to the predictability and legal certainty of the regulation. It is not entirely clear why the Council has chosen for this solution.[92]

Pursuant to Article 20a(2) of the Brussels II*ter*-Proposal the parties can already determine in a marriage contract the applicable law to their possible divorce by means of a *professio iuris*. Even before the marriage takes place the parties can choose the applicable law. De Boer has posed the following questions that arise in this respect:

> [H]ow can the parties assess the consequences of an agreement that must be carried out, if at all, in a distant future they do not want to contemplate as yet, under circumstances they cannot possibly foresee? Can one of the spouses later opt out of the agreement without the cooperation of the other spouse? Which law governs the issues of consent or the principle of *rebus sic stantibus* when raised during the divorce proceedings?[93]

Such questions are certainly not easy to answer. Nevertheless, allowing a *professio iuris* on divorce in a marriage contract does compel to answer these questions.

Furthermore, it is questionable whether parties can already enter a *professio iuris* on divorce in their marriage contract in case there is not, or not yet, question of an international marriage.[94] In other words, would it be possible for two Italians who currently live in Italy and do not intend to move abroad in any near future to enter a *professio iuris* on divorce in their marriage contract? Article 20a(2) does not shed light on this issue.[95] An issue that is closely linked hereto is whether Article 20a permits (future) spouses to choose the law of an intended habitual residence. The current wording of Article 20a does not seem to permit such a choice.

5.5.2.4 The *Professio Iuris* as an Accurate Reflection of the Intention of the Parties

The choice of the applicable law to divorce can be a delicate issue: the parties should be well aware of the consequences of their choice. This is equally a point of

---

92 Most probably the introduction of the possibility for the spouses to choose the applicable law to divorce during the divorce proceedings met with resistance of the Member States. However, the impossibility to examine the comments of the delegations of the Member States on the Brussels II*ter*-Proposal as part of the negotiations in the Council obscures the true motives.

93 De Boer 2008a, pp. 330–331.

94 See for the definition of an international marriage *supra* Sect. 2.1.

95 It should be noted that there is, incidentally, not much to choose for the parties in such a case: they can only choose their national law as the applicable law to their divorce pursuant to Article 20a(1) of the Brussels II*ter*-Proposal.

concern to the European Parliament, whose resolution contains the following statement:

> It must be ensured that the choice made by the parties is an enlightened one, i.e. that both spouses are duly informed of the practical implications of their choice. In this regard, consideration needs to be given to the best way of ensuring that comprehensive, reliable information is made available [...] before the act is signed. Access to information must also be provided, irrespective of each spouse's financial situation. It must be ensured that both spouses receive comprehensive, accurate information concerning the implications of their choice of jurisdiction and the law applicable to divorce, especially since the Member States' laws differ considerably in a number of respects.[96]

The existing differences in the substantive laws of the Member States as regards the grounds and conditions for divorce and the consequences attached to divorce concerning maintenance obligations, parental responsibility and matrimonial property make it impossible for the parties to gain a view of the opportunities and implications. The situation is far too complex to assume that the parties will be able to know their way about. Therefore, the requirement to provide information on the (practical) implications of the *professio iuris* to both spouses is to be welcomed.[97]

However, some critical remarks in this respect are also called for. In the first place the question should be asked to what extent the choice of law on divorce should take the possible implications for ancillary matters into account. It is not obvious that the choice of law rules on divorce should do so.

Secondly, it must be stressed that spouses do have their own responsibility as regards their choice of the applicable law to divorce. If their choice no longer reflects their intentions, the spouses are free to make a new *professio iuris*. The Council draft determines in this regard in Article 20a(2) that an agreement designating the applicable law may be concluded and modified at any time.

A situation which must be distinguished in this respect is the one in which the chosen substantive law has been amended. In such a situation the spouses should be protected. Witness the following consideration of its Explanatory Statement, the European Parliament holds similar concerns in this respect:

> [...] since laws can and do change, it may be that an agreement designating the applicable law which was signed at a given moment no longer meets the legitimate expectations of the parties at the time at which it should deploy its effects, since the legislation of the Member State in question has in the meantime been amended.[98]

Such situations may arise because of the time factor of Article 20a(2): quite some time may have lapsed between the agreement and the divorce. In the meantime the chosen law can be amended. A second consequence of the time

---

[96] Explanatory Statement to the Report of the European Parliament of 19 September 2008, A6-0361/2008, p. 19.

[97] See equally Kohler 2008b, p. 195.

[98] See equally Explanatory Statement to the Report of the European Parliament of 19 September 2008, A6-0361/2008, p. 19.

factor as foreseen by Article 20a(2) of the Brussels II*ter*-Proposal is that it may lead to the application of a certain legal system with which the spouses had a close connection at the time of the agreement of the *professio iuris*, but with which no close connection exists at the time of the divorce.[99]

The formal requirements of Article 20a(2) are meant to ensure that the parties are aware of the consequences of their choice.[100] However, it is questionable whether the Brussels II*ter*-Proposal actually succeeds in this respect, as many questions remain unanswered. Therefore, more safeguards might need to be introduced to ensure that the *professio iuris* accurately reflects the intention of the parties; e.g. the court may be obliged to inform whether the parties still agree on their choice.

5.5.3 The Applicable Law in the Absence of a Choice by the Parties

The Brussels II*ter*-Proposal puts the possibility to choose the law applicable to divorce first. Consequently, only in the absence of a *professio iuris* in accordance with Article 20a, the law which is applicable is determined pursuant to Article 20b of the Brussels II*ter*-Proposal. Divorce will be governed by the law of the country with which the spouses are deemed to be most closely connected.[101] Article 20b stipulates:

> In the absence of choice pursuant to Article 20a, divorce and legal separation shall be subject to the law of the State:
> a. where the spouses have their common habitual residence, or failing that,
> b. where the spouse had their last common habitual residence insofar as one of them still resides there, or failing that,
> c. of which both spouses are nationals, or, in the case of United Kingdom and Ireland, both have their "domicile", or failing that,
> d. where the application is lodged.

In the absence of a *professio iuris*, the applicable law to divorce is determined on the basis of a hierarchical scale of connecting factors. Unlike the general jurisdictional connecting factors contained in Article 3(1) of the Brussels II*bis*-Regulation that are alternative, the connecting factors of Article 20b of the Brussels II*ter*-Proposal are hierarchic, meaning that the latter can be applied only in the absence of the prior.

Article 20b Brussels II*ter*-Proposal refers in the first place to the law of the country of the common habitual residence of the spouses, or failing that, to the law

---

99 See equally Beyer 2007, p. 23.

100 Explanatory Memorandum to the Brussels II*ter*-Proposal, p. 9.

101 See Explanatory Memorandum to the Brussels II*ter*-Proposal, p. 9; see also Recital 10b of the Preamble to Council draft of the Brussels II*ter*-Proposal of 23 May 2008.

of the country of their last common habitual residence insofar as one of them still resides there. In the absence of both of these connecting factors, the law of the common nationality of the spouses will apply. If the spouses also do not have a common nationality either, the law of the forum (*lex fori*) is designated. In the following these connecting factors will be discussed separately.

5.5.3.1 Habitual Residence

Habitual residence has gained a prominent position as connecting factor in the Brussels II*ter*-Proposal. Article 20b refers firstly to the law of the country of the common habitual residence of the spouses, or failing that, to the law of the country of their last common habitual residence insofar as one of them still resides there.

The (last) place of common habitual residence of the spouses is considered as an appropriate connecting factor on the European level: it corresponds with the EU policy striving for an integration of persons that live outside their home countries and it forms an appropriate response to the needs of a mobile Europe.[102] Moreover, habitual residence does not — as opposed to nationality — depend on national definitions. Consequently, the use of habitual residence as connection factor is of more avail to the establishment of a common European choice of law.[103] Furthermore, the reference to the law of the habitual residence of the spouses generally leads to the application of the law with which they have a close connection; with this law they are to a certain extent familiar and its application generally corresponds to their expectations. Finally, the petition for divorce will often be filed in the State of the habitual residence of the spouses, which permits the competent court to apply its own substantive law.[104] The use of habitual residence as a connecting factor thus synchronises jurisdiction and applicable law.[105]

The European Council has added the limitation to the possibility to connect to the last common place of habitual residence of Article 20b(b) that such connection can only take place 'provided that that period did not end more than 1 year before the court was seised'.[106] This limitation seems a valuable addition to Article

---

[102] See Dethloff 2004, p. 563; Rüberg 2005, p. 157: '*In einem immer mehr zusammenwachsenden Europa, in dem die Integration der Bürger großgeschrieben wird und in dem das Ziel eine fortschreitende Angleichung der Rechtsordnungen ist, wird die Anknüpfung an das Recht des gewöhnlichen Aufenthaltsortes den Interessen der Parteien am besten gerecht*'. See equally Martiny 2007, pp. 88–89; Baetge 2008, p. 82; Calvo Caravaca and Carrascosa González 2009, p. 59.

[103] See equally Baetge 2008, p. 88.

[104] Cf., Bonomi 2007, pp. 780–781. The Explanatory Memorandum to the Brussels II*ter*-Proposal, p. 10 equally mentions this circumstance.

[105] This does not only hold for the divorce, but also for other areas that are connected to divorce. E.g. habitual residence is equally the main connecting factor for maintenance obligations, see Article 3 of the Maintenance Regulation (jurisdiction) and Article 3 of the Hague Protocol on the Law Applicable to Maintenance Obligations (the choice of law).

[106] Council Document No. 9712/08 JUSTCIV 106 of 23 May 2008, p. 14.

20b(b), as it ensures that the last common habitual residence still reflects a close connection, which is the foundation of the Brussels II*ter*-Proposal. Suppose a Polish couple who has resided in Lithuania for several years. However, the husband cannot adjust to the Lithuanian way of living and decides to move back to Poland. The wife remains in Lithuania. Consequently, if she files for divorce 3 years after her husband has returned to Poland, it can hardly be said that Lithuanian law provides for a 'substantial' connection with the divorce in question, even though it is their last common habitual residence. Therefore, the limitation introduced by the Council will definitely limit the risk of reference to a legal system that does not reflect a substantial connection.

The reference to the habitual residence leads to the question what actually is to be understood by the notion of habitual residence in European context. The meaning of the connecting factor habitual residence is generally regarded as varying on the basis of the quality of the person it relates to and the context in which it plays a role.[107] The concept of habitual residence is equally part of the current Brussels II*bis*-Regulation, but nevertheless it is not defined in the Regulation.[108] The ECJ has given the following definition to the term habitual residence in other fields of law:

> the place of habitual residence is that in which the [person] concerned has established, with the intention that it should be of a lasting character, the permanent or habitual centre of his interests. For the purposes of determining habitual residence, all the factual circumstances which constitute such residence of the [person] concerned must be taken into account.[109]

It follows from this interpretation of the notion habitual residence that, on the one hand, the intention to reside in a certain place could be relevant only when the situation *de facto* would confirm it, but, on the other hand, it could also allow immediate acquisition of habitual residence, without a specific length of time being required.[110] Consequently, habitual residence is a very flexible notion that allows for reference to a legal system which is closely connected to the case at issue. However, its factual character makes it difficult to determine whether or not a person has changed his habitual residence, which may lead to legal uncertainty.[111]

---

[107] Cf., Fiorini 2008, p. 197; Strikwerda 2008, p. 81; Stone 2002, p. 378.

[108] See on this issue: Richez-Pons 2005, pp. 355–360; Lamont 2007, pp. 261–281; Ricci 2008, pp. 207–219.

[109] See *inter alia* ECJ Case 13/73 *Angenieux* et al. v. *Hakenberg* [1973] ECR 935, para 32; ECJ Case C-297/89 *Rigsadvokaten* v. *Ryborg* [1989] ECR I-1943, para 19; ECJ Case C-452/93 *Fernández* v. *Commissio*, [1994] ECR I-4295, para 22; ECJ Case C-90/97 *Swaddling* v. *Adjudication Office* [1999] ECR I-1075, para 29; Case C-372/02 *Adanez-Vega* v. *Bundesanstalt für Arbeit* [2004] ECR I-10761, para 37; Case T-298/02 *Herrero Romeu* v. *Commission* [2005] ECR II-4599, para 51; Case C-66/08 *Kozłowski* [2008] ECR I-06041, para 54. See McEleavy 2008, pp. 278–290, for an extensive analysis of habitual residence in European case law.

[110] See ECJ Case C-90/97 *Swaddling* v. *Adjudication Office* [1999] ECR I-1075, para 30.

[111] Cf., Knot 2008, p. 196, who regards the factual character of habitual residence as its strength, but at the same time as its flaw.

It is questionable whether the abovementioned definition of habitual residence is suitable for family law purposes, as this is a very sensitive area of law that differs from social law, the area in which the ECJ has developed the definition of habitual residence. The respective provisions pursue different aims. So far the ECJ has, however, not clarified the extent to which this definition can be transposed to matrimonial matters.[112] In a recent case the ECJ did determine that its case law relating to the concept of habitual residence in other areas of European Union law cannot be directly transposed in the context of the assessment of the habitual residence of children for the purposes of Article 8(1) of the Brussels II*bis*-Regulation. Within this framework the Court gave the following interpretation to the concept of habitual residence:

> The 'habitual residence' of a child, within the meaning of Article 8(1) of the Regulation [i.e. the Brussels II*bis*-Regulation; NAB], must be interpreted as meaning that it corresponds to the place which reflects some degree of integration by the child in a social and family environment. To that end, in particular the duration, regularity, conditions and reasons for the stay on the territory of a Member State and the family's move to that State, the child's nationality, the place and conditions of attendance at school, linguistic knowledge and the family and social relationships of the child in that State must be taken into consideration. It is for the national court to establish the habitual residence of the child, taking account of all circumstances specific to each individual case.[113]

This definition of the habitual residence is specially geared to that of the child and cannot be copied indiscriminately to that of the spouses. In the first place, the emphasis the earlier definition of habitual residence has placed on the intentions of the persons concerned is better conceivable for adults than for children.[114] Secondly, with regard to parental responsibility the ratio of selecting the state of habitual residence is in the 'best interest of the child'. The courts of the Member State in which the child is habitually resident are generally best placed, for reasons of proximity, to judge what is in the interests of the child.[115] However, with respect to matrimonial matters, there is no similar guiding principle to help identifying the place of habitual residence of the spouses.

Consequently, the definition of habitual residence, as given in the *A.*-case, needs some adjustment in order to be used in matrimonial matters. Most of the factors that are mentioned in this case can very well be taken as point of departure, but the intentions of the parties concerned — on which the definition of habitual residence as previously given by the ECJ places strong emphasis — play an important role as well.

---

[112] It is to be noted that the French *Cour de Cassation* adopted this definition of the ECJ as regards the notion of habitual residence in matrimonial matters. See Cour de Cassation — Première chambre civile, 14 December 2005 ('*la résidence habituelle* [...] *se définit comme le lieu où l'intéressé a fixé, avec la volonté de lui conférer un caractère stable, le centre permanent ou habituel de ses intérêts*').

[113] ECJ Case C-523/07 *A* [2009] ECR I-02805, para 37.

[114] Cf., the Opinion of the Advocate General in Case C-523/07, para 36.

[115] Recital No. 12 of the Preamble to the Brussels II*bis*-Regulation.

Does this current definition of habitual residence meet the purposes of the Brussels II*ter*-Proposal as regards the choice of law? In accordance with its case law, the ECJ will take into account the context and the purpose of the legislation in question.[116] In matrimonial matters two different approaches underlie the jurisdictional rules, on the one hand, and the choice of law rules, on the other. Whereas the aim of the jurisdictional rules is to facilitate access to court, the choice of law rules are based on the approach of the closest connection. In order to achieve the desired *Gleichlauf*, i.e. the situation in which the competent court applies its own substantive law, the notion of habitual residence needs to be defined in such a way as to reconcile these two approaches. From this perspective, it is to be noted that the current definition of habitual residence — formulated in the framework of the jurisdictional rules — is too non-factual for choice of law purposes,[117] as the acquisition of habitual residence does not require a certain period of residence, which as such gives rise to the risk of manipulation.[118]

Therefore, the concept of habitual residence should for the choice of law purposes of the Brussels II*ter*-Proposal be interpreted as ensuring that it accurately designates the law with which there is a strong, current and — to some extent — lasting tie. The most pragmatic solution for choice of law purposes to help identifying the most appropriate law would simply be to add a presumption to the use of this connecting factor. E.g. a person having his residence in a given state for a period of at least 1 year is presumed to also have his habitual residence in that state.[119] This will provide certainty and ensure that an appropriate degree of connection exists.

From the foregoing it is clear that the term habitual residence is a question of fact to be appreciated by the court in each individual case. There is a risk of varying interpretations between the Member States as long as the ECJ has not given a definition expressly tailored to the Brussels II*ter*-Proposal. The lack of such clear-cut definition might lead to possible arbitrary interpretations by the courts of the Member States. Consequently, the lack of such a definition is not very conducive to legal certainty and predictability.[120]

---

[116] See ECJ Case 283/81 *Cilfit Srl* et al. v. *Ministry of Health* [1982] ECR 3415, paras 19–20; Case C-98/07 *Nordania Finans and BG Factoring* [2008] ECR I-1281, para 17.

[117] The link established between a person and a certain country through habitual residence on the basis of its current definition is too weak to meet the requirements set up for the choice of law. See equally Gaertner 2006, p. 134.

[118] Cf., McEleavy 2008, pp. 291–292.

[119] See with regard to the choice of law on succession, in which a same solution has been proposed: Ten Wolde 2004, p. 508; Ten Wolde and Knot 2006, p. 31.

[120] Cf., Stone 2002, p. 387 with regard to the Brussels II-Regulation: '*the absence of an explicit definition seems regrettable, since it tends to undermine the harmonising effect of the measures*'.

5.5.3.2 Nationality

In the absence of a common habitual residence and a last common habitual residence in which one of the spouses still resides, Article 20b(c) Brussels II*ter*-Proposal refers to the common nationality of the spouses.

The connection to the common nationality of the spouses raises several questions.[121] What happens if one of the spouses (or both of them) has more than one nationality? Is the Proposal limited to the law of the country with which spouses are most closely connected? In other words, can the court apply an effectivity test in order to assess which nationality reflects the closest connection?[122] The Brussels II*ter*-Proposal does not take any position as to the question how to deal with cases of multiple nationalities. This issue has been discussed in the Council and in its draft of 18 April 2008 a recital concerning multiple nationalities has been added to the Preamble to the Brussels II*ter*-Proposal. The solution found is to leave the question of how to deal with cases of multiple nationalities to the national law of the Member States.[123]

This solution is not very conducive to uniformity. Hence, the solution found for issues of multiple nationalities is not likely to lead to legal certainty and predictability. Instead, a more uniform approach should be employed, e.g. if faced with multiple nationalities, the competent court should apply an effectivity test.[124] In applying the effectivity test the national courts are obliged to take into account the purposes of the Brussels II*ter*-Proposal, i.e. applying the most closely connected law to divorce.

Moreover, one can also wonder whether the court has the authority to apply an authenticity test to a single nationality of the spouses: is the court to assess whether the spouses still have a real connection to their country of origin? In this connection one can think of refugees, where the application of the common national law is not obvious, even though they still possess their nationality. Application of the national law in such a case would therefore violate the principle of closest connection.

Where in national context the application of an effectivity test or an authenticity test can seem obvious from the perspective of the principle of closest connection,

---

[121] See also Ibili 2006, p. 744.

[122] Cf., Case C-168/08 *Laszlo Hadadi (Hadady)* v. *Csilla Marta Mesko, married name Hadadi (Hadady)* [2009] ECR I-06871. In this case the ECJ held with regard to a jurisdictional issue of multiple nationalities that Article 3 of the Brussels II*bis*-Regulation precludes that only the effective nationality can be taken into account in applying that provision. The system of jurisdiction established in the Brussels II*bis*-Regulation 'is not intended to preclude the courts of several States from having jurisdiction. Rather, the coexistence of several courts having jurisdiction is expressly provided for, without any hierarchy being established between them.' See on this case V. Van den Eeckhout, 'Het beroep op het bezit van een nationaliteit in het geval van dubbele nationaliteit', *NTER* 2009, pp. 307–316.

[123] Recital No. 5c of the Preamble to the Brussels II*ter*-Proposal. See Council Document No. 8587/08 JUSTCIV 73 of 18 April 2008.

[124] See equally Siehr 2005, pp. 33–34.

in European context this might run counter to the principle of non-discrimination: any discrimination on the grounds of nationality is prohibited (Article 18 TFEU). The use of nationality as a connecting factor in European context has been subject of a lively debate by legal doctrine.[125]

According to the European Court of Justice the principle of non-discrimination is not concerned with disparities which may result from divergences between the laws of the Member States, but rather with the fact that all persons subject to those laws must be treated equally, i.e. the laws must be applied in accordance with objective criteria and without regard to nationality.[126] However, the principle of non-discrimination does not prevent the Member States from using nationality as a connecting factor to determine the law applicable to a certain case, provided that such designation is made without considering the content of the law that is designated as applicable. The principle of non-discrimination is thus not harmed in case of neutral choice of law rules that refer to the national law of the person(s) involved: it distinguishes between persons with different nationalities but it does not add further differences to the detriment of EU citizens. A unilateral approach, however, delimits the scope of application of particular substantive rules and could create distinctions which risk being considered discriminatory.[127]

The Court of Justice has confirmed this interpretation on several occasions.[128] With regard to international family law, the ECJ has implicitly maintained in *Garcia Avello* and *Grunkin-Paul* that the use of nationality as connecting factor is compatible with the European principle on non-discrimination.[129] In these cases the European Court of Justice pointed out that 'although, as Community law stands at present, the rules governing a person's surname are matters coming within the competence of the Member States, the latter must none the less, when exercising that competence, comply with Community law.'[130] Even though the Court did not explicitly consider the use of nationality as a connecting factor, it is clear that — as long as no discriminatory differentiation on grounds of nationality is made — the use of nationality as such is not contrary to Article 18 TFEU. Therefore, the mentioned cases support the conclusion that it is very likely that the ECJ would

---

[125] See, *inter alia*, Drobnig 1970, Fischer 1991, Roth 1991, Schulz 2000, Puljak 2003, Ballarino and Ubertazzi 2004, Bogdan 2007, Schmidt 2008.

[126] ECJ Case 14/68 *Walt Wilhelm and others* v. *Bundeskartellamt* [1969] ECR 1, para 13.

[127] Cf., Meeusen 2007b, p. 294.

[128] ECJ Case C-339/89 *Alsthom Atlantique* v. *Compagnie de Construction Mécanique Sulzer SA* [1991] ECR I-107; ECJ Case C-305/92 *Albert Hoorn* v. *Landesversicherungsanstalt Westfalen* [1994] ECR I-1525; ECJ Case C-214/94 *Ingrid Boukhalfa* v. *Bundesrepublik Deutschland* [1996] ECR I-2253; and ECJ Case C-208/00 *Überseering BV* v. *Nordic Construction Company GmbH* [2002] ECR I-9919.

[129] ECJ Cases C-148/02 *Garcia Avello* v. *État belge* [2003] ECR I-11613 and C-353/06 *Grunkin-Paul* [2008] ECR I-07639.

[130] *Garcia Avello*, paras 25 and 26; and *Grunkin-Paul*, para 16.

consider the use of nationality as a connecting factor that is compatible with European law.[131]

From a strictly legal point of view, the use of nationality as a connecting factor offers, in terms of certainty, immense advantages over the use of habitual residence. A change of nationality can nearly always be verified by official documents. Habitual residence is much more difficult to determine with certainty — both for the person concerned and for the authorities — since it largely depends on the intentions of the person(s) involved which may be hard to prove. Further, the notion of habitual residence differs widely and may even give rise to controversies within one state. Furthermore habitual residence can be changed more or less overnight. Nationality on the other hand is much more stable: a person must generally have a domicile in a county for a certain number of years before being able to acquire nationality.

The current debates on the adherence to the principle of nationality in private international law rest upon a fundamental conflict and show that the application of the national law of the parties is in the middle of two contradictory developments.[132] On the one hand, the progressive process of integration — which is one of the principal objectives of the European choice of law — questions the justification of the application of the national law of the parties. On the other hand, the increasing internationalisation of society — which is accompanied by more and more awareness of diversity — seems to be a valid argument in favour of the application of the national law of the parties. The European choice of law rules have to strike a balance between these two developments.

The fundamental principles of the connection to the nationality can be traced back to Mancini, who regarded the application of the national law as a way of respecting the differences between sovereign states.[133] He argued that these differences would only be sufficiently taken into consideration if the applicable law in a private international law dispute was determined by the national law of the parties. In the course of time, the connection of the national law of the parties has increasingly given way to the reference to the most closely connected law, which is not *per se* the national law of the parties. Although it is beyond doubt that nationality serves as an objective and proportional criterion in the field of family law, as it responds to the ties between a State and its nationals, to the idea of a close connection and to the necessary stability of personal status,[134] the closest connection may very well require the application of another law.

---

[131] See further Puljak 2003, pp. 195–196; Ballarino and Ubertazzi 2004, pp. 105–106; Lehmann 2008, p. 149.

[132] Cf., Gaertner 2008, p. 233.

[133] See on Mancini, Jayme 1980; and Jayme 1981, pp. 145–155.

[134] See also Hohloch 2007, p. 266; and Meeusen 2007b, p. 293.

5.5.3.3 The *Lex Fori*

The *lex fori* is the last step of the cascade rule of Article 20b Brussels II*ter*-Proposal.

The fact that several Member States have indicated a strong preference for the application of their own substantive law in divorce cases makes it hardly surprising that, in the negotiations on the Brussels II*ter*-Proposal, various attempts have been made in order to reach a compromise in awarding a more prominent role to the *lex fori*.[135] One of those attempts has led to the insertion of a new Article in the Brussels II*ter*-Proposal, functioning as a remedy for situations in which the applicable law 'does not provide for divorce'.[136] In such cases, the *lex fori* will apply:

> 1. Where the law applicable pursuant to Article 20a and 20b does not provide for divorce or does not grant one of the spouses because of his or her gender equal access to divorce or legal separation, the law of the forum shall apply.[137]

Proceeding from the principle of the closest connection, this provision is far from being welcomed. By means of this provision, which is clearly based on the principle of *favor divortii*, the neutral foundation of the choice of law rules on divorce of the Brussels II*ter*-Proposal is disrupted. It is not meant as an adjustment of the closest connection. De Boer considers this provision as an expression of a European policy, supporting divorce at least as an *ultimum remedium* that cannot be denied on the sole ground that it is not allowed in the state with which the spouses are supposed to be most closely connected.[138]

The introduction of this provision is surrounded by uncertainties, e.g. what does the wording 'does not provide for divorce' mean? Can it equally entail that a legal system which requires a waiting period of a few years may qualify as 'not providing for divorce' because the divorce cannot be directly pronounced? From several documents it is clear that this situation would not qualify as a situation in which the applicable law does not provide for divorce, as the provision only

---

[135] See also De Boer 2008a, pp. 327–328.

[136] This attempt has evolved during the negotiations from the addition of an extra paragraph to Article 20b to the insertion of a completely new Article. The issue is discussed for the first time in Council Document No. 5274/07 JUSTCIV 4 of 12 January 2007, p. 7, which added a second paragraph to Article 20b stipulating that where the law applicable pursuant to para 1 (a), (b) or (c) does not provide for divorce, the law of the forum shall apply. In the jurisdictional provisions of the Brussels II*ter*-Proposal the introduction of the *forum necessitatis* is based on this same concern. See Article 7a, introduced in Council Document No. 13445/07 JUSTCIV 250 of 3 October 2007, p. 6.

[137] Article 20b-1 on the application of the law of the forum; see Council Document No. 9712/08 JUSTCIV 106 of 23 May 2008, p. 15.

[138] De Boer 2008a, p. 336. See also Silberman 2008, p. 2012.

applies to situations in which the applicable law does not provide for divorce at all.[139]

In the Council this provision has been a subject of debate, considering the following extract: '[F]uture work shall examine whether it would not be necessary to expressly indicate that the lex fori shall apply where [...] the foreign law does not provide for divorce.'[140] As the provision has been maintained until the last Council draft on the Brussels II*ter*-Proposal, it was apparently deemed necessary to expressly indicate that the *lex fori* applies if the applicable law does not provide for divorce.[141]

However, should not the reference to a legal system which does not provide for divorce simply be accepted as a consequence of the choice of law system? The choice of law system of the Brussels II*ter*-Proposal offers the parties the opportunity to choose the law applicable to their divorce, by which they can designate a legal system which does provide for divorce.

If such a provision is deemed necessary at all, a more just solution to this problem would be to proceed to the next alternative connecting factor provided for by Article 20b and not automatically to the *lex fori*. This solution implies a less fierce disruption of the neutral foundation of the unified choice of law on divorce on the principle of the closest connection.

Another attempt to further the role of the *lex fori* in divorce proceedings was made by the French delegation, proposing to introduce a facultative choice of law:

1. In the absence of a choice pursuant to Article 20a, where neither of the parties has requested application of another law, lex fori shall apply.
2. If either of the spouses has requested application of another law, divorce and legal separation shall be subject to the following law:
   a. the law of the spouses' common habitual residence or, failing that,
   b. the law of the spouses' common nationality or, failing that,
   c. the law of the spouses' last common habitual residence, insofar as one of them still resides there or, failing that,
   d. the lex fori.[142]

This proposal would allow the courts, in the absence of a *professio iuris*, to apply the *lex fori* as long as neither party has requested the application of the law

[139] In Council Document No. 7144/07 JUSTCIV 47 of 9 March 2007 the Presidency suggests 'a recital clarifying that the provision covers cases where the applicable law does not know the concept of divorce *at all* [...]' (emphasis added). The Council draft on the Brussels II*ter*-Proposal of 23 May 2008 added such recital in No. 9b of the Preamble: '[W]here the Regulation refers to the fact that the applicable law does not provide for divorce, this should be interpreted in such a way that the applicable law does not know the concept of divorce at all'.

[140] Guidelines of the Presidency of the Council, Council Document No. 8549/07 JUSTCIV 91 of 17 April 2007, para 19.

[141] Yet again the impossibility to examine the comments of the delegations of the Member States on the Brussels II*ter*-Proposal as part of the negotiations in the Council obscures the true motives.

[142] Council Document No. 6258/07, to know from Council Document No. 7144/07 JUSTCIV 47 of 9 March 2007, p. 9, footnote 2.

designated by Article 20b.[143] The advantage of this system is that the application of foreign law can be omitted if neither party has invoked that law and, often, the application of foreign law is quite a job.[144] However, there are several objections that can be raised against the doctrine of facultative choice of law. Most importantly, the doctrine of facultative choice of law would affect the basic premise of the choice of law, i.e. both forum law and foreign law are eligible for application.[145] Moreover, the doctrine of facultative choice of law would equally harm the principle of the closest connection, on which the common choice of law rules are based.

The French proposal on the introduction of a facultative choice of law on divorce in the European Union was removed from the last Council draft of 23 May 2008.

The systematic application of the *lex fori* to any (international) divorce certainly has its advantages: its simplicity and effectiveness contribute to a fast settlement of the case and to a correct application of the divorce law.[146] Yet starting from the principle of the closest connection these advantages cannot convince. In the first place, the systematic application of the *lex fori* disturbs the presumed equality of local and foreign law, which is generally acknowledged as one of the premises of private international law. Furthermore, recourse to a mechanical and inflexible rule that does not take into consideration the specific circumstances of the case — other than the place where the court is seised — seems inappropriate in terms of the *rationale* of the principle of the closest connection behind the application of a particular law.[147]

However, the application of the *lex fori* as a last resort option for cases where the other connecting factors are not applicable, as proposed in Article 20b, is appropriate. The *lex fori* can, if it is seen in connection with the jurisdictional rules of the Brussels II*bis*-Regulation, be considered to represent the necessary close connection.

5.5.3.4 *Ex Officio* Authority?

Does the competent court have *ex officio* authority to apply Article 20b of the Brussels II*ter*-Proposal, provided that the parties fail to make a *professio iuris* and do not even plead the application of a certain law pursuant to Article 20b of the Brussels II*ter*-Proposal? This seems to be presupposed in the Proposal.

---

143 See in general on facultative choice of law: De Boer 1996; Mostermans 2004.

144 See further *infra* Sect. 5.6 on the difficulties surrounding the application of foreign law.

145 See further *infra* Sect. 6.5.3.2, where the question whether the field of a European choice of law on divorce is suitable for a facultative choice of law will be elaborated upon.

146 Cf., e.g., De Boer 1996, pp. 304–308; Gaertner 2008, p. 215 ff.

147 See e.g. North 1980, p. 82 ff; Rüberg 2005, p. 112 ff; Pertegás 2007, pp. 321–326; Looschelders 2008, p. 349.

However, the Member States' traditions strongly vary on this point.[148] There is a difference in particular between common law countries — where foreign law is to a certain extent on the same footing as the facts — and civil law countries — where the general approach is that the court applies the choice of law rules and foreign law *ex officio* (on the basis of the principle of *ius curia novit*).[149] There are, moreover, numerous variations of both approaches. But the question is whether the Brussels II*ter*-Proposal entails an implicit obligation to apply the choice of law and foreign law *ex officio* or whether this is still an issue of national civil procedure.[150]

The fact that the proposed choice of law rules on divorce will be part of a regulation implies that these rules should be applied *ex officio*. As seen in the previous chapter, a regulation has as main characteristic that it is binding in its entirety and directly applicable in all Member States.[151] Furthermore, the principle of solidarity contained in Article 4(3) second sentence EU-Treaty would require that courts apply foreign law *ex officio*.[152] From these characteristics one can conclude that the unified European choice of law rules is to be applied *ex officio*.[153] In addition, the uniform application of the common choice of law rules in all Member States equally requires the *ex officio* authority of the courts to apply the common rules.[154]

Moreover, does the competent court have the authority to assess whether the connecting factor to which Article 20b refers actually provides for a substantial connection? The same can be asked for the *professio iuris* of Article 20a.[155]

The choice of law rule of Article 20b is based on the approach of the closest connection. Obviously, the connecting factors as laid down in Article 20b are

---

[148] Cf., Fiorini 2008, p. 197; Kreuzer 2008, p. 6 ff.

[149] See for an elaborate comparative analysis: Geeroms 2004. See also Hausmann 2008.

[150] Cf., with regard to the Rome II-Regulation, Kramer 2008, pp. 414–424, spec. at pp. 418–419. A Commission Statement attached to the Rome II-Regulation provides that the Commission, being aware of the differences in this regard between the Member States, will publish at the latest 4 years after the entry into force of this Regulation a horizontal study on the application of foreign law in civil and commercial matters, and take appropriate measures if necessary. Such study would, therefore, also encompass the application of foreign law in the field of family law. See also Communication from the Commission to the European Parliament and the Council, An area of freedom, security and justice serving the citizen, COM(2009) 262 final, p. 12: '*the proper functioning of the European judicial area sometimes requires a national court to apply the law of another Member State. The Union must consider how to avoid the current disparity in practices in this area*'.

[151] See *supra* Sect. 4.4.4.3.

[152] Cf., with regard to Article 10 EC-Treaty Jänterä-Jareborg 2003, p. 367 ff.

[153] See also Kreuzer 2008, p. 6 and pp. 8–9.

[154] Cf., Siehr 2008, p. 86: '*Denn was nützt eine schöne Vereinheitlichung, wenn das vereinheitlichte Kollisionsrecht und das anwendbare Privatrecht in den Mitgliedstaaten unterschiedlich gehandhabt werden?*'

[155] Cf., *supra* Sect. 5.5.2.4 with regard to the question how to ensure that the *professio iuris* is an accurate reflection of the intentions of the parties.

solely an assumption of a close connection.[156] However, what happens if the spouses are more closely connected to the country of their common nationality, even though they have their common habitual residence elsewhere? On the basis of Article 20b of the Brussels II*ter*-Proposal the court should in this case apply the law of the country of the common habitual residence of the spouses. But this seems to contravene the principle of the closest connection.

The Council has only dealt marginally with this issue. As seen above, the question of multiple nationalities has been left to the national law of the Member States.[157] There will most certainly be more cases in which the circumstances of the case justify the assumption that the case is more closely connected to another country than the one designated by the choice of law rules. For example a person can very well be estranged of his country of origin: in such a case the connecting factor of nationality does not reflect a close connection. Moreover, should the specified effective nationality of a person also be submitted to an authenticity test in order to determine whether or not the connection to the country of this nationality provides for the necessary close connection? The Brussels II*ter*-Proposal does not provide for any mechanism to adjust the result of the reference of the case according to Article 20b.

Since the absence of answers to these issues will not be too conducive to legal certainty and predictability, the European legislature has to respond to them. Otherwise Member States might be inclined to interpret the rationale of the choice of law in such a way that it will support their own preferences. An interference of the European Court of Justice then has to be awaited in issues resulting from such lack of clarity for uniformity to arise.

Article 20b of the Brussels II*ter*-Proposal would benefit from the insertion of an extra paragraph stipulating that 'where it is clear from all the circumstances of the case that the divorce is manifestly more closely connected with a country other than that indicated in paragraph 1, the law of that other country shall apply'.[158] On the one hand, such a correcting mechanism carries the risk with it as regards legal certainty and predictability, but, on the other hand, it would imply a just adjustment of the result of the connection with a certain legal system in the light of the principle of the closest connection.[159] Even though such a correcting mechanism leaves a considerable margin of appreciation to the national courts of the Member States, it does imply a just interpretation of the regulation from the perspective of the principle of the closest connection. It is beyond doubt that such manifest closer connection should not be assessed on the basis of substantive law concerns, but exclusively on the basis of factual and geographical factors. Consequently, this

[156] Cf., Rüberg 2005, p. 173.

[157] Supra Sect. 5.5.3.2.

[158] Cf., Article 4(3) of the Rome I-Regulation and Article 4(3) of the Rome II-Regulation. See equally Kohler 2008b, p. 195.

[159] See also Rüberg 2005, p. 188 ff, who considers such correcting mechanism as a means to provide for '*Einzalfallgerechtigkeit*', i.e. the means to ensure justice at individual level.

correcting mechanism should have a reasonably high threshold in order to displace the otherwise applicable law: it should be demonstrated that the particular case has only a very slight connection to the law designated as applicable and has a much closer connection to another law. If necessary, the European Court of Justice can adjust possible excesses committed by national courts of the Member States.

Finally, the Brussels II*ter*-Proposal does not contain any provision for situations in which the applicable law is the law of a state with more than one legal system. For example, Article 20b of the Brussels II*ter*-Proposal may designate 'American' law as the applicable law. However, there is no 'American' divorce law, as each State of the USA autonomously provides for substantive divorce law.

The Council proposed to introduce a special provision on this issue in Article 20f:

1. Where a State comprises several territorial units, each of which has its own rules of law in respect of divorce and legal separation, each territorial unit shall be considered as a State for the purposes of identifying the law applicable under this Regulation.
2. A Member State within which different territorial units have their own rules of law in respect of divorce and legal separation shall not be required to apply this Regulation to conflicts solely between the laws of such units.[160]

This provision is certainly a valuable addition, as it provides for clarity and legal certainty and ensures a more uniform application of the choice of law rules throughout the European Union.

5.5.4 Date of Reference

The connecting factors of the original Brussels II*ter*-Proposal are not completed with a date of reference. Both the Council and the European Parliament have filled this gap and completed the choice of law rules with a date of reference.

In case of a *professio iuris* the habitual residence or the nationality of either spouse needs to be present at the time of the conclusion of the agreement.[161] This date of reference is fairly strange, as the agreement on the law applicable to divorce can be concluded already before divorce proceedings have commenced (Article 20a(2) Brussels II*ter*-Proposal). The existence of the connection to the habitual residence or to the nationality of either spouse is thus not reviewed at the time of the divorce, but at the time of the conclusion of the agreement. However, possibly the spouses do no longer have any connection to the chosen law at the time of the divorce. The application of the chosen law will then conflict with the principle of the closest connection. From the perspective of the latter principle the time the court is seised would be a better date of reference.

---

[160] See the Council draft on the Brussels II*ter*-Proposal of 23 May 2008.

[161] See Council Document No. 9712/08 JUSTCIV 106 of 23 May 2008, pp. 12–13; and the Legislative Resolution of the European Parliament of 21 October 2008, A6-0361/2008, Amendments 18–22.

With regard to the law applicable to divorce in the absence of a *professio iuris* the habitual residence or nationality of either spouse needs to be present at the time the court is seised.[162]

The addition of a date of reference is generally a good proposal. A fixed date of reference will provide for more clarity and, hence, have a favourable effect towards strengthening legal certainty and the predictability of results.

5.5.5 The Law Applicable to Divorce: Synthesis

The alternatives out of which spouses can choose pursuant to Article 20a are hardly different from the laws that would apply according to Article 20b in the absence of a choice.[163]

According to Article 20a the parties can choose the law of the last common habitual residence, if one of the spouses still lives there, the law of the common habitual residence, the national law of either spouse or the *lex fori*. If the spouses have not made a *professio iuris* according to Article 20a, the law applicable to divorce is determined on the basis of the scale of connecting factors of Article 20b. In the latter situation the divorce is governed by the law of the country of the common habitual residence of the spouses, or failing that, by the law of the country of their last common habitual residence insofar as one of them still resides there. In the absence of both these connecting factors, the law of the common nationality of the spouses applies. If the spouses do not have a common nationality either, the law of the forum (*lex fori*) is designated.[164]

A comparison of these provisions shows that Article 20a allows the parties to choose the national law of *either* spouse, while Article 20b refers to the *common* national law of the parties.[165] The main difference is that the parties may choose a law that would not be applicable under Article 20b, either because they have chosen an alternative that would not be the primary law in the absence of a *professio iuris*, or because the circumstances at the time of the choice were distinct from those at the time of divorce.

5.6 The Application of Foreign Law

The proposed choice of law rules of the Brussels II*ter*-Proposal can lead to the application of foreign law. The application of foreign law can result either from a valid *professio iuris* pursuant to Article 20a or from the cascade rule of Article 20b.

---

[162] See Council Document No. 9712/08 JUSTCIV 106 of 23 May 2008, p. 14; and the Legislative Resolution of the European Parliament of 21 October 2008, A6-0361/2008, Amendments 27–29.

[163] See equally De Boer 2008a, p. 330.

[164] See *supra* Sects. 5.5.2 and 5.5.3, respectively.

[165] See further on Article 20b *supra* Sect. 5.5.3.

According to the Commission the application of the law designated by Article 20b will in most cases coincide with the *lex fori*:

> [T]he fact that the rule is based in the first place on the habitual residence of the spouses and, failing that, on their last common habitual residence if one of them still resides there will result in the application of the law of the forum in the majority of cases.[166]

However, Article 20b does not preclude the application of foreign law.[167]

In every cross-border case in which foreign law is designated the court is faced with the problem that it is generally not acquainted with the content of the foreign law. From the point of view of those Member States that systematically apply the *lex fori* to any divorce, the application of foreign law is surrounded by several disadvantages. In the first place, it will take much longer to settle cases as the court needs to inquire thoroughly into and understand the content of the foreign law. Moreover, the costs of the proceedings will increase significantly. The settlement rates will furthermore decrease because of the uncertainty and unpredictability that is strongly connected with the lack of knowledge of the foreign law.[168] Finally, in many countries substantive law and procedural law are strongly interconnected: the choice of law rules refer to the application of substantive law only. Consequently, courts have to apply the substantive law of the country with which the couple has the closest connection, but will apply their own procedural law to the case.[169]

There is no denying that the listed disadvantages certainly hold an element of truth: ascertaining the content of and applying foreign laws may be a long, costly and difficult process.[170] There may therefore be merit in the simple and pragmatic approach of systematically applying the *lex fori*. Yet this cannot be a reason to abandon the principle of the closest connection.

Article 20c of the Brussels II*ter*-Proposal contains a provision on the application of foreign law, which determines that the court may make use of the European Judicial Network where the law of another Member State is applicable. The Council deleted this provision in its drafts of the Brussels II*ter*-Proposal and it suggested that it be removed to a recital.[171]

---

166 Explanatory Memorandum to the Brussels II*ter*-Proposal, p. 10.

167 See also Kohler 2008a, p. 1678.

168 See Hodson 2008b, p. 10. See also Gaertner 2006, p. 107 ff; and the report of April 2009 of the British Centre for Social Justice, 'European Family Law: Faster Divorce and Foreign Law', p. 16 ff, available at: www.centreforsocialjustice.org.uk.

169 See Hodson 2008a, p. 177.

170 See equally Fiorini 2008, pp. 188–189.

171 Council Document No. 5274/07 JUSTCIV 4 of 12 January 2007, p. 8. See recital No. 10c of the Preamble to the Brussels II*ter*-Proposal.

5.7 Public Policy Exception

The proposed choice of law rules of the Brussels II*ter*-Proposal are meant to have universal application. The choice of law rules could, therefore, lead to the reference to the law of either a Member State or a third country. Consequently, the problems described above in relation to the public policy exception with regard to the Dutch choice of law rules on divorce, can occur *mutatis mutandis* in relation to the public policy exception in European context.[172] These problems mainly occur in relation to non-Western legal systems: the principle of equality between men and women clashes fairly often with certain non-egalitarian rules of Islamic law. Repudiation is the most significant example in this respect.

The Brussels II*ter*-Proposal contains the following public policy exception in Article 20e:

> The application of a provision of the law designated by this Regulation may be refused only if such application is manifestly incompatible with the public policy of the forum.

The wording 'manifestly incompatible' expresses that the public policy exception must be seen as an *ultimum remedium*.[173]

Article 20e of the Brussels II*ter*-Proposal refers to the public policy notion of the forum. However, the national approaches to the public policy exception differ greatly from one Member State to another. Practice in certain Member States shows that more restrictive foreign laws are excluded through the application of the public policy exception. It is also not inconceivable that courts from more 'conservative' Member States would equally rely on their public policy exception to exclude the application of very liberal foreign divorce laws.[174]

Kreuzer argued that the current differences in application of the public policy exception between the Member States are to diminish with the development of the jurisprudence of the European Court of Justice and the European Court on Human Rights.[175] But in such a sensitive area as divorce, where the substantive laws of the Member States are based on conflicting policies,[176] the differences in the application of the public policy exception could very well prove to be persistent.

Consequently, doubts can be cast on how the reference to the public policy exception of the forum state could lead to uniform decisions.[177] Two possible solutions to this problem are suggested.

---

[172] See *supra* Sect. 2.5.

[173] Cf., De Boer 2008b, p. 296.

[174] See Romano 2006, pp. 500–501.

[175] Kreuzer 2008, p. 46.

[176] See *supra* Sect. 5.2.1.

[177] See equally Cadet 2004, p. 9: '*l'application de l'exception d'ordre public risque de se développer, mettant en péril les objectifs d'espace judiciaire unifié au sein de l'Union européenne*'.

The first alternative would be to refer to the European public policy exception. However, does such exception exist? In other words, is there a distinct category of *European* values and interests, or do the values and interests of each Member State coincide with those of the European Union?

The European Union system does have its own public policy that is formed by the fundamental freedoms, European citizenship, human rights and the principles of non-discrimination and subsidiarity.[178] But it is not clear whether or not there is a specific European public policy requiring the defence of European values and interests, to the extent that they do not coincide with those of the forum.[179] Yet with regard to divorce the content of the European *ordre public* is highly uncertain.[180]

The reference to a European public policy exception would have the advantage that the European Court of Justice can provide for a uniform interpretation of this concept.

The second alternative suggested in literature is for the Member States to reach a basic agreement on what can and cannot constitute a 'manifest incompatibility' with the public policy in the sense of Article 20e Brussels II*ter*-Proposal.[181] However, such an agreement does not seem to be very realistic, given the strongly diverging views on the concept of divorce in the various Member States.

One of the most far-reaching agreements in this respect is to envisage the impossibility for the courts of a Member State to invoke its public policy exception as to refuse to apply the law of another Member State: e.g. 'the application of a provision of the law of a Member State designated by this Regulation shall not be refused on the ground of public policy.'[182] In an area of freedom, security and justice the exclusion of the public policy exception in cases in which the law of a Member State is designated as the applicable law would mean a major step forward, as it would express a deep-rooted belief in the fundamental fairness of the divorce laws of the Member States.[183] In fact, such a definition would imply that the public policy exception of Article 20e of the Brussels II*ter*-Proposal can only be invoked in cases in which the law of a third country is designated as the applicable law.[184] Yet it is highly questionable whether such a definition can be

[178] See on this issue: Thoma 2007, p. 120 ff; Reichelt 2007, pp. 7–11. Cf., ECJ case C-7/98 *Krombach* v. *Bamberski* [2000] ECR I-01935.

[179] Cf., De Boer 2008b, p. 328.

[180] See equally Kroll 2007, p. 335. See generally on the European public policy in choice of law matters: Basedow 2004.

[181] See also Martiny 2006, p. 132; Jänterä-Jareborg 2008, p. 339.

[182] Cf., Leible 2009, pp. 68–69.

[183] See Meeusen 2008, pp. 332–333.

[184] The Commission Proposal for the Maintenance Regulation contained such a provision, COM(2005) 649 final. Article 20 of this proposal stipulated: '[T]he application of a provision of the law designated by this Regulation may be refused only if such application is manifestly incompatible with the public policy ('*ordre public*') of the forum. *However, the application of a provision of the law of a Member State designated by this Regulation shall not be refused on such a ground*' (emphasis added). This provision has, however, disappeared since the law applicable to maintenance obligations is removed from the Maintenance Regulation and is instead determined by the Hague Protocol on the law applicable to maintenance obligations.

reached between the Member States considering the delicate issues surrounding divorce, e.g. the issue of same-sex marriages, the impossibility to dissolve a marriage pursuant to Maltese law and the concept of fault-based divorce recognised in a number of Member States.[185] Furthermore, the Member States cannot be expected to apply the law of another Member State if this would violate their national fundamental values.[186]

The subsequent question to be answered is what happens if the public policy exception of Article 20e is successfully invoked? Can the competent court apply the *lex fori* or is it required to proceed to the next alternative connecting factor?

In order to prevent the problem described above of courts applying the public policy exception so as to apply their own more liberal or restrictive divorce law, the competent court should only fall back on the *lex fori* if it is the only acceptable solution.[187]

To sum up, one can conclude that the protection of the current provision on public policy is uncertain, as it leaves (too) much room to the national preferences of the Member States.

5.8 Does the Proposal Attain the Objectives as Set Out by the Commission in the Explanatory Memorandum to the Brussels II*ter*-Proposal?

In Section 5.3 above the five objectives the Brussels II*ter*-Proposal attempts to attain have been set forth. Below the question whether these objectives are actually attained with the proposed choice of law rules will be analysed.

- *Providing for a Clear and Comprehensive Legal Framework*

This objective is very ambitious and is not attained by the Brussels II*ter*-Proposal.

The exclusion of a certain type of marriage in advance, i.e. same-sex marriages, implies that a solution is found only for the dissolution of a — albeit large — part of the existing marriages. As mentioned above, the exclusion of same-sex marriages seems to contradict the overall objective of the Brussels II*ter*-Proposal to provide for a comprehensive legal framework in matrimonial matters in the European Union: a solution is not found for all marriages.[188] Consequently, the existing problems resulting from the lack of unified rules on the law applicable to divorce as indicated by the Commission will continue with regard to the

[185] See Working Document on the law applicable in matrimonial matters of the European Parliament of 21 June 2007, p. 6.

[186] Cf., De Boer 2008b, pp. 323–325.

[187] See Kreuzer 2008, pp. 46–47.

[188] Recital No. 5 of the Preamble to the Brussels II*ter*-Proposal. See further *supra* Sect. 5.4.2.

dissolution of same-sex marriages, be it on a smaller scale given the fact that currently solely three Member States provide for same-sex marriages in their legislation.[189]

Moreover, considering the substantial number of obscurities surrounding the Brussels II*ter*-Proposal, the legal framework can hardly be considered to be clear. To name a few, the issues of multiple nationalities, of *ex officio* authority of the courts, of the application of the public policy exception of the forum and of the definition of the concept of habitual residence have incited to quite some debate and no (satisfying) answer is found to solve these issues.

- *Strengthening Legal Certainty and Predictability*

The proposed choice of law rules of the Brussels II*ter*-Proposal ensure that in principle in all Member States the same law is applied to an international divorce in the European Union, irrespective of which court is seised. Consequently, it can definitely be said that the Brussels II*ter*-Proposal attains the objective of strengthening legal certainty and predictability.

However, the achievement of this objective is relatively limited: the outcome of a case can only be predicted once a specific jurisdiction has been seised. The common choice of law rules on divorce cannot achieve uniform results if the case can be brought before the courts of both an EU-Member State and a third country. Certainty and predictability can thus only be ensured in intra-European cases, in which the requesting party has no access to a court outside the EU.[190]

Furthermore, equally the lack of a common approach to general issues, such as the application of foreign law and the public policy exception, does constitute an obstacle for the attainment of this objective.[191] The fact that the Member States can follow their own approach to such issues does not strengthen legal certainty, since it involves less predictability for the parties concerned. As a result, the proposed choice of law rules on divorce of the Brussels II*ter*-Proposal is not yet truly crystallised.

Legal certainty and predictability in international divorce cases are, finally, not only dependent on the law applicable to divorce. Legal certainty and predictability imply that parties know which law will govern their divorce and the consequences thereof. Consequently, ancillary matters, such as parental responsibility and

---

189 Belgium, the Netherlands, Sweden and Spain provide for same-sex marriage. Some other Member States, among which Portugal, currently consider the introduction of same-sex marriage. Yet, there are also a few Member States, such as Latvia, Lithuania and Poland that are strongly opposed to same-sex marriage.

190 Cf., De Boer 2009, p. 302.

191 Such open questions need not necessarily all be clarified in the legislative act itself. One could in this respect envisage the development of a more elaborate Explanatory Memorandum or a 'Guide to Good Practice' accompanying the legislative act. Cf., thesis No. 6 appended to Knot 2008: '*Europese wetgeving op het gebied van het internationaal privaatrecht dient, wil het ooit de kwaliteit van de in het kader van de Haagse Conferentie tot stand gebrachte verdragen benaderen, te worden voorzien van een uitgebreide(re) toelichting; dit komt de rechtszekerheid ten goede*'.

maintenance obligations, are of equal importance when it comes to legal certainty and predictability in international divorce cases.[192] However, the scope of the Brussels II*ter*-Proposal is limited to divorce and does not cover its consequences.

- *Increasing Flexibility*

By introducing a limited degree of party autonomy, the Brussels II*ter*-Proposal has definitely increased flexibility. By means of the *professio iuris* introduced by Article 20a spouses are offered the opportunity to choose the law applicable to their divorce.

Because the possibilities out of which the spouses can choose are limited, the spouses are not offered full flexibility. The limitation of the *professio iuris* is well reasoned: there should be a (close) connection between the divorce in question and the law to be applied.

Consequently, the Brussels II*ter*-Proposal succeeds in increasing flexibility.

- *Ensuring Access to Court*

The fourth objective of the Brussels II*ter*-Proposal seeks to improve access to court in matrimonial proceedings. In this respect reference is made to the possibility to choose the competent court in divorce cases and to the introduction of a uniform and exhaustive rule on residual jurisdiction.

However, as both these matters fall outside the scope of this study, they have not been analysed in-depth. Therefore, it is impossible to ascertain whether the proposed rules of the Brussels II*ter*-Proposal have attained this objective.

- *Preventing a 'Rush to Court'*

The proposed choice of law rules ensure that, wherever the spouses file their petition for divorce, the courts of a Member States will normally apply the same substantive law. Consequently, the risk of forum shopping for a (more) favourable substantive divorce law is severely limited. The Brussels II*ter*-Proposal has largely shut the door to forum shopping as regards the applicable law to divorce.

But, as argued in Section 4.3.1 above, forum shopping mostly occurs if a great deal of money is involved. With respect to divorce, forum shopping will mostly arise for ancillary claims, such as maintenance obligations and the division of matrimonial property. Therefore, forum shopping in matrimonial matters is likely to continue as long as the choice of law rules on maintenance obligations and on matrimonial property have not been unified.[193]

It can, consequently, be stated that the Brussels II*ter*-Proposal can only partly attain the specified objective of preventing a 'rush to court', as the lack of uniform

[192] See equally Fiorini 2008, p. 194.

[193] For both these fields of law legislative measures on the European level are in the pipeline. See Maintenance Regulation and Green Paper on Matrimonial Property. The Maintenance Regulation will most probably apply from 18 June 2011 (cf., Article 76 of the Maintenance Regulation).

rules applicable to the consequences of the divorce will lead to a continuing rush to court and to forum shopping.[194]

Overall, the conclusion is that the Brussels II*ter*-Proposal does achieve its objectives quite well. However, some of the objectives set by the Proposal seem too ambitious to be attained by this single instrument.

5.9 Conclusion

This chapter contains an analysis of the proposed choice of law rules on divorce of the Brussels II*ter*-Proposal.

The Brussels II*ter*-Proposal provides in Article 20a for the opportunity for the spouses to choose the law applicable to their divorce. This *professio iuris* is limited to a number of legal systems that (are deemed to) express a close connection. The *professio iuris* is also formally limited: both the form and the time of the agreement are bound to specific requirements.

In the absence of *professio iuris* pursuant to Article 20a by the parties, the applicable law to divorce is determined by Article 20b of the Brussels II*ter*-Proposal. The latter Article contains a cascade rule entailing in the first place the application of the law of the common place of habitual residence of the spouses. In the absence of a common place of habitual residence, Article 20b refers to the law of the last common place of habitual residence of the spouses insofar as one of them still resides there. In the absence of both these connecting factors, the divorce is governed by the common national law of the spouses. If the spouses do not have a common nationality either, the *lex fori* will apply.

The analysis of the choice of law rules of the Brussels II*ter*-Proposal has shown that there are still many difficulties to be clarified. The fact that quite a number of issues are left to national law is not very conducive to clarity and legal certainty.

The Brussels II*ter*-Proposal aspired to attain five objectives: providing for a clear and comprehensive legal framework, strengthening legal certainty and predictability, increasing flexibility, ensuring access to court and preventing a rush to court. The Brussels II*ter*-Proposal succeeds quite well in attaining these objectives. However, some of the objectives set by the Proposal seem too ambitious to be attained by this single instrument: as no choice of law rules on the consequences of divorce are established, legal certainty and predictability are not entirely strengthened and a rush to court and forum shopping for the latter issues will continue.

---

194 The European Economic and Social Committee has suggested to deal with all consequence of divorce in one single instrument; see its Opinion on the Proposal of 13 December 2006, SOC/253, n. 4.3. See equally Fiorini 2008, p. 195. See further *infra* Sect. 8.2.3.

References

Regulations, Conventions, Reports and Other Documentary Sources

Brussels II*bis*-Regulation. Council Regulation (EC) No. 2201/2003 of 27 November 2003 on Jurisdiction and Enforcement of Judgments in Matrimonial Matters and Matters of Parental Responsibility, [2003] OJ L338/1

Brussels II*ter*-Proposal. Proposal for a Council Regulation amending Regulation (EC) No. 2201/2003 as regards jurisdiction and introducing rules concerning applicable law in matrimonial matters, COM(2006) 399 final

EPEC Study on divorce. Study to inform a subsequent Impact Assessment on the Commission proposal on jurisdiction and applicable law in divorce matters, undertaken by EPEC, April 2006 available at: http://ec.europa.eu/justice_home/news/consulting_public/divorce_matters/study.pdf

European Convention on Human Rights. European Convention on Human Rights concluded at Rome at 4 November 1950, *Trb.* 1951, No. 154

EU-Treaty. Treaty on the European Union of 7 February 1992, [1992] OJ C191/1 (original version), [2010] OJ C83/13 (consolidated version)

Green Paper on Divorce. Green Paper on applicable law and jurisdiction in divorce maters, COM(2005) 82 final

Green Paper on Matrimonial Property. Green Paper on conflict of laws regarding matrimonial property regimes, including the question of jurisdiction and mutual recognition, COM(2006) 400 final

Hague Protocol on the Law Applicable to Maintenance Obligations. Protocol on the Law Applicable to Maintenance Obligations of 23 November 2007. Protocol to the Hague Convention of 23 November 2007 on the International Recovery of Child Support and Other Forms of Family Maintenance

House of Lords Rome III Report. House of Lords—European Union Committee, *Rome III—Choice of Law in Divorce*, 52nd Report of Session 2005–2006 (HL Paper 272) December 2006

Impact Assessment on Divorce. Commission Staff Working Document—Annex to the proposal for a Council Regulation amending Regulation (EC) No. 2201/2003 as regards jurisdiction and introducing rules concerning applicable law in matrimonial matters, SEC(2006) 949

Maintenance Regulation. Council Regulation (EC) No. 4/2009 of 18 December 2008 on jurisdiction, applicable law, recognition and enforcement of decisions and cooperation in matters relating to maintenance obligations, [2009] OJ L7/1

Books and Articles

Antokolskaia MV (2006) The search for a common core of divorce law: state intervention v. spouses' autonomy. In: Martín-Casals M, Ribot J (eds) The role of self-determination in the modernisation of family law in Europe. Documenta Universitaria, Girona, pp 33–58

Baetge D (2008) Auf dem Weg zu einem gemeinsamen europäischen Verständnis des gewöhnlichen Aufenthalts. In: Baetge D et al (eds) Die richtige Ordnung. Festschrift für Jan Kropholler zum 70. Geburtstag. Mohr Siebeck, Tübingen, pp 77–88

Ballarino T, Ubertazzi B (2004) On *Avello* and other judgments: a new point of departure in the conflict of laws? Yearbook of Private International Law, pp 85–128

Basedow J (2000) The communautarization of the conflict of laws under the treaty of Amsterdam. CMLR 37:687–708

Basedow J (2004) Die Verselbständigung des europäischen ordre public. In: Coester M et al (eds) Privatrecht in Europa. Vielfalt, Kollision, Kooperation. Festschrift für Hans Jürgen Sonnenberger zum 70. Geburtstag. Verlag C.H. Beck, München, pp 291–319

Basedow J (2008) The recent developments of the conflict of laws. In: Basedow J et al (eds) Japanese and European Private International Law in Comparative Perspective. Mohr Siebeck, Tübingen, pp 4–18

Bergé JS (2003) L'avenir communautaire du droit international privé des conflits de lois', In: La réception du droit communautaire en droit privé des Etats Membres, Bruylant, Brussel, pp 206–233

Beyer M (2007) Handlungsfelder der deutschen EU-Ratspräsidentschaft im Familienrecht—Die europäischen Verordnungsvorschläge zum internationalen Scheidungs— und Unterhaltsrecht. Forum Familienrecht, pp 20–27

Boele-Woelki K (2008a) Europese unificatie conflictenrecht echtscheiding van de baan. FJR 30:261

Boele-Woelki K (2008b) To be or not to be: enhanced cooperation in international divorce law within the European Union. Victoria University of Wellington Law Review, pp 779–792

Boele-Woelki K, Curry-Sumner I, Jansen M, Schrama W (2007) Huwelijk of geregistreerd partnerschap? Kluwer, Deventer

Boele-Woelki K, González Beilfuss C (2007) Brussels II bis: its impact and application in the member states. Intersentia, Antwerpen

Bogdan M (2007) The EC Treaty and the use of nationality and habitual residence as connecting factors in international family law. In: Meeusen J et al (eds) International family law for the European Union. Intersentia, Antwerpen, pp 303–317

Bonomi A (2007) Le divorce en droit communautaire entre règles de droit international privé et objectifs de droit matériel. In: Epiney A et al (eds) Die Herausforderung von Grenzen. Festschrift für Roland Bieber. Nomos, Baden-Baden, pp 771–783

Borrás A (2005) Le droit international privé communautaire: réalités, problèmes et perspectives d'avenir. Recueil des Cours 317:313–536

Brilmayer L (1995) The role of substantive and choice of law policies in the formation and application of choice of law rules. Recueil des Cours 252:9–112

Cadet F (2004) La gestion de l'internationalité par les méthodes communautaires: vers un droit international privé unifié dans l'Union européenne? Petites Affiches 57:3–12

Calvo Caravaca AL (2006) The private international law of the European community. In: Pereznieto Castro L et al (eds) Tradition and innovation of private international law at the beginning of the third millennium. Liber in memoriam of professor Friedrich K. Juenger. Juris Publishing, New York, pp 23–44

Calvo Caravaca AL, Carrascosa González J (2009) La Ley aplicable al divorcio en Europa: el futuro reglamento Roma III. Cuadernos de Derecho Transnacional, pp 36–71

Carbonneau TE (1978) The New Article 310 of the French civil code for international divorce actions. The American Journal of Comparative Law 26(3):446–460

Curry-Sumner I (2005) All's well that ends registered? Intersentia, Antwerpen

De Boer ThM (1993) De wisselwerking tussen materieel recht en conflictenrecht. Preadvies uitgebracht voor de Nederlandse Vereniging voor Rechtsvergelijking, No. 47. Kluwer, Deventer

De Boer ThM (1996) Facultative choice of law. The procedural status of choice-of-law rules and foreign law. Recueil des Cours 257:225–427

De Boer ThM (2001) Prospects for European conflicts law in the twenty-first century. In: Borchers PJ, Zekoll J (eds) International conflicts of laws for the third millennium, essays in honor of Friedrich K. Juenger. Transnational Publishers, Ardsley, pp 193–226

De Boer ThM (2008a) The second revision of the Brussels II regulation: jurisdiction and applicable law. In: Boele-Woelki K, Sverdrup T (eds) European challenges in contemporary family law. Intersentia, Antwerpen, pp 321–341

De Boer ThM (2008b) Unwelcome foreign law: public policy and other means to protect the fundamental values and public interests of the European Community. In: Malatesta A et al (eds) The external dimention of EC private international law in family and succession matters. CEDAM, Milan, pp 295–330

De Boer ThM (2009) The purpose of uniform choice-of-law rules: the Rome II regulation. NILR 56:295–332

Dethloff N (2004) Europäische Vereinheitlichung de Familienrechts. Archiv für die civilistische Praxis, pp 544–568

Drobnig U (1970) Verstößt das Staatsangehörigkeitsprinzip gegen das Diskriminierungsverbot des EWG-Vertrages? RabelsZ, pp 636–662

Fiorini A (2008) Rome III—choice of law in divorce: is the Europeanization of family law going too far? International Journal of Law, Policy and the Family 22:178–205

Fischer G (1991) Gemeinschaftsrecht und kollisionsrechtliches Staatsangehörigkeitsprinzip. In: von Bar C (ed) Europäisches Gemeinschaftsrecht und Internationales Privatrecht. Carl Heymanns Verlag, Cologne, pp 157–182

Gaertner V (2006) European choice of law rules in divorce (Rome III): an examination of the possible connecting factors in divorce matters against the background of private international law developments. Journal of Private International Law 2:99–136

Gaertner V (2008) Die Privatscheidung im deutschen und gemeinschaftsrechtlichen Internationalen Privat- und Verfahrensrecht (diss. Heidelberg). Mohr Siebeck, Tübingen

Gaudemet-Tallon H (2007) Incertaines familles, incertaines frontières: quel droit international privé? In: Mélanges en l'honneur de Mariel Revillard: liber amicorum. Defrénois, Paris, pp 147–168

Geeroms S (2004) Foreign law in civil litigation: a comparative and functional analysis. Oxford University Press, Oxford

Hausmann R (2008) Pleading and proof of foreign law—a comparative analysis. The European Legal Forum I-1-13

Heinze C (2008) Bausteine eines Allgemeinen Teils des europäischen Internationalen Privatrechts. In: Baetge D et al (eds) Die richtige Ordnung, Festschrift für Jan Kropholler. Mohr Siebeck, Tübingen, pp 105–127

Hodson D (2007) Rome III: subsidiarity, proportionality and the house of Lords. IFL, pp 32–34

Hodson D (2008a) Rome III and applicable law EU proposals scrapped: filling the vacuum. IFL 1:177–179

Hodson D (2008b) A Practical Guide to International Family Law. Jordan Publishing, Bristol.

Hohloch G (2007) Rechtswahl als Anknüpfungsprinzip (Zur Bedeutung des Parteiwillens im europäischen Internationalen Privatrecht). In: Frantzen T et al (eds) Rett og toleranse: festskrift til H.J. Thue. Gyldendal Akademisk, Oslo, pp 257–270

Ibili F (2006) Van 'Brussel II' en 'Brussel II*bis*' naar 'Brussel II*ter*'; voorstel tot introductie van forumkeuze en conflictenregels in het IPR-scheidingsprocesrecht. WPNR, pp 743–745

Jayme E (1980) Pasquale Stanislao Mancini: internationales Privatrecht zwischen Risorgimento und praktischer Jurisprudenz. Gremer, Ebelsbach

Jayme E (1981) Mancini heute—Einige Betrachtungen. In: Bernstein H et al (eds) Festschrift für Konrad Zweigert. Mohr, Tübingen, pp 145–155

Jayme E, Kohler C (2007) Europäisches Kollisionsrecht 2007: Windstille im Erntefeld der Integration. IPRax, pp 493–506

Jänterä-Jareborg M (2003) Foreign law in national courts: a comparative perspective. Recueil des Cours 304:181–385

Jänterä-Jareborg M (2008) Jurisdiction and applicable law in cross-border divorce cases in Europe. In: Basedow J et al (eds) Japanese and European Private International Law in Comparative Perspective. Mohr Siebeck, Tübingen, pp 317–343

Knot JG (2008) Internationale boedelafwikkeling Over het toepasselijke recht op de afwikkeling van nalatenschappen (diss. Groningen). Kluwer, Deventer

Kohler C (2003) Der europäische Justizraum für Zivilsachen und das Gemeinschaftskollisionsrecht. IPRax, pp 401–412

Kohler C (2008a) Zur Gestaltung des europäischen Kollisionsrecht für Ehesachen: Der steinige Weg zu einheitlichen Vorschriften über das anwendbare Recht für Scheidung und Trennung. Zeitschrift für das gesamte Familienrecht 55:1673–1681

Kohler C (2008b) Einheitliche Kollisionsnormen für Ehesachen in der Europäische Union: Vorschläge und Vorbehalte. Familie Partnerschaft und Recht, pp 193–196

Kramer XE (2008) The Rome II regulation on the law applicable to non-contractual obligations: the European private international law tradition continued. NIPR 26:414–424

Kreuzer K (2008) Was gehört in den Allgemeinen Teil eines Europäischen Kollisionsrechtes? In: Jud B et al (eds) Kollisionsrecht in der Europäischen Union. Jan Sramek Verlag, Wien, pp 1–62

Kroll K (2007) Scheidung auf europäisch?—Die (derzeit) nicht scheidbare Ehe im IPR. Das Standesamt, pp 330–336

Kropholler J (2000) Der Renvoi im vereinheitlichten Kollisionsrecht. In: Gottwald P et al (eds) Festschrift für Dieter Henrich. Verlag Ernst und Werner Gieseking, Bielefeld, pp 393–402

Kropholler J (2006) Internationales Privatrecht, 6th edn. Mohr Siebeck, Tübingen

Lamont R (2007) Habitual residence and Brussels II*bis*: developing concepts for European private international family law. Journal of Private International Law 3:261–281

Lazic V (2008) Recent developments in harmonizing 'European private international law' in family matters. European Journal of Law Reform 10(1):75–96

Lehmann M (2008) What's in a name? *Grunkin-Paul* and beyond. Yearbook of Private International Law 10:135–164

Leible S (2009) Rom I und Rom II: Neue Perspektiven im Europäischen Kollisionsrecht. Zentrum für Europäisches Wirtschaftsrecht, Bonn

Looschelders D (2008) Scheidungsfreiheit und Schutz des Antragsgegners im Internationalen Privat—und Prozessrecht. In: Baetge D et al (eds) Die Richtige Ordnung Festschrift für Jan Kropholler zum 70, Mohr Siebeck, Geburtstag, Tübingen, p 349

Martiny D (2006) Ein Internationales Scheidungsrecht für Europa. In: Freitag R et al (eds) Internationales Familienrecht für das 21. Jahrhundert. Sellier. European Law Publishers, München, pp 119–135

Martiny D (2007) Objectives and values of (private) international law in family law. In: Meeusen J et al (eds) International family law for the European Union. Intersentia, Antwerpen, pp 69–99

McEleavy P (2004) The communitarization of divorce rules: what impact for English and Scottish law? ICLQ, pp 605–642

McEleavy P (2008) Applicable law and relations with third states: The use and application of habitual residence. In: Malatesta A et al (eds) The external dimension of EC private international law in family and succession matters. CEDAM, Milan, pp 269–294

Meeusen J (2007a) What has it got to do necessarily with the European Union?: international family law and European (economic) integration. The Cambridge Yearbook of European Legal studies 2006–2007, pp 329–355

Meeusen J (2007b) Instrumentalisation of private international law in the European Union: towards a European conflicts revolution? European Journal of Migration and Law 1:287–305

Meeusen J (2008) Public policy in European private international law: in response to the contribution of Professor Th.M. de Boer on "Unwelcome foreign law". In: Malatesta A et al (eds) The external dimensions of EC private international law in family and succession matters. CEDAM, Milan, pp 331–335

Mostermans PMM (2004) Optional (facultative) choice of law? Reflections from a Dutch perspective. NILR 51:393–410

Mostermans PMM (2006) Echtscheiding, 3rd edn. Kluwer, Deventer

North P (1980) The Development of rules of private international law in the field of family law. Recueil des Cours 166:9–117

Oderkerk AE (2006) Het Groenboek inzake het toepasselijke recht en de rechterlijke bevoegdheid in echtscheidingszaken. NIPR 24:119–128

Paulino Pereira FR (2007) "Rome III": La compétence juridictionnelle et la loi applicable en matière matrimoniale. Revue du Marché commun et de l'Union européenne, pp 390–394

Pertegás M (2007) Beyond nationality and habitual residence, other connecting factors in European private international law in family matters. In: Meeusen J et al (eds) International Family Law for the European Union. Intersentia, Antwerpen, pp 319–340

Puljak MP (2003) Le droit international privé à l'épreuve du principe communautaire de non-discrimination en raison de la nationalité. Presse Universitaires d'Aix Marseille, Aix-en-Provence

Reichelt G (2007) Zur Kodifikation des Europäischen Kollisionsrechts—am Beispiel des ordre public. In: Reichelt G (ed) Europäisches Gemeinschaftsrecht und IPR. Manzsche, Wien, pp 5–11

Remien O (2001) European private international law, the European community and its emerging area of freedom, security and justice. CMLR 38:53–86

Ricci C (2008) Habitual residence as a ground of jurisdiction in matrimonial disputes: from Brussels II-*bis* to Rome III. In: Malatesta A et al (eds) The external dimension of EC private international law in family and succession matters. CEDAM, Milan, pp 207–219

Richez-Pons A (2005) Habitual residence considered as a European harmonization factor in family law (regarding the "Brussels II-*bis*" regulation). In: Boele-Woelki K (ed) Common core and better law in European family law. Intersentia, Antwerpen, pp 355–360

Romano GP (2006) Développements récents en matière d'état des personnes. La bilatéralité éclipsée par l'autorité. RCDIP 95:457–519

Roth WH (1991) Der Einfluß des Europäischen Gemeinschaftsrechts auf das Internationale Privatrecht. RabelsZ 55:623–673

Rüberg S (2005) Auf dem Weg zu einem europäischen Scheidungskollisionsrecht (diss. Konstanz), available at http://www.ub.uni-konstanz.de/kops/volltexte/2005/1694/pdf/Rueberg.pdf

Rühl G (2008) Rechtswahlfreiheit im europäischen Kollisionsrecht. In: Baetge D et al (eds) Die richtige Ordnung. Festschrift für Jan Kropholler zum 70. Geburtstag. Mohr Siebeck, Tübingen, pp 187–209

Sauveplanne JG (1990) 'Renvoi', international encyclopedia of comparative law, private international law, Chapter 6, vol III. Mohr, Tübingen

Schmidt C (2008) Das Staatsangehörigkeitsprinzip in Europa. Die Vereinbarkeit der kollisionsrechtlichen Staatsangehörigkeitsanknüpfung mit dem gemeinschaftsrechtlichen Diskriminierungsverbot. Nomos, Baden-Baden

Schulz M (2000) Verfassungsrechtliche Vorgaben für das Kollisionsrecht in einem Gemeinsamen Markt. Peter Lang, Frankfurt am Main

Siehr K (2005) General problems of private international law in modern codifications: *de lege lata* and *de lege europea ferenda*. Yearbook of Private International Law 7:17–61

Siehr K (2008) Die Kodifikation des Europäischen IPR—Hindernisse, Aufgaben und Lösungen. In: Jud B et al (eds) Kollisionsrecht in der Europäischen Union. Jan Sramek Verlag, Wien, pp 77–95

Silberman LJ (2008) Rethinking rules of conflict of laws in marriage and divorce in the United States: what can we learn from Europe? Tulane Law Review 82:1999–2019

Stone P (2002) The developing EC private international law on family matters. Cambridge Yearbook of European Legal Studies 4:373–412

Stone P (2004) The Rome II Proposal on the law applicable to non-contractual obligations. The European Legal Forum, pp 213–228

Strikwerda L (2008) Inleiding tot het Nederlandse Internationaal Privaatrecht, 9th edn. Kluwer, Deventer

Struycken AVM (2000) Het Verdrag van Amsterdam en de Haagse Conferentie voor internationaal privaatrecht. WPNR 6421:735–745

Thoma I (2007) Die Europäisierung und die Vergemeinschaftung des nationalen ordre public. Mohr Siebeck, Tübingen

Ten Wolde MH (2004) Will professionals in other countries be able to rely on a European certificate of inheritance for all purposes? In: Les Successions Internationales dans l'UE. Perspectives pour une Harmonisation Deutschen Notarinstitut (DNotI), Würzburg, pp 503–514

Ten Wolde MH (2009) Inleiding Nederlands en Europees Internationaal Privaatrecht, Deel A Algemeen deel en materieel IPR Personen-, familie- en erfrecht. Groningen, Hephaestus

Ten Wolde MH, Knot JG (2006) European international law of succession. Groningen, Hephaestus

Vonken APMJ (2006) De internationale beslissingsharmonie nader beschouwd. Tijdschrift voor Privaatrecht 43:9–125

Chapter 6
The Failure of the Establishment of a Common European Choice of Law on Divorce

6.1 Introduction

The previous chapter analysed the Brussels II*ter*-Proposal; it enhances *inter alia* the introduction of common European choice of law rules on divorce. These rules introduce a limited possibility for the spouses to designate by a common agreement the law applicable to their divorce. In the absence of such a choice, the applicable law is determined on the basis of a cascade rule based in the first place on habitual residence.

The preceding analysis has shown that the Brussels II*ter*-Proposal contains quite some issues that still need to be clarified. Some of these issues have been highly debated during the many Council meetings on the Brussels II*ter*-Proposal. However, since the beginning of the negotiations in 2006, consensus in the Council appeared difficult to reach.[1] A number of Member States have taken an obstructive stance with regard to a unified choice of law on divorce: Malta, for example, has repeatedly made clear to be unwilling to support a European regulation on the law which is applicable to divorce because of its substantive law approach.[2] The United Kingdom and Ireland have both declined to opt-in and, hence, do not participate.[3] Some other Member States, among which are the Netherlands, Sweden and the Czech Republic, have threatened to use their power of veto in order to prevent the Brussels II*ter*-Proposal from entering into force.

---

[1] The Brussels II*ter*-Proposal has even been referred to as a 'political minefield'. See 'Justice and Home Affairs: EU divorce legislation too tricky to tackle', *European Report*, No. 3332, 22 June 2007.

[2] Cf., *supra* Sect. 5.2.1: Malta is the only Member States that does not provide for divorce at all in its legislation. Maltese law does provide for legal separation.

[3] The United Kingdom and Ireland do not participate in measures pursuant to Title V of the third part of the Treaty on the Functioning of the European Union. Pursuant to a Protocol both countries do have the possibility to join these measures by means of an 'opt in' clause. See further *supra* Sect. 4.6.1.

N.A. Baarsma, *The Europeanisation of International Family Law*,
DOI: 10.1007/978-90-6704-743-2_6, © T.M.C. Asser press, The Hague,
The Netherlands, and the author 2011

Measures in the field of international family law need a unanimous Council decision.[4] But 'insurmountable difficulties' precluded the required unanimity on the Brussels II*ter*-Proposal.[5] Some of these difficulties could have been solved by means of amendments of the provisions of the Proposal. Other problems underlying the Brussels II*ter*-Proposal are by contrast more fundamental and have ultimately led to the failure of the establishment of a unified choice of law on divorce.[6] Ironically speaking, the European Union is thus split over divorce.

In this chapter the question 'where did it go wrong?' will be dealt with. Three distinct issues which underlie the failure to reach an agreement on the Brussels II*ter*-Proposal can be distinguished: the position of Malta (Section 6.2), the question of Union competence as regards the choice of law on divorce (Section 6.3) and a complicated methodological problem (Section 6.4). To two of these issues a solution was indeed found during the negotiations in the Council. Ultimately the methodological problem proved to be insurmountable.

In June 2008 the Slovenian Presidency has concluded that all possibilities for a compromise have been exhausted.[7] The procedure on enhanced cooperation has consequently been launched and has resulted in the Regulation on enhanced cooperation in the field of divorce (Section 6.5). However, it is debatable whether this conclusion could have been taken as true. At the end of this chapter (Section 6.6) the issue of possible alternatives for yet another compromise in the field of a unified choice of law on divorce will be elaborated upon.

6.2 The Position of Malta

In the whole debate on the establishment of unified choice of law rules on divorce, Malta occupies a special position. In its legislation Malta does not provide for divorce at all and it has repeatedly declared to oppose any proposal that would oblige the Maltese courts to apply foreign law to circumvent its ban on divorce. However, Malta did adopt the Brussels II*bis*-Regulation. Although Malta was obliged to accept the latter regulation as part of the *acquis communautaire* at acceding to the European Union, the introduction of the Brussels II*bis*-Regulation did not really lead to much debate in Malta.[8] By contrast to the latter Regulation, Malta did have problems with the Brussels II*ter*-Proposal.

The Council has tried to find a solution to this Maltese problem. Firstly, the possibility of an opt out, which would exempt the Maltese courts from applying

---

4 See *supra* Sect. 4.4.5.

5 See Press Release of the 2887th Meeting of the Justice and Home Affairs Council of 24 and 25 July 2008, p. 23, available at: http://ue.eu.int/uedocs/NewsWord/en/jha/102007.doc.

6 Paulino Pereira 2007, p. 394.

7 See background note of the Justice and Home Affairs Council of 5–6 June 2008, pp. 7–8, at: http://www.eu2008.si/en/News_and_Documents/Background_Information/June/0506_JHA.pdf.

8 See Farrugia 2007, p. 205.

that part of the regulation on applicable law, has been considered.[9] But the Committee on Civil Law Matters (Rome III) concluded that an opt out was not a feasible option. Any opt out would have to be considered in the light of two specific criteria, i.e. an objective justification and a temporary nature. The concerns raised by Malta could not be met by means of a derogation of a temporary nature. Moreover, most Member States considered that it was difficult to objectively justify an opt out in the context of a European instrument that aims at unifying the national choice of law rules of the Member States.[10]

During the negotiations in the Council it has been stressed that the Brussels II*ter*-Proposal does not establish the legal institution of divorce in a Member State which does not know such institution nor does it oblige a Member State to introduce divorce in its national law.[11] Following on this statement the Council made another attempt to solve the Maltese problem by means of the addition of a special provision to the Brussels II*ter*-Proposal stipulating that

> nothing in this Regulation shall oblige the courts of a Member State whose law does not provide for divorce [...] to pronounce a divorce by virtue of the application of this Regulation.[12]

This last attempt obviously had the desired effect: at the Justice and Home Affairs Council Meeting of 26 January 2008 Malta indicated that it no longer intended to oppose the Brussels II*ter*-Proposal.[13]

As a counterpart to this solution to the Maltese problem, a provision functioning as a remedy for situations in which the applicable law 'does not provide for divorce' has been inserted in the Brussels II*ter*-Proposal. In such cases, the *lex fori* will apply:

> 1. Where the law applicable pursuant to Article 20a and 20b does not provide for divorce or does not grant one of the spouses because of his or her gender equal access to divorce or legal separation, the law of the forum shall apply.[14]

Although the arrangement of this provision is not desirable from a methodological perspective,[15] it is to be applauded that Malta and the other Member States have reached this compromise.

---

[9] Council Document No. 8038/08 JUR 48 and JUSTCIV 62 of 2 April 2008.

[10] See Council Document No. 9985/08 JUSTCIV 106 of 29 May 2008, para 11, p. 4.

[11] See Council Document No. 8549/07 JUSTCIV 91 of 17 April 2007, p. 6.

[12] Article 20e-1 as proposed in Council Document No. 8587/08 JUSTCIV 73 of 18 April 2008. This issue appeared for the first time in Council Document No. ST 8028/07 JUSTCIV 75 of 30 March 2007.

[13] 'Justice and Home Affairs: Rome III: Swedish opposition not yet insurmountable', *European Report*, No. 3458, 28 January 2008.

[14] Article 20b-1 on the application of the law of the forum; see Council Document No. 9712/08 JUSTCIV 106 of 23 May 2008, p. 15. See further on this provision *supra* Sect. 5.5.3.3.

[15] See further *supra* Sect. 5.5.3.3.

6.3 The Problem of Competence

The second problem underlying the failure to reach a consensus on a common choice of law on divorce concerns the competence of the European legislature. As seen above, the competence of the European legislature as regards the Brussels II*ter*-Proposal was based on Article 65 EC-Treaty.[16] Article 65(b) EC-Treaty granted the European Community the competence to enact measures on the choice of law. However, this competence was subject to certain limits: it must concern rules in the field of judicial cooperation in civil matters, be necessary for the proper functioning of the internal market and promote the compatibility of the rules applicable in the Member States on conflict of laws. In addition, the principles of subsidiarity and proportionality must be fulfilled.

The Czech Republic, the Netherlands and the United Kingdom did not consider the European legislature to be competent on the subject of the unification of the choice of law on divorce.[17] Their objections concern two different aspects: the fulfilment, on the one hand, of the internal market requirement and, on the other, of the principles of subsidiarity and proportionality.

6.3.1 Does the Internal Market Require a Unified Choice of Law on Divorce?

Currently each Member State autonomously provides for rules on the law applicable to divorce. But these rules differ from one Member State to another.[18]

According to the European Commission the absence of unified choice of law rules on divorce is characterised by a lack of legal certainty and predictability for the spouses, insufficient party autonomy, the risk of results that do not correspond to the legitimate expectations of the citizens, the risk of difficulties for Community citizens living in third States, and the risk of rushing to court.[19] As a means to eliminate these shortcomings, the European Commission has proposed the introduction of unified choice of law rules on divorce.

The Dutch Parliament objected to the assumption that the nature and scope of these problems are so serious as to constitute an obstacle to the proper functioning of the internal market, thereby necessitating the establishment of the proposed measure:

> According to the figures of the European Commission, an estimated 170,000 "international" divorce proceedings take place each year. It follows that approximately 340,000

---

[16] Cf., *supra* Sect. 4.7.

[17] See the Annex to the COSAC Report for the precise concerns raised by these Member States.

[18] See further *supra* Sect. 5.2.2.

[19] See Green Paper on Divorce, pp. 3–6.

people are faced each year with the conflict-of-law rules of the Member States, which is equivalent to some 0.074% of the EU population (about 457 million). The possible scope of the (potential) obstacles to the free movement of persons in the internal market should therefore not be overestimated.

The question of in what percentage of these 170,000 cases the differences between national conflict-of-law rules actually result in the problems identified by the European Commission, including lack of legal certainty and the "rush to court", is disregarded. For example, it is evident from the answers to the questions in the "Green Paper on applicable law in divorce matters" that there is no (statistical) proof available of the "rush to the courts" in the majority of the Member States that have responded to the Green Paper. [...] It may therefore be considered very probable that the problems outlined by the European Commission do not occur in all the 170,000 divorce proceedings concerned.

Both Chambers also have insufficient evidence that the supposed problems do *actually* constitute an obstacle to the free movement of persons or even represent a *potential* obstacle to the proper functioning of the internal market. Both Chambers therefore have serious doubts about the opportuneness of the decision to choose Article 65 of the EC Treaty as the legal basis for the proposed Regulation.[20]

The European Commission responded to these concerns by challenging the statistical derivations of the Dutch Parliament: the dimension of the problems needs to be considered in the light of the free movement of persons. Only a fraction of the total EU population currently makes use of this right. Therefore, a comparison of the number of international divorces with the total number of divorces is more revealing: the approximately 170,000 international divorce proceedings that take place each year in the EU represent roughly 19% of all divorces.[21]

The question whether the internal market requires a common choice of law on divorce should indeed be considered in the context of the free movement of persons. This is a fundamental freedom that enhances the internal market and that contributes to the establishment of a proper European judicial area.[22]

---

[20] *Kamerstukken I/II* 2006–2007, 30 671, E and No. 5. The English translation was provided in the Dutch response to the COSAC Report; see its Annex, p. 92. The fulfillment of the internal market requirement of Article 65 EC was equally questioned by both the Czech Parliament ('*It is arguable to what extent a measure in the area of family law fulfills the last criterion, i.e. how unification of the conflict-of-law rules applicable in matrimonial matters contributes to the proper functioning of the internal market.* [...] *neither the explanatory memorandum nor the impact assessment to the proposal removes doubts* [*about; NAB*] *the necessity of a Community legal instrument regulating such conflict-of-law rules.*') and the British House of Lords ('[...] *the House of Lords EU Committee doubts whether the Commission's statistical analysis provides a sufficient basis on which to act.*'); see Annex to the COSAC Report, pp. 24–25 and 120, respectively.

[21] See the letter of the Vice-President of the European Commission of 7 December 2006, *Kamerstukken I/II*, 2006–2007, 30 671, F and No. 6: '*De omvang van het probleem in het licht van het vrije personenverkeer kan niet worden gemeten aan de totale bevolking van de EU, aangezien slechts een fractie van die bevolking thans gebruik maakt van het recht om naar een andere lidstaat te verhuizen in verband met werk. Een vergelijking van het aantal echtscheidingsgevallen waarbij collisieregels een rol spelen, met het totale aantal echtscheidingen is veelzeggender. Geschat wordt dat jaarlijks zo'n 170 000 «internationale» echtparen in Europese Unie scheiden, wat neerkomt op ongeveer 19% van alle echtscheidingen.*'

[22] See more elaborately *supra* Sect. 4.7.2.

As part of the question whether the unified choice of law on divorce complies with the internal market requirement of Article 65 EC, the European Union Committee of the British House of Lords has expressed serious doubts concerning the reliability of the European Commission's statistical analysis:

> 18. Only 13 Member States could provide the information requested and in five cases not for the full period of time (four years) requested. Significantly only one large Member State (Germany) responded. The UK was unable to do so because it does not keep the sort of statistics requested by the Commission. Whether it is safe to extrapolate for the whole Union on the basis of the Commission's study has been questioned. Practitioners expressed concern that the responses from smaller Member States with high numbers of foreign residents (such as Luxembourg and Belgium) may have skewed the statistics. [...] How, in the apparent absence of statistical data from any large Member State save Germany, the Commission can state that "the rates of international marriages and divorces do not vary enormously amongst the larger EU countries" is extraordinary.
> 19. Even if there are some 170,000 international divorces each year, doubts have been expressed as to whether this is sufficient to justify the action being proposed: what the Commission's statistics do not reveal is the number or percentage of cases where the question of applicable law has been a problem.
> [...]
> 28. [A] second concern is that the rules in Rome III could apply to cases which may have little connection with the Internal Market.
> 29. [...] the substantial variations in the figures would not seem to justify the conclusions drawn for the whole Union. The statistics are not a safe basis on which to act.[23]

To my knowledge, the Commission has never responded to these concerns.[24] However, as long as these concerns have not been refuted, they undeniably damage the credibility of the basis of the Community action.[25]

It should be borne in mind, however, that not only the scale of the problems resulting from the lack of unified choice of law rules on divorce has incited the Commission to regulate this field. A common European choice of law on divorce should be seen in a broader perspective, i.e. the realisation of a common judicial area that makes life easier for the EU citizens.[26] Moreover, the principle of mutual recognition also plays an important part in this respect:

> [T]he harmonisation of conflict-of-law rules facilitates the mutual recognition of judgments. The fact that courts of the Member States apply the same conflict-of-law rules to

[23] See House of Lords Rome III Report, pp. 8–11. The Commission's proposal on a Council Decision authorising enhanced cooperation in the area of the law applicable to divorce and legal separation, COM(2010) 104 final/2 shows that the previous statistical analysis was in fact slightly overdone. See p. 6 of the proposal: 'In 2007 there were 1 040 000 divorces in the 27 Member States of the European Union, of which 140 000 (13%) had an 'international' element.'

[24] The reason that the Commission has not responded to these concerns is probably that the concerns have been published in a Report of the House of Lords. The House of Lords has not adopted a formal reasoned opinion as such. See the Annex to the COSAC-Report, p. 120.

[25] The same goes for the already observed inconsistency in the percentage representing the number of international divorces in the EU: is it 16 or 19%? See *supra* note 236 of Chap. 4.

[26] See Impact Assessment on Divorce, p. 28.

determine the law applicable to a given situation reinforces the mutual trust in judicial decisions given in other Member States.[27]

Although both the objective of the realisation of a common judicial area and the principle of mutual recognition do shed light on the reasons for the establishment of a unified choice of law on divorce, they do not relate to the internal market requirement of Article 65 EC-Treaty.

In Chapter 4 above, it became clear that the latter requirement should not be interpreted too strictly and can be complied with rather easily. A stimulating effect towards the internal market is already enough for a Community act to comply with the internal market requirement. The shortcomings indicated by the Commission and the three other defaults hinder the free movement of persons. Therefore, the unification of the choice of law rules on divorce will remove an obstacle to the free movement of persons and will, hence, contribute to the proper functioning of the internal market.[28]

6.3.2 Fulfilment of the Principles of Subsidiarity and Proportionality

The Explanatory Memorandum to the Brussels II*ter*-Proposal justifies the fulfilment of the principles of subsidiarity and proportionality:

- **Subsidiarity principle**
  The objectives of the Proposal cannot be accomplished by the Member States but require action at Community level in the form of common rules on jurisdiction and applicable law. Jurisdiction rules as well as conflict-of-law rules must be identical to ensure the objective of legal certainty and predictability for the citizens. Unilateral action by Member States would therefore run counter this objective. There is no international convention in force between Member States on the question of applicable law in matrimonial matters. The public consultation and the impact assessment have demonstrated that the scale of the problems addressed in this proposal is significant and that it concerns thousands of citizens each year. In light of the nature and the scale of the problem, the objectives can only be achieved at Community level.
- **Proportionality principle**
  The Proposal complies with the principle of proportionality in that it is strictly limited to what is necessary to achieve its objectives. [...]
- **Choice of instrument**
  With regard to the type of legislative instrument, the nature and the objective of the proposal require the form of Regulation. The need for legal certainty and predictability calls for clear and uniform rules. The proposed rules on jurisdiction and applicable law are detailed and precise and require no implementation into national law. To leave Member States any margin of discretion for the implementation of these rules would endanger the objectives of legal certainty and predictability.[29]

---

[27] Explanatory Memorandum to the Brussels II*ter*-Proposal, p. 2.

[28] See *supra* Sect. 4.7.2.

[29] Explanatory Memorandum to the Brussels II*ter*-Proposal, p. 7. See further *supra* Sect. 4.4.4 on the principles of subsidiarity and proportionality.

Yet some Member States consider the Brussels II*ter*-Proposal in breach of the principles of subsidiarity and proportionality.[30] In November 2006 COSAC held a 'Subsidiarity and Proportionality Check' of the Brussels II*ter*-Proposal. The result of this check was that the great majority of the participating parliaments did not consider the Brussels II*ter*-Proposal to be in breach of the principles of subsidiarity and proportionality. However,

> some parliaments found that the Commission did not sufficiently justify the need for the proposed legislation with regard to the legal basis, given that Art. 65 TEC applies only in so far as it is necessary for the proper functioning of the internal market. Some of the concerns raised when checking subsidiarity and proportionality of the proposal seem to rather refer to the question of legal basis than to the principles of subsidiarity and proportionality.[31]

The COSAC Report rightly emphasised that some of the concerns expressed by the Member States with regard to the principles of subsidiarity and proportionality seem to rather challenge the legal basis of the Brussels II*ter*-Proposal.[32]

The Netherlands is one of the Member States that has raised concerns about the fulfilment of the principle of subsidiarity.[33] In the view of the Dutch Parliament, the problems indicated in the Green Paper on divorce resulting from the absence of unified choice of law rules on divorce cannot be sufficiently solved on the level of choice of law.[34] These problems can in essence be reduced to differences in the substantive divorce laws of the Member States. Therefore, the encountered problems should be solved by unifying the Member States' substantive divorce

---

[30] E.g. the Czech Republic, the Netherlands and the United Kingdom.

[31] See the Conclusion of the COSAC Report, p. 14.

[32] The European Union Committee of the British House of Lords did frankly admit that in their view the concerns regarding the Brussels II*ter*-Proposal raise both *vires* and subsidiarity questions. See House of Lords Rome III Report, p. 10.

[33] See the Reply of the Dutch government to the Green Paper on Divorce, p. 2. Available at: http://ec.europa.eu/justice_home/news/consulting_public/divorce_matters/contributions/contribution_netherlands_en.pdf. A special Dutch Temporary Commission on Subsidiarity has examined the European Commission's Proposal as to compatibility with the principles of subsidiarity and proportionality and has concluded that the Brussels II*ter*-Proposal does not comply with these principles, *KamerstukkenI/II* 2005-06, 30 671, D and No. 4. See for an in-depth analysis of the Dutch concerns raised with regard to the principles of subsidiarity and proportionality: Pontier 2007, pp. 203–216.

[34] The Czech Chamber of Deputies agreed with this point of view, although it considers the Brussels II*ter*-Proposal 'disputable' in terms of the principle of subsidiarity. See the Annex to the COSAC Report, p. 25: '*The Commission's effort towards the unification of conflict-of-law rules (that Commission wrongly designates this as "harmonization") can be considered as a step towards the harmonization of family law of the Member States, since the main objective of the proposal, i.e. "legal certainty and predictability" can be attained in full only through the complete harmonization of substantive family law of the Member States.*'

laws. The Dutch Parliament concluded accordingly that the provisions on choice of law should be deleted from the Brussels II*ter*-Proposal.[35]

The Dutch Parliament rightly stresses that the diverging substantive divorce laws of the Member States are the very source of the encountered problems. Accordingly, the unification of the substantive law provisions on divorce of the Member States would certainly solve the problems pointed out.[36] However, the European Union has no competence to unify substantive law, since measures to be taken under Article 81 TFEU are limited to those having 'cross-border implications'.[37] Due to this lack of competence, no progress can be made. The establishment of a common choice of law on divorce would mean a step forward and a, albeit partial, solution to the problems observed.[38] Furthermore, even if the EU was competent to unify substantive family law, it is highly doubtful whether a unification of the substantive divorce laws of the Member States is feasible considering the large differences in this respect.[39] It should be noted that there are some tendencies towards convergence of the substantive divorce laws of the Member States, even though the common core of divorce law in Europe is currently rather scarce.[40] Possibly these tendencies towards convergence may make a unification of the choice of law on divorce more feasible in the future.

It is, however, somewhat strange that the Dutch Parliament has not at an earlier stage opposed the establishment of European rules on jurisdiction and on recognition and enforcement in matrimonial matters (the Brussels II(*bis*)-Regulation). Theoretically speaking, the same line of reasoning would apply to these issues. Moreover, it would equally apply to other issues: why has the Dutch Parliament not adduced this line of reasoning with regard to the choice of law on, e.g., maintenance obligations? From the Dutch reply to the relevant Green Paper no similar objections can be derived.[41] Nevertheless the problems encountered in this field of law equally originate from diverging substantive law of the Member States.[42] One can therefore question whether the concerns raised by the

---

[35] See *Kamerstukken I/II* 2006–2007, 30 671, E and No. 5.

[36] See on the unification of substantive family law in general *inter alia* Boele-Woelki 1997 and Antokolskaia et al. 1999.

[37] See *supra* Sect. 4.4.2.

[38] Cf., the letter of the Vice-President of the European Commission of 7 December 2006, *Kamerstukken I/II* 2006–07, 30 671, F and No. 6.

[39] See for a broad overview of these differences *supra* Sect. 5.2.1.

[40] See Boele-Woelki et al. 2004; Antokolskaia 2006, p. 357 ff; and Boele-Woelki 2007, pp. 265–267. See also the efforts of the Commission on European Family Law (CEFL).

[41] See for the Dutch reply to the Green Paper on maintenance obligations (COM(2004) 254 final): www.europapoort.nl/9345000/1/j9vvgy6i0ydh7th/vg7slw5im1tl?key=vguwawrau0qt.

[42] This differentiation can, however, be explained by the fact that maintenance is a field of law that is less sensitive than divorce, as it verges on the law of obligations and — unlike divorce — the substantive laws of the Member States on maintenance obligations resemble each other to a large extent. An account of the Member States' laws on maintenance obligations is available on the European Judicial Network website: http://ec.europa.eu/civiljustice/maintenance_claim/maintenance_claim_gen_en.htm.

Netherlands in this respect are actually meant to challenge the principles of subsidiarity and proportionality, or whether they in fact imply a substantive objection against the Brussels II*ter*-Proposal considering the *favor divortii* prevailing in Dutch (private international) law.[43]

The European Union Committee of the British House of Lords has raised concerns as regards both the principle of subsidiarity and the principle of proportionality. The latter Committee considers the Brussels II*ter*-Proposal in breach of the principle of subsidiarity as the Commission's statistical analysis is not reliable.[44] In its view the principle of proportionality is neither complied with, as:

> 30. [...] the objective might be achieved by less simpler, possibly less prescriptive, means.
> 31. It has been suggested that if the jurisdictional rules (Brussels II) were to be improved then it would not be necessary to harmonise applicable law rules.[45]

Also to this objection the Commission has, to my knowledge, never responded.[46] The marginal justification of the fulfilment of the principle of proportionality in the Explanatory Memorandum to the Brussels II*ter*-Proposal does not succeed satisfactorily in refuting this objection.

The Czech Chamber of Deputies considers the Brussels II*ter*-Proposal 'disputable' in terms of the principle of proportionality, as it questions whether the European Union is the appropriate level for the harmonisation of the choice of law on divorce[47]:

> [...] the form of the international convention adopted by the Hague Conference on Private International Law is probably the most appropriate and widely acceptable form in the field of international family law. There is no doubt that a regulation-with regard to its direct effect and direct applicability-represents a more effective tool, but if we accede to the unification of conflict-of-law rules on divorces, we should not limit the rules only to the Member States. It is not just a problem of the European Union, it is an international problem. In addition, Denmark is not participating in the adoption of this proposal, so the unification of conflict-of-law rules in the whole European Union is just illusory.[48]

---

[43] Cf., the letter of the Minister of Foreign Affairs of 2 October 2006. *Kamerstukken II*, 2006–2007, 22 112, No. 465. In this letter the Minister states: *'De kans is niet gering dat het resultaat van de onderhandeling zal zijn een regeling van het conflictenrecht die minder gunstig is dan de huidige Nederlandse regeling, en dat aldus voor echtgenoten in Nederland meer barrières worden opgeworpen om uit elkaar te gaan dan thans het geval is.'*

[44] See *supra* Sect. 6.3.1.

[45] See House of Lords Rome III Report, p. 11.

[46] Cf., *supra* note 24 of Chap. 5.

[47] Although the Czech Republic considers this concern as an issue of proportionality, it is rather an issue of subsidiarity, as it regards the question of the appropriate level to achieve the policy objectives and to address the problems in the current situation. See further on the content of the principles of subsidiarity and proportionality *supra* Sect. 4.4.4.

[48] See Resolution of the Czech Chamber of Deputies, Annex to the COSAC Report, p. 25.

The Czech Republic thus considers the Hague Conference on Private International Law to be the most appropriate level to unify the choice of law on divorce. If there would already be a convention on this issue that could be ratified by the Member States or if there would be tangible prospects of such a convention, it would certainly be preferable that the choice of law on divorce be dealt with through a Hague convention.[49] However, in divorce there is neither a convention nor any prospect to it.

Although the Commission has not succeeded in satisfactorily justifying the fulfilment of the principles of subsidiarity and proportionality, these principles seem to have been fulfilled as regards the unified choice of law on divorce.[50] As no Member State acting alone is able to solve any problems created by the lack of uniform choice of law rules on divorce in Europe, the problems mentioned above can best be solved at the Community level. Consequently, the Community is actually competent to enact common choice of law rules on divorce.

Furthermore, even the Brussels II*ter*-Regulation — suppose that it enters into force — would be challenged non-compliance with the principles of subsidiarity and proportionality, it is doubtful what the consequences of such challenge will be. As seen above, the European legislature has a margin of appreciation with regard to the principles of subsidiarity and proportionality: a measure can only be reviewed on the grounds of these principles if it is manifestly inappropriate.[51] Since the Commission has shown in the Brussels II*ter*-Proposal that it has taken account of both principles, it is not likely that the Court of Justice will find it to be in breach of either principle.[52]

6.3.3 *Problem of European Competence Solved?*

In addition to the solution found to the problem concerning the position of Malta, also the problem of competence seems to have been 'solved', considering the following statement as a result of the Justice and Home Affairs Council meeting of 26 January 2008:

---

[49] Cf., the issue of maintenance obligations. A European Regulation applies to the issues of jurisdiction and recognition and enforcement in the matter of maintenance obligations. Ancillary to the 2007 Hague Convention on the Recovery of Child Support a separate Protocol on the law applicable to maintenance obligation has been concluded. In accordance with Article 24 of the Protocol, the European Council will most probably sign it on behalf of the European Community; see the Proposal for a Council decision on the conclusion by the European Community of the Protocol on the Law Applicable to Maintenance Obligations, COM(2009) 81 final. See further *infra* Sect. 8.4.4.3.

[50] See further *supra* Sect. 4.7.2.

[51] See *supra* Sect. 4.4.4.

[52] See also Fiorini 2008, pp. 185–186.

> Both the Netherlands and Malta, two [...] countries that were known previously to have reservations, signalled at the meeting that they do not intend to oppose the text.[53]

Consequently, it appears that the initial opposition of the Member States against the Brussels II*ter*-Proposal due to the lack of Community competence with regard to a common choice of law on divorce would not have obstructed the adoption of the Brussels II*ter*-Proposal.[54]

As seen above, the alleged lack of Community competence was one of the reasons of the opposition of both the United Kingdom and Ireland against the Brussels II*ter*-Proposal. Accordingly, both Member States did not avail themselves of their opportunity to opt into the Brussels II*ter*-Proposal. But, due to the special position of the United Kingdom and Ireland with regard to judicial cooperation in civil matters, their participation is no *conditio sine qua non* for the establishment of a common choice of law on divorce. Consequently, the Brussels II*ter*-Proposal could have been adopted without the participation of these Member States.[55]

As far as the Netherlands is concerned, it has apparently decided to give up its initial opposition against the Brussels II*ter*-Proposal.[56] Despite its objections, the Netherlands has continued to 'labour for a final compromise that would fit to the current Dutch views on choice of law on divorce and that would, therefore, be acceptable to the Netherlands.'[57] According to the Dutch Minister of Justice, the

---

[53] 'Justice and Home Affairs: Rome III: Swedish opposition not yet insurmountable', *European Report*, No. 3458, 28 January 2008.

[54] However, it cannot be stated with certainty that the problem of competence is solved, as the position of the Czech Republic in this respect is unclear. Possibly the Czech Republic never intended to use its power of veto with regard to the Brussels II*ter*-Proposal, considering the following statement in the Presidency Agenda of January 2009: '[*T*]*he Czech Republic participated in the negotiations with the parliamentary reservations.*'; see: http://www.justice2009.cz/en/justice-2009/redakce/presidency-agendas/civil-agenda/c66.

Yet, the mentioned statement can also be interpreted in a way that the Czech Republic has possibly felt that it should remain neutral on such politically sensitive issue while holding the European Presidency (first half of 2009). Consequently, the position of the Czech Republic as regards the Brussels II*ter*-Proposal remains unclear.

[55] Cf., the Maintenance Regulation has equally been adopted without the United Kingdom having opted in. Ireland did, however, opt into this Regulation. See Recitals Nos. 46 and 47 of the Preamble to the Maintenance Regulation. On 3 February 2009, after the adoption of the Maintenance Regulation, the United Kingdom has requested the Commission to opt in. The Commission has agreed to the UK's participation on 21 April 2009. The difference is, however, that the Maintenance Regulation does not provide for choice of law rules. Although the first draft of the Maintenance Regulation did contain a regulation on the law applicable to maintenance obligations, the adopted Regulation refers as regards the applicable law to the Hague Protocol on the law applicable to maintenance obligations of 23 November 2007. The United Kingdom did, however, not opt in (yet) to this Protocol. The Protocol will, by contrast, apply to Ireland.

[56] See also Boele-Woelki 2008b, p. 785: '*Ultimately, the Netherlands reluctantly accepted the Rome III proposal, although it strongly supported the* lex fori *camp.*'

[57] See letter of the State Secretary of Justice of 2 July 2008 to the Committee on Justice and Home Affairs of the Dutch Upper House of the Parliament (No. 5551493/08/6). This letter can be found at: http://www.europapoort.nl/9345000/1f/j9vvgy6i0ydh7th/vhcedoimzey0.

Netherlands has accordingly advocated in COREPER[58] to bring up anew the French proposal on the law applicable to divorce in the absence of a *professio iuris*. This proposal would allow the courts to apply the *lex fori* as long as neither party requests the application of the law designated by Article 20b Brussels II*ter*-Proposal.[59] However, in COREPER there was no inclination to reconsider the French Proposal.[60] This position of the Dutch Parliament once again endorses that it can be questioned whether the Dutch concerns are actually meant to challenge the European legislature's competence or rather imply a substantive opposition against the Brussels II*ter*-Proposal.[61]

6.4 The Methodological Problem

The last problem under discussion is the methodological problem, which is strongly connected to the different choice of law approaches to divorce that currently exist within the European Union. As indicated above, the EU Member States can be broadly divided into two categories.[62] The first category is constituted by Member States that determine the applicable law to divorce on the basis of the approach of the closest connection. The majority of the Member States belong to this category.[63] In the second category, the Member States systematically apply their own national law (*lex fori*) in international divorce proceedings.[64]

---

[58] COREPER ('Comité des représentants permanents') is a European institution preparing the decision-making of the Council. It is a permanent liaison body for the exchange of information between the national administrations and the institutions of the European Communities. See further Kapteyn and VerLoren van Themaat 1998, p. 193 ff.

[59] Cf., *supra* Sect. 5.5.3.3 on the French proposal. See also *infra* Sect. 6.5.3.2.

[60] *Kamerstukken II* 2007–08, 23 490, No. 510, Parliamentary Report of a General Consultation, p. 6.

[61] The Minister of Foreign Affairs has furthermore indicated that the decision of the United Kingdom and Ireland not to opt into the Brussels II*ter*-Proposal is an obstacle to the Netherlands: '*Een Nederlands belang is ook dat het Verenigd Koninkrijk en Ierland een "opt-in"-verklaring afleggen.*' See Letter of the Minister of Foreign Affairs of 2 October 2006, *Kamerstukken II*, 2006–2007, 22 112, No. 465. Strangely enough, this argument has not been raised with regard to the Maintenance Regulation, which has been adopted without the United Kingdom having opted in to it.

[62] See *supra* Sect. 5.2.2. Two Member States do not come under the two categories mentioned: France applies unilateral choice of law rules which only determine when French law applies and Malta does not provide for divorce in its substantive law and does, hence, not have any choice of law rules on this issue either.

[63] These Member States are: Austria, Belgium, Bulgaria, Estonia, Germany, Greece, Hungary, Italy, Lithuania, Luxemburg, the Netherlands, Spain, the Czech Republic, Poland, Portugal, Romania, Slovakia and Slovenia.

[64] Seven Member States belong to this category: Cyprus, Denmark, Finland, Ireland, Latvia, Sweden and the United Kingdom.

The choice of law rules of the Member States cannot be seen in isolation of their substantive divorce laws: the objectives that the substantive divorce laws are meant to achieve (partly) influence the arrangement of the related choice of law rules. As seen above, the objectives of the substantive divorce laws of the Member States differ fundamentally. They range from the rigid position of Malta that does not permit divorce at all, to the liberal attitude of Sweden, where divorce will be granted without a specific ground being required. In between, there is a wide variety of conditions, such as mutual consent, or in the absence of an agreement, a *de facto* separation for at least six months in the Czech Republic to five years in Cyprus.[65]

These profound differences in approach as regards divorce between the Member States constitute a serious obstacle to the establishment of unified choice of law rules in this area.[66]

The Commission has decided to unify the choice of law rules on divorce on the basis of the principle of the closest connection.[67] The principle of closest connection requires such arrangement of the choice of law rules that they lead to the application of a law to which both spouses are connected.[68] Yet, the Commission does not explain the rationale behind this approach. Most probably the unified choice of law on divorce is based on the approach of the closest connection for the fact that the majority of the Member States currently propagate this approach. However, a recent evaluation of the private international law rules on divorce of eight European countries has shown that in all of them the application of the *lex fori* was general or quasi-general.[69]

Although the analysis below will show that the principle of the closest connection is the best approach for the common choice of law on divorce, the lack of explanation of the chosen approach is not likely to contribute to its acceptation by the Member States that currently adhere to the *lex fori* approach.

Which choice of law methodology should underlie the European choice of law on divorce?

De Boer considers both the principle of party autonomy and the principle of functional allocation not suitable as a basis for common choice of law rules on divorce, as both principles would encounter difficulties: the social policies underlying the substantive divorce laws of the Member States are too

---

65 A very broad classification of the substantive divorce laws of the Member States is given above in the table included in Sect. 5.2.1.

66 See also Rüberg 2005, p. 106 ff; Bonomi 2007, pp. 779–780; Boele-Woelki 2008b, pp. 784–785; De Boer 2008, p. 334 ff; Kohler 2008b, p. 195. See more general Cadet 2004, p. 9.

67 See the Green Paper on Divorce, p. 7.

68 *Supra* Sect. 2.4.

69 Romano 2006, pp. 457–519. It is to be noted that seven of these countries are EU Member States and only one of them (the United Kingdom) expressly adheres to the *lex fori* approach. Cf., the position of the Netherlands, which currently belongs to the category of States that determine the applicable law on the basis of the closest connection. However, in its reply to the Green Paper on Divorce it has advocated a *lex fori* approach. See on this issue already De Boer 2001, p. 211.

divergent.[70] With regard to the principle of functional allocation — i.e. the choice of law approach based on the function of the corresponding substantive law, mainly in order to protect the weaker party — he rightly stresses that in case of divorce the weaker party cannot be allocated.

De Boer regards the introduction of the principle of party autonomy, which allows the spouses to choose between alternative laws, useless as long as the result to be favoured is not agreed upon: dissolution of the marriage at the request of either spouse, or preservation of the marriage as long as possible. The Member States which adhere to a *favor matrimonii* approach are not likely to approve the principle of party autonomy: allowing the spouses to choose the law applicable to their divorce *de facto* evidently implies that party autonomy will often be used to choose a 'divorce-friendly' law.[71] But does this necessarily mean that the principle of party autonomy is unsuitable as such for an area in which the substantive law approaches of the Member States differ greatly?

Strikingly, during the preparatory phase of and the negotiations on the Brussels II*ter*-Proposal the introduction of party autonomy in the field of divorce did not seem to be highly opposed.[72] This at least suggests that the diverging substantive law approaches do not necessarily constitute an insurmountable barrier to the introduction of the principle of party autonomy.

In European context the principle of party autonomy should be considered as a principle of European private international law that aims to allow parties to more

---

[70] See De Boer 2008, p. 336: '*The principle of party autonomy can hardly be reconciled with the notion that divorce cannot be granted on the grounds of mutual consent, a that view still prevails in a number of member states. The principle, allowing a choice between alternative laws, is useless as long as we are not agreed on the result to be favoured: dissolution of the marriage at the mere request of either spouse, or preservation of the marital status as long as possible. The principle of functional allocation, calling for the application of the law of the weaker party's social environment, cannot be resorted to either, because it is impossible to mark either husband or wife as the weaker party.* [...] *That leaves us — at least as a basis for unification — with the neutral choice-of-law criterion of the closest connection.*'

[71] See equally Bonomi 2007, p. 783. Bonomi argues furthermore that allowing party autonomy would join the development in several Member States of increasingly submitting divorce to the free disposal of the spouses: '*Sur le plan des principes, elle peut cependant se justifier si l'on considère que dans la plupart des Etats la dissolution du mariage au cours des dernières décennies a été de plus en plussoumise à la disponibilité des époux. L'évolution en grande partie achevée en Europe du principe de divorce par faute, voire de la prohibition du divorce, en faveur d'un régime fondé sur le constat de la rupture irréversible de la communauté conjugale, l'introduction de procédures facilitées en cas de requête conjointe et plus récemment, l'admission, même dans des pays traditionnellement restrictifs, de mécanismes presque automatiques de divorce, fondés sur la simple requête unilatérale de l'un des époux et sans aucun véritable pouvoir de contrôle de la part de l'autorité compétente sont autant de manifestations d'une véritable métamorphose du droit de divorce. Dans ce contexte, l'attribution aux époux, dans des situations internationales, du droit de désigner la loi applicable n'est, pour la plupart des pays européens, pas choquante.*' See equally Kohler 2008b, p. 195.

[72] Cf., Oderkerk 2006, pp. 124–125; Boele-Woelki 2008b, p. 784. It must be admitted that some Member States (e.g. Finland) did support the introduction of the *professio iuris* on divorce in their reply to the Green Paper on Divorce, but they wished to limit the choice to the *lex fori*.

or less fashion their legal relationships to their own needs. All current and proposed European regulations providing for choice of law rules contain the possibility to choose the applicable law as principal rule.[73]

Moreover, according to Bonomi the introduction of a *professio iuris* on divorce would be no more than to openly recognise the party autonomy that is currently already indirectly provided for by the Brussels II*bis*-Regulation:

> Il convient d'ajouter que, dans les faits, les époux, et même l'un seul d'entre eux bénéficient d'ores et déjà de la liberté de déterminer (au moins indirectement) le droit applicable au divorce, dans la mesure où ils peuvent saisir l'un ou l'autre des tribunaux compétents sur la base du Règlement "Bruxelles II-*bis*". Ils peuvent exercer ce choix en fonction du droit qui sera finalement appliqué au fond à leur demande de divorce. Face à un tel *forumshopping*, mieux vaut reconnaître ouvertement le droit de désigner le droit applicable, car cela permet de mieux garantir la sécurité et la prévisibilité du droit.[74]

Consequently, the area of divorce does not seem to necessarily be opposed to the introduction of the principle of party autonomy.

In view of the formal requirement of the *professio iuris* as regards its form — a common agreement is required pursuant to Article 20a(2) of the Brussels II*ter*-Proposal — not all parties will be able to use the possibility to choose the law applicable. Therefore, the common choice of law should contain a provision that determines the law applicable to divorce in the absence of a *professio iuris*.

In this regard the fact that divorce is an area in which the substantive law approaches of the Member States differ greatly does truly affect the arrangement of the choice of law. The common choice of law rules should be neutral, i.e. rules which are blind to the result they achieve in terms of substantive law. Only in case of neutral choice of law rules the Member States are likely to ignore the strong social policies that underlie their choice of law rules.[75] Choice of law rules which are based on the principle of the closest connection are - in principle - neutral. The principle of the closest connection does not make any distinction on the basis of the content or the source of the applicable law, and neither between foreigners or 'own' citizens.[76] A legal relationship is referred to a certain legal system by means of specific objective criteria, i.e. connecting factors, determining with which jurisdiction a certain type of legal relationship has the closest connection. The principle of the closest connection does imply that the choice of law rules may sometimes lead to the reference of a specific case to a foreign legal system. However, some Member States take the position that they do not want their courts to apply foreign divorce law, since such law might be more restrictive or more liberal than their own law. These Member States wish to continue to apply their own substantive law (the *lex fori*) to any divorce requested in their courts, regardless of the nationality or the place of habitual residence of the

---

[73] See further *infra* Sect. 8.4.3.

[74] Bonomi 2007, pp. 774–775.

[75] Cf., De Boer 2008, p. 336.

[76] See Pontier 1997, p. 377.

spouses.[77] Although the decision of the United Kingdom and Ireland not to opt in to the Brussels II*ter*-Proposal for this reason could have been foreseen, also other Member States strongly opposed the Brussels II*ter*-Proposal for this reason.[78] The strongest opponent in this respect, Sweden, has repeatedly declared that it is not willing to accept the application of any other law than its own liberal law in international divorce cases.[79] Kohler has pointed out that this position does not show much willingness to cooperate in the framework of the European integration and, moreover, that it contravenes the principle of mutual trust:

> Kritisch betrachtet werden muss die Haltung, die sich grundsätzlich gegen die Anwendung fremden Rechts in Ehesachen wendet. [...] Diese Haltung nimmt das Recht und die Identität anderer an einer auslandsverknüpften Situation beteiligten Staaten und Personen nicht ernst und wirkt im globalen Zusammenhang provinziell. In einer Integrationsgemeinschaft wie der Europäischen Union steht sie im Widerspruch zu dem vom Gemeinschaftsgesetzgeber und vom *EuGH* hervorgehobenen Grundsatz des gegenseitigen Vertrauens, das die Mitgliedstaaten einander entgegen bringen sollen und das auf der vorausgesetzten Gleichwertigkeit der Rechtsordnungen beruht.[80]

Although Kohler rightly stresses that the refusal of some Member States to apply any other law than their own does not express much willingness to cooperate, the emphasis on the violation of the principle of mutual trust can be questioned. Does the principle of mutual trust actually entail that Member States can no longer propagate a *lex fori*-approach? This seems a too extensive interpretation of this principle, as a refusal to apply foreign law does not necessarily infringe the equivalence of the legal systems of the Member States.

There is yet no denying that the Council was confronted with the problem that some Member States refused to apply foreign law and it has—by means of a compromise — tried to give the *lex fori* a more prominent position in the Brussels II*ter*-Proposal, *inter alia* by the addition of the possibility to apply the *lex fori* in

---

[77] This resistance is (partly) connected with the universal character of the proposed choice of law rules, as they can designate the law of a Member State or the law of a third State. See further *supra* Sect. 5.4.1.1. In extra-European cases it might happen that the applicable law is the law of a country where, for instance, religion (such as the Islam) plays a central role, which might disrespect the principle of the equality of the spouses. See on this issue Boele-Woelki 2008b, p. 784.

[78] See also Kohler 2008a, p. 1678.

[79] See e.g. www.thelocal.se/9784/20080126/. Jänterä-Jareborg 2008, p. 340 has listed the three intertwined objections on which Sweden's opposition is primarily based. Firstly, according to Swedish law the right to divorce is a fundamental right. Secondly, the Swedish Parliament considers that the Brussels II*ter*-Proposal does not pay due regard to the effects of immigration from countries outside of the European Union and the importance of integration and equality. Finally, as far as forum shopping or rush to court occur, it is not motivated by the differences between the Member States' choice of law rules on divorce. Decisive is instead what rules apply to the various ancillary claims to divorce. The Brussels II*ter*-Proposal does not solve this essential problem.

[80] Kohler 2008b, p. 196. Cf., Israël 2001, p. 141, who regards the application of a foreign Member State's law as a *comitas Europaea*, which is consequence of the principle of mutual recognition.

cases in which the applicable law does not provide for divorce.[81] However, such an addition is no longer in line with the objective of neutral choice of law rules. And that is exactly where the next series of problems start. A revealing statement in this respect has come from two Irish authors who regard the Brussels II*ter*-Proposal as having swept aside any prospect of reconciliation between spouses who have links to other EU jurisdictions by imposing a *favor divortii* regime.[82]

The neutrality of the choice of law rules of the Brussels II*ter*-Proposal can, therefore, be questioned: although the initial Proposal of the Commission did succeed in establishing neutral choice of law rules, the negotiations in the Council and the resulting amendments give the opposite impression and seem to rather propagate a *favor divortii* approach.[83]

The resistance of the Member States against the Brussels II*ter*-Proposal at issue consequently seems to be the result of a lack of agreement as to its methodological approach.

In respect of the desirable neutrality of the European choice of law on divorce the following two remarks must be made.

In the first place, the question must be asked to what extent a neutral regulation of the choice of law on divorce is still within the bounds of the possible.[84] The Brussels II*bis*-Regulation, currently providing for rules on jurisdiction and on recognition and enforcement in matrimonial matters and in matters of parental responsibility, clearly reflects the intention to facilitate the dissolution of a marriage.[85] Some even consider both the jurisdictional rules and the rules on recognition and enforcement to be based on a *favor divortii* approach.[86] Article 3 of the Brussels II*bis*-Regulation contains seven alternative grounds for jurisdiction, which has the effect that the spouse who wishes to obtain a divorce may have several options as regards the competent court. From the automatic recognition of foreign decisions on divorce (Article 21 et seq Brussels II*bis*-Regulation) it is even

---

81 See *supra* Sect. 5.5.3.3.

82 McNamara and Martin 2006, p. 16 who even refer in this respect to divorce as '*a commodity that can be bought on the European market*'. Such reaction was already predicted by Meeusen 2007, p. 343.

83 See equally Kohler 2008b, pp. 195–196: '*Während in dem Vorschlag der Kommission eine materielle Aufladung der Anknüpfungen vermieden wird, zeigen* [...] *die bisherigen Arbeiten in dem Rat ein anderes Bild. Hier stehen sich* favor divortii [...] *gegenüber*.' See also Fiorini 2008, p. 193 observing that '*the proposal is based on a number of substantive presuppositions: there is a right to divorce, divorce should be egalitarian, easy, and quick,* à la carte.'

84 Provided that neutral choice of law rules can be provided for at all; very sceptic on this issue is De Boer 2004, pp. 39–55.

85 Cf., Van den Eeckhout 2004, pp. 58–59; Van den Eeckhout 2008a, pp. 89–90. The proposed amendments of the jurisdictional rules in the Brussels II*ter*-Proposal liberalise these rules even more by introducing the possibility of a choice of court (Article 3a Brussels II*ter*-Proposal) and the *forum necessitatis* (Article 7a Brussels II*ter*-Proposal).

86 See e.g. Kohler 2001, p. 41 ff; Mostermans 2006, p. 2 ff (with regard to jurisdiction) and pp. 74–75 (with regard to recognition and enforcement); Bonomi 2007, p. 771 ff; Shannon 2007, pp. 149–150.

more clear that the Brussels II*bis*-Regulation is inspired by a *favor divortii* approach: the rules on recognition only apply to decisions granting a divorce and not to those rejecting a divorce.

Furthermore, De Boer has entered upon the question whether the principle of the closest connection can be considered as the best approach of the unification of choice of law rules in an area in which strong social policies determine the content of the corresponding substantive law.[87] Since the policies of the Member States with regard to divorce can be considered as being largely incompatible, the results of such a neutral choice of law would prove to be unsatisfactory — not to say unacceptable — in cases in which the applicable foreign law is directly conflicting with the *lex fori*, as it proves to be too liberal or too restrictive. As a consequence, the national courts will be tempted to fall back on escape devices, such as the public policy exception in order to circumvent the application of foreign law.[88] This certainly is a conceivable risk. However, as argued above, a possible solution to this problem would be for the Member States to reach a basic agreement on what can and cannot constitute a 'manifest incompatibility' with the public policy in the sense of Article 20e Brussels II*ter*-Proposal. Such an agreement should largely remove the mentioned problem. The mentioned objections do not convince and, hence, the principle of the closest connection seems to remain the most suitable basis for the common choice of law.[89]

In the end, this methodological problem has led to the failure to reach an agreement on the Brussels II*ter*-Proposal.[90] Consequently, two possible solutions were left so as to overcome the resulting paralysis: either to abandon the Proposal, or to search for alternatives. The Council has chosen for the latter solution.

6.5 Will There be a Common Choice of Law on Divorce in the EU in the Future?

Now that it has become clear that the Commission's Proposal and the attempts the Council has made to reach consensus on the issue of a unified system of choice of law on divorce have all been rejected, the question arises whether there are any alternatives.

While looking for alternatives, the question that inevitably comes up is whether the European Union actually needs common choice of law rules on divorce. After all, one could conclude that the current regulation on recognition, pursuant to which divorces issued in one Member State have to be recognised in all other Member States independently from the law applied (Article 21 in conjunction with

[87] De Boer 2008, p. 339.

[88] Ibid., p. 339.

[89] See *supra* Sect. 5.7.

[90] See equally Boele-Woelki 2008a, p. 261.

Article 25 Brussels II*bis*-Regulation), suffices. In other words, what is the purpose of choice of law rules if a divorce pronounced in one Member State can be recognised throughout the European Union after all?

Kohler is very clear on this issue. Already strongly opposed to the *Anerkennung statt IPR*-approach in general,[91] he has specifically argued for the urgency of the establishment of common choice of law rules on divorce, considering the different interests that are involved as regards affairs of status:

> Die Pflicht zur Anerkennung kollisionsrechtlich abweichender Entscheidungen bewirkt in Übrigen eine Verdrängung der Verweisungsnormen des Anerkennungsstaates des dortigen internationales Privatrechts. Dies kann in personenstandsrechtlichen Materien, in denen es nicht nur um Individualinteressen geht, zur kritikwürdigen Widersprüchen innerhalb der Rechtsordnung des Anerkennungsstaates führen. Um diese empfindliche Schwäche der Rechtsvereinheitlichung in der EU zu beseitigen, ist die Schaffung einheitlicher Kollisionsnormen vordringlich.[92]

Besides, as has already been discussed in Section 4.4.4.2 above, the need for choice of law rules on divorce is explained by the fact that these rules actually have a proper function, mainly as regards the achievement of justice. In addition, the choice of law equally plays an important part in terms of legal certainty and predictability for the spouses. Therefore, it is important to continue to look for alternatives in order to establish a unified choice of law on divorce.

In July 2008 the procedure on enhanced cooperation was commenced so as to overcome the paralysis that has resulted from the failure to reach a consensus on the issue of a unified choice of law on divorce. This procedure will be discussed below in Section 6.5.1.

There may nevertheless have been more alternatives to overcome the deadlock that has arisen in the establishment of unified choice of law rules on divorce in the EU. Hereinafter the conceivable alternatives will be inquired into, in connection with the question whether the discussed alternative is feasible, and if so desirable. The following alternatives will be discussed: limiting the scope of application of the choice of law to intra-European cases (Section 6.5.2), the *lex fori in foro proprio*-approach, the 'French proposal' and other means to enhance the role of the *lex fori* (Section 6.5.3), and, finally, the possibility of a less stringent interpretation of the principle of the closest connection (Section 6.5.4).

---

[91] Cf., Kohler 2003, p. 412. See further on this approach *supra* Sect. 4.4.4.2.

[92] Kohler 2008a, p. 1675. See equally Kohler 2002, pp. 711, 713: '*Es muß in das Bewußtsein gerückt werden, daß bei divergierenden Kollisions-und Sachrecht der Mitgliedstaaten die Anerkennung und Vollstreckung fremder Entscheidungen ohne Rücksicht auf das angewendete Recht zu Widersprüchen führt, welche die Kohärenz der nationalen Rechtsordnungen in Frage stellen und die gerade im Familien- und Erbrecht häufig nicht erträglich sind. Sind aufgrund der einheitlichen Zuständigkeitsregeln die Gerichte mehrerer Mitgliedstaaten mit divergierenden Kollisionsnormen konkurrierend zuständig, so bestimmt die Wahl des Gerichts zugleich das anwendbare Recht, ohne daß dem in dem oder den Anerkennungsstaaten entgegengetreten werden könnte.*'

6.5.1 Enhanced Cooperation

In June 2008 the Slovenian Presidency concluded that all possibilities for a compromise on the establishment of a common choice of law on divorce have been exhausted.[93] Accordingly, the Justice and Home Affairs Council of 5 and 6 June 2008 confirmed somewhat cryptically:

> A large majority of Member States supported the objectives of this proposal for a Council Regulation [i.e. the Brussels II*ter*-Proposal; NAB]. Therefore and due to the fact that the unanimity required to adopt the Regulation could not be obtained, the Council established that the objectives of Rome III cannot be attained within a reasonable period by applying the relevant provisions of the Treaties. Work should continue with a view to examining the conditions and implications of possibly establishing enhanced cooperation between Member States.[94]

It is the first time in history that some of the national parliaments have threatened to exercise their power of veto awarded by ex-Article 67(5) EC-Treaty (now: Article 81(3) TFEU).

In an attempt to reach yet another compromise, the idea of enhanced cooperation has been launched. This procedure allows a group of Member States to move ahead in one particular area, even though other states are opposed. In July–August 2008, nine Member States (Austria, Bulgaria, Greece, Spain, Italy, Luxembourg, Hungary, Romenia and Slovenia) formally requested enhanced cooperation, asking the Commission to legislate for a common standard for divorces of international couples on their territory. In January 2009, France also addressed a similar request. In March 2010, Greece withdrew its request.[95] Thus the proposed mechanism just managed the required number of 'at least' nine participating Member States. In the meantime five other Member States decided to participate as well: Belgium, Germany, Latvia, Malta and Portugal.

Enhanced cooperation is regulated by Article 20 of the EU-Treaty and Articles 326 to 334 of the Treaty on the Functioning of the European Union. Although the Treaty of Amsterdam already provided for the possibility of enhanced cooperation, it is the first time such a procedure has started.[96] The procedure is meant to be a 'last resort'-option, any subsequent agreement reached is open to all other Member States; the Commission is placed under an active responsibility to ensure that

---

[93] See background note of the Justice and Home Affairs Council of 5–6 June 2008, pp. 7–8, available at: http://www.eu2008.si/en/News_and_Documents/Background_Information/June/0506_JHA.pdf.

[94] See EU Council Factsheet on decisions in civil law matters, p. 2, available at: http://www.consilium.europa.eu/ueDocs/cms_Data/docs/pressData/en/jha/101000.pdf.

[95] See Commission proposal for a Council Decision authorising enhanced cooperation in the area of the law applicable to divorce and legal separation, COM(2010) 104 final/2, p. 3.

[96] See for analysis of the procedure of enhanced cooperation: Prinssen 2008, spec. 62–67; and Amtenbrink and Kochenov 2009.

Member States are encouraged to participate.[97] According to Article 329 TFEU the Member States intending to establish enhanced cooperation themselves should address a request to the Commission. It will then be up to the Commission to make a proposal to the Council based on the request. Subsequently, the Council has to authorise the establishment of enhanced cooperation acting by qualified majority. An important element is that the enhanced cooperation should aim to further the objectives of the Union, protect its interests and reinforce its integration process (Article 20(1) EU-Treaty). According to the Commission, these requirements are complied with by establishing enhanced cooperation in the field of divorce.[98] However, one can have doubts whether the creation of a 'divided' European area in the field of the choice of law on divorce would reinforce the Union's integration process.[99]

In March 2010, the European Commission published the proposal on enhanced cooperation in the field of divorce. Because of the lapse of time between the request of the mentioned Member States and the actual proposal and because of a number of statements from the Commission, this proposal was published rather unexpectedly. However, the proposal on enhanced cooperation is one of the first actions undertaken by the new EU Justice Commissioner Ms. Reding.[100]

The European Commission initially proved to be willing to examine favourably the formal request of the Member States to present a proposal for enhanced cooperation. The Commission did not want to indicate beforehand what the terms of such a proposal might be.[101] It stressed that it would consider the request in the light of the political, legal and practical aspects of a proposal of this nature. At the informal Council meeting of 15 and 16 January 2009 the possibility of enhanced cooperation in the field of the choice of law on divorce was discussed. The discussions made clear that the Member States are divided on the issue.[102] During this meeting the Commission has postponed the procedure.[103] Apparently it wishes to

---

97 See Kortenberg 1998, p. 833, stating that '*closer cooperation must* [...] *be temporary, and everything possible should be done to allow those States who are not part of an initial group to join in as soon as possible.*'

98 See Commission proposal for a Council Decision authorising enhanced cooperation in the area of the law applicable to divorce and legal separation, COM(2010) 104 final/2, pp. 3–12.

99 See equally Boele-Woelki 2008b, p. 789.

100 See: http://blog.divorce-online.co.uk/?p=534: '*incoming EU justice commissioner Viviane Reding said she would present a demand for "enhanced cooperation" in this area within three months of taking office.*'

101 See Council Document No. 11984/08 JUSTCIV 150 of 23 July 2008, para 14.

102 See *Kamerstukken II* 2008–2009, 23 490, No. 541, p. 5: '*De meeste ministers die het woord voerden, gaven aan weinig heil te zien in versterkte samenwerking voor Rome III. Daarbij merkten enkelen op dat het familierecht nu juist een terrein is waar samenwerking met minder dan 27 lidstaten geen goede optie is, anderen wilden versterkte samenwerking op dit gebied niet uitsluiten, maar benadrukten dat de groep van deelnemende landen dan wel belangrijk groter moet zijn dan het minimum van 8 lidstaten. Weer andere landen hielden vast aan hun wens tot versterkte samenwerking.*'

103 At this meeting the then Commissioner for justice and home affairs, Mr. Barrot, declared that there was, as yet, not enough support. See: www.dw-world.de/dw/article/0,,3950713,00.html.

avoid creating a 'divided' European area.[104] In June 2009 it seemed as if the Commission did not intend to present a proposal for enhanced cooperation; instead, it announced to present a revised proposal for a regulation.[105] Furthermore, the Stockholm Programme also seemed to hint at the establishment of a common EU-wide choice of law on divorce.[106]

The EU nevertheless moved ahead with enhanced cooperation and in December 2010 the Regulation on enhanced cooperation in the field of divorce. This regulation essentially reproduces the choice of law rules as introduced by the failed Brussels II*ter*-Proposal (if compared to the last Council draft of the Brussels II*ter*-Proposal of 23 May 2008): although a number of issues which have been pointed out as problematic in the previous chapter have been addressed,[107] the possible legal systems out of which the spouses can choose have remained the same as well as the cascade rule providing for the applicable law in the absence of a *professio iuris*.

The choice of law provisions on divorce and legal separation of this regulation will apply in fourteen Member States[108] as from 21 June 2012.[109]

Is the Regulation on enhanced cooperation in the field of the choice of law on divorce to be welcomed? Foremost, it is regrettable that the Member States failed to agree on a common choice of law on divorce, for reaching a consensus is obviously to be preferred. However, the mechanism of enhanced cooperation allows at least a number of Member States to proceed and maybe the advantages of their enhanced cooperation will persuade other Member States to join the

---

[104] See Vandystadt 2009, p. 11; 'Brussels seeks compromise over divorce laws proposal', *Times of Malta* of 28 March 2009, available at: http://www.timesofmalta.com/articles/view/20090328/local/brussels-seeks-compromise-over-divorce-laws-proposal: '*In a bid to secure a deal, EU Justice Commissioner Jacques Barrot said the Commission intended to present a fresh proposal on transnational divorce, known technically as Rome III, without resorting to the mechanism of enhanced cooperation requested by 10 member states.*'

[105] See: http://blog.divorce-online.co.uk/?p=205. However, from a communication of the Commission of 10 June 2009 it seemed strangely enough as if the Brussels II*ter*-Proposal was still pending. See the Communication from the Commission to the Council, the European Parliament, the European Economic and Social Committee and the Committee of the Regions on Justice, Freedom and Security in Europe since 2005: An Evaluation of the Hague Programme and Action Plan of 10 June 2009, COM(2009) 263 final, p. 12: '*A legislative proposal on the law applicable to divorce (known as 'Rome III') is being discussed in the Council and Parliament.*'

[106] See Stockholm Programme, p. 24: 'the European Council considers that the process of harmonising conflict-of-law rules at Union level should also continue in areas where it is necessary, like separation and divorces.' However, the Commission considers that using enhanced cooperation is in line with this statement in the Stockholm Programme; see Commission Proposal for a Council Decision authorising enhanced cooperation in the area of the law applicable to divorce and legal separation, COM(2010) 104 final/2, p. 12.

[107] E.g. the application of the *lex fori* if the foreign applicable law 'does not provide for divorce' is defined more clearly in Article 10 of the regulation on enhanced cooperation. Cf., *supra* Sect. 5.5.3.3.

[108] Austria, Belgium, Bulgaria, France, Germany, Hungary, Italy, Latvia, Luxemburg, Malta, Portugal, Romania, Slovenia and Spain.

[109] Cf., Article 21 of the Regulation on enhanced cooperation in the field of divorce.

cooperation. Yet, now the Regulation on enhanced cooperation largely mirrors the failed Brussels II*ter*-Proposal it is highly unlikely that all Member States will eventually join the cooperation.

Moreover, enhanced cooperation certainly has more shortcomings. There is a risk that it will result in an even more complicated situation than the current one, namely in a patchwork of rights, powers and procedures which will be complicated for legal practitioners and their clients.[110] In addition, the major risk is the precedent that enhanced cooperation in the field of divorce creates for all future EU projects on international family law, such as matrimonial property and succession.[111]

Finally, Boele-Woelki has pointed out to the risk that the enhanced cooperation can be established not only by those Member States supporting the Brussels II*ter*-Proposal, but:

> [...] then another group of Member States might move in a different direction. Those who favour the *lex fori* approach, for instance, might come up with a new Rome III proposal which contains the uncomplicated rule that the competent court can apply its own law provided that the parties have not chosen the applicable law [...] This would then result in two Rome III instruments which contain different rules for the applicable law. Undoubtedly this would create uncontrollable layers of complexity. In addition another important detail should be kept in mind: the enhanced cooperation cannot become exclusive; any other Member State must be able to join the original group at a later stage and also a switch from one instrument to the other should be possible.[112]

Although this risk theoretically exists, it is not very likely to occur in view of the role of the Commission in the initiation of enhanced cooperation. It is not very probable that the Commission would allow other Member States to establish enhanced cooperation on a different basis. Furthermore, allowing two different enhanced cooperation instruments on one issue would clearly be contrary to the requirements posed by Article 20(1) EU-Treaty, as it would neither further the objectives of the Union nor reinforce its integration process.

The Commission is aware of the possible disadvantages, but 'considers that the benefits of using enhanced cooperation in the area of the law applicable to divorce and legal separation are numerous compared to the option of the status quo and that the advantages in this particular case of enhanced cooperation outweigh the possible disadvantages.'[113] It must be admitted that, now the establishment of a common choice of law on divorce had clearly arrived at an impasse, it is better to have some Member States sharing a choice of law system in the field of divorce than none. In the situation of enhanced cooperation between the nine participating Member States, the twenty-six different choice of law regimes that currently exist

---

[110] The Estonian government even fears that enhanced cooperation would 'open up a Pandora's box'. See http://www.eubusiness.com/news-eu/1217000821.83/.

[111] See also Boele-Woelki 2008a, p. 261; Mansel et al. 2009, p. 9.

[112] Boele-Woelki 2008b, p. 790.

[113] See Commission Proposal for a Council Decision authorising enhanced cooperation in the area of the law applicable to divorce and legal separation, COM(2010) 104 final/2, p. 12.

in the twenty-six Member States that participate in judicial cooperation in civil matters would reduce to eighteen different legal regimes.[114]

As mentioned above, there may have been more alternatives to overcome the deadlock that has arisen in the establishment of unified choice of law rules on divorce in the EU. These alternatives will be discussed below.

6.5.2 Limitation of the Scope of Application to Intra-European Cases

In the foregoing it became clear that the European Union is competent to enact universal choice of law rules. In addition, the establishment of universal choice of law rules certainly offers advantages, specifically in terms of ease of use of the European choice of law and of legal certainty.[115]

Although these advantages are clear, the Brussels II*ter*-Proposal has shown that it is questionable whether such a universal scope of application is feasible. After all, the major obstacle in the adoption of a common European choice of law on divorce (for Sweden) was that it could possibly lead to the application of foreign law to an international divorce case.[116] As regards the universal scope of the common choice of law on divorce of the Brussels II*ter*-Proposal Beaumont has questioned

> whether it is really necessary for the proper functioning of the internal market to apply foreign law on divorce from outside the Community when the connection with the Community is quite slim [...]. In quite a number of cases only one party is connected with the Community and it is also possible that quite a lot of the issues surrounding the marriage might not be connected with the Community. You could therefore have a situation where non-EU law is being applied under this instrument and it is certainly arguable as to whether that is necessary for the proper functioning of the internal market.[117]

Would a restriction of the scope of application of the common choice of law to strictly intra-European situations[118] have solved the observed problems?

The resistance of Sweden — the strongest opponent in this respect — was to a considerable extent connected to the possible application of foreign law to divorce. In extra-European cases it might happen that the applicable law is the law of a state where, for instance, religion (such as the Islam) plays a central role, which might

---

[114] Ibid., p. 9.

[115] See *supra* Sect. 5.4.1.1.

[116] Cf., *supra* Sect. 6.4. Sweden repeatedly expressed the fear that its courts would be obliged to apply 'Iranian divorce law'. See e.g. Küchler 2006.

[117] P. Beaumont in response to Q5 in the Minutes of Evidence taken before the Select Committee on the European Union (Sub-Committee E), 18 October 2006; appendix to the House of Lords Rome III Report.

[118] Provided that this restriction can be made; as seen in Sect. 5.4.1.1 above, the differentiation between intra- and extra-European cases is intricate.

disrespect the principle of equality of the spouses. The restriction of the scope of application to intra-European cases could thus provide for a solution to this issue. However, it does not remove Sweden's other principle objection to the Brussels II*ter*-Proposal, which is related to the fact that according to Swedish law the right to divorce is a fundamental right, which should not way be obstructed at all. The application of a less liberal divorce law of another Member State, such as Irish law, could then still encounter difficulties in Sweden.

Therefore, the limitation of the scope of application of the Brussels II*ter*-Proposal to intra-European cases will not provide for a solution to Sweden's opposition.

Moreover, the jurisdictional rules of the Brussels II*bis*-Regulation would oppose such a limitation of the scope of application of the common choice of law rules on divorce to intra-European cases. These jurisdictional rules do not only apply to Union citizens, but also to third country nationals, as the competence of the courts of the Member States is pursuant to Article 3(1)(a) of the Brussels II*bis*-Regulation primarily based on the habitual residence of the spouses.[119] A limitation of the scope of application of the choice of law to intra-European cases could then very well lead to the situation in which the common jurisdictional rules determine that the court of a Member State is competent, but in which the common choice of law rules do subsequently not apply.

6.5.3 Enhancing the Role of the Lex Fori

6.5.3.1 The *Lex Fori in Foro Proprio*-Approach

According to De Boer the future European choice of law on divorce should meet the following three conditions: it needs to be simple, to be in line with the objectives of choice of law harmonisation and to allow the Member States to preserve their respective own ideological views on divorce.[120] Only one choice of law rule meets all these requirements: a choice of law rule referring solely to the *lex fori*. De Boer thus proposes for matters of international divorce — in the absence of a *professio iuris* — the introduction of *Gleichlauf*, i.e. the situation in which the competent court applies its own national substantive rules on divorce.[121]

This approach, also referred to as the *lex fori in foro proprio*-approach, implies that a particular court, designated by specific rules, applies its national substantive

[119] See Mansel 2003, pp. 144–145; Ancel 2007, p. 7.

[120] De Boer 2008, p. 339 ff.

[121] This idea is equally supported by the German Senate and the British International Committee of Resolution. See respectively Bundesrat 3 November 2006, Ratsdok. 11818/06, Drucksache 531/06 (Beschluss), para 3 and the Reply of Resolution to the Green Paper on Divorce, available at: http://ec.euro-pa.eu/justice_home/news/consulting_public/divorce_matters/contributions/contribution_icr_en.pdf.

law to the case.[122] The approach thus involves the ascertainment of the appropriate forum, the *forum legis*, i.e. 'the forum which, owing to its contacts with the parties or the case, can properly apply its own law'.[123] For traditional continental Europe this approach would imply a shift in private international law thinking towards a jurisdictional approach: the search for the *forum legis* will become the primary objective of private international law instead of the search for the applicable law.

According to De Boer there are two convincing arguments that argue in favour of adopting the *lex fori in foro proprio*-approach on the European Union level.[124] Firstly, no Member State will have any objection to applying its own substantive divorce law. Secondly, one of the main objectives of the European unification of the choice of law on divorce is, according to the Commission, to strengthen legal certainty and predictability.[125] In international divorce cases, spouses should know in advance which law will apply to their divorce; such certainty and predictability can be achieved by the *lex fori in foro proprio*-approach.[126] No requesting party or respondent could be unduly surprised if a national court applies its own substantive law. A regulation that requires all Member States to apply the *lex fori* in divorce cases, unless the parties themselves have chosen the applicable law, will put an end to the discordance between the choice of law rules of the Member States.

The *lex fori in foro proprio*-approach implies a shift of attention from choice of law criteria, determining whether forum law or foreign law applies, to jurisdictional standards, determining whether or not the forum may assume jurisdiction. Introducing this approach for matrimonial matters on the European level would entail two important turnovers in the current jurisdictional approach of the Brussels II*bis*-Regulation.

In the first place, the *lex fori in foro proprio*-approach necessitates an amendment of the current rules on jurisdiction of the Brussels II*bis*-Regulation, as coordination between the choice of law and jurisdiction is necessary. Considering the existing alternative grounds of jurisdiction of Article 3 of the Brussels II*bis*-Regulation, it must be recognised that the *lex fori in foro proprio*-approach will render it impossible for any spouse involved in an international marriage, and particularly for the spouse that does not initiate the divorce proceedings, to really

---

122 This approach is originally advocated by Ehrenzweig. See *inter alia* Ehrenzweig 1960; Ehrenzweig 1965; and Ehrenzweig 1967.

123 Ibid.

124 De Boer 2008, p. 339.

125 See Explanatory Memorandum to the Brussels II*ter*-Proposal, pp. 3–4; see also *supra* Sect. 5.3.

126 De Boer is in general very sceptic concerning the strengthening of legal certainty and predictability; see De Boer 2008, p. 321 ff, on 'the myth of certainty and predictability'. See *supra* Sect. 5.8, in which is argued that legal certainty and predictability with regard to divorce are not only dependent on the law which is applicable to divorce.

predict which law will be applied to the divorce.[127] The *lex fori in foro proprio*-approach would thus involve either a reduction of the current grounds of jurisdiction of Article 3 of the Brussels II*bis*-Regulation or an allocation of an order of precedence of these jurisdiction grounds.[128] The allocation of a hierarchy is to be preferred to the reduction of the grounds of jurisdiction, as it would contribute to the ascertainment of the most appropriate court to hear the case, i.e. the *forum legis*. This would be the court of that Member State with which the spouses have the closest connection. The competent court would then apply its own substantive law on the basis of the principle of the closest connection. This approach would ideally be accompanied by a provision on a *forum non-conveniens*, i.e. a court has the discretionay power to refuse to hear a case that has been brought before it, if there is a more appropriate forum available to the parties. Such a provision will ensure that the *lex fori in foro proprio*-approach will be fully pursued.

In the second place, as the *lex fori in foro proprio*-approach implies a shift in private international law thinking, it is highly questionable if the current jurisdictional standards of the Brussels II*bis*-Regulation are suitable to serve the specific choice of law objectives.[129] The jurisdictional grounds of the Brussels II*bis*-Regulation are based on 'the principle of a genuine connection between the person and the Member State'.[130] However, it is not clear whether this genuine connection needs to be proven *in concreto*. The Borrás Report seems to assume that nationality and habitual residence express *eo ipso* a substantial connection.[131] This assumption is equally endorsed to by a recent judgment of the European Court of Justice, holding that for the purposes of determining jurisdiction under Article 3(1)(b) in case of spouses who hold more than one nationality, not only the more effective nationality is to be taken into account.[132] Consequently, pursuant to Article 3 of the Brussels II*bis*-Regulation jurisdiction may already be assumed on the basis of a very tenuous connection to the forum. But such a tenuous connection to a certain country contradicts the objectives of the *lex fori in foro proprio*-approach: it does not ensure that the applicable law complies with the principle of the closest connection.

---

[127] In this respect Fiorini 2008, p. 189 pointed out that this approach does not bring any changes with respect to legal certainty and predictability if the couple or family is particularly mobile. However, of all people this category of persons should be aware of the issues surrounding questions of international family law and one can, therefore, wonder whether this category of persons needs special protection.

[128] See equally German Bundesrat 3 November 2006, Ratsdok. 11818/06, Drucksache 531/06 (Beschluss), para 3.

[129] See equally Gaertner 2008, pp. 222–223; Pocar 2007, p. 250. See already Eyl 1965 arguing that the rationale behind jurisdictional rules is different from the choice of law influencing factors.

[130] See the Borrás Report, para 30.

[131] Cf., De Boer 1999, p. 246; Hau 2000, p. 1337; Schack 2001, p. 624. .

[132] ECJ Case C-168/08 *Laszlo Hadadi* (*Hadady*) [2009] ECR I-06871. See equally the Opinion of Advocate General Kokott in this case.

An important disadvantage of the introduction of the *lex fori in foro proprio*-approach in the Union context is that it contravenes the current objectives of the Brussels II*bis*-Regulation. It currently provides for several grounds of jurisdiction that are objective, alternative and exclusive, *inter alia* implying that none of the grounds should take precedence over the others.[133] The introduction of a hierarchy of jurisdiction as part of the *lex fori in foro proprio*-approach would, consequently, run counter to the rationale of the jurisdictional rules of the Brussels II*bis*-Regulation. The grounds for jurisdiction would then no longer be alternative. Therefore, the introduction of the *lex fori in foro proprio*-approach would imply a rigorous break with the current objectives of the Brussels II*bis*-Regulation. An entirely new system would have to be established so as to ensure that solely the most closely connected forum has jurisdiction to hear the international divorce case so as to justify that the competent court applies its own law.

Moreover, equally a reduction of the present alternative jurisdictional grounds is not a suitable solution. It would not alleviate the problems resulting from the absence of common choice of law rules on divorce without severely limiting access to court.[134] A reduction of the jurisdictional grounds would, furthermore, not remove the risk of forum shopping and of a rush to court.[135] The reduction of the jurisdictional grounds thus contradicts the objectives of the Brussels II*ter*-Proposal.

In national legal systems the exclusive application of the *lex fori* has the disadvantage that it could easily lead to limping relationships, i.e. couples that are considered as being divorced in one state and as still being married in another.[136] However, in the European context this disadvantage is less present considering the principle of mutual recognition of Member States' decisions on divorce (Article 21 et seq Brussels II*bis*-Regulation).

The introduction of the *lex fori in foro proprio*-approach on the subject of divorce would thus demand a total turnover of the current theory, structure and arrangement of European private international law.[137] A shift should be made towards a more jurisdictional approach of private international law than has been employed so far. It is highly questionable whether such a turnover is feasible, considering that it would equally entail a reassessment of the jurisdictional

---

[133] See the Borrás Report, paras 28 and 29. The ECJ has confirmed the exclusive character of the jurisdictional grounds of Article 3 of the Brussels II*bis*-Regulation in case C-68/07 *Sundelind Lopez* v. *Lopez Lizazo* [2007] ECR I-10403, para 28.

[134] By contrast, the Brussels II*ter*-Proposal has explicitly embraced 'ensuring access to court' as one of the objectives it seeks to attain. See Explanatory Memorandum to the Brussels II*ter*-Proposal, pp. 3–4. See also *supra* Sect. 5.3.

[135] This brings Kreuzer 2006, p. 80 to the conclusion that a unification of the choice of law rules can prevent forum shopping and a race to the court in a better and more practical way than attempts to do so through jurisdictional methods.

[136] Cf., Eyl 1965, p. 11.

[137] Supposing that there is a theory underlying the European private international law at all. See on this issue further *infra* Chap. 8

grounds of the Brussels II*bis*-Regulation. Finally, the introduction of the *lex fori in foro proprio*-approach would also imply a clean break with the current general characteristics of European private international law.[138]

6.5.3.2 The 'French Proposal' After All?

As seen above, the Dutch Parliament has in COREPER tried to bring up anew the French proposal on a European choice of law on divorce.[139] This proposal enhances the application of the *lex fori* in Article 20b:

1. In the absence of a choice pursuant to Article 20a, where both parties enter an appearance and neither requests application of another law, divorce and legal separation shall be subject to the *lex fori*.
2. In other cases, divorce and legal separation shall be subject to:w
   a. the law of the spouses' common habitual residence or, failing that,
   b. the law of their common nationality or, failing that,
   c. the law of the spouses' last common habitual residence, insofar as one of them still resides there or, failing that,
   d. the *lex fori*
   The application of a law other than the lex fori [defined according to the criteria laid down in paragraph 2] must be requested before any claim or defence on the merits
3. Where the law applicable to paragraphs 1 and 2 does not provide for divorce, the lex fori shall apply to the application for divorce.[140]

As discussed in Section 5.5.3.3, the French proposal would imply the introduction of a facultative choice of law in the European Union.[141] Pursuant to the facultative choice of law the court solely applies the choice of law at the request of either party.

Although this approach certainly offers advantages in terms of quality and rapidity of judicial decisions, it has four important shortcomings.[142]

[138] See for these characteristics *infra* Sect. 8.4.3.

[139] See *supra* Sect. 6.3.3. This proposal of the Dutch Parliament is striking, considering the negative stand of the Dutch Standing Committee on the doctrine of facultative choice of law. See Staatscommissie 2002, para 27. See in general on the doctrine of the facultative choice of law De Boer 1996.

[140] Council Document No. 11295/07 JUSTCIV 183 of 28 June 2007, p. 10, footnote 31. This provision came up for the first time in Council Document No. 6258/07, to know from Council Document No. 7144/07 JUSTCIV 47 of 9 March 2007, p. 9, footnote 2.

[141] See in general on the question whether or not to introduce the doctrine of the facultative choice of law in European context: Van den Eeckhout 2008b, pp. 258–262.

[142] See for an enumeration of the objections against a facultative choice of law: Staatscommissie 2002, para 27.

The facultative choice of law firstly affects the basic premise of choice of law, i.e. both forum law and foreign law are equally eligible for application. Secondly, this approach may have a negative effect on the balance in the procedural position of the parties resulting from their unequal financial possibilities. For the parties do not always have the same (financial) means to examine whether raising the issue of the choice of law might lead to the application of a foreign law that is more advantageous to his or her cause than the law of the forum. Thirdly, the doctrine of facultative choice of law would equally harm the principle of the closest connection, on which the common choice of law rules should be based.[143] Finally, the doctrine of facultative choice of law fails to give the parties certainty as to the applicable law before moving to another country. Such certainty can be gained by reference to the choice of law.[144]

Compared to the *lex fori in foro proprio*-approach, the doctrine of the facultative choice of law does grant the spouses more flexibility, as either by means of a valid *professio iuris* or at the mere request of either spouse the application of the *lex fori* can be set aside. However, all the other shortcomings mentioned with regard to the *lex fori in foro proprio*-approach equally apply to the French proposal. Mainly the problems of a rush to court and forum shopping will not be solved, unless the jurisdictional grounds of Article 3 of the Brussels II*bis*-Regulation will either be strongly reduced or be ordered in priority.

6.5.3.3 Other Means to Enhance the Role of the *Lex Fori*

In one of its drafts, the Council has included an 'escape clause' favouring the application of the *lex fori*.[145] This escape clause could solely apply in case Article 20b determines that the divorce is governed by the law of the last habitual residence of the spouses insofar as one of them still resides there. The clause substitutes the law of the last common habitual residence of the spouses for the *lex fori*, on three conditions:

> By derogation to paragraph 1(b), the law of the forum shall apply where:
> (a) one of the spouses so requests; and
> (b) during their marriage, the spouses had their last habitual residence in the State referred to in paragraph 1(b) for less than [three] years; and
> (c) the requesting spouse has a substantial connection with the Member State of the court seised by virtue of the fact that he or she

---

[143] Cf., *supra* Sect. 6.4.

[144] Cf., Ten Wolde 2009, pp. 55–56.

[145] Council Document No. 11295/07 JUSTCIV 183 of 28 June 2007, p. 9. In the last Council draft of 23 May 2008 this escape clause had been removed.

(i) has been habitually resident in that Member State for at least [ten] years, provided that that period did not end more than [three] years before the court is seised; or
(ii) is a national of that Member State.

This exception to Article 20b(1)(b) Brussels II*ter*-Proposal attempts to reconcile a policy-oriented approach, i.e. allowing the application of the 'divorce-friendly' *lex fori*, with the principle of the closest connection. But such a compromise should be rejected from a methodological perspective.[146] What the escape clause intends to achieve is a quick and easy divorce pursuant to forum law and not an adjustment of the principle of the closest connection.

6.5.4 Less Stringent Interpretation of the Principle of the Closest Connection

A next possible solution to the indicated problems could be to resort to a less stringent interpretation of the principle of the closest connection. In order to achieve its objective to provide for a clear and comprehensive legal framework, the Brussels II*ter*-Proposal gives a detailed interpretation of the principle of the closest connection. Article 20b contains a cascade rule providing for connecting factors that are assumed to reflect a close connection.

An alternative would be to draw up a choice of law rule on divorce that resembles Articles 3 and 4 of the former Rome Convention on contractual obligations. With regard to the law applicable to contractual obligations, the freedom of choice was the cornerstone of the Rome Convention. In the absence of the parties' choice as to the applicable law the legal relationship was governed by the law which is most closely connected to the contract.[147] Article 4(2) of the Rome Convention subsequently gave a presumption of the most closely connected law.

With regard to unified choice of law on divorce a similar approach could be operated. Most of the Member States could agree on allowing the spouses a limited degree of party autonomy. Therefore, it seems feasible to retain the *professio iuris*. However, most resistance existed concerning the applicable law in the absence of a choice by the parties. The principle of the closest connection is the most suitable basis for the common choice of law.[148] The abovementioned approach entails that for cases in which the spouses have not made a *professio iuris*, a compromise could be made by referring to the law with which the spouses in question are most

[146] Cf., De Boer 2008, p. 329.

[147] Article 3 of the Rome Convention stipulates that a contract shall in principle be governed by the law chosen by the parties. Article 4(1) of the latter Convention determines that, in the absence of a *professio iuris*, a contract shall be governed by the law of the country with which it is most closely connected. Article 4(2) stipulates that a contract is presumed to be most closely connected to the place where the party performing the service characterising the contract has his habitual residence.

[148] See *supra* Sect. 6.4.

closely connected. Subsequently, the provision on the applicable law can give a presumption of the closest connection: the law of the state where the spouses have their common habitual residence at the time the court is seised, or failing that the law of the State where the spouses had their last common habitual residence provided that that period did not end more than one year before the court was seised and insofar as one of them still resides there. Such presumption of the closest connection should be helpful in order to allocate the most closely connected law. However, the presumption is refutable: it can be discarded should a certain case be more closely connection to another country.

This approach certainly has disadvantages, most importantly its subjectivity and unpredictability.[149] When it is left to the court to establish the closest connection on the basis of the actual circumstances, the interpretation will most certainly be coloured by national preferences. It is very tempting to give much weight to circumstances that point to the jurisdiction whose law one prefers and to discount those that point elsewhere in order to circumvent the application of a more liberal or a more restrictive law. When such a choice of law rule is applied, the choice of law process is wide open to manipulation. The ultimate effect is that parties are not able to predict which law will apply to their divorce and this will not have a favourable effect on legal certainty.[150]

For exactly these reasons, the conversion of the Rome Convention into the Rome I-Regulation was accompanied by the amendment of the provision on the law applicable to contractual obligations in the absence of a *professio iuris*.[151] In the Rome I-Regulation the most closely connected law referred to in Article 4 is specified for certain types of contracts.[152] The Explanatory Memorandum to the Rome I-Regulation elucidates this specification:

> [T]he proposed changes seek to enhance certainty as to the law by converting mere presumptions into fixed rules and abolishing the exception clause. Since the cornerstone of the instrument is freedom of choice, the rules applicable in the absence of a choice should be as precise and foreseeable as possible so that the parties can decide whether or not to exercise their choice.[153]

---

[149] See Hatfield 2005, p. 4. See equally De Boer 1996, pp. 278–279.

[150] By contrast, one of the objectives of the Brussels II*ter*-Proposal is to strengthen legal certainty and predictability. See *supra* Sect. 5.3.

[151] Practice has also shown that Article 4 of the Rome Convention affords national courts plenty of opportunity to continue to apply the choice of law rule on contract they used to apply before the Convention entered into force, whether that rule is based on the principle of the characteristic performance, as in the Netherlands, or on the proper law of the contract approach, as in the United Kingdom, or on the presumptive will of the parties, as in Germany. Cf., De Ly 1996.

[152] Article 4(1) specifies the applicable law based on the principle of the closest connection for different categories of contracts (e.g. contract of sale, contract of carriage, contract relating to intellectual property, etc.). For contracts that are not specified by Article 4(1) a special choice of law rule is provided for in Article 4(2).

[153] See Explanatory Memorandum to the Rome I-Regulation, COM(2005) 650 final, p. 5.

Article 4(3) of the Rome I-Regulation does foresee that in the event that a country other than that indicated in the previous paragraphs is manifestly more closely connected to the contract, the law of that other country will apply.

Would a choice of law rule similar to Article 4 of the Rome I-Regulation be helpful to overcome the current deadlock in the establishment of a unified system of choice of law on divorce? Although the addition of a clause similar Article 4(3) of the Rome I-Regulation to the Brussels II*ter*-Proposal is to be welcomed from the point of view of the principle of the closest connection,[154] this approach is not likely to result in a choice of law rule that differs from Article 20b of the Brussels II*ter*-Proposal. Since the Member States could not accept this choice of law rule, the approach concerned will not help to overcome the existing deadlock.

Consequently, with regard to a unified choice of law rule on divorce a provision referring to the most closely connected law, specified by a presumption of this law, would not be a suitable alternative to the failed Brussels II*ter*-Proposal, because it does not really involve a change of the choice of law provision. Replacing the choice of law provisions with a provision that refers solely to the most closely connected law would not be a suitable alternative either, as it involves too much uncertainty.

6.5.5 *Synthesis*

From the foregoing it appears that the Slovenian Presidency of the Council has rightly concluded that all possibilities for a compromise on a unified choice of law system have been exhausted after all.[155] The present divergences of opinion that exist between the Member States with regard to a unified choice of law on divorce are fundamental and cannot be overcome easily.

All the possible alternatives that have been discussed above are either unfeasible or have major (practical) drawbacks.

In the field of the choice of law on divorce the enhanced cooperation is the 'last resort'-option, which the mechanism is intended to be. Yet since the Regulation on enhanced cooperation essentially reproduces the choice of law as introduced by the failed Brussels II*ter*-Proposal, the prospect of all Member States participating in the cooperation is near to utopian.

6.6 Conclusion

This chapter contains an analysis of the failure to reach consensus on unified choice of law rules on divorce (the Brussels II*ter*-Proposal). Three distinct problems that underlie the failure of the establishment of common choice of law rules

[154] Cf., *supra* Sect. 5.5.3.4.

[155] See Press Release of the 2887th Meeting of the Justice and Home Affairs Council of 24 and 25 July 2008, p. 23.

on divorce have been distinguished. In the first place, the position of Malta — the only Member State that does not provide for divorce in its substantive legislation — posed problems. Moreover, doubts existed concerning the EU competence in the field at hand: mainly the fulfilment of the internal market requirement on the one hand and the fulfilment of the principles of subsidiarity and proportionality on the other posed problems. During the negotiations in the Council both these problems seem to have been solved. The last problem observed is the most problematic, as it touches upon the methodological approach of the common choice of law rules. The large differences in substantive law on divorce of the Member States seem to require the adoption of neutral choice of law rules. However, not all Member States agree with such an approach, as they wish to continue to apply the *lex fori*.

The fundamental discord between the Member States concerning the Brussels II*ter*-Proposal has led to the search for alternatives. The alternatives that have been discussed above, *inter alia* enhancing the role of the *lex fori* and interpreting the principle of the closest connection in a less stringent way, do not lead to a proper or feasible solution. Therefore, an alternative to the establishment of a common choice of law does not currently seem to be present. Apparently, the European Union as a whole is not yet ready for a common choice of law on divorce. Consequently, the procedure on enhanced cooperation is the 'last resort' for establishing some form of cooperation between the Member States in the field of the choice of law on divorce. But the establishment of enhanced cooperation in the field of divorce does create a possibly impeding precedent for all future EU projects on international family law, such as matrimonial property and succession.

References

Regulations, Conventions, Reports and other Documentary Sources

Borrás Report. Explanatory Report on the Convention on Jurisdiction and the Recognition and Enforcement of Judgments in Matrimonial Matters, [1998] OJ C221/27

Brussels II-Convention. Convention on jurisdiction and recognition and enforcement in matrimonial matters of 28 May 1998, [1998] OJ C221/1

Brussels II-Regulation. Council Regulation (EC) No. 1347/2000 of 29 May 2000 on jurisdiction and the recognition and enforcement of judgments in matrimonial matters and in matters of parental responsibility for children of both spouses, [2000] OJ L160/19

Brussels II*bis*-Regulation. Council Regulation (EC) No. 2201/2003 of 27 November 2003 on Jurisdiction and Enforcement of Judgments in Matrimonial Matters and Matters of Parental Responsibility, [2003] OJ L338/1

Brussels II*ter*-Proposal. Proposal for a Council Regulation amending Regulation (EC) No. 2201/2003 as regards jurisdiction and introducing rules concerning applicable law in matrimonial matters, COM(2006) 399 final

COSAC Report. Report of the subsidiarity and proportionality check on the Brussels II*ter*-Proposal organised in November 2006 by COSAC, Report No. 1/2006. The COSAC-Report and the Annex thereto are available at: http://www.cosac.eu/en/info/earlywarning/doc/results/

EPEC Study on divorce. Study to inform a subsequent Impact Assessment on the Commission Proposal on jurisdiction and applicable law in divorce matters, undertaken by EPEC, April 2006 available at: http://ec.europa.eu/justice_home/news/consulting_public/divorce_matters/study.pdf

Green Paper on Divorce. Green Paper on applicable law and jurisdiction in divorce maters, COM(2005) 82 final

Green Paper on Matrimonial Property. Green Paper on conflict of laws regarding matrimonial property regimes, including the question of jurisdiction and mutual recognition, COM(2006) 400 final

House of Lords Rome III Report. House of Lords - European Union Committee, *Rome III - Choice of Law in Divorce*, 52nd Report of Session 2005-06 (HL Paper 272) December 2006

Impact Assessment on Divorce. Commission Staff Working Document – Annex to the proposal for a Council Regulation amending Regulation (EC) No. 2201/2003 as regards jurisdiction and introducing rules concerning applicable law in matrimonial matters, SEC(2006) 949

Regulation on enhanced cooperation in the field of divorce. Council Regulation (EU) No. 1259/2010 of 20 December 2010 implementing enhanced cooperation in the area of the law applicable to divorce and legal separation, OJ L343/10

Staatscommissie (2002). Staatscommissie voor het Internationaal Privaatrecht, Rapport Algemene Bepalingen IPR, Report of 1 June 2002, available at: http://www.justitie.nl/onderwerpen/wetgeving/over_wet-geving/privaatrecht/commissies-privaatrecht/staatscommissie-ipr.aspx

Books and Articles

Amtenbrink F, Kochenov D (2009) Towards a more flexible approach to enhanced cooperation. In: Ott A, Vos E (eds) Fifty years of European integration: foundations and perspectives. T.M.C. Asser Press, The Hague, pp 181–200

Ancel JP (2007) La libre circulation de la famille en Europe. Petites Affiches 199:4–7

Antokolskaia MV (2006) Harmonisation of family law in Europe: a historical perspective. Intersentia, Antwerpen

Antokolskaia MV, De Hondt W, Steenhoff G (1999) Een zoektocht naar Europees familierecht. Kluwer, Deventer

Boele-Woelki K (1997) The road towards a European family law. Electronic Journal of Comparative Law 1.1:1–12

Boele-Woelki K (2007) Building on convergence and coping with divergence. In: Antokolskaia MV (ed) Convergence and divergence of family law in Europe. Intersentia, Antwerpen, pp 253–268

Boele-Woelki K (2008a) Europese unificatie conflictenrecht echtscheiding van de baan. FJR 30:261

Boele-Woelki K (2008b) To be or not to be: enhanced cooperation in international divorce law within the European Union. Victoria University of Wellington Law Review 39:779–792

Boele-Woelki K et al (2004) Principles of European family law regarding divorce and maintenance between former spouses. Intersentia, Antwerpen

Bonomi A (2007) Le divorce en droit communautaire entre règles de droit international privé et objectifs de droit matériel. In: Epiney A et al (eds) Die Herausforderung von Grenzen. Festschrift für Roland Bieber. Nomos, Baden-Baden, pp 771–783

Cadet F (2004) La gestion de l'internationalité par les méthodes communautaires: vers un droit international privé unifié dans l'Union européenne? Petites Affiches 157:3–12

De Boer ThM (1996) Facultative choice of law. The procedural status of choice-of-law rules and foreign law. Recueil des Cours 257:225–427

De Boer ThM (1999) Brussel II: een eerste stap naar een communautair IPR. FJR 21:246

De Boer ThM (2001) Prospects for European conflicts law in the twenty-first century. In: Borchers PJ, Zekoll J (eds) International conflicts of laws for the third millennium, essays in honor of Friedrich K. Juenger. Transnational Publishers, Ardsley, pp 193–226

De Boer ThM (2004) Forum preferences in contemporary European conflicts law: the myth of a 'neutral choice'. In: Mansel H-P et al (eds) Festschrift für Erik Jayme. Sellier. European Law Publishers, München, pp 39–55

De Boer ThM (2008) The Second revision of the Brussels II Regulation: jurisdiction and applicable law. In: Boele-Woelki K, Sverdrup T (eds) European challenges in contemporary family law. Intersentia, Antwerpen, pp 321–341

De Ly F (1996) Het Balenpers-arrest en de eenvormige uitleg van artikel 4 (5) EVO. In: Schmidt GE, Freedberg-Schwartzburg JA (eds) Het NIPR geannoteerd, Annotaties opgedragen aan Dr. Mathilde Sumampouw. T.M.C. Asser Instituut, The Hague, pp 125–133

Ehrenzweig AA (1960) Lex fori—basic rule in the conflict of laws. Michigan Law Review 58:637–688

Ehrenzweig AA (1965) A proper law in a proper forum: a "restatement" of the "lex fori approach". Oklahoma Law Review, pp 340–352

Ehrenzweig AA (1967) Private international law. A comparative treatise on American international conflicts law, including the law of admiralty. General part, vol 1. Sijthoff, Leyden

Eyl HR (1965) Internationale echtscheiding in Nederland. Scheltema & Holkema N.V, Amsterdam

Farrugia R (2007) The impact and application of the Brussel II bis Regulation in Malta. In: Boele-Woelki K, González Beilfuss C (eds) Brussels II bis: its impact and application in the Member States. Intersentia, Antwerpen, pp 205–216

Fiorini A (2008) Rome III—choice of law in divorce: is the Europeanization of family law going too far? International Journal of Law, Policy and the Family 22:178–205

Gaertner V (2008) Die Privatscheidung im deutschen und gemeinschaftsrechtlichen Internationalen Privat- und Verfahrensrecht (diss. Heidelberg). Mohr Siebeck, Tübingen

Hatfield HN (2005) Private international law concepts in divorce. American Journal of Family Law 19(2):4

Hau W (2000) Das System der internationalen Entscheidungszuständigkeit im europäischen Eheverfahrensrecht. Zeitschrift für das gesamte Familienrecht 47:1333–1341

Israël J (2001) Europees internationaal privaatrecht. De EG, een comitas Europaea en 'vrijheid, veiligheid en rechtvaardigheid'. NIPR 19:135–149

Jänterä-Jareborg M (2008) Jurisdiction and applicable law in cross-border divorce cases in Europe. In: Basedow J et al (eds) Japanese and European Private International Law in Comparative Perspecive. Mohr Siebeck, Tübingen, pp 317–343

Kapteyn PJG, VerLoren van Themaat P (1998) Introduction to the law of the European Communities, 3rd edn. edited and further revised by L.W. Gormley. Kluwer Law International, London

Kohler C (2001) Status als Ware: Bemerkungen zur europäischen Verordnung über das internationale Verfahrensrecht für Ehesachen. In: Mansel HP (ed) Vergemeinschaftung des Europäischen Kollisionsrecht. Carl Heymanns Verlag, Köln, pp 41–53

Kohler C (2002) Auf dem Weg zu einem europäischen Justizraum für das Familien- und Erbrecht. Zeitschrift für das gesamte Familienrecht 41:709–714

Kohler C (2003) Der europäische Justizraum für Zivilsachen und das Gemeinschaftskollisionsrecht. IPRax 23:401–412

Kohler C (2008a) Zur Gestaltung des europäischen Kollisionsrecht für Ehesachen: Der steinige Weg zu einheitlichen Vorschriften über das anwendbare Recht für Scheidung und Trennung. Zeitschrift für das gesamte Familienrecht 55:1673–1681

Kohler C (2008b) Einheitliche Kollisionsnormen für Ehesachen in der Europäische Union: Vorschläge und Vorbehalte. Familie Partnerschaft und Recht, pp 193–196

Kortenberg H (1998) Closer Cooperation in the Treaty of Amsterdam. CMLR 35:833–854

Kreuzer K (2006) Zu Stand und Perspektiven des Europäischen Internationalen Privatrechts. RabelsZ 70:1–88
Küchler T (2006) Member States attack divorce law scheme. Available at: http://euobserver.com/9/22882
Mansel HP (2003) Das Staatsangehörigkeitsprinzip im deutschen und gemeinschaftsrechtlichen Internationalen Privatrecht: Schutz der kulturellen Identität oder Diskriminierung der Person? In: Jayme E (ed) Kulturelle Identität und Internationales Privatrecht. C.F. Müller Verlag, Heidelberg, pp 119–154
Mansel HP, Thorn K, Wagner R (2009) Europäisches Kollisionsrecht 2008: Fundamente der Europäischen IPR-Kodifikation. IPRax 29:1–23
McNamara R, Martin F (2006) Brussels calling: the unstoppable Europeanisation of Irish family law. Irish Journal of Family Law 9:8–21
Meeusen J (2007) What has it got to do necessarily with the European Union?: international family law and European (economic) integration. The Cambridge Yearbook of European Legal Studies 2006–2007, pp 329–355
Mostermans PMM (2006) Echtscheiding, 3rd edn. Kluwer, Deventer
Oderkerk AE (2006) Het Groenboek inzake het toepasselijke recht en de rechterlijke bevoegdheid in echtscheidingszaken. NIPR 24:119–128
Paulino Pereira FR (2007) Rome III: La compétence juridictionnelle et la loi applicable en matière matrimoniale. Revue du Marché commun et de l'Union européenne, pp 390–394
Pocar F (2007) Quelques remarques sur la modification du règlement communautaire no. 2201/2003 en ce qui concerne la competence et la loi applicable au divorce. In: Mélanges en l'honneur de Mariel Revillard. Defrénois, Paris, pp 245–252
Pontier JA (1997) Conflictenrecht: grondslagen, methoden, beginselen en belangen (diss. Amsterdam). Ars Aequi Libri, Nijmegen
Pontier JA (2007) Verantwoording van Europese IPR-wetgeving: 'Rome III'. Herziening Brussel IIbis, subsidiariteit en evenredigheid. In: Feteris ET (ed) 'Alles afwegende....' : bijdragen aan het Vijfde Symposium Juridische Argumentatie 22 juni 2007 te Rotterdam. Ars Aequi Libri, Nijmegen, pp 203–216
Prinssen JM (2008) Flexibiliteit in het Verdrag van Lissabon. In: Meeusen J et al (eds) Het Verdrag van Lissabon: de Europese impasse doorbroken (?). Intersentia, Antwerpen, pp 57–75
Romano GP (2006) La bilatéralité éclipsée par l'autorité. Développements récents en matière d'état des personnes. RCDIP 95:457–519
Rüberg S (2005) Auf dem Weg zu einem europäischen Scheidungskollisionsrecht (diss. Konstanz). Available at: http://www.ub.uni-konstanz.de/kops/volltexte/2005/1694/pdf/Rueberg.pdf
Schack H (2001) Das neue internationale Eheverfahrensrecht in Europa. RabelsZ 65:615–633
Shannon G (2007) The impact and application of the Brussel II bis Regulation in Ireland. In: Boele-Woelki K, Borrás A (eds) Brussels II bis: its impact and application in the Member States. Intersentia, Antwerpen, pp 145–166
Ten Wolde MH (2009) Inleiding Nederlands en Europees Internationaal Privaatrecht, Deel A Algemeen deel en materieel IPR Personen-, familie- en erfrecht. Hephaestus, Groningen
Van den Eeckhout V (2004) Communitarization of private international law: tendencies to "liberalize" international family law. Tijdschrift@ipr.be 51–70. Article available at https://openaccess.leidenuniv.nl/bitstream/1887/16146/2/Microsoft+Word+-+engelsveerleiprtijdschriftdefinitief.doc%5B1%5D.pdf
Van den Eeckhout V (2008a) Het Hof van Justitie als steun en toeverlaat in tijden van Europeanisatie van het ipr? NTER, pp 84–90
Van den Eeckhout V (2008b) Europeanisatie van het ipr: aanleiding tot herleving van discussies over facultatief ipr, of finale doodsteek voor facultatief ipr? NIPR 26:258–262
Vandystadt N (2009) Cross-border divorce: we want to avoid enhanced cooperation. Europolitics (3715):11

Chapter 7
The Dutch and the European Choice of Law Rules on Divorce Compared

7.1 Introduction

In the chapters two and three above, the Dutch choice of law rules on divorce and on the termination of registered partnerships have been discussed respectively. In the three chapters that followed, the European dimension of both international family law in general as the choice of law on divorce in particular were highlighted.

Whereas the field of private international law was previously a matter of the national competence of the Member States, the European Union has shown an increasing interest in the unification of matters of private international law in the past decades. Since 1999 the European legislature is competent to enact proper private international law rules. Aspects of international family law are also subject to this European unification process, including the choice of law rules on divorce. The latter choice of law rules have been introduced in the Brussels II*ter*-Proposal. As became clear in the previous chapter, the Member States have not succeeded in reaching a compromise on the issue of a common choice of law on divorce. Consequently, a unified European choice of law on divorce will probably be still quite a long time coming.

Even though the adoption of the Brussels II*ter*-Proposal has been cancelled, the comparison between the Dutch and the European system of the choice of law on divorce remains of importance to the general question of this research. This comparison will be helpful to answer the question whether from the attempt to unify the choice of law on divorce on the European level some more general directions can be deduced as regards the European methodology of international family law at large.[1] In addition, the comparison pursues two specific objectives: on the one hand, to reveal the precise obstacles of the Brussels II*ter*-Proposal from Dutch perspective to the European legislature and, on the other hand, to answer the

[1] This issue will be dealt with in Chap. 8.

N.A. Baarsma, *The Europeanisation of International Family Law*,
DOI: 10.1007/978-90-6704-743-2_7, © T.M.C. ASSER PRESS, The Hague,
The Netherlands, and the author 2011

question whether the Dutch government has rightly opposed the introduction of a common choice of law on divorce.

This chapter will address the similarities and differences between the choice of law systems on divorce of the Netherlands and of the European Union. These similarities and differences will be analysed and — if possible — explained. The comparison at issue between an existing system and a system being 'in the process of formation' is — by its very nature — an imbalanced one. Obviously, the Dutch system is much more evolved than the European, which is a very logical consequence of the fact that the European system has not entered into force (yet). The Dutch choice of law rules on divorce, by contrast, already exist since 1981 and many judicial decisions have given shape to the regulation of the Choice of Law Act on Divorce.

The comparison of the two systems will commence in Section 7.2 with a number of general observations. Subsequently, the comparison will concentrate on the following aspects: the composition of the choice of law rules on divorce (Section 7.3), the applicable law by choice of the parties (Section 7.4), the formal requirements of the *professio iuris* (Section 7.5) and the applicable law in the absence of a *professio iuris* (Section 7.6). Finally, Section 7.7 will elaborate on the question whether the Netherlands has rightly opposed the Brussels II*ter*-Proposal. An important reason for the Netherlands to be set against the common choice of law rules is that it has decided to adhere to the *lex fori*-approach in the future.[2] In 1995 the Dutch Standing Committee on Private International Law has proposed to amend the choice of law rule on divorce, which has been taken up in the Dutch Proposal on Private International Law of September 2009. Pursuant to this proposal Dutch law (the *lex fori*) will apply in all divorce cases, unless (one of) the spouses has opted for the application of their common national law. Throughout this chapter the choice of law rules of the Brussels II*ter*-Proposal will be compared to both Article 1 CLAD and its proposed amended version.

In the following the European choice of law rules that have been laid down in the last Council draft on the Brussels II*ter*-Proposal will be taken as point of departure.[3]

As seen above, the Brussels II*ter*-Proposal solely designates the applicable law to divorce and to legal separation and it does not apply to the termination of registered partnerships.[4] Consequently, hereinafter a comparison will only be drawn between the Brussels II*ter*-Proposal and the Dutch choice of law rules on

[2] See *supra* Sect. 2.6 and the Reply of the Dutch Government to the Green Paper on Divorce, p. 2. This Reply is available at: http://ec.europa.eu/justice_home/news/consulting_public/divorce_mat-ters/news_contributions_divorce_matters_en.htm. See equally Oderkerk 2006, p. 124.

[3] This draft has been annexed to this study as Appendix No. 2.

[4] See *supra* Sect. 5.4.2.3.

divorce. No comparison will be made with the Dutch choice of law rules on the termination of registered partnerships.[5]

7.2 General Observations

Before comparing the current Dutch and the proposed European choice of law on divorce as regards their content, three general observations will be placed on some characteristics that strike in the comparison of these two systems. The first observation concerns the arrangement of the choice of law. Secondly, the foundation of the Dutch and the European choice of law on divorce will be compared. The third observation, finally, relates to the scope of application of the two legal systems.

7.2.1 Arrangement of the Choice of Law: General and Specific Provisions

A remarkable difference between the European and the Dutch system of the choice of law on divorce is that the Brussels II*ter*-Proposal as such is more comprehensive. Whereas the Dutch law contains solely one provision on the choice of law (Article 1 of the CLAD), the Brussels II*ter*-Proposal contains eight provisions on the issue (Articles 20a–20f of the Proposal). For many issues the Dutch Choice of Law Act on Divorce does not contain any specific provision; in Dutch law the general doctrines of private international law, such as *renvoi* and the public policy exception, have been arranged on a more general level. However, many of these general doctrines have thus far remained uncodified.[6] The Brussels II*ter*-Proposal, on the contrary, does make an explicit mention of the general doctrines of private international law. The explicit mention of these general doctrines in European context can be explained by the absence of an already existing private international law system. The European legislature only has the competence to enact measures in the field of private international law since 1999.[7] Ever since, the European

---

[5] In Sect. 7.2.3 one exception to this exclusion will be made in order to answer the question whether it is a lost opportunity that the Brussels II*ter*-Proposal does not apply to the termination of registered partnerships.

[6] It is to be noted that the Dutch Proposal on Private International Law contains several stipulations on the latter doctrines in its general provisions (Articles 1–17). See on these general provisions also Staatscommissie 2003.

[7] See *supra* Sect. 4.2 on the development of the European legislature's competence in the field of private international law.

Union has put this power to good use by producing a large number of instruments in the field of private international law. But the European Union is currently establishing its own private international law system in a very fragmented way by regulating several sub-fields of private international law separately.[8] Consequently, a coherent system underlying the European system of private international law is lacking.[9] As a result there is at present no European approach to the general doctrines of private international law.[10]

Recently several academics have plunged into the development of general provisions of European private international law, derived from the existing and proposed instruments in the field of private international law.[11] The creation of general provisions of private international law is to be welcomed, as it prevents the same general issues from being subject to different approaches in the separate instruments.[12]

Although the Dutch choice of law rules have been embedded in a national system, in which the latter doctrines have been arranged for on a more general level, there is very well case for the structure of the Brussels II*ter*-Proposal. In the absence of codified provisions on the general doctrines of private international law on a general level, the structure of the Brussels II*ter*-Proposal is to be preferred: at a single glance all relevant provisions are available. Nevertheless ideally it is most preferable to establish the structure as envisaged by the Dutch legislature in which all provisions — both the general and the specific ones — are assembled in one Act.[13]

---

[8] According to Fiorini the reason for this 'atomization' is '*that it will be easier to achieve consensus on these issues taken in isolation than it would have been had work been undertaken on a wider area of family law*'. See Fiorini 2008b, p. 195. Separate instruments have been or will be established in the following sub-fields of private international law: contractual obligations, non-contractual obligations, divorce, maintenance obligations, wills and succession and matrimonial property.

[9] Cf., Fiorini 2008a, p. 7: '*Although the unification of private international law is very much a priority for the Community, work in this area is proceeding in a very disjointed fashion.* [...] *Indeed coordination between the various dossiers, a very arduous exercise, is at best weak and superficial if not completely inexistent; the unification of private international law rules in Europe is very much proceeding* via *a piecemeal approach* [...].' See on this issue further *infra* Sect. 8.4.1.

[10] See *infra* Sect. 8.4.4.2 for a discussion *de lege ferenda* of these general doctrines.

[11] See *inter alia* Leible 2007; Heinze 2008; Kreuzer 2008; Sonnenberger 2008; and Leible 2009.

[12] See Siehr 2008, p. 92. Currently there is a risk that, due to the present fragmented unification of European private international law, a coherent approach of the general doctrines of private international law may never arise. Theoretically, in each Regulation a distinct approach on these general doctrines can be adopted; e.g. *renvoi* may be excluded in one instrument, yet permitted in another.

[13] This holds true for Dutch as well as for European private international law. Cf., for such European system Boele-Woelki 2008, p. 783.

7.2.2 Foundation of the Choice of Law on Divorce

Both the current Dutch and the proposed European choice of law on divorce are based on the principle of the closest connection. The Dutch rules are furthermore based on the principle of *favor divortii*, entailing that the choice of law rules aim to favour the possibility to obtain a divorce.[14]

The situation for the Brussels II*ter*-Proposal is somewhat different. The substantive law on divorce varies so much from one Member State to another, that solely a neutral approach as regard the choice of law on divorce can be followed in European context. This neutral approach implies the establishment of choice of law rules that are blind to the result they achieve in terms of substantive law. In the previous chapter it became clear, however, that one can wonder whether the European choice of law rules are actually neutral. Although the Commission has introduced a neutral choice of law approach, the compromises that have been made in the Council have altered this neutral point of departure.[15] This friction is the very source of the failure of the establishment of a European unified system of choice of law on divorce.[16] The European choice of law on divorce should not be based on or have any tendency towards the principle of *favor divortii*, but it should instead consist of strictly neutral rules.

7.2.3 Scope of Application

In the discussion on the scope of application of both systems two specific issues arise. The first concerns the dissolution of same-sex marriages and the second the termination of registered partnerships.

With regard to the dissolution of same-sex marriages neither the Dutch nor the European choice of law on divorce provides for a satisfactory basis.

The Dutch choice of law rules on divorce pre-date the substantive law reform concerning the opening of the marriage to same-sex couples.[17] According to the Dutch Standing Committee on Private International Law Article 1 of the CLAD equally applies to the dissolution of same-sex marriages.[18] Although the Dutch

---

[14] See Werkgroep IPR NVvR 1993, p. 137; Boele-Woelki 1994, pp. 173–174; Vlas 1996, p. 200; and Mostermans 2006, p. 41. See further *supra* Sect. 2.2.3.

[15] Examples of these compromises having a *favor divortii* tendency can be found in the solutions to the situations in which the applicable law does not provide for divorce. Both the jurisdictional rules and the choice of law rules of the Brussels II*ter*-Proposal contain a provision for the latter situations: the introduction of the *forum necessitatis* in international divorce cases (Article 7a) and the application of the *lex fori* as a remedy for cases in which the applicable law does not provide for divorce (Article 20b-1).

[16] See further *supra* Sect. 6.4.

[17] See *supra* Sect. 2.2.2.

[18] Staatscommissie 2001, Sect. 8, p. 15.

legislature will in all probability follow the advice of the Standing Committee, there is currently no clarity as regards the question whether Article 1 of the CLAD applies to same-sex marriages. The Dutch legislature is namely not bound by the Standing Committee's advice. Article 56 of the Dutch Proposal on Private International Law changes this situation, as it will apply to the dissolution of same-sex marriages.

Unfortunately, the Brussels II*ter*-Proposal does not provide for a clear and concise regulation with respect to the dissolution of same-sex marriages.[19] The proposal is rather halfhearted in this respect: it does not determine the law applicable to marriage.[20] Consequently, the definition of marriage and the conditions of the validity of a marriage are left to the national law of the Member States. This position leaves discretion to each individual Member State, which may apply the proposed choice of law rules to the dissolution of any type of marriage it recognises. Considering the position of many Member States as regards the institution of same-sex marriage, it is likely that the majority of the Member States will not apply the choice of law rules of the Brussels II*ter*-Proposal to the dissolution of the latter type of marriage.

The position of same-sex marriages is, therefore, not well arranged for in neither system. Obviously, this is not a desirable situation, as it leads to legal uncertainty and to legal inequality for same-sex spouses.

With regard to the issue of the termination of registered partnerships the question can be asked whether it is a lost opportunity that the termination of registered partnerships is not covered by the Brussels II*ter*-Proposal. With respect to this question a distinction must be made between its desirability and its feasibility.[21]

In Section 4.3.1 a number of objectives have been listed that would be fulfilled by the unification of the choice of law in the European context. Such unification would increase legal certainty, contribute to decisional harmony, grant better protection to the legitimate expectations of the parties, minimise the risk of limping relationships and enable the achievement of justice. These objectives would fully apply to the unification of the choice of law on the termination of registered partnerships and mainly the arguments of increasing legal certainty and preventing the risk of limping relationships are very convincing. Consequently, such unification would certainly be desirable.

---

[19] See *supra* Sect. 5.4.2.2.

[20] See Press Release No. 8364/07 (Presse 77) of the 2794th Council Meeting of Justice and Home Affairs held in Luxembourg 19–20 April 2007, p. 11. See equally Article 20e-1 of the Brussels II*ter*-Proposal: 'Nothing in this Regulation shall oblige the courts of a Member State whose law [...] does not recognise the marriage in question for the purposes of divorce proceedings to pronounce a divorce by virtue of the application of this Regulation.'

[21] See the analysis of whether it is desirable, and if so possible, to strive for the unification or harmonisation of private international law rules in the field of non-marital registered relationships in general by Curry-Sumner 2005, spec. p. 517 ff.

However, the feasibility of a European unification of the choice of law rules on the termination of registered partnerships is quite a different matter. This question is divisible into two distinct issues: on the one hand, the question whether the issue at hand is suitable for European unification at all and, on the other, whether the Brussels II*ter*-Proposal could be extended to the termination of registered partnerships.

In the first place, the question must be asked whether a unified choice of law on the termination of registered partnerships is feasible at all. The most difficult task in this respect would be to agree on a definition of the registered partnership to be regulated or to specify its main characteristics. Not all EU Member States have currently legally regulated the issue of registered partnerships.[22] In addition, the national regulations in this field of law of the Member States that have introduced the registered partnership or a similar institution largely differ.[23] These two circumstances make it very hard to reach consensus on the issue.[24] The EU Member States can in imitation of the issue of same-sex marriages equally decide to leave the definition of a registered partnership to the discretion of each individual Member States. However, this would probably not lead to legal certainty and predictability. A European unification of the choice of law rules on the termination of registered partnerships does therefore not seem to be feasible.

Should such unification be feasible, it is in addition questionable whether the Brussels II*ter*-Proposal is the most suitable instrument for the regulation of this issue. In other words, are the proposed choice of law rules on divorce suitable to be extended to the termination of registered partnerships or does the latter category demand for a different approach?

Dutch law has regulated the termination of registered partnerships in a separate Act, which did try to conform as much as possible to the equivalent rules on divorce.[25] The conformity in Dutch law of the choice of law rules on registered partnership to those on marriage is accounted for by the resemblance of these two institutions.[26] In other countries such resemblance between marriage and registered partnership is not always present. In some countries the institution of registered partnership is considered merely to create a simple contractual relationship, while in other legal systems the institution determines personal status. Therefore, the institution of registered partnership demands for a different instrument on the Euro-pean level. As the institution of the registered partnership does not *per se* resemble the marriage, it makes no sense with regard to the choice of law rules on

---

[22] As seen in note 11 of Chap. 3, currently 14 EU Member States have enacted some form of registered partnership.

[23] In this respect the termination of registered partnerships differs from the dissolution of same-sex marriages. Although the institution of same-sex marriage has not been regulated by many Member States, the national regulations of the Member States that have regulated the institution largely correspond.

[24] Cf., *supra* Sect. 3.2. See also Curry-Sumner 2005, p. 530.

[25] See *supra* Sects. 3.3.2 and 3.4.1.

[26] See *supra* Sects. 3.3.3 and 3.4.3.

the termination of registered partnerships to try to join the latter rules on divorce. Arguably different choice of law rules should be adopted with regard to the termination of registered partnerships than the ones on divorce on the European level. It might moreover be easier to establish common choice of law rules on this issue in a separate instrument, which would also provide for jurisdictional rules and rules on recognition and enforcement. Furthermore, such a separate instrument should not be limited to the issue of the termination of registered partnerships, but should equally cover other issues related to registered partnerships, such as its establishment.

Consequently, the fact that the choice of law rules of the Brussels II*ter*-Proposal do not apply to the termination of registered partnerships is not to be considered a lost opportunity. Already with the scope of application being limited to divorce and legal separation, it proved to be impossible to reach consensus between the Member States. It is thus not hard to imagine which fate that a project on the unification of the choice of law rules on the termination of registered partnerships would currently meet.

7.3 Structure and Composition of the Choice of Law Rules on Divorce

The underlying structure of the current Dutch and the European choice of law on divorce is similar: party autonomy is regarded as the prevailing principle. Only in the absence of a *professio iuris* on divorce, the applicable law to divorce is determined by a cascade rule, which is based on the principle of the closest connection.[27]

However, despite this similarity of the structure, the composition of the current Dutch and European choice of law on divorce differs. The European system contains two separate provisions regulating the *professio iuris* on divorce and the applicable law to divorce in the absence of such a choice (Articles 20a and 20b of the Brussels II*ter*-Proposal respectively). This division makes perfectly clear that the *professio iuris* is the principal rule of the Proposal. The Dutch system, on the other hand, does not possess such a clear organisation: the fact that party autonomy is the prevailing principle is more or less hidden.[28] It follows from Article 1(4) CLAD that the spouses, irrespective of their nationality or their place of habitual residence, can always opt for Dutch law as the law applicable to their divorce.

[27] Both the alternatives out of which parties can choose with regard to the law applicable to divorce as well as the cascade of connecting factors are not identical in the Dutch and the European choice of law on divorce, see further *infra* Sects. 7.4 and 7.6 respectively.

[28] Cf., Van Rooij 1981, p. 424.

In the event that the spouses possess a common nationality, they can equally choose the application of this common national law on the basis of Article 1(2), second sentence of the CLAD.

It requires little explanation that the composition of the European choice of law on divorce is preferable to the Dutch one. By means of the organisation of the choice of law, the European system provides much more clarity in two ways. In the first place, from the composition of the Brussels II*ter*-Proposal it is clear that party autonomy is its principal rule, as it clearly states that Article 20b only applies in the absence of a *professio iuris* on the basis of Article 20a. In the second place, equally the alternatives out of which the spouses can choose have been articulated more clearly, simply by listing them in one and the same section. Therefore, the European choice of law on divorce succeeds better in providing clarity and legal certainty for the spouses.

The structure of the proposed amendment of the Dutch choice of law on divorce will differ greatly from the Brussels II*ter*-Proposal. Party autonomy will no longer be the prevailing principle of the Dutch choice of law on divorce. Instead its principal rule will be the application of Dutch law. This rule will only be derogated from in case (one of) the spouses chooses the application of their common national law. The composition of this amendment is a better reflection of the structure of the choice of law on divorce though: it clarifies the principal rule and the possible exception to it.

7.4 The Spouses' Choice as to the Applicable Law

Pursuant to the Dutch choice of law on divorce and to the Brussels II*ter*-Proposal the spouses have the opportunity to choose the law applicable to their divorce. However, as the current and proposed Dutch choice of law differ in this respect, the comparison with the Brussels Ii*ter*-Proposal will be drawn separately.

7.4.1 Current Dutch Choice of Law on Divorce

It is clear from the previous paragraph that both the Dutch and the European choice of law on divorce regard party autonomy as the prevailing principle. Another similarity is that the Dutch as well as the proposed European provision on the spouses' choice as to the applicable law do not allow spouses to choose any law as the applicable law to their divorce: the *professio iuris* is limited.

Dutch law grants the spouses the following possibility to choose the applicable law to their divorce; the parties can choose between:

- Dutch law (Article 1(4) CLAD); and
- the spouses' common national law (Article 1(2), second sentence CLAD).

The Brussels II*ter*-Proposal offers some more option to the spouses. Article 20a provides for the following alternatives out of which the spouses can choose:

- the law of the State where the spouses are habitually resident;
- the law of the State where the spouses were last habitually resident insofar as one of them still resides there;
- the law of the state of the nationality of either spouse; and
- the law of the Member State where the court is seised

In Section 2.3.1 above the limitation of the possibility to choose the applicable law to divorce according to Dutch law has been questioned. In general a limitation of the legal systems out of which the spouses can choose is appropriate in view of the requirement of the existence of a connection between the spouses and the law to be applied to their divorce. However, from this perspective the limitation of the alternatives out of which the spouses can choose according to Dutch law is not very convincing. The Brussels II*ter*-Proposal succeeds better in this respect by allowing the spouses more options as regards the legal systems out of which they can choose. All the alternatives of Article 20a(1) of the Brussels II*ter*-Proposal meet the requirement of reflecting a (close) connection between the spouses and the law to be applied to their divorce. The greater freedom of choice as proposed in the Brussels II*ter*-Proposal should be welcomed with regard to increasing flexibility for the spouses and, not in the least, to legal certainty. By means of the *professio iuris* the parties can assure the application of a certain law to their divorce, leading in consequence to more legal certainty.

The preceding analysis in the Chapters 2 and 5 above has shown that the *professio iuris* of the Dutch choice of law on divorce is based on a completely different foundation — *favor divortii* — than the *professio iuris* of the European choice of law on divorce — increasing flexibility for the spouses. The alternatives out of which the spouses can choose according to Article 20a of the Brussels II*ter*-Proposal do more justice to the underlying objective than the ones according to Dutch law. An extension of the alternatives out of which the spouses can choose should also be considered in Dutch law. The principle of *favor divortii* would most certainly benefit from it: the spouses both have more opportunities to influence the law applicable to their divorce. Moreover, the spouses who both wish to get divorced and who are offered the opportunity to influence the law to be applied to their divorce are likely to choose the law most favourable to divorce in their case.

7.4.2 Proposed Dutch Choice of Law on Divorce

In contrast to Article 1 CLAD the possibility to choose the applicable law to divorce is no longer the principal rule of Article 56 of the Dutch Proposal on Private International Law, but merely the exception to it. The *professio iuris* will be limited to the law of the common nationality of the spouses. As the amendment involves that Dutch law will apply in any cross-border divorce case, the possibility to choose Dutch law is no longer of use.

The difference with the *professio iuris* of the current choice of law on divorce is that the limitation of the *professio iuris* of its proposed amendment does not seem to be inspired by the principle of *favor divortii* — of which the principal rule is the expression — but rather by motives relating to the prevention of limping legal relationships.[29] The rationale is that the application of the spouses' common national law will increase the chance that the divorce will be recognised in their country of origin.[30]

Although the proposed amendment of Article 1 CLAD will certainly ensure that Dutch law will be applied in the vast majority of international divorce cases, the rationale behind the limitation of the *professio iuris* is not obvious. According to the Dutch Standing Committee on Private International law the extension of the alternatives out of which the spouses can choose would produce a too complicated choice of law rule.[31] Yet wouldn't the principle of *favor divortii* be better served if the parties have a less limited choice as to the applicable law? Furthermore, what difference does it make for the court to apply the common national law of the spouses or yet the law of their common habitual residence? In both cases the court would, in derogation from Dutch law, apply foreign law to divorce.

Compared to Article 20a of the Brussels II*ter*-Proposal the degree of party autonomy pursuant to the proposed Dutch rule is even further restricted.

7.5 Formal Requirements of the *Professio Iuris*

Large differences exist between the Dutch and the European rules with regard to the formal requirements of the *professio iuris*. Three aspects of the formal requirements are to be distinguished: the first one relates to the form of the choice (Section 7.5.1), the second to the impossibility to impliedly choose the applicable law (Section 7.5.2) and the third to the time of the choice (Section 7.5.3).

7.5.1 Form of the Professio Iuris

With regard to the form of the *professio iuris* there are two major differences between the European and the current Dutch rules.

---

[29] This thought currently also underlies Article 1(2), second sentence CLAD, by virtue of which the spouses can choose the application of their common national law.

[30] It is to be noted that this same argument would equally apply to the place of the common habitual residence of the spouses.

[31] See Staatscommissie 1995, p. 5.

In the first place, Dutch law does not require a specific agreement between the spouses on the *professio iuris*. By contrast, Article 20a(2) of the Brussels II*ter*-Proposal does require a specific agreement: the *professio iuris* must be determined by a written agreement that has been dated and signed by both parties.

The second difference as regards the form of the *professio iuris* concerns the explicit consent of both spouses.[32] According to Article 20a(2) of the Brussels II*ter*-Proposal the agreement on the *professio iuris* on divorce can only be made jointly. A unilateral choice by one of the spouses cannot meet the requirements posed by Article 20a(2). The explicit consent of both spouses on the designation of a certain legal system as the law applicable to divorce is thus required. Conversely, in addition to a joint choice of the spouses, Articles 1(2) and 1(4) of the CLAD do allow a unilateral, but uncontested, choice of one spouse. Consequently, Dutch law does not require a common choice of the spouses and, hence, no explicit consent between them either. Although Dutch law does actually require the consent of the spouses with regard to the law applicable to divorce, the court will rather easily assume such consent.

The proposed amendment of the Dutch choice of law rule on divorce does not involve an alteration of the requirements as to the form of the *professio iuris*. It maintains the requirement of a choice 'that has been made jointly by the parties or such a choice remains uncontested by one of the parties'. The proposal did add an extra paragraph determining that the choice as to the applicable law should be made expressly or be sufficiently clear from the wording of the initiatory petition or the written defence.[33]

The different requirements as regards the form of the *professio iuris* make clear that, whereas under Dutch law the parties can benefit from the opportunity to choose the applicable law in any divorce case, be it a case on a petition of one spouse or on their joint application, this is not the case under European law. Pursuant to Article 20a of the Brussels II*ter*-Proposal the parties who wish to initiate divorce proceedings on the basis of mutual consent will benefit the most from the possibility to choose the applicable law, save for those cases in which the agreement on the *professio iuris* has been concluded upon before the marriage or during happier times of the marriage. The requirement of a joint choice as to the applicable law forces the parties to reach an agreement, which — on the average — will not be an easy task in the absence of mutual consent.

The formal requirements as regards the form of the *professio iuris* as posed by the Brussels II*ter*-Proposal are as a result considerably stricter than the Dutch ones.

The absence of strict formal requirements as regards the *professio iuris* in Dutch law can be explained by the principle of *favor divortii*. Given the thought of this principle — i.e. the possibility to dissolve the marriage is favoured — it is not surprising that Dutch law does not require any strict formalities to be complied

---

[32] See equally Ibili 2006, p. 744.

[33] This requirement is mainly meant to prevent the assumption of an implied *professio iuris*. See further *infra* Sect. 7.5.2.

with regarding the form of the *professio iuris*. For the absence of strict formal requirements encourages the choice for the application of the Dutch — 'divorce-friendly' — law.

By contrast, the introduction of the *professio iuris* on divorce in the Brussels II*ter*-Proposal is based on other principles.[34] In this respect the two most important objectives of the Brussels II*ter*-Proposal are, on the one hand, increasing flexibility and party autonomy and, on the other, strengthening legal certainty and predictability. A balance between these two objectives must be found with respect to the regulation of the *professio iuris* and the stricter approach regarding the form of the agreement is a logical consequence of this balance. The objective of increasing flexibility would entail a (considerable) number of legal systems out of which the spouses can choose. However, the *professio iuris* pursuant to Article 20a of the Brussels II*ter*-Proposal is not without limitation: it is restricted by virtue of both the objective of strengthening legal certainty and predictability and the principle of the closest connection in order to ensure the application of a law with which the spouses have a close connection. The objective of strengthening legal certainty and predictability furthermore requires a strict framework within which the agreement should be concluded. A carefully contemplated decision on the *professio iuris* on divorce is — given its possible implications — desirable and it is certainly conducive to legal certainty. As the formal requirements of Article 20a(2) of the Brussels II*ter*-Proposal compel to a contemplated choice on the law applicable to divorce both the objective of increasing flexibility and the objective of strengthening legal certainty are complied with.

7.5.2 Implied Choice of the Spouses as to the Applicable Law

Both Dutch and European law do not allow an implied choice as to the law applicable to divorce. Yet the reason for not allowing such a choice differs between the current Dutch law and the Brussels II*ter*-Proposal. There is yet no difference between the Brussels II*ter*-Proposal and the proposed Dutch provision in this respect.

The exclusion of an implied choice is a good cause, since the application of a certain legal system to the divorce can have far-reaching consequences. Parties must have been aware of all these (possible) consequences. Even though an explicit choice as to the applicable law does not fully guarantee that the parties are actually aware of the consequences of their choice, the chance that they will be unduly surprised is more remote than in case of an implied choice.

Moreover, as already argued above, a *professio iuris* presumes that the parties have been aware, firstly, of the possibility of the option to choose the law applicable to their divorce and, secondly, of the consequences that such a choice

[34] See *supra* Sect. 5.3 on the objectives underlying the Brussels II*ter*-Proposal.

might involve.[35] Therefore, the competent court should not assume a *professio iuris* in cases in which parties did not intend it: the fact that parties did not make any explicit mention as regards the applicable law cannot be seised in order to assume an implied choice for the application of a certain legal system. In addition, it is not in the least certain that the parties have been aware of the international character of their divorce.[36]

Consequently, the assumption of an implied choice as to the applicable law to divorce is not desirable.

7.5.2.1 Comparison to the Current Dutch Law

Whereas pursuant to the current Dutch law an implied choice might be within the bounds of the possible in the absence of strict formal requirements on the *professio iuris*, the formal requirements of Article 20a(2) of the Brussels II*ter*-Proposal demanding an written agreement between the spouses on the law to be applied to their (possible) divorce already before the divorce proceedings have commenced preclude the assumption of an implied choice.

7.5.2.2 Comparison to the Proposed Dutch law

The third paragraph of Article 56 of the Dutch Proposal on Private International Law contains the following provision:

> A choice of law as meant in the preceding paragraph [*i.e.* the *professio iuris* for the common national law of the spouses; NAB] should be made expressly or be sufficiently clear from the terms used in the petition or the written defence.

This provision clearly relates to the issue of the implied choice as to the applicable law. In 1993 the Working Group on Private International Law of the Netherlands Association for the Administration of Justice has determined that a *professio iuris* can only be made by means of an explicit reference or be otherwise sufficiently clear from the wording of the initiatory petition.[37] Article 56 of the Dutch Proposal on Private International Law reflects this position.

As the formal requirements of the *professio iuris* are tightened in Article 56 of the Dutch Proposal on Private International Law, the regulation of the issue of the implied choice is actually very similar to the proposed European rule: neither one allows the assumption of an implied choice as to the applicable law.

---

[35] See *supra* Sects. 2.3.4.2 and 5.5.2.2 respectively.

[36] Cf., with regard to the Dutch choice of law on divorce Vonken (Groene Serie Personen- en familierecht) Article 1 CLAD, n. 3.4.

[37] Werkgroep IPR NVvR 1993, pp. 145 and 147–148.

7.5.3 Time of Choice as to the Applicable Law

Another important formal requirement of the *professio iuris* concerns the time factor, i.e. the question as of when and until when the *professio iuris* can be validly made.

Although the Dutch Choice of Law Act on Divorce currently does not contain any specific provision with regard to the time of choice, it is clear from the parliamentary history that a *professio iuris* on divorce can only be made in the course of the divorce proceedings. According to Dutch law a *professio iuris* on the law applicable to divorce in a marriage contract has no legal consequences. However, pursuant to Dutch law a *professio iuris* can still be agreed upon before the court during the proceedings, provided that there is case of defended divorce proceedings. In case of default of appearance the requesting party must make the *professio iuris* in the initiatory petition on divorce in order to make sure that the respondent is informed.[38]

The proposed amendment of Article 1 CLAD does expressly provide for a time factor: the choice as to the applicable law has to be made 'during the proceedings'. The introduction of the time factor is thus an expression of the already existing practice in this regard.

By contrast, the situation as regards the time factor is virtually completely opposite under the Brussels II*ter*-Proposal. Pursuant to Article 20a(2) Brussels II*ter*-Proposal the agreement on the *professio iuris* can be concluded at the latest at the time the court is seised, thus at any time before the divorce proceedings have started. This requirement entails that a marriage contract is a document *par excellence* in which the choice as to the applicable law to divorce can be made. Article 20a(4) contains a specific provision with regard to extending the time-limit to the course of the divorce proceedings. Whether the parties can take advantage of this extended time-limit depends on the law of the forum. Consequently, the spouses may not be in a position to designate the applicable law before the court in the course of the divorce proceedings in each Member State.[39]

The position that both these legal systems take with regard to the time factor of the *professio iuris* thus differs greatly. In Section 5.5.2.3 the possibility introduced by Article 20a(2) of the Brussels II*ter*-Proposal to determine the law applicable to a possible divorce in a marriage contract has already been questioned.[40]

The Dutch position with regard to the time factor of the *professio iuris* on divorce is to be preferred, as it ensures that the choice is made by (one of) the spouses at the time the divorce actually occurs. If one carries the Dutch position to European law, it would mean that the application of a legal system to the divorce

---

[38] Cf., Memorandum of Reply (MvA), *Kamerstukken II* 1980–1981, 16 004, No. 7, p. 3. See equally Wendels 1983, pp. 70–71; Mostermans 2006, p. 43; Vonken (Groene Serie Personen- en familierecht) Article 1 CLAD, n. 3.3.

[39] See further *supra* Sect. 5.5.2.3.

[40] Cf., De Boer 2008, pp. 330–331.

with which the spouses have a close connection at the time of the divorce is equally ensured. The consequence of the time factor as foreseen by Article 20a(2) of the Brussels II*ter*-Proposal is that it may lead to the application of a certain legal system with which the spouses had a close connection at the time of the agreement, but with which no close connection exists at the time of the divorce. For the circumstances at the time of the divorce and those at the time of the conclusion of the marriage contract can be as different as night and day.[41]

7.6 The Law Applicable to Divorce in the Absence of a *Professio Iuris*

According to Article 1 of the CLAD and to Articles 20a and 20b of the Brussels II*ter*-Proposal, the law applicable to divorce is determined by a cascade rule only in the absence of a *professio iuris*. The respective rules provide for the reference of an international divorce case to the legal system with which it is most closely connected. The current Dutch law and the Brussels II*ter*-Proposal will be compared in Section 7.6.1 below.

Article 56 of the Dutch Proposal on Private International Law provides by contrast for a completely different approach: the exclusive application of the *lex fori* (i.e. Dutch law) to any cross-border divorce case. In Section 7.6.2 this proposal will be compared to the Brussels II*ter*-Proposal.

7.6.1 Current Dutch Choice of Law on Divorce

Both the current Dutch and the proposed European choice of law rules on divorce are based on the principle of the closest connection. The Dutch rules are furthermore based on the principle of *favor divortii*.

In order to determine the law applicable to divorce in the absence of a *professio iuris*, both systems provide for a cascade rule. However, the order in the cascade of the two systems does differ. According to the current Dutch law (Article 1(1) to (3) of the CLAD), an international divorce is governed by:

1. the law of the state of the common nationality of the spouses or, in the absence thereof,

[41] See *supra* Sect. 5.5.4, where the proposed date of reference with regard to the *professio iuris* has been criticised. The existence of a connection between the spouses and the law to be applied is reviewed at the time of the conclusion of the agreement and not at the time of the divorce, which seems to contravene the principle of the closest connection, on which the Brussels II*ter*-Proposal is based.

2. the law of the state of the common habitual residence of the spouses or, in the absence thereof,
3. Dutch law.

The cascade rule of Article 20b of the Brussels II*ter*-Proposal determines that an international divorce is governed by:

1. the law of the state of the common habitual residence of the spouses or, in the absence thereof,
2. the law of the state in which the spouses were last habitually resident provided that that period did not end more than one year before the court was seised and provided that one of the spouses still lives there or, in the absence thereof,
3. the law of the state of the common nationality of the spouses or, in the absence thereof,
4. the law of the state where the court is seised (the *lex fori*).

What strikes one most is that both the Dutch and the European choice of law rule on divorce make use of the same connecting factors: habitual residence and nationality. Moreover, both systems use the *lex fori* as a last resort option.

However, whereas the Dutch choice of law rule uses the nationality of the spouses as a primary connecting factor, Article 20b of the Brussels II*ter*-Proposal awards this position to the habitual residence of the spouses. This difference of approach can be explained by two factors. In the first place, the Dutch choice of law rule on divorce was established in 1981: at that time the principle of nationality was still predominating in international family law. This prevalence explains the priority that has been given to nationality as a connecting factor in the CLAD, even though the principle of residence has obtained an important supplementary role in the Dutch choice of law on divorce.[42]

Secondly, the objectives of the European Union, in which the fundamental freedom of movement of persons is to be guaranteed, incite to a more flexible approach with regard to the choice of law.[43] In addition, habitual residence does not — as opposed to nationality — depend on national definitions, but is rather an autonomous concept.

An important difference between the Dutch and the European choice of law on divorce arises in the situation in which the choice of law rules designate a law that does not provide for divorce. According to Dutch law the consequence is that the Dutch court cannot pronounce the divorce; it is a consequence that should be accepted in view of the advantage of the simplicity of the system.[44] The Brussels II*ter*-Proposal provides in this regard for a special provision that functions as a remedy for situations in which the applicable law 'does not provide for divorce'.

---

[42] See further *supra* Sect. 2.4.1.

[43] See *supra* Sect. 5.5.3.2.

[44] Explanatory Memorandum (MvT), *Kamerstukken II* 1979–1980, 16 004, No. 3–4, p. 11. See further *supra* Sect. 2.4.

In such cases, the *lex fori* will apply.[45] Proceeding from the principle of the closest connection, this provision is far from being welcomed. By means of this provision, which is clearly based on the principle of *favor divortii*, the neutral foundation of the choice of law rules on divorce of the Brussels II*ter*-Proposal is disrupted.[46] If such a provision is deemed necessary at all, a more just solution would be to proceed to the next alternative connecting factor provided for and not automatically to the *lex fori*.

Remarkably enough, the issue at hand shows a *favor divortii* tendency of the Brussels II*ter*-Proposal and not of the Dutch choice of law on divorce. Since the European provision has clearly been inserted by way of compromise, the *favor divortii* tendency is most probably not the consequence of a deliberate policy.

Another important difference between the Dutch and the European choice of law on divorce is that Dutch law awards more authority to the court to assess whether the designated law actually complies with the principle of the closest connection. In case of a single nationality, the Dutch court is to apply an authenticity test (*realiteitstoets*, Article 1(2) CLAD) in order to determine whether either of the parties manifestly lacks a 'real societal connection' with the country of his or her nationality. The Dutch court needs to apply a similar test in case of multiple nationalities, i.e. the effectivity test (*effectiviteitstoets*, Article 1(3) CLAD), in order to assess with which of the states of which the person involved possesses the nationality is most closely connected. In applying both these tests the court needs to take all the circumstances of the case into consideration.[47]

The Brussels II*ter*-Proposal does not provide for any such 'correcting' tools to assess whether the designated law reflects a close connection. In the negotiations on the Brussels II*ter*-Proposal this issue has only been dealt with marginally; solely the question of multiple nationalities has been subject of debate in the Council. However, it has been decided to leave this issue to the national laws of the Member States.[48] Otherwise the Brussels II*ter*-Proposal does not contain any (other) correcting mechanisms concerning other situations in which the case proves to be manifestly more closely connected with another country than the one that is referred to by Article 20b. In Section 5.5.3.4 above it has been argued that Article 20b of the Brussels II*ter*-Proposal would benefit from the insertion of an extra paragraph stipulating that 'where it is clear from all the circumstances of the

[45] See Article 20b-1 on the application of the law of the forum. See Council Document No. 9712/08 JUSTCIV 106 of 23 May 2008, p. 15. 'Where the law applicable pursuant to Article 20a and 20b does not provide for divorce or does not grant one of the spouses because of his or her gender equal access to divorce or legal separation, the law of the forum shall apply.'

[46] See *supra* Sect. 5.5.3.3.

[47] See further *supra* Sects. 2.4.2.1 and 2.4.2.2 on the authenticity and effectivity test respectively.

[48] Recital No. 5c of the Preamble to the Brussels II*ter*-Proposal. See Council Document No. 8587/08 JUSTCIV 73 of 18 April 2008. See further *supra* Sect. 5.5.3.2.

case that the divorce is manifestly more closely connected with a country other than that indicated in paragraph 1, the law of that other country shall apply'.[49] It is beyond doubt that such manifest closer connection should not be assessed on the basis of concerns regarding substantive law, but exclusively on the basis of factual and geographical factors. Even though such a correcting tool could encourage the tendency of the courts to apply their own law and carry a risk with it as regards legal certainty and predictability, these drawbacks should be accepted in light of its favourable effects on the principle of the closest connection.

This difference between the Dutch and the European choice of law system shows that Article 1 CLAD is a better expression of the principle of the closest connection. Although this principle underlies both systems, its effect on the choice of law rules on divorce differs in this respect. By providing correcting tools, the 'static' result of the choice of law rule referring to a certain legal system can be adjusted in order to attain the designation of the most closely connected law. The difference at issue between the two systems can also be partly explained by the principle of *favor divortii* prevailing in Dutch law, as the correcting tools of Article 1(2) and (3) CLAD can equally serve to realise the *favor divortii*.[50]

7.6.2 Proposed Dutch Choice of Law on Divorce

The amendment of the Dutch choice of law on divorce involves a drastic change of the choice of law approach adhered to so far in the Netherlands. Instead of the reference to the most closely connected law, the amendment provides for the exclusive application of Dutch law in international divorce cases.

The approach of the proposed Dutch choice of law on divorce therefore differs from the Brussels II*ter*-Proposal, which is based on the principle of the closest connection. The proposed Dutch choice of law on divorce on the contrary moves away from the approach of the closest connection and adheres to the *lex fori*-approach.

Consequently, whereas the approach of the current Dutch choice of law on divorce and the Brussels II*ter*-Proposal is similar, this does not hold true for the approach of the proposed Dutch choice of law on divorce and the Brussels II*ter*-Proposal. These two proposed systems are therefore miles apart as regards their choice of law approach. The opposition of the Netherlands against the Brussels II*ter*-Proposal can very well be explained by this difference of approach. In the next paragraph this opposition will be analysed in more detail.

[49] Cf., Article 4(3) of the Rome I-Regulation and Article 4(3) of the Rome II-Regulation.

[50] See *supra* Sect. 2.4.2.1.

7.7 Has the Netherlands Rightly Opposed the Brussels II*ter*-Proposal as Regards Its Content?

In the previous chapter it was argued that the objections that have been raised by the Netherlands as regards the lack of EU competence in the field of a unified choice of law on divorce actually rather imply a substantive objection against the Brussels II*ter*-Proposal motivated by the principle of *favor divortii* prevailing in Dutch law.[51] In other words, the Netherlands has opposed the establishment of the common European choice of law rules on divorce on the basis of its content; it was feared that the common choice of law would be less favourable towards divorce than current Dutch law.[52]

Therefore, the question that can be posed on the basis of the preceding comparison between the current Dutch and the proposed European choice of law on divorce is whether the Netherlands rightly opposed the establishment of the common European choice of law rules. That is, does the Brussels II*ter*-Proposal actually put up more barriers for spouses that wish to obtain a divorce in the Netherlands?

Although the Dutch Minister of Foreign Affairs referred to the *current* law,[53] i.e. Article 1 of the CLAD, a distinction must be made between the current choice of law on divorce and its proposed amendment in order to gain a clear understanding of the expressed fear. For the answer to the question whether the Brussels II*ter*-Proposal actually puts up more barriers for spouses wishing to get divorced in the Netherlands fully depends upon which of these two systems is taken as point of departure.

7.7.1 The Current Dutch Choice of Law on Divorce

The comparison between the current Dutch choice of law on divorce and the Brussels II*ter*-Proposal has shown that the Dutch system is considerably more flexible with regard to the *professio iuris* on divorce. Even though Dutch law does not provide for as many alternative legal systems out of which the spouses can choose as the Brussels II*ter*-Proposal, the *professio iuris* as such is easier to establish pursuant to Dutch law. Compared to Dutch law the formal requirements of Article 20a(2) of the Brussels II*ter*-Proposal imply a substantial complication

[51] See *supra* Sects. 6.3.2 and 6.3.3.

[52] See the letter of the Minister of Foreign Affairs of 2 October 2006, *Kamerstukken II* 2006–2007, 22 112, No. 465: '*De kans is niet gering dat het resultaat van de onderhandeling zal zijn een regeling van het conflictenrecht die minder gunstig is dan de huidige Nederlandse regeling, en dat aldus voor echtgenoten in Nederland meer barrières worden opgeworpen om uit elkaar te gaan dan thans het geval is.*'

[53] Ibid.

for the spouses, mainly since these requirements do not accept a unilateral choice as to the applicable law.

However, these stricter European formal requirements as regard the *professio iuris* do not *per se* imply deterioration. A carefully considered choice as to the law applicable to divorce cannot do any harm given its possible implications as regards the grounds and the conditions for divorce, which, as seen in Section 5.2.1 above, vary considerably among the Member States. Although the stricter requirements of Article 20a(2) can thus be endorsed, the question remains whether they involve that the Brussels II*ter*-Proposal is less favourable than Dutch law. It cannot be denied that the stricter formal requirements do actually raise a barrier as compared to the present Dutch law, which does not require any agreement of the spouses as to the applicable law.

Section 7.6.1 above has shown that the cascade rule of Article 20b of the Brussels II*ter*-Proposal provides for the same connecting factors to determine the applicable law to divorce in the absence of a *professio iuris* as the ones that are currently employed by the CLAD. The sole difference is the order occupied by the connecting factors in the hierarchy of applicability.

The application of Article 20b of the Brussels II*ter*-Proposal would not bring much change for the Dutch courts as regards the interpretation of the connecting factors. The connecting factor of nationality is a clear-cut concept and not subject to any specific European interpretation. Moreover, the Dutch and European choice of law both employ the same definition of the concept of habitual residence, i.e. habitual residence has to be determined on the basis of the specific circumstances of the case. In both systems the permanency of the actual residence and the intentions of the person in question are to be taken into consideration.[54]

Therefore, the cascade rule of Article 20b of the Brussels II*ter*-Proposal is not less favourable than the current Dutch choice of law rule on divorce of Article 1 CLAD.

Finally, it should be mentioned that Article 20b of the Brussels II*ter*-Proposal will more often lead to the application of Dutch law than Article 1 CLAD. The latter Article refers in the first place, in the absence of a *professio iuris,* to the application of the common national law of the spouses to divorce. As the jurisdictional rules of the Brussels II*bis*-Regulation apply pursuant to Dutch law in all situations,[55] the competence of the court is mostly established on the basis of the habitual residence of both spouses or of either spouse. Consequently, Article 1 CLAD may regularly lead to the application of foreign law. From this perspective Article 20b of the Brussels II*ter*-Proposal — which refers to the law of the place of habitual residence — should thus mean a step forward instead of backward.

---

[54] See Sects. 2.4.3 and 5.5.3.1 respectively.

[55] Article 4(1) of the Dutch Code of Civil Procedure extends the rules of the Brussels II*bis*-Regulation analogously to all questions of international jurisdiction in matrimonial matters.

7.7.2 The Proposed Dutch Choice of Law on Divorce

An important reason for the Netherlands to be set against the Brussels II*ter*-Proposal is that it has decided to adhere to the *lex fori*-approach in the future.[56] Article 20b of the Brussels II*ter*-Proposal refers to the application of the *lex fori* solely in case of absence of the provided connecting factors. However, this approach seems to differ considerably from the proposed Dutch choice of law rule on divorce, which stipulates that Dutch law will be applied in all cases, unless (one of) the parties have chosen the application of their common national law.

Yet, according to the European Commission the competent court will often apply its own substantive law pursuant to the choice of law rule of Article 20b of the Brussels II*ter*-Proposal, as the petition for divorce will generally be filed in the state in which the spouses habitually reside.[57] All six jurisdictional grounds of Article 3(1)(a) of the Brussels II*bis*-Regulation use the habitual residence of (one of) the spouses as a connecting factor. Nationality as a connecting factor for jurisdictional purposes only comes into play in case of a common nationality of the spouses (Article 3(1)(b)). As the international competence of the court is thus mainly grafted onto criteria based on habitual residence, the *lex fori* and the *lex domicilii* often correspond.

However, this assumption of the Commission is open to objections, as only the first two indents of Article 3(1)(a) of the Brussels II*bis*-Regulation correspond to Article 20b(a) and (b) of the Brussels II*ter*-Proposal. The latter provision is restricted to the common or the last common habitual residence of the spouses, whereas Article 3(1)(a) of the Brussels II*bis*-Regulation equally refers to the habitual residence of either spouse for the purposes of assuming jurisdiction. From this perspective the assumption that the competent court can apply its own substantive divorce law in the majority of cases is not that obvious. Most probably in many cases the competence of the court is established on the basis of Article 3(1)(a) first or second indent of the Brussels II*bis*-Regulation, but this is not in the least certain.

Consequently, one cannot state with certainty that the European choice of law on divorce is less favourable than Article 56 of the Dutch Proposal on Private International Law.

7.7.3 Synthesis

From the foregoing it is clear that the answer to the question whether the Brussels II*ter*-Proposal actually puts up more barriers for spouses that wish to get divorced in the Netherlands is dependent on the system that has been taken as point of departure.

---

[56] See *supra* Sect. 2.6. See equally Oderkerk 2006, p. 124.

[57] Explanatory Memorandum to the Brussels II*ter*-Proposal, p. 10 and the Impact Assessment on Divorce, p. 26. See equally Lagarde 2004, p. 238; Beyer 2007, p. 23; Bonomi 2007, pp. 780–781; Lazic 2008, p. 90.

In comparison with the current Dutch choice of law on divorce, the position of the Netherlands that the Brussels II*ter*-Proposal puts up more barriers for spouses that wish to get divorced in the Netherlands does not seem to be justified. The preceding analysis of the similarities and differences between the two systems has shown that the European choice of law rules are not *per se* stricter than the Dutch ones, save for the formal requirements of the *professio iuris*. Despite the different underlying principles and the differing accents that have been laid, the Brussels II*ter*-Proposal does not seem to bring many disadvantageous consequences for the Netherlands. The European choice of law on divorce is, therefore, not really less favourable than Article 1 of the CLAD.

However, this conclusion does not hold true for Article 56 of the Dutch Proposal on Private International Law. Pursuant to this provision the Dutch court should, in the absence of a *professio iuris* for the common national law of the spouses, always apply Dutch law in cross-border divorce cases. Although the analysis above has shown that the cascade rule of Article 20b of the Brussels II*ter*-Proposal will lead to the application of the *lex fori* in many cases, the point of departure of the latter proposal differs greatly from the intended amendment of the Dutch choice of law on divorce. It is, therefore, not possible to state with certainty that the Brussels II*ter*-Proposal is less favourable to divorce than Article 56 of the Dutch Proposal on Private International Law.

7.8 Conclusion

Although on the face the current Dutch and the proposed European choice of law on divorce may seem to differ, both systems have many characteristics in common. The underlying structure of both these systems is similar: party autonomy is regarded as the prevailing principle. Only in the absence of a *professio iuris* on divorce, the applicable law to divorce is determined by the choice of law rules, which are based on the principle of the closest connection in both systems. The main differences are to be found in the further details of the regulations.

Article 20a of the Brussels II*ter*-Proposal provides the spouses with more alternative legal systems out of which they can choose as regards the law to be applied to their divorce than Dutch law does. However, the formal requirements of the *professio iuris* posed by Article 20a(2) of the Brussels II*ter*-Proposal are stricter. These requirements differ as regards both the form of the *professio iuris* as the time within which the choice as to the applicable law must be made from Dutch law, which does not demand very strict formal requirements to be complied with.

As far as the situation in the absence of a *professio iuris* is concerned, the current Dutch and the European choice of law rules bear quite some resemblance to each other. The law applicable to divorce is in both systems determined by a cascade rule, in which the same connecting factors are employed. However, the order of hierarchy of the connecting factors differs. Whereas habitual residence is used as the primary connecting factor in Article 20b of the Brussels II*ter*-Proposal, Article 1 of the CLAD has assigned it a secondary position. Another important difference between the two systems is the absence in the Brussels II*ter*-Proposal of correcting mechanism so as to ensure the application of the law with which the spouses are most closely connected.

However, there are considerable differences between the Brussels II*ter*-Proposal and the proposed amendment of the Dutch choice of law on divorce. Firstly, the intended amendment of the Dutch choice of law will no longer regard the principle of party autonomy as the prevailing rule. Furthermore, while the Brussels II*ter*-Proposal is based on the principle of the closest connection, Article 56 of the Dutch Proposal on Private International Law is based on the *lex fori*-approach.

Chapter 6 showed that the Netherlands opposed the Brussels II*ter*-Proposal for fear of a less favourable choice of law on divorce than Dutch law currently provides for. The analysis in this chapter made clear that whether or not this fear is justified depends on the system which has been taken as a point of departure: the current Dutch choice of law rule of Article 1 CLAD or its proposed amendment. The observed fear is not really justified in comparison with the current Dutch choice of law on divorce. But compared to Article 56 of the Dutch Proposal on Private International Law which adheres to the *lex fori*-approach, the fear of the Netherlands seems to be more justified. Although the application of the Brussels II*ter*-Proposal may in the vast majority of cases lead to the application of forum law, it may very well lead to the application of foreign law considering both the *professio iuris* of Article 20a and the cascade rule of Article 20b of the Brussels II*ter*-Proposal.

References

Regulations, Conventions, Reports and Other Documentary Sources

Brussels II*ter*-Proposal. Proposal for a Council Regulation amending Regulation (EC) No. 2201/2003 as regards jurisdiction and introducing rules concerning applicable law in matrimonial matters, COM(2006) 399 final

Choice of Law Act on Divorce. Act of 25 March 1981, *Stb.* 1981, No. 166, containing a regulation of the choice of law rules on the dissolution of the marriage and on legal separation and the recognition thereof, *Wet conflictenrecht Echtscheiding*

Choice of Law Act on Registered Partnerships. Act of 6 July 2004, *Stb.* 2004, Nos. 334 and 621, containing a regulation of the choice of law with regard to the registered partnership, *Wet conflictenrecht Geregistreerd Partnerschap*

Dutch Proposal on Private International Law. Vaststelling en invoering van Boek 10 (Internationaal privaatrecht) van het Burgerlijk Wetboek, *Kamerstukken II* 2009–2010, 32 137, No. 2

Green Paper on Divorce. Green Paper on applicable law and jurisdiction in divorce maters, COM(2005) 82 final

Staatscommissie (1995). Staatscommissie voor het Internationaal Privaatrecht, Advies inzake Wet conflictenrecht echtscheiding, Report of 28 March 1995

Staatscommissie (2001). Staatscommissie voor het Internationaal Privaatrecht, Internationaal privaatrecht in verband met de openstelling van het huwelijk voor personen van hetzelfde geslacht, Report of 1 December 2001

Staatscommissie (2003). Staatscommissie voor het Internationaal Privaatrecht, Voorontwerp van Wet houdende consolidatie van regelgeving betreffende het Internationaal Privaatrecht, the state of affairs on 1 November 2003

The reports of the Dutch Standing Committee on Private International Law are available at: http://www.justitie.nl/onderwerpen/wetgeving/over_wetgeving/privaatrecht/commissies-privaatrecht/staatscommissie-ipr.aspx

Werkgroep IPR NVvR (1993). Werkgroep Internationaal Privaatrecht van de Nederlandse Vereniging voor Rechtspraak, Knelpunten bij de toepassing van artikel 1 Wet Conflictenrecht Echtscheiding. Trema, 129–151

Books and Articles

Beyer M (2007) Handlungsfelder der deutschen EU-Ratspräsidentschaft im Familienrecht -Die europäischen Verordnungsvorschläge zum internationalen Scheidungs- und Unterhaltsrecht. Forum Familienrecht, pp 20–27

Boele-Woelki K (1994) Der *favor divortii* im Niederländischen internationalen Scheidungsrecht. In: Boele-Woelki K (ed) Comparability and Evaluation, Liber Amicorum D. Kokkini-Iatridou. Nijhoff, Dordrecht, pp 167–181

Boele-Woelki K (2008) To be or not to be: enhanced cooperation in international divorce law within the European Union. Victoria University of Wellington Law Review 39:779–792

Bonomi A (2007) Le divorce en droit communautaire entre règles de droit international privé et objectifs de droit matériel. In: Epiney A et al (eds) Die Herausforderung von Grenzen. Festschrift für Roland Bieber. Nomos, Baden-Baden, pp 771–783

Curry-Sumner I (2005) All's well that ends registered? Intersentia, Antwerpen

De Boer ThM (2008) The second revision of the Brussels II Regulation: jurisdiction and applicable law. In: Boele-Woelki K, Sverdrup T (eds) European challenges in contemporary family law. Intersentia, Antwerpen, pp 321–341

Fiorini A (2008a) The codification of private international law in Europe: could the community learn from the experience of mixed jurisdictions? Electronic Journal of Comparative Law 12:1–16

Fiorini A (2008b) Rome III—Choice of law in divorce: is the Europeanization of family law going too far? International Journal of Law, Policy and the Family 22:178–205

Heinze C (2008) Bausteine eines Allgemeinen Teils des europäischen Internationalen Privatrechts. In: Baetge D et al (eds) Die richtige Ordnung, Festschrift für Jan Kropholler. Mohr Siebeck, Tübingen, pp 105–127

Ibili F (2006) Van 'Brussel II' en 'Brussel II*bis*' naar 'Brussel II*ter*'; voorstel tot introductie van forumkeuze en conflictenregels in het IPR-scheidingsprocesrecht. WPNR 6685:743–745

Kreuzer K (2008) Was gehört in den Allgemeinen Teil eines Europäischen Kollisionsrechtes? In: Jud B et al (eds) Kollisionsrecht in der Europäischen Union. Jan Sramek Verlag, Wien, pp 1–62

Lagarde P (2004) Développements futurs du droit international privé dans une Europe en voie d'unification: quelques conjectures. RabelsZ 68:225–243

Lazic V (2008) Recent Developments in Harmonizing 'European Private International Law' in Family Matters. European Journal of Law Reform 10:75–96

Leible S (2007) Der Beitrag der Rom II-Verordnung zu einer Kodifikation der allgemeinen Grundsätze des Europäischen Kollisionsrecht. In: Reichelt G (ed) Europäisches Gemeinschaftsrecht und IPR. Manzsche, Wien, pp 31–54

Leible S (2009) Rom I und Rom II: Neue Perspektiven im Europäischen Kollisionsrecht. Zentrum für Europäisches Wirtschaftsrecht, Bonn

Mostermans PMM (2006) Echtscheiding, 3rd edn. Kluwer, Deventer

Oderkerk AE (2006) Het Groenboek inzake het toepasselijke recht en de rechterlijke bevoegdheid in echtscheidingszaken. NIPR 24:119–128

Siehr K (2008) Die Kodifikation des Europäischen IPR—Hindernisse, Aufgaben und Lösungen. In: Jud B et al (eds) Kollisionsrecht in der Europäischen Union. Jan Sramek Verlag, Wien, pp 77–95

Sonnenberger HJ (2008) Randbemerkungen zum Allgemeinen Teil eines europäisierten IPR. In: Baetge D et al (eds) Die richtige Ordnung, Festschrift für Jan Kropholler. Mohr Siebeck, Tübingen, pp 227–246

Van Rooij R (1981) Wetgeving internationale echtscheidingen. Ars Aequi 30:420–429

Vlas P (1996) Echtscheiding in het IPR: de peildatum en het bijzondere geval. Ars Aequi 47:196–202

Vonken APMJ (Groene Serie Personen- en familierecht) Titel 9, Internationaal Privaatrecht. Internationale Echtscheidingen. Groene Serie Privaatrecht, Personen- en familierecht (Electronic database Plaza Kluwer Juridisch en Fiscaal, looseleaf)

Wendels A (1983) Internationale echtscheidingen. W.E.J. Tjeenk Willink, Zwolle

Chapter 8
A Unified System of International Family Law in the European Union: Which Way Forward?

8.1 Introduction

The field of international family law currently has a predominantly national nature: the EU Member States provide for autonomous rules in this field of law.

However, this situation will probably change in the future, as the European Commission develops a common European system of international family law. According to the Hague Programme, instruments in the field of family law including divorce, maintenance, and matrimonial property should be completed by the year 2011.[1] With the Maintenance Regulation and the accompanying Hague Protocol determining the law applicable to maintenance obligations, the Brussels II*ter*-Proposal and the Green Paper in the field of matrimonial property the establishment of such a common system is taking shape more and more. Moreover, also issues such as personal status, names and adoption have been mentioned as future areas of Union action in the field of private international law.[2] Although the introduction of the common choice of law rules on divorce was not as successful as the Commission had hoped, its intentions as regards issues of international family law are clear: this field of law will be 'Europeanised'. However, the failure to reach a compromise on the Brussels II*ter*-Proposal will certainly have its repercussions on the establishment of and the negotiations over other issues of international family law to be arranged for. Yet whether this is an unfavourable development remains to be seen. Section 8.2 therefore aims to detect the pitfalls of the Brussels II*ter*-Proposal.

---

[1] The Hague Programme, p. 13. The Commission also published the Proposal for a Succession Regulation. This Proposal will; however, not be taken into consideration in the following analysis, since the law of succession is regarded as a matter distinct from family law (see the Explanatory Memorandum to this Proposal, p. 3).

[2] See Communication from the Commission to the Council and the European Parliament establishing for the period 2007–2013 a framework programme on Fundamental Rights and Justice, COM(2005) 122 final, p. 67.

N.A. Baarsma, *The Europeanisation of International Family Law*,
DOI: 10.1007/978-90-6704-743-2_8, © T.M.C. ASSER PRESS, The Hague,
The Netherlands, and the author 2011

When discussing the future of European international family law, one of the primary questions is what the European Union actually wishes to attain by Europeanising this field of law (Section 8.3). From these aims and objectives some guidelines for the future unification of issues of international family law will be tried to be derived. In view of the consequences which the unified choice of law in family matters may have, legal doctrine has emphasised not to proceed too fast and to firstly lay a theoretical foundation for European private international law.[3] For the risk exists that the current — fragmented — approach will not allow for the development of a coherent system of European international family law and it will inevitably lead to problems of definition of the respective fields of application.[4] Section 8.4 will therefore seek to instigate the development of such a coherent system of international family law.

Finally, in Section 8.5 a number of recommendations resulting from the analysis on the Europeanisation of international family law will be made to the EU legislature.

8.2 What can be Learned from the Brussels II*ter*-'Adventure'?

The preceding three chapters showed that the development of a unified system of choice of law on divorce is not an easy task; on the contrary, it turns out to be a rather slippery path.[5] It proved to be impossible to reach a consensus between the Member States on the issue of the law applicable to divorce.

As a means to overcome the resulting paralysis, the procedure on enhanced cooperation has been launched and has resulted in the establishment of the Regulation on enhanced cooperation in the field of divorce. This regulation allows a group of Member States to move ahead in the area of the choice of law on divorce, while others have the possibility either to join the cooperation or to stay behind.

This paragraph analyses the lessons that can be drawn from the experience of the failed attempt to establish a common choice of law on divorce. The analysis in Chapter 6 above on the failure of unified choice of law rules on divorce has shown that the most important bottleneck was the lack of agreement between the Member States on the methodological and theoretical foundation of a unified system of the choice of law on divorce, mainly because of the differences in the substantive law approach of the Member States.[6] Initially also the position of Malta, the only Member State that does not provide for divorce in its national legislation, and the

---

[3] See e.g. Kohler 2003, p. 409: '*Die wirkliche Herausforderung, der sich der Gemeinschaftsgesetzgeber stellen muss, betrifft die Formulierung einer Politik für das Gemeinschaftskollisionsrecht*'; Vlas 2003, p. 393 (with regard to the private international law aspects of succession); Gaudemet-Tallon 2005, p. 168; Pontier 2005, p. 25; Dethloff 2007, p. 995.

[4] Cf., Gaudemet-Tallon 2005, p. 168; Fiorini 2008b, p. 195.

[5] Cf., Baarsma 2009, p. 14.

[6] See *supra* Sect. 6.4.

issue of competence with regard to the unification of the choice of law posed problems. During the negotiations in the Council to both these problems a solution was found.[7]

In this paragraph the failure of an agreement between the Member States on the Brussels II*ter*-Proposal will be analysed on a more general level in order to draw lessons from it. After the discussion of some general aspects (Section 8.2.1), Section 8.2.2 will elaborate on the question of transparency. Finally, the influence of the interrelationship between divorce and other fields of family law on the establishment of a single instrument in one area will be discussed (Section 8.2.3).

8.2.1 General

The Brussels II*ter*-Proposal has been described as too ambitious.[8] Boele–Woelki has accordingly observed that whether this holds true undeniably depends on the aims and objectives of the legislative measure to be taken.[9] She further noted that

> [I]n trying to achieve these aims the unification of private international law rules within the European Union as such and at all costs should never be a goal in itself. The content of the rules is more important. In addition, it should be respected that for some Member States higher values than the uniformity of rules and a coherent approach prevail.[10]

Obviously Boele-Woelki touches here upon a very important issue: the sole goal of Europeanisation of the choice of law rules should not take place at the expense of the content of these rules. However, the Union legislature tends to adhere to a functional approach of the unification of the private international law rules: the Europeanisation of this field of law is aimed at European integration.[11] Therefore, the risk that the Europeanisation of the choice of law in a certain area is considered as a goal in itself is certainly present. It should nevertheless be noted that the goal of Europeanisation of the choice of law does already include more objectives, such as enhancing legal certainty and predictability, the prevention of limping relationships and reducing the risk of forum shopping.

The Brussels II*ter*-Proposal showed that one of the main difficulties with regard to the Europeanisation of international family law is that it is very dependent on

---

[7] See *supra* Sects. 6.2 and 6.3, respectively.

[8] See Fiorini 2008b questioning whether the Europeanisation of family law is going too far.

[9] See Boele-Woelki 2008, pp. 785, 786. See on the aims and objectives of European international family law *infra* Sect. 8.3.

[10] Boele-Woelki 2008, p. 786. See also Duintjer Tebbens 2002, p. 184: '*Insgesamt ergibt sich das Bild eines EG-Gesetzgebers, der sich begierig auf das IPR richtet und […] mehr an quantitativem Scoren als an der guten Qualität und Funktionsfähigkeit der Rechtssetzungsprodukte interessiert zu sein scheint.*'

[11] See *infra* Sect. 8.3.

political will.[12] The Member States were highly divided as to the content of the unified choice of law on divorce, which originated from the different substantive law approaches of the Member States.[13] Although the substantive divorce laws of the Member States differ, within the European Union a spouse seeking a divorce will sooner or later obtain it, irrespective of the applicable law, in all of the Member States (with the exception of Malta). In addition, the methodological approach of the common choice of law plays an important role as well: do the EU Member States wish to further a distinct policy with regard to divorce by means of unified choice of law? Or is their position in this respect completely neutral, i.e. excluding any *favor* tendency? The latter point of view does, however, require consensus on the possible application of foreign law, as any solution that does not automatically lead to the application of the *lex fori* would otherwise fail. A question that needs to be answered furthermore is which result the unified choice of law rules on divorce actually mean to achieve: 'substantive justice', i.e. the designation of a law that achieves a certain result, or 'conflicts justice', i.e. designating the law that represents the closest connection in an 'objective', impartial way?[14]

The question can be asked why the Member States did succeed in establishing common choice of law rules in other fields of law, such as contractual obligations (Rome I) and maintenance obligations, without any of such methodological problems. This can partly be accounted for by the fact that these other fields of law are less sensitive than divorce and the differences between the substantive laws of the Member States on these issues are — on the average — also less strong. The lack of any methodological problems in these fields of law may explain why the Commission probably thought that the unified choice of law on divorce could easily be established.

This difficulty surrounding the Brussels II*ter*-Proposal shows that a more fundamental discussion between the Member States as regards the methodology of the choice of law should precede the actual proposal establishing a unified choice of law.

The failure of the Brussels II*ter*-Proposal has led to a more fundamental discussion in the Council. During the informal meeting of the Justice and Home Affairs Council of 15 and 16 January 2009 the question on the future of judicial cooperation in family matters was under discussion.[15] The discussion subsequently showed that many Member States hold a rather reserved attitude in regards to the future of judicial cooperation in family law. Matrimonial property, child protection and adoption have been mentioned as fields of family law of which the private international law aspects should be regulated on the European level. However,

---

[12] Cf., *supra* Sect. 1.1

[13] See *supra* Sect. 6.4. See also Hess 2010, p. 435: '*Die Hauptursache sind die Unterschiede der materiellen Scheidungsrechte der EG-Mitgliedstaaten.*'

[14] See further on this question *infra* Sect. 8.4.3.

[15] See Press Release of the Informal Meeting of the Justice and Home Affairs Council of 15–16 January 2009 held in Prague, p. 1. Available at http://www.eu2009.cz/scripts/file.php? id=9958& down=yes. See also *Kamerstukken II* 2008–09, 23 490, No. 537, p. 7.

many Member States proved to have no need of new European rules in the field of international family law.[16] Consequently, the Europeanisation of issues of international family law has become even more delicate than it already was.[17]

The Commission may have slightly underestimated the establishment of common choice of law rules in the field of divorce. The previous experience with the unification of issues of international family law has shown that the road towards the adoption of a European instrument in this field of law is certainly not easy. The Brussels II-Regulation — containing common European rules on jurisdiction and on recognition and enforcement in matrimonial matters and in matters of parental responsibility — has taken quite some time to come into force: work on drafting this instrument began already in 1992 and the regulation has only entered into force on 1 March 2001.

8.2.2 Transparency

As seen above, one of the obstacles in the negotiations over the Brussels II*ter*-Proposal was whether the European Community was actually competent to unify the choice of law rules on divorce.[18] Mainly the question to what extent the internal market needs such unified choice of law rules was pressing. Although this issue has lost some of its importance by the entry into force of the Treaty on the Functioning of the European Union, which has removed the imperative character of the internal market requirement, the analysis of the problem in Section 6.3 proved the significance of the justification of the legal basis of the Union action.

In this regard the European Commission does not always justify satisfactorily whether the requirements of Article 81 TFEU have been fulfilled. If the legislative proposal is already accompanied by a clarification justifying the legal basis of the issue concerned, this justification is often not satisfactory.[19] Two examples of such statements are:

> [...] the objectives of this Regulation cannot be sufficiently achieved by the Member States and can therefore be better achieved by the Community. This Regulation does not go beyond what is necessary to achieve those objectives.[20]

---

[16] See *KamerstukkenII* 2008–2009, 23 490, No. 541, p. 5. The European Council has responded to this opposition of some Member States in the Stockholm Programme; see the Stockholm Programme, p. 24: 'the European Council considers that the process of harmonising conflict-of-law rules at Union level should also continue in areas where it is necessary.'

[17] Cf., Sect. 1.1.

[18] See *supra* Sect. 6.3.

[19] This critique is often expressed, see *inter alia* Schack 2001, pp. 618–619; Duintjer Tebbens 2002, pp. 177–180; Vigand 2005, pp. 145–147; Meeusen 2007, p. 337; Fiorini 2008a, pp. 7–8; Knot 2008, p. 166. With regard to the Brussels II*ter*-Proposal this critique is also shared by some national parliaments; see the COSAC-Report, pp. 12–13.

[20] Recital No. 5 of the Preamble to the Brussels II-Regulation.

> The proper functioning of the internal market creates a need, in order to improve the predictability of the outcome of litigation, certainty as to the law applicable and the free movement of judgments, for the conflict-of-law rules in the Member States to designate the same national law irrespective of the country of the court in which an action is brought.[21]

Moreover, the statistics used to underline the necessity of Union action in a certain area and reliable derivations thereof are of crucial importance to the credibility of the basis of the Union action. As already observed above, the reliability of the statistics and of the resulting derivations with regard to the number of international divorce cases in the European Union have been questioned.[22] The European Union Committee of the British House of Lords has expressed serious doubts concerning the reliability of the European Commission's statistical analysis:

> Only 13 Member States could provide the information requested and in five cases not for the full period of time (4 years) requested. Significantly only one large Member State (Germany) responded. The UK was unable to do so because it does not keep the sort of statistics requested by the Commission. Whether it is safe to extrapolate for the whole Union on the basis of the Commission's study has been questioned. Practitioners expressed concern that the responses from smaller Member States with high numbers of foreign residents (such as Luxembourg and Belgium) may have skewed the statistics. [...] How, in the apparent absence of statistical data from any large Member State save Germany, the Commission can state that "the rates of international marriages and divorces do not vary enormously amongst the larger EU countries" is extraordinary.[23]

This statement clearly undermines the European Commission's statistical analysis.

Furthermore, there is an inconsistency in the percentage representing the number of international divorces in the European Union: in the course of time the Commission seemed to juggle with the figures. While according to the Impact Assessment the estimated 170,000 international divorces that take place each year in the European Union represent about 16% of the total number of divorces,[24] soon after these same 170,000 divorces all of a sudden represent 19% of all divorces.[25]

It cannot be denied that these two statistical concerns damage the credibility of the basis of the Union action in the field of choice of law on divorce. The Brussels II*ter*-Proposal therefore shows that in sensitive areas of law, such as the choice of

---

[21] Recital No. 6 of the Preamble to the Rome II-Regulation.

[22] See *supra* Sect. 6.3.1.

[23] See House of Lords Rome III Report, para 18.

[24] See Impact Assessment on Divorce, p. 13.

[25] See the letter of the Vice-President of the European Commission of 7 December 2006, *Kamerstukken I/II*, 2006–2007, 30 671, F and No. 6.

law on family matters, a clear and reliable reasoning behind the Union's action is required.[26]

8.2.3 Interrelationship with Other Areas of (International) Family Law

The Brussels II*ter*-Proposal provides for uniform choice of law rules on divorce and legal separation. Marriage annulment is excluded from its scope of application, even though the jurisdictional rules of the Brussels II*bis*-Regulation do apply to marriage annulment.[27] Moreover, although the Brussels II*ter*-Proposal regulates the law applicable to divorce, strangely enough the preliminary question of the existence of a marriage is not provided for. The latter issue has been left to the discretion of the Member States.[28]

Besides, the Brussels II*ter*-Proposal deals with the choice of law on divorce alone and in most countries the court deciding on the divorce will go on to determine financial applications including maintenance, pension sharing and the division of the matrimonial property. Furthermore, if present, the latter court will also make arrangements concerning the parental responsibility over the child(ren). Consequently, given the ties between these fields of law it is argued that divorce and all the ancillary aspects need to be seen and dealt with together.[29]

The Commission has declared to be aware of the interrelationship between divorce and the ancillary financial matters. After displaying the activities that have been launched in the fields of maintenance obligations and matrimonial property, the Commission expressly stated that it:

---

[26] Although it is not certain whether the Brussels II*ter*-Proposal has had any direct influence on this inquiry, but the British House of Lords has questioned the transparency of the EU legislative proposals in general. See the House of Lords European Union Committee, Sub-committee E (Law and Institutions), 'Inquiry into the initiation of EU legislation', April 2008; available at: http://www.publications.parliament.uk/pa/ld200708/ldselect/ldeucom/150/15002.htm.

The EU itself also seems to put more emphasis on the transparency of its work. Article 15(1) TFEU determines that 'in order to promote good governance and ensure the participation of civil society, the Union institutions, bodies, offices and agencies shall conduct their work as openly as possible.' Although this provision is not new (ex Article 255 EC-Treaty), it received a more prominent place in the Treaty on the Functioning of the European Union.

[27] See recital No. 6 of the Preamble to the Brussels II*ter*-Proposal. See equally Explanatory Memorandum to the Brussels II*ter*-Proposal, pp. 7, 9. See further on the exclusion of marriage annulment from the scope of application of the Brussels II*ter*-Proposal *supra* Sect. 5.4.2.1.

[28] See Press Release No. 8364/07 (Presse 77) of the 2794th Council Meeting of Justice and Home Affairs held in Luxembourg 19–20 April 2007, p. 11.

[29] See Boele-Woelki 2008, p. 783; Fiorini 2008b, p. 195; Jänterä-Jareborg 2008, p. 340. See also the German Bundesrat 3 November 2006, Ratsdok. 11818/06, Drucksache 531/06 (Beschluss), pp. 1–2; and the Opinion of the European Economic and Social Committee on the Brussels II*ter*-Proposal of 13 December 2006, SOC/253, n. 4.3.

> [...] is aware that the question of applicable law in divorce matters cannot be examined in isolation from these ancillary matters [i.e. maintenance obligations and matrimonial property; NAB] and will therefore carefully consider the interrelationship between the different issues when preparing future projects.[30]

Although currently several Union instruments in the field of international family law are being developed, no parallel development seems to be taking place. The current approach is rather fragmented. Moreover, not all ancillary matters are the subject of unification, e.g. the law applicable to parental responsibility. According to Weber this fragmented approach can be explained by virtue of the fact that it will be easier to achieve consensus on these issues taken in isolation than it would have been had work been undertaken on a wider area.[31] However, a more systematic approach is called for, as unnecessary overlap and contradiction should be avoided.[32]

8.3 Aims and Objectives of European International Family Law

The development of European private international law rules raises the question on what goals the European Union wishes to further by such a proper system. In other words, are there any specific aims and objectives to be achieved by the private international law rules adopted by the European Union, as compared to the traditional ones? This question can be answered with a straightforward 'yes'.

Section 4.3 above has disclosed the objectives pursued by the unification of the choice of law at the European level. Besides the general objectives that would be fulfilled by any choice of law unification,[33] the European system of international family law strives for four specific objectives.[34]

In the first place, one of the principal objectives of the European Union as a whole is the creation of an internal market. Indeed, private international law exists for the purpose of the establishment and functioning of the internal

[30] See Commission Staff Working Document — Annex to the Green Paper on applicable law and jurisdiction in divorce matters, SEC(2005)331 of 14 March 2005, p. 3.

[31] Weber 2004, pp. 228–229. See equally Fiorini 2008b, p. 195.

[32] See further *infra* Sect. 8.4.1.

[33] See *supra* Sect. 4.3.1 on the objectives that would be fulfilled by Europeanising the choice of law: such unification would increase legal certainty, it might provide for the uniformity of decisions, it would grant better protection to the legitimate expectations of the parties, it would prevent the development of limping relationships and, finally, it would enable the achievement of justice.

[34] See *supra* Sect. 4.3.2.

market.[35] Initially this objective kept the role of the EU in the development of common rules of international family law fairly limited. The introduction of the Union citizenship was a milestone in this respect, taking the development of European rules on international family law one step further by detaching the principle of free movement of persons from its purely economic connotation. Compared to a traditional private international law system, the European system of private international law is in this regard utilised to promote, rather than just to manage international mobility of citizens. Secondly, the establishment of the area of freedom, security and justice meant another (major) step forward, in particular the creation of a European judicial area, in which international family law occupies a prominent position. The third objective disclosed is the principle of mutual recognition. Although this principle seems to give more priority to the development of common rules on the recognition and enforcement of foreign judgments in the EU, it has two important characteristics that equally influence the European choice of law. The first is that by virtue of this principle the legal traditions and systems of the Member States should be respected. The second characteristic is that on the basis of the principle of mutual recognition European law assumes an equivalence of the legal norms of the Member States. Finally, the EU strives for the protection of stability interests, which is particularly important for the realisation of the internal market, as the fundamental freedoms can solely be ensured if the exercise of those freedoms does not involve the loss of legal positions that have already been acquired in another Member State.

The coordinating interest of the abovementioned specific aims and objectives pursued by the Europeanisation of international family law seems to be the promotion of European integration.[36]

Ever since the establishment of the European Economic Community the process of European integration is at the center of European law.[37] European integration was founded on the principles of the free movement of goods, capital and services, but also of people. Since the EEC-Treaty of 1958, European citizens living in (what is now) the European Union have enjoyed progressively stronger rights to move freely, to reside and work in other EU Member States.[38] Pursuant to Article 1 of the EU-Treaty the European Union is 'in the process of creating an

[35] Ex Article 65 EC-Treaty limited the competence of the European legislature to enact measures of private international law to those 'necessary for the proper functioning of the internal market'. The current provision (Article 81 TFEU) has abandoned this imperative character, but does still refer to the internal market (particularly when necessary for the proper functioning of the internal market).

[36] Cf., as regards this interest in the field of international civil procedure, Hess 2001, p. 389 ff; and Hess 2010, p. 4 ff and 81 ff.

[37] Cf., the Preamble to the EU-Treaty: 'RESOLVED to mark a new stage in the process of European integration undertaken with the establishment of the European Communities'.

[38] Cf., Borrás Report, para 1: '[…] *integration is now no longer purely economic and is coming to have an increasingly profound effect on the life of the European citizen* […]. *The issue offamily lawtherefore has to be faced as part of the phenomenon of European integration.*'

ever closer Union among the peoples of Europe.' This process entails the transfer of increasingly far-reaching policy areas and of the corresponding powers to the European Union.

The creation of a European system of private international law equally contributes to this process of integration.[39] Private international law can very well help shape the policy options embodied in the EU legal order. The development of the Union's competence as described in Section 4.2 clearly shows the increasing transfer of powers: the first tentative efforts were taken in the Treaty of Maastricht, through which judicial cooperation in civil matters became an element of European cooperation. The Treaty of Amsterdam actually transferred competence in the field of private international law to the European Union, but formally limited this power in Article 65 EC-Treaty. Furthermore, the EC-Treaty introduced a new objective, namely the creation of an area of freedom, security and justice. The Treaty on the Functioning of the European Union, finally, removed the imperative character of the internal market requirement and thereby formally expanded the legal basis of Union action in the field of judicial cooperation in civil matters.

Viewed from the aim of European integration, the development of a European system of international family law should ultimately lead to the construction of a genuine European judicial area in which all citizens are able to assert their rights, irrespective of the Member State where they reside. This assertion of rights implies the identification of the competent jurisdiction, the designation of the applicable law and the effective enforcement of judgments in all areas of international family law.[40]

In fact this broad aim of European integration does not seem to pose any limitations on the development of common choice of law rules on issues of family law. Because of this broad aim the risk exists that the European system of private international law is not an end in itself (a better private international law), but a means to an end (European integration).[41] In other words, there is a risk of a too functional approach as regards the Europeanisation of international family law. Consequently, the European legislature should make sure not to fully subordinate the Europeanisation of this field of law to the sole goal of European integration.

---

[39] That private international law is the instrument *par excellence* for the purposes of integration has been demonstrated by Hay et al. 1986. See also Fentiman 2008, p. 2041 ff, spec. p. 2045: '*It* [*i.e. EU private international law; NAB*] *is to create a further building block in the edifice of European integration.*' Fentiman reasons from the ECJ Case C-281/02 *Owusu* v. *Jackson* [2005] ECR I-01383.

[40] Cf., Communication from the Commission to the European Parliament and the Council, An area of freedom, security and justice serving the citizen, COM(2009) 262 final, p. 10 ff.

[41] Cf., Jayme 2000, p. 168; Kohler 2001, pp. 41–53; Van den Eeckhout 2008, p. 8; and Fentiman 2008, p. 2041 ff.

From the foregoing it is clear that there are a reasonably high number of goals and objectives that can be discerned. These aims and objectives can roughly be divided into three categories:

1. Aims related to the promotion of European integration (such as the principle of mutual recognition and the establishment of the area of freedom, security and justice).
2. Aims ensuing from European law (such as the principle of non-discrimination on grounds of nationality, respect for human rights, respect for the national identities of the Member States); and
3. Aims attached to any choice of law unification (such as increasing legal certainty and predictability, the prevention of forum shopping and enabling the achievement of justice).

Besides these 'general' aims, which apply to any European choice of law instrument, the protection of specific interests will come into play depending on the field of family law at issue. For example, in the choice of law on divorce the principle of gender equality plays an important part, whereas in the choice of law on adoption the protection of the best interests of the child is of major importance. Also the following other interests may be acknowledged in one or more fields of international family law: the protection of incompetent persons, the protection of the weaker party and increasing party autonomy.

This high number of objectives leads to the question whether there is a hierarchy between them. Such hierarchy would certainly be helpful, as in a particular case the objectives to be fulfilled may even conflict: e.g. the protection of the weaker party may lead to the establishment of a choice of law rule that is not the most suitable one for the establishment of the area of freedom, security and justice or to increase predictability. However, it is very hard to make any general statement on this issue, since in every subfield of international family law different interests play a part.

8.4 The Methodology of European International Family Law

This paragraph will focus on the quest for a specific methodology for the European system of international family law. In the first place, the need for a theoretical foundation of the European system of international family law will be elaborated upon (Section 8.4.1). The EU system of international family law would constitute a full part of European law, which has repercussions on its content. Therefore, the unique character of the European Union and its consequences for the development of a common European system of international family law will be analysed (Section 8.4.2). Thirdly, Section 8.4.3 will disclose the general characteristics of European international family law that can be deduced from the instruments that have been introduced and proposed so far. Finally, the initial impetus will be given to the development of a proper method of European international family law (Section 8.4.4).

8.4.1 The Need for a Theoretical Foundation of European International Family Law

There is no denying that the establishment of an EU system of international family law is on the European agenda.[42] Despite the recent setback of the failure to adopt the Brussels II*ter*-Proposal, it is beyond doubt that an EU system of international family law will see the light of day sooner or later. Presumably, besides the areas that have already been regulated or been 'fixed' in European policy plans — i.e. maintenance obligations, divorce and matrimonial property — more fields of international family law will be Europeanised in the future. Although several Member States have recently stated to have no need for new unified European rules in the field of international family law,[43] one day the Commission will undoubtedly attempt yet again to Europeanise new fields of international family law.[44]

As mentioned above, the current approach of Europeanisation of international family law is not very coherent. Two distinct factors seem to underlie this lack of coherence.

One of the problems of establishing a coherent common system of international family law is the procedure through which a legislative measure is established. The European Commission initiates the legislative procedure by making a proposal to adopt a specific instrument. This proposal is probably designed and structured in a certain direction so as to achieve a specific goal (such as the aims and objectives observed above). Subsequently, many compromises are made in the Council in order to have all the Member States accept the instrument. Many instruments are, consequently, not achieved by a specific methodological form and content but instead by moving from compromise to compromise in order to reach unanimity among the Member States.[45]

---

42 See the Hague Programme.

43 See *KamerstukkenII* 2008-2009, 23 490, No. 541, p. 5.

44 Cf., Rühl 2008, p. 187: '*Es bedarf keiner hellseherischen Fähigkeiten, um angesichts dieser Entwicklungen vorauszusagen, dass das Kollisionsrecht in wenigen Jahren nahezu vollständig vergemeinschaftet sein wird.*'

45 See Borrás 2007, p. 56 ff; Fiorini 2008b, p. 192. Cf. in this regard, De Boer 2008b, p. 993. Jayme and Kohler 2000, p. 465 also indicate that a further difficulty in this respect is that within the European Commission different Directorates-General are involved in the Europeanisation of the choice of law: '*Die Aufgabenverteilung innerhalb der Kommission trägt nicht zu einer kohärenten Entwicklung bei. Neben der Generaldirektion Justiz und Inneres, die für Rechtsakte nach Art. 61 Buchst. c) EGV zuständig ist, bereiten die Generaldirektionen Binnenmarkt und Verbraucherschutz in ihrem jeweiligen Bereich Rechtsakte vor, die auch das Kollisionsrecht berühren. Hier kommt es zu Spannungen* [...].' See for this point of view equally Schaub 2005, p. 329. Under the Treaty of Lisbon the judicial cooperation has received an own Commissioner (Justice, Fundamental Rights and Citizenship).

Therefore, the essence of the lack of a clear methodology of the common choice of law may already be found in the legislative procedure leading to the adoption of a specific instrument in the field of international family law.

In addition, a second factor that does not contribute to the development of a coherent European system of international family law is the approach of the Commission as regards its unification. As already observed, the unification of European private international law is currently very much proceeding via a piecemeal approach with no *Kodifikationsidee*.[46] This approach can be explained by two reasons: it will be easier to achieve consensus on the issues taken in isolation and the unification of issues of international family law remains very sensitive as is proven time and again.[47] Obviously the Commission has to be very careful not to overplay its hand: the Member States all hold a power of veto in the field of international family law pursuant to Article 81(3) TFEU.

However, the separate legislative development of the instruments will inevitably lead to fragmentation. Unnecessary overlap and contraction should be avoided. A more systematic approach is, therefore, desirable, particularly from the perspective of legal certainty and predictability.[48] Moreover, the ease of use of the common choice of law rules would also benefit from a more systematic approach.

A lack of coherence between the different European choice of law instruments is obviously undesirable.[49] This view is endorsed by the Stockholm Programme:

> The European Council also highlights the importance of starting work on consolidation of the instruments adopted so far in the area of judicial cooperation in civil matters. First and foremost the consistency of Union legislation should be enhanced by streamlining the existing instruments. The aim should be to ensure the coherence and user-friendliness of the instruments, thus ensuring a more efficient and uniform application thereof.[50]

Although this initiative should be applauded, it does not alter the fact that a proper and sound methodology of European international family law should be developed in order to overcome the abovementioned risk. For a comprehensive and consistent choice of law system requires that there is a basic agreement on the

---

[46] Cf., Siehr 2005, p. 95; and Jayme and Kohler 2006, pp. 540–541.

[47] The current fragmentation of the choice of law can also be explained by the priority that is awarded to the different subfields of international family law; see Asín Cabrera 2004, p. 173: '*le réalisme impose de procéder* step by step *de manière qu'il soit possible de bien définir et sélectionner les secteurs prioritaires d'intervention eu égard au bon fonctionnement du marché intérieur et, partant, à la réalisation d'un espace européen.*' See equally Weber 2004, pp. 228–229.

[48] Cf., Martiny 2007, p. 98; Fiorini 2008b, p. 195; Rühl 2008, p. 188.

[49] See equally Ehle 2002.

[50] See Stockholm Programme, p. 24. See also already Communication from the Commission to the European Parliament and the Council, An area of freedom, security and justice serving the citizen, COM (2009) 262 final, p. 5: '[T]he achievement of a European area of justice must be consolidated so as to move beyond the current fragmentation'.

determination of the applicable law.[51] From this point of view, the development of a European system of international family law actually raises several general questions related to the establishment of a new private international law instrument:

> How do they [i.e. the legislators; NAB] determine whether a policy-oriented rule is called for, or whether a neutral approach will do? When do they opt for one type of rule rather than another one, and why? Do they articulate their views on the objectives of the rules to be created? Is their final draft consistent with those views? And to what extent does political compromise taint the coherence between the purpose of the rules as originally conceived and their expression conceived in subsequent amended versions?[52]

Evidently the question is what a 'proper and sound methodology' of European international family law should enhance. Considering the problems that the European legislature Union faces surrounding the establishment of common international family law rules, this question is obviously not easy to answer.

In the following the initial impetus to such answer will be given. An important point of departure is the character of the European Union, which is clearly of relevance to the development of a proper European methodology on international family law. This character will be discussed in the next paragraph.

8.4.2 Unique Character of the European Union

The European Union constitutes a unique supranational organisation. It is for the first time in history that the sovereign Member States of an intergovernmental organisation have voluntarily transferred so much of their sovereignty.[53] As a result of this transfer of sovereignty the European Union is now for a large part a supranational organisation, which has many traits of a federation. Although the EU is not a federation in the strict sense, it is far more than a free-trade association such as ASEAN, NAFTA or Mercosur. Moreover, the EU has many attributes that are associated with independent countries: its own flag, anthem, motto and founding date (Europe Day), as well as an incipient common foreign and security policy in its dealings with other nations.[54] In the future, many of these nation-like

---

[51] The analysis of the failure to reach a compromise on the establishment of a common choice of law on divorce has shown that precisely this basic agreement was lacking. See further *supra* Sect. 6.4.

[52] De Boer 2009, p. 299.

[53] It is to be noted that the transfer of powers from the Member States to the Union is of an irreversible nature. See ECJ Case 7/71 *Commission* v. *France* [1971] ECR 1003.

[54] See for this definition of the EU, the World Fact Book of the American Central Intelligence Agency (CIA): https://www.cia.gov/library/publications/the-world-factbook/geos/ee.html.

characteristics of the Union are likely to be further developed.[55] The European Union is often characterised as a new and separate entity that strongly differs from all other existing regional and international organisations. Therefore, the character of the European Union can be defined as unique.[56]

What is the significance of the EU's unique character for the Europeanisation of private international law?

In the first place, it should be borne in mind that private international law is traditionally a 'national' field of law. In other words, private international law is in many states part of their legal order. Even when a state has ratified international conventions containing rules of private international law, these conventions are solely integrated in that state's legal order according to its constitutional procedure on account of the wish of that state to do so.[57] National private international law rules can furthermore be intended to define the personal and spatial scope of application of the national substantive law rules.[58]

The creation of the EU legal order has greatly changed this perspective. It is widely accepted that the European Treaties and the secondary legislation can be regarded as constituting a single legal order. The Union's system is distinguished from — but not unconnected with — the legal orders of its Member States. European law is therefore often identified as an own legal order. Its enforceability is greatly advanced by the doctrines of direct legal effect and primacy: European law is directly enforceable in the courts of the Member States and prevails over national law.[59] These characteristics of EU law equally apply to the EU private international law rules.

From the foregoing it is clear that the European Union stands midway between a sovereign state and an intergovernmental organisation. This characteristic entails that the unification of private international law by the European Union cannot be compared with any other unification process and is, consequently, unprecedented.[60]

---

[55] E.g. the Treaty of Lisbon introduced in the EU-Treaty a High Representative of the Union for Foreign Affairs and Security Policy to coordinate the Union's foreign policy with greater consistency and to present a united position on EU policies (Article 18 EU-Treaty).

[56] Cf., Santer 1999, p. 15: '*L'Union européenne, ce n'est pas un Etat, mais c'est une construction politique originale regroupant des nations séculaires qui veulent, à juste titre, préserver leurs différences.*' See equally Traest 2003, pp. 32–33.

[57] Cf., Borrás 2005, pp. 324–325.

[58] See, e.g., Siehr 2008, p. 85.

[59] See Jessurun d'Oliveira 2003, p. 268; Calvo Caravaca 2006, pp. 28–29. The European Court of Justice has often held that the Treaties have called into being a new, distinctive legal order, see *inter alia* ECJ Case 26/60 *Van Gend en Loos* [1963] ECR 1; ECJ Case 6/64 *Costa* v. *ENEL* [1964] ECR 585; ECJ Cases 90 and 91/63 *Commission* v. *Luxembourg and Belgium* [1964] ECR 625; ECJ Cases C-6 and 9/90 *Francovich* et al. v. *Italy* [1991] ECR I-3365. See in general on these doctrines Kapteyn and VerLoren van Themaat 1998, p. 551 ff.

[60] See Poillot-Peruzzetto 2005, p. 31: '*La communautarisation par la méthode conflictuelle opérée par le règlement propose une expérience nouvelle puisqu'il s'agit de construire des règles de structure sans* lex fori *de base.*' See equally Badiali 1985, p. 37 ff.; Basedow 2005, p. 280.

The organisation with which the European Union could in this regard be compared with is the Hague Conference on Private International Law. In developing common private international law rules, these two institutions share a number of specific goals, such as increasing legal certainty and contributing to the uniformity of decisions. However, the very essence of their respective approaches differs. In the first place, the Member States of the Hague Conference did not transfer any power to the Conference. Furthermore, the European Union attaches the pursuance of more specific political goals to the development of its proper system of private international law, such as the functioning of the internal market and the establishment of the area of freedom, security and justice.[61]

Besides, the European Union can be compared neither to a sovereign state nor to a federation, such as the USA, that develops its own system of private international law.[62]

This unprecedented process of Europeanisation which is currently taking place entails two specific difficulties. In the first place, it must be admitted that, because of the lack of harmonisation of the substantive law at Union level, a great challenge arises as to how to develop a common system of private international law for 27 Member States.[63] Moreover, all the persons involved in the development of the EU private international law rules are still primarily connected to their respective national legal order and will yet slowly know their way around in the specific merits and needs of the European legal order, which differs by its very nature from the national ones.[64]

The different character of European private international law equally involves a change in thinking. Whereas many national private international law systems are based on a 'nationalistic' perspective, the European system of private international law should be established on a more international, European perspective: the EU system of private international law 'transcends' the national interests of the Member States.[65]

---

[61] See further on the relationship between the European Union and the Hague Conference on Private International Law and the different levels of integration pursued *infra* Sect. 8.4.4.3.

[62] See further on the relationship between (American) federalism and choice of law notably the publications of Brilmayer and Yntema. See also Baxter 1963, pp. 1–42. See very recently Symeonides 2010.

[63] Cf., Siehr 2008, p. 85 has argued that the absence of a substantive law poses a great advantage, as a correct choice of law system should not be based on a specific substantive law, but should be neutral instead. See equally Basedow 2008, p. 8: '*For the first time the legislative decisions relating to choice of law will be made by a legislator who is not responsible for the substantive law in that field. For the twenty-seven national laws of its Member States, the Community acts like a referee who has to be strictly neutral. He may even pursue objectives other than those of the single players.*'

[64] See Kadner Graziano 2002, pp. 10–14; Siehr 2008, p. 81; Basedow 2009, p. 458.

[65] Cf., Mills 2009, p. 12 ff. This perspective is not entirely new, as the treaties that are agreed upon in the Hague Conference on Private International Law can also be considered as efforts to find coordinated solutions between different countries.

It is thus clear that the European Union has a unique character. Does it influence the arrangement of the European private international law rules? Below two specific issues that are related to this question will be dealt with. In the first place, the question is whether the unique character of the European Union will not be better guaranteed by the establishment of an intra-European system of international family law (Section 8.4.2.1). The second sub question that will be discussed is whether and to what extent the EU system of international family law should respect the existing legal diversity of the sovereign Member States (Section 8.4.2.2).

8.4.2.1 An Intra-European Choice of Law System?

The special character of the European Union justifies the question whether the specific European aims and objectives distinguished above would not be better served by the establishment of an intra-European choice of law system. Such a limited scope of application of the European choice of law could then be used in order to strongly promote these specific EU aims and objectives.

The unification of international family law in European context seems to lay on a paradox. Universally applicable choice of law rules, which currently seem to be the norm,[66] aim at regulating cross-border family relations, regardless of the countries with which the persons involved are connected. On the contrary, the objectives of European international family law seem to suggest that the cross-border family relations are only to be regulated in a European context with little regard to the rest of the world.[67] It is not clear then why the requirements which are typical of the structure of the internal market or of the creation of the European judicial area should have impact in relation to third countries.

The development of an intra-European system of international family law would offer the possibility to establish a European system of private *interregional* law, which might allow for a closer cooperation between the Member States on the basis of the principle of mutual trust.[68] One of the advantages of such an intra-European choice of law system is that the promotion and advancement of the specific European objectives, such as the creation of the European judicial area, can be ensured.[69] However, are these European aims and objectives actually better served with specific intra-European choice of law rules? According to the EU legislature these aims and objectives require not only the Europeanisation of the choice of law rules for intra-European cases, but also of those rules concerning

---

[66] Cf., *infra* Sect. 8.4.3.

[67] See Pataut 2008, p. 123.

[68] See for the advantages of a private interregional law system, Ten Wolde 2004, pp. 504–506. See Spamann 2001 for an explorative analysis of the establishment of an intra-European choice of law.

[69] Cf., Vonken 2006, p. 48.

extra-European cases. This argument relies on the view that differing rules dealing with extra-European cases may still have an indirect and undesirable effect distorting the internal market and the European judicial area.[70]

It thus seems that the specific EU aims and objectives of private international law are not per se better served with the limitation of the scope of application of the common choice of law to intra-European cases. Consequently, the establishment of an intra-European choice of law is not recommendable, especially if one takes into account that the efficiency of the EU system of choice of law would highly benefit from a universal scope of application. Indeed, the establishment of universal choice of law rules would certainly offer advantages.[71]

The application of the same law to one and the same legal relationship by the courts of the Member States is the ultimate goal of the European unification of private international law. It would encourage parties to effectively make use of their basic freedoms assigned by the European Treaties, which would in turn improve the proper functioning of the internal market. This holds true for both intra-European situations and for situations involving third States.

Furthermore, universal choice of law rules has the advantage that the EU and its Member States make a uniform appearance *vis-à-vis* third countries. In all Member States of the European Union the same choice of law rules will be applied to a certain case, regardless of the nature of the case, i.e. whether it concerns an intra- or an extra-European case. Such a situation would certainly make things less complicated: it would facilitate the application of the choice of law rules and would, accordingly, be conducive to legal certainty.

Thirdly, it may generally be doubted whether a differentiation between intra- and extra-European cases is to be recommended, as there will most certainly be cases in which it is very hard to decide whether a certain situation concerns an intra- or an extra-European case. If universal choice of law rules would be established, it would not be necessary to make the intricate differentiation between intra- and extra-European relationships.[72]

Finally, the current jurisdictional rules of the Brussels II*bis*-Regulation and the Maintenance Regulation are not restricted to intra-European cases. A limitation of the scope of application of the choice of law to intra-European cases could then very well lead to the situation in which the common jurisdictional rules determine that the court of a Member State is competent, but in which the common choice of law rules do subsequently not apply. Such a situation is clearly undesirable.

---

[70] Cf., Fletcher 1982, p. 52 ff; Duintjer Tebbens 1990, p. 65 ff; Kreuzer 2006, pp. 65–66. See also ECJ Case C-281/02 *Owusu* v. *Jackson* [2005] ECR I-01383, spec. paras 33 and 34, in which the court considered the distinction between intra- and extra-European cases. The ECJ held that the purpose of the Brussels I-Convention was not solely to ensure the free movement of judgments between the Member States, but also to facilitate the functioning of the internal market. This latter objective was, however, not served only in intra-European cases, but by the uniform application of the Convention's rules on jurisdiction in any case.

[71] See already Sect. 5.4.1.1 above.

[72] See *supra* Sect. 5.4.1.1 for a number of examples.

It is to be noted that the mentioned concerns with respect to the limitation of the scope of application of the choice of law to intra-European cases can partly be met by the establishment of a choice of law instrument in which both intra- and extra-European legal relationships are regulated, but which provides for different rules for each of the two situations. In other words, in intra-European situations a different connecting factor may be applied than in extra-European situations.[73] However, this does not circumvent the need of a precise distinction between intra- and extra-European cases, which is truly intricate. Besides, since the European aims and objectives do not require the establishment of an intra-European choice of law system, it is not necessary to make the mentioned distinction.

8.4.2.2 Respect for the Existing Legal Diversity

Regardless of all the competences that have been transferred to the European Union, the Member States have remained sovereign states with their own legal systems and traditions. Besides, each Member State is, within the boundaries of European law, still free to pursue its own (legal) development. The respect for the diversity of these national systems is the cornerstone of the European integration in the field of justice.[74] This follows from Article 4(2) EU-Treaty, which determines that the Union shall respect the national identities of the Member States. In particular, the area of freedom, security and justice — the framework within which European private international law rules are established — is to be build upon respect for the different legal systems and traditions of the Member States (Article 67(1) TFEU).

Do these provisions have any influence on European international family law? The 'national identity' of the Member States in the context of Article 4(2) EU-Treaty refers to their distinguishing features.[75] To what extent is the legal system of a state part of its national identity?[76]

---

[73] Cf., Ten Wolde 2004, p. 504; and Ten Wolde and Knot 2006, p. 29, arguing that the intra-European choice of law is to be based on principles that differ from those on which the choice of law rules in relation to third states are based.

[74] See the Hague Programme, p. 11, in which the Council indicated that the progressive development of a European judicial culture was to be based on the diversity of legal systems and unity through European law.

[75] See Hilf 1995, spec. p. 163: '*Nationale Identität stellt ab auf das subjektive Zusammengehörigkeitsgefühl, das sich in einem Volk aus historischen, wirtschaftlichen, religiösen oder sonstigen soziokulturellen Unterschieden zu anderen Nationen bildet*.' See equally Uhle 2004, spec. pp. 475–476. Cf., the German *Bundesverfassungsgericht* (the Constitutional Court) held in its judgment of 12 October 1993 (BVerfGE 89, 155, the so-called *Maastricht-Urteil*, para 109) that the national identity of the Member States concerns their independence and sovereignty ('*die Unabhängigkeit und Souveränität der Mitgliedstaaten*').

[76] See generally on this question Friedman 1975.

Law has been defined as 'a part of the cultural web that shapes and defines people's lives.'[77] Indeed, their lives are shaped by the values embodied and given effect through the legal order.[78] Law is thus culturally defined. What is culture then?

> Culture gives people a sense of who they are, of belonging, of how they should behave, and what they should be doing. Culture impacts behaviour, morale, [...] and includes values and patterns that influence [...] attitudes and actions.[79]

This definition shows that culture influences many aspects of life, such as attitude, social organisation and thought patterns. Thought patterns in turn affect the process of reasoning, be it legal or otherwise. What is perfectly logical, self-evident and reasonable for one culture may be offensive, illogical and unreasonable for any other. Consequently, the cultural background of a state strongly influences its legal system and understanding.[80] The legal system can thus be considered as a mirror of a state and of its culture.[81] Therefore, the legal system of a state definitely forms part of its national identity.

Law must always be considered in a specific cultural context. Neither economically oriented private law nor family law can be viewed as independent of culturally shaped values or ideals. However, few — if any — fields of law form a more clear expression of culture than family law.[82] Divorce is a good example of a culturally coloured legal concept. As seen above, throughout the European Union there are currently five grounds for divorce present in the legal systems of the Member States.[83] On one end of the spectrum there is the divorce based on fault (divorce as a sanction) and, on the other end, there is divorce on demand (divorce as a right). Whereas it is not easy to have a marriage dissolved in the catholic Member States such as Cyprus, Poland and Ireland, and not permitted at all in Malta, there are virtually no obstacles to divorce in more liberal Member States such as Sweden and the Netherlands.

The European Union secures the respect for the legal diversity of its Member States — and thus for their national identities — in two distinct ways.[84] In the first place, the national peculiarities of the substantive family laws of the Member States are left untouched. Apart from the lack of competence to unify issues of substantive law, it is questionable whether a European unification of substantive family law would be feasible, as quite often the field of family law is described as

---

77 See Haltern 2003, p. 15: '*Recht ist Teil des kulturellen Gewebes, das unser Leben prägt und definiert.*'

78 Cf., Mills 2009, p. 256.

79 Moran et al. 2007, p. 6.

80 See ibid., p. 61.

81 See e.g. Sanada 1989, p. 128.

82 See Thue 1996, p. 59; Poillot-Peruzzetto and Marmisse 2001, p. 465; Dethloff 2003, p. 59.

83 See *supra* Sect. 5.2.1.

84 It is not certain to what extent the EU legislature particularly had the respect for the national identity of the Member States in mind in this regard.

being too deeply rooted in the national legal cultures, which would prevent any attempt to unification.[85] By not interfering in the substantive family laws of the Member States the European Union respects the existing cultural diversity in its territory.[86] By pursuing the unification of private international law — a field of law that coordinates the diversity of national laws[87] — the EU urges to respect the peculiarities of each legal system.

Secondly, the common choice of law rules would respect the diversity by allowing the application of foreign law.[88] In this respect KOHLER has observed that the refusal of some Member States to apply foreign law (*i.c.* with regard to divorce) — and thus automatically excluding the application of the laws of other states — does not express much willingness to cooperate, which is after all one of the key features of European integration.[89] The willingness to apply foreign law — certainly in intra-European cases — ensues from the principle of mutual recognition and expresses the trust in the fundamental equivalence of the legal systems.[90] The European choice of law rules on issues of family law that have been enacted and proposed so far do not exclude the application of foreign law. Therefore, this characteristic of the European choice of law expresses that the diversity of the Member States' legal systems is respected.[91] Yet the attempt to unify the choice of law on divorce has shown that the willingness to apply foreign law is under great pressure.[92] Considering the importance of the application of foreign law from the perspective of the respect for legal diversity, the European legislature needs to make great efforts to ensure that this feature occupies an important place in the choice of law.

---

85 Cf., *supra* Sect. 1.1.

86 Poillot-Peruzzetto and Marmisse 2001, p. 465: '*Organiser et structurer un corpus de règles de droit international privé en matière familiale permettrait d'assurer l'unité dans la diversité, de maintenir les spécificités en coordonnant les systèmes.*'

87 Cf., *supra* Sect. 1.1.

88 It is to be noted that also a restrictive application of the public policy exception may reflect the respect for the legal diversity. Cf., the resolution of the Institute of International Law on 'Cultural differences and ordre public in family private international law' of 2005, available at: http://www.idi-iil.org/idiE/navig_chon2003.html.

The European choice of law in family matters meets this requirement: it does allow the public policy exception, but only in cases in which it the application of the applicable law would be *manifestly incompatible* with the public policy. Both Article 13 of the Protocol on the Law Applicable to Maintenance Obligations and Article 20e of the Brussels II*ter*-Proposal contain this limitation.

89 Kohler 2008b, p. 196.

90 Although, as indicated in Sect. 6.4 above, the principle of mutual trust does not seem to require that Member States can no longer propagate a *lex fori*-approach, since a refusal to apply foreign law does not necessarily infringe the equivalence of the legal systems of the Member States.

91 It is to be noted that this feature may incline to a different regulation of intra-European and extra-European legal relationships, as the Member States may be more willing to apply foreign law in the former cases.

92 See *supra* Sect. 6.4.

Although the question of the respect for the legal diversity is justified in light of the European motto of 'unity in diversity', Mankowski has rightly stressed that legal scholars tend to overestimate the cultural element that can be attributed to the law.[93]

However, in the European context one should not be surprised that many — if not all — Member States will search for the protection of fundamental characteristics of their own legal system (such as the marriage open to couples regardless of their sex), which are part of their national identity.[94] The Brussels II*ter*-Proposal has shown that, even though the proposed choice of law rules are aimed neither at replacing nor at harmonising the national substantive divorce laws, the unification of the choice of law can lead to strong resistance of the Member States.[95] This attitude of the Member States can be explained by the search for the respect of their national identity.

Consequently, despite the danger that the significance of the respect for the legal diversity is slightly overestimated by legal scholars, it does play an important part in the Europeanisation of the choice of law on family issues.

8.4.2.3 'United in Diversity'

From the previous paragraph it is clear that the EU legislature has to respect the existing legal diversity. In establishing unified choice of law rules on family law the same legislature is, however, also required to observe the motto 'united in diversity'.

A particular issue that comes into play in this regard is the fact that within the European Union both common and civil law systems exist.[96] According to Fiorini the common European choice of law has to show a 'mixedness' of these two legal traditions:

> Given that the European Union involves legal systems belonging to both the common and the civil law tradition, and that the very aim of private international law is the coordination of legal systems, it would seem rather sensible that European private international law should borrow from both traditions and therefore display characteristics of *mixedness*.[97]

---

[93] Mankowski 2004, p. 284. See also already Henrich 2001, p. 444.

[94] See equally Gaudemet-Tallon 2002, pp. 175–176; De Groot and Rutten 2004, p. 282; Siehr 2008, p. 85.

[95] In this respect the strong interconnection between substantive law and the choice of law plays an important part. See *supra* Sect. 6.2, in which the position of Malta has been discussed. Malta is the only Member State that does not provide for divorce in its legislation. Malta fiercely opposed the Brussels II*ter*-Proposal, as it feared that the adoption of common choice of law rules would oblige the Maltese courts to apply foreign law in order to circumvent its ban on divorce. A special provision was added to the Brussels II*ter*-Proposal so as to solve the Maltese problem in order to prevent Malta from using its power of veto.

[96] In the EU the following Member States are common law jurisdictions: the United Kingdom, Ireland, Cyprus and (in some but not all respects) Malta.

[97] Fiorini 2008a, p. 3.

Given a number of recent common law publications, in which the ECJ has been reproached of tending to adopt a 'civil law based approach',[98] it seems wise to consider such mixedness, which would certainly contribute to the adherence to the European motto 'united in diversity'. However, what does it mean in practice?

The experience of the Louisiana private international law code shows that it is not impossible to establish a private international law system that successfully mixes common and civil law features.[99] Symeonides concluded that this code did not aspire to resolve the 'eternal tension' between common and civil law traditions, but that it could reconcile the two traditions and provide a framework for them for an interactive coexistence.[100] The Louisiana private international law code has managed to find 'an independent third path between the common law and the civil law paths'.[101] This 'third path' is best illustrated by the balance struck between the principles of legal certainty and flexibility.

Broadly speaking common law systems lay strong emphasis on the notion of flexibility, whereas in civil law systems, on the contrary, the notion of certainty prevails. The Louisiana private international law code provides for three distinct techniques to strike a balance between these notions: in the first place, the use of alternative connecting factors (e.g. 'a marriage is valid in the state where contracted, or in the state where the parties were first domiciled as husband and wife, shall be treated as valid [...]'),[102] secondly, the use of 'soft' connecting factors (e.g. application of the most closely connected law), and, thirdly, the use of escape clauses (e.g. exception to the designated law if it is manifestly clear that the circumstances of the case are more closely connected to another law').[103]

---

[98] See Mance 2007, p. 87 ff. Mance specifically refers to the following cases: ECJ Case C-116/02 *Erich Gasser* v. *Misat* [2003] ECR I-14693; ECJ Case C-159/02 *Turner* v. *Grovit* [2004] ECR I-03565; and ECJ Case C-281/02 *Owusu* v. *Jackson* [2005] ECR I-01383. See for a similar view: Hartley 2005, pp. 813–828.

[99] Equally Book Ten of the Civil Code of Quebec is a successful fruit of a private international law codification in a mixed legal system. See on this Act, Glenn 1996, pp. 231–268.

[100] Symeonides 1993; Symeonides 2009.

[101] See Symeonides 2009, p. 1054.

[102] Rules that employ alternative connecting factors authorise the court to apply the law of the country which produces the preferred substantive result (e.g. upholding the marriage).

[103] See Symeonides 2009, pp. 1061–1062. Moreover, the Louisiana code has introduced two other 'innovative' features. In the first place, there is a careful combination and interplay between, on the one hand, rules that specifically designate the applicable law for certain cases or issues and, on the other hand, a general 'approach', namely a list of factors providing courts with guided directions and discretion in selecting the applicable law. Secondly, the Louisiana code calls for an issue-by-issue analysis: rather than seeking to choose a law as if all aspects of the case were in dispute, the focus is on the narrow issues where a conflict exists and, subsequently, to proceed accordingly. Depending on the circumstances of the case, this analysis may lead either to the application of the law of the same country to all issues, or to the application of the laws of different countries to different issues in the same case ('*dépeçage*').

Can the Louisiana experience serve as a model for the European choice of law methodology?

The Louisiana code shows that three specific techniques can be used to strike a balance between the common and civil law traditions: the use of alternative connecting factors, the use of soft connecting factors and the use of escape clauses. The balance between certainty and flexibility is in this regard absolutely crucial.[104] The ultimate goal of a unified choice of law system is that in all Member States the same national law is applied to an international family dispute in the European Union, irrespective of which court is seised. In this context the use of alternative connecting factors is not suitable, as it will not lead to the mentioned goal of the European private international law system. Every connecting factor of the choice of law rule containing alternative connecting factors can refer to the applicable law in random order, which fails to give the parties certainty as to the applicable law before making use of their right to free movement. It is to the discretion of the court to determine which legal system produces the desired result. However, what happens if several legal systems would produce this result? Do the parties have any say in this matter? If so, this approach may have a negative effect on the balance in the procedural position of the parties resulting from their unequal financial possibilities. For the parties do not always have the same (financial) means to examine which of the connecting factors leads to the application of the law that is most advantageous to his or her cause. Consequently, the use of alternative connecting factors does not provide for a proper balance between certainty and flexibility. This same conclusion holds true for the second technique mentioned — the use of soft connecting factors; leaving the courts the discretion to determine the most closely connected law on the basis of the circumstances of the case has disadvantages, most importantly its subjectivity and unpredictability.[105]

The third technique — the use of escape clauses — could, however, very well lead to a solution. The European Union should develop choice of law rules that refer to the law of the closest connection but that are also adaptable to the circumstances of the case. Although such a correcting mechanism carries the risk with it as regards legal certainty and predictability, on the other hand, it would imply a just adjustment of the result of the connection with a certain legal system in light of the principle of the closest connection. However, this possibility should have a reasonably high threshold in order to displace the otherwise applicable law: it should be demonstrated that the particular case has only a very slight connection to the law designated as applicable and has a much closer connection to another

---

[104] See equally Basedow 2008, p. 17: '*flexibility without certainty means anarchy. Flexibility and certainty have to be brought in balance*.'

[105] Cf., *supra* Sect. 6.5.4. For exactly these reasons the Rome I-Regulation amended the provision on the law applicable to contractual obligations, which was previously governed by the law which was most closely connected to the contract.

law.[106] By means of a combination of strict rules and a flexible possibility to displace the presumptively applicable law in favour of the principle of the closest connection, the European choice of law on family issues should attempt to attain an appropriate balance between certainty and flexibility and, accordingly, between the common and civil law traditions.[107]

8.4.3 General Characteristics of European International Family Law De Lege Lata

From the development of European choice of law rules in the field of family law so far, some general characteristics can be deduced. These characteristics are present in the adopted instrument on maintenance, the Brussels II*ter*-Proposal and they can partly be deduced from the Commission's Green Paper on matrimonial property.

In general the prime characteristic of the EU's choice of law approach is its strong emphasis on legal certainty, uniformity and predictability.

Without having the intention to enumerate exhaustively the general characteristics of the European choice of law rules in the field of family law, the following five characteristics can be distinguished:

- *adherence to the Savignyan choice of law methodology*

The autonomous private international law systems of the majority of the continental Member States of the European Union basically follow the classical Savignyan choice of law approach: the choice of law rules designate the law of the country with which the case is most closely connected.[108] Yet other Member States, such as the United Kingdom, Ireland and Cyprus, follow a different choice of law approach: their choice of law rules exclusively designate the *lex fori* as the applicable law.

The choice of law rules that have been enacted and proposed so far show that the European Union adheres to the classical choice of law approach, as the common choice of law rules are based on the principle of the closest

---

[106] See Sect. 5.5.3.4 above, in which is argued in favour of the insertion of such an escape clause in the common choice of law on divorce.

[107] Cf., Basedow 2008, pp. 17–18 who refers in this respect to the *technique of presumption and rebuttal*.

[108] Although many countries have developed and 'materialised' their private international law in the course of time, which led to the disappearance of the requirement that a choice of law rule should be abstract and neutral, the classical Savignyan method remained the basis of their private international law systems. See e.g. Kadner Graziano 2003; De Boer 2004, spec. p. 41 on the 'inroads on the tenets of traditional choice of law'.

connection.[109] The basis of the determination of the applicable law to an international case is that the legal systems involved are equally and evenly eligible for application.

- *The achievement of 'conflicts justice'*

The European choice of law rules in the field of family law are — just as any legal provision — aimed at achieving justice. In the context of private international law the reference to justice can entail either 'substantive justice' or 'conflicts justice'.[110] The achievement of substantive justice refers to the solution of a case that is considered the most 'just' in a direct, material sense (*das sachlich beste Recht*). However, in European context the reference to substantive justice makes no sense, as it should not involve a determination of whether one legal system gives a more just outcome of the case than another.[111] Instead it should 'merely' ensure the application of the legal system that is most appropriate to the resolution of the case, which is indicated by the term conflicts justice (*das räumlich beste Recht*). In European private international law — an area which includes different jurisdictions with diverging laws — justice thus characterises a legal environment which enables the predictability of which courts will be competent and which law will be applied in a given case.[112]

The aim of achieving conflicts justice by the European choice of law is already clear from the EC-Treaty, as it provides the legal basis for the unification of private international law and not of substantive law of the Member States.[113] In the European choice of law there is, consequently, no room for the designation of *das*

---

[109] See *inter alia* Kohler 2003, p. 409; Schaub 2005, p. 335: '*Methodischer Ausgangspunkt des europäischen Kollisionsrechts ist nach wie vor der Savigny'sche Ansatz: Zunächst wird nach Rechtsverhältnissen, also sachrechtlichen Kategorien, systematisiert, um bestimmte Anknüpfungsgegenstände zu schaffen. Für diese werden anschließend — ausgehend vom Prinzip der engsten Verbindung — Anknüpfungspunkte ermittelt.*'; Michaels 2006, p. 3: '*What the EU legislates in the realm of private international law is, in shape and approach, widely compatible with traditional private international law.*'; Pocar 2008, p. 15: '[…] *the method of conflict of laws remains formally unchanged*'; Leible 2009, p. 7: '*Der "Triumpf" des klassischen Kollisionsrechts.*' According to Ballarino and Ubertazzi 2004, p. 124 ff equally the European Court of Justice has shown a clear preference towards this method, which results from the case *Garcia Avello* (ECJ Case C-148/02 [2003] ECR I-11613).

[110] This idea was defended by Zweigert: see Zweigert 1948, p. 50; Zweigert 1973, pp. 283–299. See equally Kegel 1953; and Symeonides 2001.

[111] There are, however, exceptions; see e.g. the choice of law rules in EU labour law. See further on these rules Susanti 2008, p. 82 ff.

[112] See equally Basedow 2009, p. 458.

[113] Cf., Weber 2004, pp. 234–235; Basedow 2009, p. 457.

sachlich beste Recht, the law which achieves substantive justice in the individual case.[114]

- *The choice of law contains* 'Sachnormverweisungen'

The European choice of law rules that have been enacted and proposed so far contain so-called *Sachnormverweisungen*, i.e. choice of law rules that refer solely to the substantive rules of the applicable law. Foreign choice of law rules are not referred to. This implies that the legal system referred to by the common choice of law rules applies, irrespective of further references by the choice of law rules of that legal system. Also if the choice of law rules of the applicable law would refer back to the law of the competent jurisdiction, such a reference cannot be accepted. Consequently, the European choice of law precludes the application of *renvoi*.[115]

- *Universal scope of application*

The aim of the European Commission is to establish a common choice of law that applies to both intra- and extra-European cases. In order to achieve this goal the scope of application of the European choice of law rules in the field of family law that have been enacted and proposed so far is universal. Such a scope of application implies that the choice of law rules are not dependent on any other link to the European Union than that the court of a Member State has jurisdiction and is by reason of this competence dealing with the case.[116]

The universal scope of application of the choice of law rules joins the wide scope of application of the European jurisdictional rules.[117] For instance, the jurisdictional rules of the Brussels II*bis*-Regulation apply not only to Union citizens, but also to third country nationals, as the competence of the courts of the Member States is pursuant to Article 3(1)(a) of the Brussels II*bis*-Regulation primarily based on the habitual residence of the spouses.[118]

---

114 De Boer is very critical on this characteristic with regard to the Rome II-Regulation. See De Boer 2008b, p. 993: '*De opstellers van de verordening hebben zich teveel laten leiden door de aanhangers van het neutrale, waardevrije IPR, waarin nog een onderscheid gemaakt wordt tussen conflictenrechtelijke en materieelrechtelijke rechtvaardigheid* [...]. *De evolutie van het conflictenrecht in Europa — een antwoord op de* conflicts revolution *in de Verenigde Staten — is kennelijk aan de Europese wetgever voorbij gegaan*'. However, Schaub does not share the opinion that the European choice of law on non-contractual obligations is 'non-normative'. See Schaub 2005, p. 335: '*Jedenfalls in den zahlreichen Eingriffsnormen und ordre public-Regelungen dieser Entwürfe* [i.e. *the proposals for the Rome I- and II-Regulations; NAB*] *und des Aussenkollisionsrechts der Gemeinschaft zeigt sich aber eine deutliche Tendenz zur Materialisierung des europäischen Kollisionsrechts. Ziel scheint nicht mehr die rein internationalprivatrechtliche Gerechtigkeit und dadurch der sachnächsten Rechtsordnung zu sein, sondern das Erreichen eines auch materiell als gerecht empfundenen Ergebnisses.*'

115 See further on *renvoi infra* Sect. 8.4.4.2.

116 See more elaborately *supra* Sects. 5.4.1.1 and 8.4.2.1 on the universal scope of application of the European choice of law.

117 See Mansel 2003, pp. 144–145.

118 The same goes for the jurisdictional rules of the Maintenance Regulation (Article 3).

- *Party autonomy*

In European choice of law party autonomy is the cornerstone in the determination of the applicable law; it is becoming a fundamental principle.[119] Leaving the parties the opportunity to choose the applicable law themselves is part of a general trend towards liberalisation in private international law, which more and more frequently recognises that it is the individual, and not the state, who can best weigh the relevant choice of law interests.[120] The *professio iuris* grants the parties involved the absolute certainty that the law they have chosen will be applied. In fact one of the core objectives of private international law is to facilitate — rather than to obstruct — the search for consensual solutions by the parties involved in family disputes.[121] The introduction of party autonomy is therefore to be welcomed.

The principle of party autonomy is certainly not a 'makeshift solution', i.e. a *solution faute de mieux*.[122] In the past the principle of party autonomy could bring a solution in case of a failure to reach a compromise on the connecting factor to be employed. However, in the European context there is no case of such situation; the principle of party autonomy has been deliberately chosen as the prevailing principle.[123] The right to choose the applicable law fits very well in the emerging area of freedom, security and justice, in which the citizen can freely exercise his rights. Party autonomy leaves the parties the possibility to shape themselves their legal relationships.[124]

Allowing (limited) party autonomy certainly has advantages: a valid *professio iuris* has the effect that the court is relieved of *ex officio* finding and applying any law other than the one chosen. This would produce a less complicated choice of law rule and even serve legal economy. Finally, party autonomy provides for the largest possible chance of the achievement of (material) justice, as not the abstract objective, but rather the subjective interests of the parties determine what is just.[125]

8.4.4 *The Methodology of European International Family law* De Lege Ferenda

In Section 4.3.2 the internal market and its four fundamental freedoms, the area of freedom, security and justice, the principle of mutual recognition and the

---

119 See *inter alia* Martiny 2007, pp. 90–91; Hohloch 2007, p. 262; Pertegás 2007, p. 329 ff; Rühl 2008, p. 209.

120 See Hohloch 2007, p. 263; Basedow 2008, p. 14 ff.

121 See Pertegás 2007, p. 321.

122 See Leible 2004.

123 See more elaborately on the theory of party autonomy, Pontier 1997, p. 275 ff.

124 Cf., Weber 2004, p. 240 ff.

125 Ibid., pp. 242–243.

protection of stability interests have been distinguished as the specific European aims and objectives of private international law. The consequential question is whether these aims and objectives involve a private international law policy of the European Union that distinguishes the new common European rules from the traditional national ones?

One of the main tasks — and at the same time difficulties — of the methodology of the European choice of law is to secure a balance between unity and diversity.[126]

It should be noted in this context that now the EU pursues the progressive development of an EU system of private international law, it can no longer get around the highly sensitive issues of family law, such as the institution of same-sex marriage.[127] Although it is hardly surprising that the European Union legislature finds it difficult to tackle these highly sensitive issues, it is not wise to continue avoiding them. Resulting from the increasing mobility of citizens, the Member States will be more and more faced with problems connected to same-sex marriages. Efficiency calls for a Union-wide solution. Moreover, the fundamental EU principles of equality and non-discrimination would also require such a solution.[128]

Again it must be admitted that the Union legislature has little room for manoeuvre in this respect, as Article 81(3) TFEU requires a unanimous Council decision on legislative instruments in the field of international family law.

When discussing the unification of international family law, the first issue that emerges is what the basic premise of the European choice of law should be. Due to the high number of objectives attached to the unified choice of law, the underlying choice of law methodology is characterised by a pluralism of methods, within which the principle of the closest connection is the point of departure (Section 8.4.4.1). Not only the specific choice of law methodology is important for the establishment of a coherent system, an EU approach to the general doctrines of

---

[126] See also Gaudemet-Tallon 2001, p. 337.

[127] Cf., Sect. 5.4.2.2 above on the halfhearted application of the proposed choice of law rules on divorce (Brussels II*ter*-Proposal) to the dissolution of same-sex marriages, i.e. leaving it to the discretion of the Member States whether or not to apply the common choice of law on divorce to the dissolution of same-sex marriages.

[128] The issue of the recognition of same-sex marriages is on the European agenda. In January 2006, the point of view of the European Commission became clear with the announcement of its vice-president, Frattini, that Member States which do not eliminate all forms of discrimination against homosexuals, including the refusal to approve 'marriage' and unions between same-sex couples, would be subject to sanctions and eventual expulsion from the EU. See: http://www.cwnews.com/news/viewstory.cfm?recnum=41919. Moreover, on 14 January 2009 the European Parliament has accepted a resolution that proposes to standardise among all Member States the legal status of same-sex relationships. See European Parliament resolution of 14 January 2009 on the situation of fundamental rights in the European Union 2004–2008 (2007/2145(INI)), p. 13. Equally the European Parliament resolution of 2 April 2009 on the application of Directive 2004/38/EC on the right of citizens of the Union and their family members to move and reside freely within the territory of the Member States (2008/2184(INI)) calls for the recognition of same-sex couples.

private international law should also be developed (Section 8.4.4.2). Finally, in Section 8.4.4.3 the relationship with the Hague Conference on Private International Law will be discussed.

8.4.4.1 Basic Premise: A Pluralism of Methods

From the foregoing it is clear that the regulation of issues of international family law in the European Union is characterised by a pluralism of objectives. As a result of the large diversity of objectives attached to European international family law also the underlying choice of law methodology is marked by pluralism.[129] Besides the adherence to the Savignyan choice of law methodology, within which neutral and multilateral choice of law rules are propagated, there is also place for a balanced policy of private international law, within which interests such as the protection of the best interests of the child, the protection of incompetent persons, the principle of gender equality and the respect for the rights of the defence may be acknowledged.[130]

The first matter of importance in the development of the European system of international family law is to provide for clear, coherent and transparent choice of law rules that ensure legal certainty.[131]

The current European choice of law rules are based on the principle of the closest connection.[132] This principle joins the abovementioned objectives of the common choice of law rules.[133] In addition, the principle of the closest connection ensures that the legal systems involved are equally and evenly eligible for application. This aspect is of great importance in the European Union, in which the principle of mutual recognition presumes an equivalence of the legal norms of the Member States.[134] Finally, an important feature of the principle of the closest connection is that it can be concretised in the majority of cases, which highly contributes to the goal to ensure certainty.

Therefore, within the observed pluralism of methods the principle of the closest connection should be the point of departure.

---

[129] Gannagé 2001, p. 13; Gaudemet-Tallon 2005, pp. 23–24. See in general on the pluralism of methods in private international law: Battifol 1973.

[130] Meeusen 2006, p. 24 rightly stresses that the adoption of European provisions on private international law within a genuine area of freedom, security and justice seems to leave scope for such a balanced policy of private international law.

[131] See equally Fiorini 2008a, p. 15.

[132] See Article 3 of the Hague Protocol on the Law Applicable to Maintenance Obligations and Article 20b of the Brussels II*ter*-Proposal. The principle of the closest connection is also the basic principle of the Rome I- and II-Regulations and the Proposal for a Succession Regulation.

[133] See equally Kohler 2003, p. 410.

[134] See *supra* Sect. 4.3.2.3.

The closest connection is to be established by the use of appropriate connecting factors providing for an objective connection.[135] The success of the choice of law methodology thus depends heavily on the adequacy of the connecting factors employed. Therefore, the identification and establishment of the connecting factors are essential tasks.[136]

The application of the most closely connected law requires the determination of what constitutes a close relationship. Family relations are first and foremost personal relations. It is therefore natural that the decisive connecting factor for the choice of law is the connection of the persons involved with a certain legal system.[137] Both the law under which a person has lived for a considerable period of time and the law of a person's place of origin can have such an impact that these legal systems may qualify for the application in cross-border cases.[138]

As has already been noted above, the lack of a substantive European family law is a great challenge for the establishment of a common choice of law.[139] For the national choice of law rules on family law always reflect to a certain extent the state of internal substantive family law. The stricter the rules of substantive family law are, the stricter the choice of law rules tend to be.[140] The choice of law methods employed by the Member States are often used to further certain national preferences.[141]

In specific issues the influence of particular principles, such as the protection of the best interests of the child and the principle of gender equality, or national preferences needs to be considered on a case by case basis. Such influence may very well lead to choice of law rules deviating from the principle of the closest connection.

---

[135] See Lagarde 1986, for his theory on the '*principe de proximité*', particularly pp. 29–126 on the principle of the closest connection in the choice of law. See for an analysis of this principle in the European context: Fallon 2005.

[136] Cf., Martiny 2007, p. 85.

[137] See also Thue 1996, p. 54; Vischer 1999, p. 7; and Henrich 2001, p. 437.

[138] In this regard some authors make a strong appeal to the respect for the cultural identity of persons. Jayme even considers that the respect for the cultural identity of persons is one of the functions of private international law. See Jayme 1995. See also Mankowski 2004, p. 282 ff.

[139] See Poillot-Peruzzetto 2005, p. 31. According to Badiali the lack of a unified substantive law even renders the development of a European system of choice of law based on the traditional private international law approach impossible. See Badiali 1985, p. 37: '*l'impossibilité d'envisager, dans les systèmes communautaires, des règles de conflit de type traditionnel est indirectement confirmée par la constatation que les systèmes en question ne contiennent pas un droit privé formulé par eux-mêmes.*'

[140] This is clearly shown by the analysis in Sect. 5.2 above on divorce in substantive and private international law of the Member States.

[141] See *inter alia* Poillot-Peruzzetto and Marmisse 2001, p. 465.

8.4.4.2 General Doctrines of Private International Law

The unification of issues of international family law does not only require the development of a proper and sound methodology, but it equally requires a proper EU approach as regards the general provisions of private international law. Otherwise the consistency of the EU system of international family law would seriously be undermined by diverging national views on the interpretation of certain general doctrines.[142] Moreover, the absence of a uniform approach as regards these doctrines is not very conducive to legal certainty.[143]

Recently several academics have plunged into the development of general provisions of European private international law, derived from the existing and the proposed instruments in the field of private international law.[144] Leible admits, however, that the hardest phase in the development of EU general provisions of private international law is yet to come with the Europeanisation of issues of international family law.[145]

From the analysis of the Brussels II*ter*-Proposal five general doctrines emerged that are of particular importance, namely the *ex officio* authority, the preliminary question, characterisation, *renvoi* and the public policy exception.[146] In the following the development *de lege ferenda* of these five general principles of European private international law will be discussed.

---

142 Cf., Jayme and Kohler 2006, p. 541: '*Trotz aller kollisionsrechtlicher Vereinheitlichungstendenzen fehlt dem europäische Kollisionsrecht bislang ein Allgemeiner Teil, der die verschiedenen gemeinschaftsrechtlichen Instrumente "verklammert".*' See equally Siehr 2008, p. 92. Currently there is a risk that, due to the present fragmented unification of European private international law, a coherent approach of the general doctrines of private international law may not arise. Theoretically, in each Regulation a distinct approach on these general doctrines can be adopted.

143 In this respect Bogdan 2006, p. 12 rightly stressed that a full uniformity of results would require much more than a unification of the choice of law rules of the Member States as such, namely equally a unified approach to a number of general doctrines of private international law.

The analysis of the Brussels II*ter*-Proposal has shown that a lack of a unified approach on the general provisions may have serious implications on the uniform interpretation and application of the common choice of law rules; see *supra* Sect. 5.4.2.2 as regards the preliminary question, Sect. 5.5.3.4 on the *ex officio* authority of the courts, Sect. 5.6 as regards the application of foreign law and Sect. 5.7 on the public policy exception.

144 See *inter alia* Leible 2007; Heinze 2008; Kreuzer 2008a; Sonnenberger 2008; and Leible 2009.

145 See Leible 2009, p. 77: '*Die beiden Rom-Verordnungen sind Bausteine für einen allgemeinen Teil eines umfassenden europäisches Kollisionsrechts. Die meisten Grundsatzfragen stellen sich in aller Schärfe freilich erst bei der anstehenden Vergemeinschaftung des IPR der familien- und erbrechtlichen Rechtsbeziehungen.*'

146 It cannot be excluded that also other general doctrines of private international law, such as adaptation and overriding mandatory provisions, come into play in issues of international family law. However, from the analysis above concerning divorce no problems as regards the latter doctrines have arisen, as a result of which they are not further deliberated upon.

- Ex officio *authority*

Does the competent court have *ex officio* authority to apply the European choice of law, provided that the parties fail to designate the applicable law themselves and do not plead the application of a certain law applicable pursuant to the European choice of law?

The fact that the choice of law will be included in a regulation implies that these rules should be applied *ex officio*. As seen above, a regulation has as a main characteristic that it is binding in its entirety and directly applicable in all Member States.[147] Moreover, the principle of solidarity contained in Article 4(3) second sentence EU-Treaty would require that courts apply the foreign law *ex officio*.[148] Furthermore, the uniform application of the common choice of law rules in all Member States equally necessitates the *ex officio* authority of the courts to apply the common rules.[149]

Consequently, the courts should be obliged pursuant to a general provision to apply the European choice of law rules *ex officio*.

- *Preliminary question*

When faced with an issue of choice of law, the competent court is usually equally faced with one or more preliminary questions. For example, in case of a divorce, the court first needs to verify whether there is actually a valid marriage: divorce is only available if the parties are married.[150]

Since one of the aims pursued by the Europeanisation of international family law is the creation of a European judicial area, an EU approach to the preliminary question would be desirable. The preliminary question actually plays a significant part in the decision on the main issue of the case and, therefore, has major consequences on the uniform application of the common choice of law rules.[151] The uniform application of the preliminary question in the European Union is thus in the interest of the unification of the choice of law in family matters: both legal certainty and predictability are highly promoted.[152]

In the absence of European choice of law rules in most issues of family law currently no autonomous response can be given to the majority of the preliminary questions that may arise. Therefore, the approach of the Union legislature in the Brussels II*ter*-Proposal — response to the preliminary question *lege fori* — is an obvious solution. Yet if it is up to the European Commission this situation will change in the future: the development of a European system of international family

[147] See *supra* Sect. 4.4.4.3.

[148] See Jänterä-Jareborg 2003, spec. p. 367 ff.

[149] Cf., Siehr 2008, p. 86.

[150] The Brussels II*ter*-Proposal provides that the question whether there is case of a marriage is to be determined by the national choice of law rules of the Member States. See Council Document No. 9712/08 JUSTCIV 106 of 23 May 2008, Article 20e-1, p. 16.

[151] Cf., Heinze 2008, p. 113 ff.

[152] See equally Sonnenberger 2008, pp. 240–241.

law is on the agenda. Once this system is established, an autonomous response to the preliminary question should be the general rule.

- *Characterisation*

The choice of law sets out specific 'connecting categories' by deciding, for instance, that maintenance obligations are governed by the law of the habitual residence of the creditor. Consequently, when the court has to determine the law applicable to a factual situation, it must first place this situation in the correct legal category before ascertaining the applicable law. This characterisation process is a question that relates to the interpretation of rules. Therefore, in European context characterisation is influenced by the general interpretative criteria developed by the Court of Justice.[153]

The ECJ developed the principle pursuant to which the meaning of the concepts and terms used in European legislation may either be established by developing autonomous notions or by reference to domestic law.[154] Unsurprisingly, the Court took the position that an autonomous definition should be preferred to the extent possible.[155] In the case *Leffler* the ECJ pointed out that

> the objective pursued by the Treaty of Amsterdam of creating an area of freedom, security and justice, thereby giving the Community a new dimension, and the transfer from the EU Treaty to the EC Treaty of the body of rules enabling measures in the field of judicial cooperation in civil matters having cross-border implications to be adopted testify the will of the Member States to establish such measures firmly in the Community legal order and thus to lay down the principle that they are to be interpreted autonomously.[156]

This case indicates that as regards issues of international family law that have been Europeanised the possibility of recourse to national law for the purpose of characterisation is precluded, save where EU law refers to, or can be interpreted as referring to, national law.

The notions used in European private international law should be primarily construed according to substantive EU law, if any such rules exist. A number of family law notions are present in free movement legislation, social security provisions, sex equality law and in the Staff Regulations as legal grounds for the application of EU law.[157] The European Court of Justice and the Court of First Instance have interpreted family law notions on several occasions, such as 'spouse', 'marriage', etc.[158]

However, the autonomous interpretation of the common choice of law precludes the automatic transposition of the above mentioned family law notions. The

---

[153] See Bertoli 2006, p. 379. See on this issue equally Audit 2004, pp. 789–816.

[154] ECJ Case 12/76 *Tessili* v. *Dunlop* [1976] ECR 1473, para 10.

[155] See ECJ Case C-27/02 *Engler* v. *Janus Versand GmbH* [2005] ECR I-481, para 33.

[156] ECJ Case C-443/03 *Leffler* [2005] ECR I-9611, para 45.

[157] See McGlynn 2000, p. 223 ff; Caracciolo di Torella 2004, p. 32 ff.

[158] ECJ Case 59/85 *Netherlands State* v. *Reed* [1986] ECR 1283; joined cases C-122/99P and C-125/99P *D and Sweden* v. *Council* [2001] ECR I-4319.

respective fields of law often pursue distinct aims. For example, whereas a polygamous marriage may very well qualify as a marriage according to the choice of law, residence rights are only assigned to one spouse and for that purpose the polygamous marriage does not qualify as a marriage (see Article 4(4) of the Family Reunification Directive).[159]

In order to promote the uniformity of application of the Union law the interpretation of the common choice of law should be interpreted autonomously.[160] The principle of equality would also require such an autonomous interpretation.[161] Moreover, the lack of autonomous interpretation of the common choice of law rules is not conducive to legal certainty and predictability and might again lead to forum shopping.

- *Renvoi*

The choice of law rules contain so-called *Sachnormverweisungen*, i.e. choice of law rules that refer solely to the substantive rules of the applicable law.[162] It is clear that there is no place for *renvoi* if the parties have chosen the law to be applied to their divorce. If they have made such a choice, the parties clearly intended that the substantive law provisions of the chosen law be applicable; their choice accordingly excludes any possibility of *renvoi* to another law.[163]

If the parties have not chosen the applicable law, it is clear that in cases in which the law of a Member State is designated as the applicable law the issue of *renvoi* does not arise. If the choice of law rules on issues of family law are unified within the European Union, all Member States apply the same choice of law rules, which means that every reference to the law of a Member State will automatically be accepted.[164]

However, the exclusion of *renvoi* is not obvious in cases in which the law of a third country is designated as the applicable law. The issue of *renvoi* arises where the common choice of law rules refer an issue to the law of another country which, under its choice of law rules in turn refers the issue back to the law of the forum (*Rückverweisung*) or to the law of yet another country (*Weiterverweisung*). The exclusion of both these forms of *renvoi* in extra-European cases has been questioned.[165] According to some *renvoi* should be accepted, at least in cases of *Rückverweisung*. Although the acceptance of a *Rückverweisung* is certainly tempting — it would allow the competent court to apply its own law — it should

159 See Council Directive 2003/86/EC on the right to family reunification, [2003] OJ L251/12.

160 Cf., ECJ Case C-523/07 *A* [2009] ECR I-02805 as regards the concept of habitual residence.

161 See also Tomasi et al. 2007, p. 374.

162 See *supra* Sect. 8.4.3. See on *renvoi* in general: Sauveplanne 1990.

163 Cf., Report on the Convention on the law applicable to contractual obligation (Giuliano-Lagarde Report), [1980] OJ C 282/1, at Article 15.

164 Cf., with regard to the European choice of law on succession, Knot 2008, pp. 200–201.

165 See Martiny 2007, p. 96; Kohler 2008a, pp. 1679–1680; and Siehr 2008, pp. 90–91.

be rejected from a methodological point of view.[166] The European choice of law rules are to be based on the principle of the closest connection. These rules have been constructed in such a way that they refer — in the view of the European legislature — to the most closely connected law.[167] From this perspective, accepting *renvoi* would be contrary to the principle of the closest connection. Moreover, Kropholler rightly points to the fact that the aim of the regulation is the development of a new, uniform choice of law, which refers directly to the applicable substantive law, and not the development of a '*Superkollisionsrecht*', which refers to the existing choice of law systems.[168] Finally, from a practical point of view also *renvoi* should be excluded, for *renvoi* would only detract from the clarity and ease of use that the uniform choice of law aims to realise, as it implies a considerable burden on legal practice.[169] Therefore, the uniform European choice of law system requires the exclusion of *renvoi*.

- *Public policy exception*

The public policy exception is meant to exclude the application of foreign law if this would result in a violation of fundamental values of the society involved.

The common choice of law rules on issues of international family law that have been enacted and proposed so far refer to the public policy notion of the forum.[170] Yet the national approaches to the application of the public policy exception differ greatly from one Member State to another, which might endanger the objective of decisional harmony.

Is it possible to refer to the European public policy exception? The advantage of the reference to a European public policy exception would be that the European Court of Justice can provide for a uniform interpretation of this concept. The European Union system does have its own public policy that is formed by the fundamental freedoms, European citizenship, human rights and the principles of

---

[166] Incidentally accepting *renvoi* would involve a strict European definition of the concept. Cf., Kropholler (2006), p. 178 stating that countries can take: '*eine verschiedene Haltung zu den einzelnen Renvoi-Fällen (Rückverweisung im engeren Sinne, Weiterverweisung, Zirkelverweisung etc.).*' Without such strict definition forum shopping is likely to occur and the uniformity of decisions is at stake. See Knot 2008, p. 126 for an overview of the different positions taken with respect to *renvoi*.

[167] See also Report on the Convention on the law applicable to contractual obligations (Giuliano-Lagarde Report), [1980] OJ C 282/1, at Article 15: '*the exclusion of renvoi is justified in international conventions regarding conflict of laws. If the Convention attempts as far as possible to localize the legal situation and to determine the country with which it is most closely connected, the law specified by the conflicts rule in the Convention should not be allowed to question this determination of place.*' Cf., with regard to Dutch private international law, Ten Wolde 2009, p. 66.

[168] Kropholler 2000, pp. 393–394. See also Rüberg 2005, pp. 104–105.

[169] Cf., Kropholler 2000, p. 394: '*Für den Ausschluss des Renvoi lässt sich außerdem anführen, dass er die Rechtsanwendung vereinfacht und der Rechtsklarheit dient.*'

[170] See Article 13 of the Hague Protocol on the law applicable to maintenance obligations, Article 20e of the Brussels II*ter*-Proposal and Article 27 of the proposed Succession-Regulation.

non-discrimination and subsidiarity.[171] However, it is not clear whether or not there is a specific European public policy requiring the defence of European values and interests, to the extent that they do not coincide with those of the forum.[172]

Consequently, in the present absence of a specific European public policy the European legislature has no other option but to refer to the public policy of the Member States. In the future this reference should be reconsidered, as it leaves (too) much room to their national preferences.[173]

8.4.4.3 Role of the Hague Conference on Private International Law

The European Union is not the only actor in the field of the unification of private international law. The most important other actor is undoubtedly the Hague Conference on Private International Law, which was established in 1893 with the mandate 'to work on the progressive unification of the rules of private international law.'[174] The result of this work is demonstrated in form of numerous Hague Conventions that have been adopted in the course of the years.

All the EU Member States are equally members of the Hague Conference on Private International Law. Since the entry into force of the Treaty of Amsterdam in 1999, the European legislature is competent to adopt measures in the field of private international law (Article 65 EC-Treaty, now Article 81 TFEU). This transfer of power equally influences the external competence of the European Union.[175] Initially the transfer of competence to the European Union was feared to stab the Hague Conference to the heart.[176] Fortunately the two organisations have sought cooperation: in 2007 the (at that time still) European Community has acceded to the Hague Conference.[177]

The Hague Conference and the European Union share the same goals to a certain extent. The ultimate goal of the Hague Conference is to strive for a world in which, despite the differences between legal systems, persons — individuals as

---

[171] See on this issue: Thoma 2007, p. 120 ff; Reichelt 2007, pp. 7–11.

[172] Cf., De Boer 2008a, p. 328.

[173] Cf., *supra* Sect. 5.7 on the protection provided by the public policy exception of the Brussels II*ter*-Proposal.

[174] See Article 1 of the Statute of the Hague Conference on Private International Law.

[175] See *supra* Sect. 4.4.3.

[176] Cf., Jayme 2000, p. 167, speaking of a possible '*Todesstoß*'.

[177] See Council Decision on the accession of the EU to the Hague Conference on Private International Law, [2006] OJ L297/1. The Statute of the Hague Conference had to be amended so as to make membership of the Conference possible for the European Union as well as for any other Regional Economic Integration Organisation to which its Member States have transferred competence over matters of private international law. See *inter alia* Preliminary Document No. 32B of May 2005 for the attention of the Twentieth Session of the Hague Conference on Private International Law on the Admission of the European Community to the Hague Conference on Private International Law, p. 3; Schulz 2007; Bischoff 2008; Van Loon and Schulz 2008.

well as companies — can enjoy a high degree of legal certainty.[178] The EU equally aims — in addition to a number of other objectives — for legal certainty and uniformity of decisions.

However, the largest difference is the model of integration of private international law that characterises these two organisations: the European Union strives for regional integration, whereas the integration pursued by the Hague Conference is global in character.[179] The cooperation between these two organisations should, therefore, be designed in such a way that the regional integration does not interfere with or impede the global integration of private international law.[180]

The accession of the European Union to the Hague Conference has provided the Union the opportunity to play a role in the global integration of private international law. Ultimately, this guarantees that the regional integration of private international law is incorporated into its global integration.

Van Loon — the Secretary General of the Hague Conference — has rightly argued in favour of a functional Europeanisation of private international law: a Union instrument in the field of private international law should only be adopted if it is strictly necessary and if it has a specific surplus value. In all other cases preference should be given to the establishment of Hague Conventions.[181] This view is to be endorsed to the extent that if there is no (concrete view on a) Hague Convention in a particular field of law that can be ratified by the Member States, the Union legislature has a free hand to develop a Union instrument in that specific area.[182]

Suppose that the EU legislature intends to establish a Union instrument in the field of registered partnerships: the developments in the Hague Conference do not indicate that there is a view of a Hague Convention in this field. The law applicable in respect of 'unmarried couples', a subject broader than registered partnerships alone, has been set on the Agenda of the Hague Conference on Private International Law. However, no priority has been given to the setting up of an instrument in this field of law by the Member States of the Hague Conference.[183] Consequently, in such situations the Union legislature should thus be able to establish a European instrument.

---

[178] See Recommendation of the European Parliament on the proposal for a Council decision on the accession of the European Union to the Hague Conference of Private International Law, A6-0250/2006, p. 6.

[179] See Traest 2003, p. 463.

[180] Cf., Boele-Woelki 1999, p. 372; Traest 2003, p. 463.

[181] Van Loon 2006, p. 101. See also already Gaudemet-Tallon 2001, pp. 332–338.

[182] Cf., Kreuzer 2008b, spec. pp. 142–143: '*Von fehlendem universalem Kollisionsrecht ist dabei auch dann auszugehen, wenn zwar eine kollisionsrechtliche Konvention mit universalem Geltungsanspruch* de iure *existiert, sich jedoch* de facto *über längere Zeit überhaupt nicht oder doch nicht über Europa hinaus durchgesetzt hat, so dass mit einer* universalen *Geltung auch in Zukunft nicht gerechnet werden kann.*'

[183] In April 2009 it was lastly confirmed that The Hague Conference leaves the issue without priority on the Agenda, see Conclusions and Recommendations adopted by the Council on General Affairs and Policy of the Conference of 31 March–2 April 2009. See further *supra* Sect. 3.2 for which reasons no Hague Convention in this field has been established yet.

The cooperation between the Hague Conference and the European Union has already achieved a success in the field of international family law. In November 2007 the Hague Protocol on the Law Applicable to Maintenance Obligations was agreed upon.[184] The European Union will ratify this Protocol, which will then determine the applicable law (see Article 15 Maintenance Regulation), and the European rules on jurisdiction and recognition and enforcement on maintenance obligations are provided for in the Maintenance Regulation.[185] Furthermore, in 2010 the 1996 Child Protection Convention will probably take effect throughout the EU, as the EU Member States shall 'take the necessary steps to deposit simultaneously their instruments of ratification or accession [...] if possible before 5 June 2010.'[186]

One of the main reasons the global integration approach of the Hague Conference should be preferred is that the field of international family law is truly global in character: families with links to the territory of the European Union are split all over the world. Many European Member States have a large foreign population originating from third countries, i.e. non-EU Member States. According to recent statistics yearly more than one and half million third country nationals immigrate into the European Union.[187] This foreign population will often possess the nationality of their country of origin. In turn, many citizens of the Member States are living more or less permanently in third countries, such as the United States of America, Canada or China. Therefore, global cooperation addressing the resulting legal problems should take high preference; the European Union should thus give priority to the development of Hague Conventions to the largest possible extent.[188]

---

184 See The Hague Protocol on the Law Applicable to Maintenance Obligation, The Hague, 23 November 2007. See on the development of this Hague Protocol and the Hague Convention of 5 November 2007 on the International Recovery of Child Support and other Forms of Family Maintenance in general: McEleavy 2008.

185 See Vlas 2009, pp. 293–295.

186 See Article 3 of Council Decision No 431/2008 of 5 June 2008 authorizing certain Member States to ratify, or accede to, in the interest of the European Community, the 1996 Hague Convention on Jurisdiction, Applicable Law, Recognition, Enforcement and Cooperation in respect of Parental Responsibility and Measures for the Protection of Children and authorizing certain Member States to make a declaration on the application of the relevant internal rules of Community law, [2008] OJ L151/36.

187 Information gathered in 2008 by Eurostat: http://epp.eurostat.ec.europa.eu.

188 Cf., the Explanatory Memorandum to the Proposal for a Succession Regulation, p. 4, where is stated: '*[T]he Hague Convention of 5 October 1961 on the conflicts of laws relating to the form of testamentary dispositions has been ratified by 16 Member States. It would be desirable for the other Member States to ratify the Convention in the interests of the Community.*' See in general also the Stockholm Programme, p. 33: '*The Union should use its membership of The Hague Conference to actively promote the widest possible accession to the most relevant Conventions and to offer as much assistance as possible to other States with a view to the proper implementation of the instruments. The European Council invites the Council, the Commission and the Member States to encourage all partner countries to accede to those Conventions which are of particular interest to the Union.*'

8.5 Synthesis: Recommendations to the EU Legislature

The preceding analysis of the establishment of an EU system of international family law yields a number of recommendations that can be made to the Union legislature.

- *Decide on an EU choice of law methodology*

From the failed Brussels II*ter*-Proposal it is clear that the lack of agreement on the choice of law methodology to be employed is the principal reason for its failure. Consequently, an agreement on the choice of law methodology needs to be reached. Such a methodology should ideally be discussed independent from any concrete legislative project. This would permit the Member States to have a general debate on the issue without the pressure of having to serve their specific national interests in a particular field of family law. Such a debate should expressly address the 'foreign law problem'.

In the establishment of a proper EU methodology of international family law two balances are of particular importance in this respect: in the first place, that between unity and diversity and, secondly, that between certainty and flexibility. Especially the latter balance is particularly important so as to ensure that the European private international law system shows traits of both common and civil law systems, as the EU involves legal systems of both these traditions. By means of a combination of strict rules and a flexible possibility to displace the presumptively applicable law in favour of the principle of the closest connection, the European choice of law on family issues should attempt to attain an appropriate balance between certainty and flexibility and, accordingly, between the common and civil law traditions.

- *More transparency is required*

The failure to reach a compromise on the Brussels II*ter*-Proposal has also shown that transparency of the reasons behind the proposal is of vital importance. Therefore, in sensitive areas of law, such as the choice of law on family matters, a clear and reliable reasoning behind the Union action is required. The absence of such reasoning makes Union legislative proposal very vulnerable, which in turn harms the credibility of its basis. More — and preferably full — transparency will remove some of the aversion that a number of Member States currently feel towards any Union activity in the field of international family law.

Furthermore, once an EU instrument containing private international law rules has been established, more transparency can be attained by the development of a more elaborate Explanatory Memorandum or 'Guide to Good Practice' that accompanies the respective instrument. The application and ease of use of the instrument will be greatly advanced by such aid.

- *More coherence is required*

The European system of international family law is currently not developed in a coherent manner, mainly because the Commission adheres to a very fragmented approach. Although this approach can very well be explained by the fact that it will be easier to achieve consensus on these issues taken in isolation than it would have been had work been undertaken on a wider area of family law, it is not very conducive to legal certainty and predictability. A more systematic approach is thus called for, as unnecessary overlap and contradiction should be avoided.[189]

It should be noted, moreover, that the current fragmented approach supplies the European legislature with an enormous amount of extra work. It could namely well be that, ultimately, once the EU's unification programme has ended, a series of streamlining reforms of the various sectors individually unified is needed in order to coordinate them. In the end the European system of private international law should ideally display the following features: coherence, logical structure, absence of contradiction, completeness, clarity and ease of use.[190]

- *The sole Europeanisation of the choice of law should not be a goal in itself*

The sole goal of Europeanisation of the choice of law rules should not take place at the expense of the content of these rules.[191] This might sound very obvious. However, the Union legislature tends to adhere to a very functional approach of the unification of the private international law rules: the Europeanisation of this field of law is aimed at European integration. The Union legislature should make sure not to fully subordinate the Europeanisation of international family law to the sole goal of European integration. For the danger exists that legal practice might otherwise be burdened with choice of law rules that are very hard to apply.

- *Participate as much as possible in the Hague Conference*

Since most family disputes are global in character, the European Union should cooperate as much as possible with the Hague Conference on Private International Law and give the ratification of Hague Conventions priority over the establishment of Union instruments.

The Union legislature should, therefore, uphold Kreuzer's maxim:

> soviel Universalität der Regelung (*ius commune universale*) wie möglich, soviel (vorrangige) europäische Regionalität der Regelung (*ius particulare europeaum*) wie nötig, um die verbindlichen Ziele der EG zu erreichen.[192]

---

189 Cf., Dethloff 2007, p. 998: '*Ziel muss es sein, der durch "Rom I, II und III"bzw". Brussel II fortfolgende" drohenden Fragmentierung entgegenzuwirken und ein kohärentes europäisches IPR-Gesetzbuch zu schaffen.*'

190 Cf., Fiorini 2008a, pp. 7–8.

191 See also Boele–Woelki 2008, p. 786.

192 Kreuzer 2006, p. 65.

8.6 To Conclude

It is clear that establishing a European system of international family law is altogether not an easy task: fundamental issues underlying such a system need to be cleared up. Although European international family law will sooner or later be realised, this will certainly still require great effort. For the development of the European system of international family law it can, therefore, in full agreement with Siehr, be concluded that:

> [D]as Ziel ist klar, es zu erreichen fordert noch viel Mühe, Zeit und Geduld.[193]

It is to be hoped that all the effort, time and patience will eventually result in a transparent and coherent system of European international family law.

References

Regulations, Conventions, Reports and Other Documentary Sources

Borrás Report. Explanatory Report on the Convention on Jurisdiction and the Recognition and Enforcement of Judgments in Matrimonial Matters, [1998] OJ C221/27

Brussels II-Regulation. Council Regulation (EC) No. 1347/2000 of 29 May 2000 on jurisdiction and the recognition and enforcement of judgments in matrimonial matters and in matters of parental responsibility for children of both spouses, [2000] OJ L160/19

Brussels II*bis*-Regulation. Council Regulation (EC) No. 2201/2003 of 27 November 2003 on Jurisdiction and Enforcement of Judgments in Matrimonial Matters and Matters of Parental Responsibility, [2003] OJ L338/1

Brussels II*ter*-Proposal. Proposal for a Council Regulation amending Regulation (EC) No. 2201/2003 as regards jurisdiction and introducing rules concerning applicable law in matrimonial matters, COM(2006) 399 final

COSAC Report. Report of the subsidiarity and proportionality check on the Brussels II*ter*-Proposal organised in November 2006 by COSAC, Report No. 1/2006. The COSAC-Report and the Annex thereto are available at: http://www.cosac.eu/en/info/earlywarning/doc/results/.

EC-Treaty. Treaty Establishing the European Community, Amsterdam 2 October 1997, [1997] OJ C340/1

EU-Treaty. Treaty on the European Union of 7 February 1992, [1992] OJ C191/1 (original version), [2010] OJ C83/13 (consolidated version)

Green Paper on Matrimonial Property. Green Paper on conflict of laws regarding matrimonial property regimes, including the question of jurisdiction and mutual recognition, COM(2006) 400 final

Green Paper on Successions and Wills. Green Paper on Succession and Wills, COM(2005) 65 final

Hague Programme. The Hague Programme: Strengthening freedom, security and justice in the European Union, [2005] OJ C53/1

---

[193] Siehr 2008, p. 83. It is to be observed that Siehr made this statement for the whole area of European private international law, not only for European international family law.

Hague Protocol on the Law Applicable to Maintenance Obligations. Protocol on the Law Applicable to Maintenance Obligations of 23 November 2007. Protocol to the Hague Convention of 23 November 2007 on the International Recovery of Child Support and Other Forms of Family Maintenance

House of Lords Rome III Report. House of Lords—European Union Committee, *Rome III—Choice of Law in Divorce*, 52nd Report of Session 2005-06 (HL Paper 272) December 2006

Impact Assessment on Divorce. Commission Staff Working Document – Annex to the proposal for a Council Regulation amending Regulation (EC) No. 2201/2003 as regards jurisdiction and introducing rules concerning applicable law in matrimonial matters, SEC(2006) 949

Maintenance Regulation. Council Regulation (EC) No. 4/2009 of 18 December 2008 on jurisdiction, applicable law, recognition and enforcement of decisions and cooperation in matters relating to maintenance obligations, [2009] OJ L7/1

Regulation on enhanced cooperation in the field of divorce. Council Regulation (EU) No. 1259/2010 of 20 December 2010 implementing enhanced cooperation in the area of the law applicable to divorce and legal separation, OJ L343/10

Proposal for a Succession-Regulation. Proposal for a Regulation of the European Parliament and of the Council on jurisdiction, applicable law, recognition and enforcement of decisions and authentic instruments in matters of Succession and the creation of a European Certificate of Succession, COM(2009) 154 final

Rome I-Regulation. Regulation (EC) No. 593/2008 of the European Parliament and the Council on the law applicable to contractual obligations (Rome I), [2008] OJ L177/6

Rome II-Regulation. Regulation (EC) No. 864/2007 of the European Parliament and the Council on the law applicable to non-contractual obligations (Rome II), [2007] OJ L199/40

Stockholm Programme. The Stockholm Programme – An open and secure Europe serving and protecting the citizens of 2 December 2009, available at: http://ec.europa.eu/justice_home/news/intro/doc/stockholm_program_en.pdf

Tampere Presidency Conclusions. Presidency Conclusions of the Tampere European Council of 15-16 October 1999, available at: http://www.consilium.europa.eu/ueDocs/cms_Data/docs/pressData/en/ec/00200-r1.en9.htm

Treaty on the Functioning of the European Union. Treaty on the Functioning of the European Union of 13 December 2007, [2010] OJ C83/46 (consolidated version)

Treaty of Lisbon. Treaty of Lisbon amending the Treaty on European Union and the Treaty establishing the European Community, 13 December 2007, [2007] OJ C306/1

Books and Articles

Asín Cabrera A (2004) 'La "communitaurisation" du droit privé de la famille: euro-chauvinisme ou intégration européenne'. In: Impérialisme et chauvinisme juridiques. Schultess, Zurich, pp 169–184

Audit B (2004) L'interprétation autonome du droit international privé. Journal du Droit International 131:789–816

Baarsma NA (2009) European choice of law on divorce (Rome III): where did it go wrong? NIPR 27:9–14

Badiali G (1985) Le droit international privé des Communautés européennes. Recueil des Cours 191:1–182

Ballarino T, Ubertazzi B (2004) On *Avello* and other judgments: a new point of departure in the conflict of laws? Yearbook of Private International Law, pp 85–128

Basedow J (2005) Spécificité et coordination du droit international privé communautaire. Comité français de droit international privé, Travaux de l'année 2002–2004. Editions Pédone, Paris, pp 275–305

Basedow J (2008) The recent developments of the conflict of laws. In: Basedow J et al (eds) Japanese and European Private International Law in Comparative Perspective, Mohr Siebeck, Tübingen, pp 4–18
Basedow J (2009) The communitarisation of private international law. RabelsZ 73:455–460
Battifol H (1973) Le pluralisme des méthodes en droit international privé. Recueil des Cours 139:75–148
Baxter WF (1963) Choice of law and the federal system. Stanford Law Review 16:1–42
Bertoli P (2006) The court of justice, European integration and private international law. Yearbook of Private International Law 8:375–412
Bischoff JA (2008) Die Europäische Gemeinschaft und die Haager Konferenz für Internationales Privatrecht. ZEuP 334–354
Boele-Woelki K (1999) De toekomst van het IPR na het Verdrag van Amsterdam. In: van Buren-Dee JM et al (eds) Privaatrecht en Gros, Intersentia Antwerpen, pp 355–375
Boele-Woelki K (2008) To be or not to be: enhanced cooperation in international divorce law within the European Union. Victoria University of Wellington Law Review, pp 779–792
Bogdan M (2006) Concise introduction to EU private international law. Europa Law Publishing, Groningen
Borrás A (2005) Le droit international privé communautaire: réalités, problèmes et perspectives d'avenir. Recueil des Cours 317:313–536
Borrás A (2007) Prinzipien des Internationalen Familienrechts. In: Reichelt G (ed) Europäisches Gemeinschaftsrecht und IPR. Manzsche, Wien, pp 55–67
Calvo Caravaca AL (2006) The private international law of the European Community. In: Pereznieto Castro L et al (eds) Tradition and innovation of private international law at the beginning of the third millennium. Liber in Memoriam of Professor Friedrich K. Juenger, Juris Publishing, New York, pp 23–44
Caracciolo di Torella E (2004) Under construction: EU family law. European Law Review 29:32–51
De Boer ThM (2004) Forum preferences in contemporary European conflicts law: the myth of a 'Neutral Choice'. In: Mansel HP et al (eds), Festschrift für Erik Jayme, Sellier. European Law Publishers, München, pp 39–45
De Boer ThM (2008a), Unwelcome foreign law: public policy and other means to protect the fundamental values and public interests of the European Community. In: Malatesta A et al (eds), The external dimention of EC private international law in family and succession matters, CEDAM, Milan, pp 295–330
De Boer ThM (2008b) De grondslagen van de Verordening Rome II. WPNR 6780:988–993
De Boer ThM (2009) The purpose of uniform choice-of-law rules: the Rome II Regulation. NILR 295–332
De Groot G-R, Rutten S (2004) Op weg naar een Europees IPR op het gebied van het personen-en familierecht. NIPR 22:273–282
Dethloff N (2003) Arguments for and against unification and harmonisation of family law in Europe. In: Boele-Woelki K, Perspectives for the harmonisation and unification of family law in Europe, Intersentia, Antwerpen, pp 37–64
Dethloff N (2007) Familien- und Erbrecht zwischen nationaler Rechtskultur, Vergemeinschaftung und Internationalität. Perspektiven für die Forschung. ZEuP, pp 992–1005
Duintjer Tebbens H (1990) Private international law and the single European market: coexistence or cohabitation? In: de Boer ThM (ed) Forty years on: the evolution of postwar private international law in Europe. Kluwer, Deventer, pp 49–69
Duintjer Tebbens H (2002) Ein Ziviljustizraum in der Europäischen Union—auf Kosten einer Aushölung der internationalen Zusammenarbeit? In: Baur JF, Mansel HP (eds) Systemwechsel im europäischen Kollisionsrecht. Verlag C.H. Beck, München, pp 171–192
Ehle B (2002) Wege zu einer Kohärenz der Rechtsquellen im Europäischen Kollisionsrecht der Verbraucherverträge (diss. Heidelberg). Peter Lang, Frankfurt am Main

Fallon M (2005) Le principe de proximité dans le droit de l'Union Européenne'. In: Le droit international privé: esprit et méthodes Mélanges en l'honneur de Paul Lagarde. Dalloz, Paris, pp 241–262
Fentiman R (2008) Choice of law in Europe: uniformity and integration. Tulane Law Review 82:2021–2051
Fiorini A (2008a) The codification of private international law in Europe: could the community learn from the experience of mixed jurisdictions? Electronic Journal of Comparative Law 12:1–16
Fiorini A (2008b) Rome III—choice of law in divorce: is the Europeanization of family law going too far? International Journal of Law, Policy and the Family 22:178–205
Fletcher IF (1982) Conflict of laws and European community law. North-Holland Publishing Company, Amsterdam
Friedman LM (1975) The legal system: a social science perspective. Russell Sage Foundation, New York
Gannagé L (2001) La hiérachie des normes et les méthodes du droit international privé (diss. Panthéon-Assas, Paris II). L.G.D.J, Paris
Gaudemet-Tallon H (2001) Quel droit international privé pour l'union européenne? In: Borchers PJ, Zekoll J (eds) International conflicts of laws for the third millennium, essays in honor of Friedrich K. Juenger. Transnational Publishers, Ardsley, pp 317–338
Gaudemet-Tallon H (2002) De l'utilité d'une unification du droit international privé de la famille dans l'union européenne? In: De Moura Ramos RM et al (eds), Estudos em homenagem à Professora Doutora Isabel de Magalhães Collaço. Livraria Almedina, Coimbra, pp 159–185
Gaudemet-Tallon H (2005) Le pluralisme en droit international privé: richesses et faiblesses (Le funambule et l'arc-en-ciel). Recueil des Cours 312:9–488
Glenn HP (1996) Codification of private international law in Quebec. RabelsZ 60:231–268
Haltern U (2003) Recht als kulturelle Existenz. In: Jayme E (ed), Kulturelle Identität und Internationales Privatrecht. C.F. Müller, Heidelberg, pp 15–50
Hartley TC (2005) The European Union and the systematic dismantling of the common law of conflict of laws. ICLQ 54:813–828
Hay P, Lando O, Rotunda RD (1986) Conflict of laws as a technique for legal integration. In: Cappelletti M et al (eds), Integration through law. Methods, tools and institutions, Book 2 political organs, integration techniques and judicial process, vol. 1. Walter de Gruyter, Berlin, pp 161–258
Heinze C (2008) Bausteine eines Allgemeinen Teils des europäischen Internationalen Privatrechts. In: Baetge D et al (eds) Die richtige Ordnung, Festschrift für Jan Kropholler. Mohr Siebeck, Tübingen, pp 105–127
Henrich D (2001) Abschied vom Staatsangehörigkeitsprinzip? In: Hohloch G et al (eds), Festschrift für Hans Stoll. Mohr Siebeck, Tübingen, pp 437–449
Hess B (2001) Die Integrationsfunktion des Europäischen Zivilverfahrensrechts. IPRax 21:389–396
Hess B (2010) Europäisches Zivilprozessrecht. C.F. Müller, Heidelberg
Hilf M (1995) Europäische Union und nationale Identität der Mitgliedstaaten. In: Randelzhofer A et al (eds) Gedächtnisschrift für Eberhard Grabitz. C.H. Beck Verlag, München, pp 157–170
Hohloch G (2007) Rechtswahl als Anknüpfungsprinzip (Zur Bedeutung des Parteiwillens im europäischen Internationalen Privatrecht). In: Frantzen T et al (eds) Rett og toleranse: festskrift til H.J. Thue. Gyldendal Akademisk, Oslo, pp 257–270
Jayme E (1995) Identité culturelle et intégration: le droit international privé postmoderne. Recueil des Cours 251:9–267
Jayme E (2000) Zum Jahrtausendwechsel: Das Kollisionsrecht zwischen Postmoderne und Futurismus. IPRax 20:165–171
Jayme E, Kohler C (2000) Europäisches Kollisionsrecht 2000: Interlokales Privatrecht oder universelles Gemeinschaftsrecht? IPRax 20:454–465
Jayme E, Kohler C (2006) Europäisches Kollisionsrecht 2006: Eurozentrismus ohne Kodifikationsidee? IPRax 537–550

Jänterä-Jareborg M (2003) Foreign law in national courts: a comparative perspective. Recueil des Cours 304:181–385
Jänterä-Jareborg M (2008) Jurisdiction and applicable law in cross-border divorce cases in Europe. In: Basedow J et al (eds) Japanese and European Private International Law in Comparative Perspective. Mohr Siebeck, Tübingen, pp 317–343
Jessurun d'Oliveira HU (2003) Towards a "European private international law? In: De Witte B, Forder C (eds) The common law of Europe and the future of legal education. Kluwer, Deventer, pp 265–283
Kadner Graziano T (2002) Gemeineuropäisches Internationales Privatrecht: Harmonisierung des IPR durch Wissenschaft und Lehre (am Beispiel der außenvertraglichen Haftung für Schäden). Mohr Siebeck, Tübingen, pp 10–14
Kadner Graziano T (2003) Aufstieg, Fall und Renaissance des internationale Perspektive im europäischen Internationalen Privatrecht—Lehren aus der Geschichte. In: Schulze R, Ajani G (eds) Gemeinsame Prinzipien des Europäischen Privatrecht. Nomos Verlagsgesellschaft, Baden-Baden, pp 41–86
Kapteyn PJG, VerLoren van Themaat P (1998) Introduction to the law of the European Communities, 3rd edn. edited and further revised by Gormley LW. Kluwer Law International, London
Kegel G (1953) Begriffs- und Interessenjurisprudenz im IPR. In: Battifol H, Lewald H (eds) Festschrift für Hans Lewald. Helbing & Lichtenhahn, Basel, pp 259–288
Knot JG (2008) Internationale boedelafwikkeling Over het toepasselijke recht op de afwikkeling van nalatenschappen (diss. Groningen). Kluwer, Deventer
Kohler C (2001) Status als Ware: Bemerkungen zur europäischen Verordnung über das internationale Verfahrensrecht für Ehesachen. In: Mansel HP (ed) Vergemeinschaftung des Europäischen Kollisionsrecht. Carl Heymanns Verlag, Köln, pp 41–53
Kohler C (2003) Der europäische Justizraum für Zivilsachen und das Gemeinschaftskollisionsrecht. IPRax 23:401–412
Kohler C (2008a) Zur Gestaltung des europäischen Kollisionsrecht für Ehesachen: Der steinige Weg zu einheitlichen Vorschriften über das anwendbare Recht für Scheidung und Trennung. Zeitschrift für das gesamte Familienrecht 55:1673–1681
Kohler C (2008b) Einheitliche Kollisionsnormen für Ehesachen in der Europäische Union: Vorschläge und Vorbehalte. Familie Partnerschaft und Recht 193–196
Kreuzer K (2006) Zu Stand und Perspektiven des Europäischen Internationalen Privatrechts. RabelsZ 70:1–88
Kreuzer K (2008a) Was gehört in den Allgemeinen Teil eines Europäischen Kollisionsrechtes? In: Jud B et al (eds), Kollisionsrecht in der Europäischen Union. Jan Sramek Verlag, Wien, pp 1–62
Kreuzer K (2008b) Gemeinschaftskollisionsrecht und universales Kollisionsrecht: Selbstisolation, Koordination oder Integration? In: Baetge D et al (eds), Die richtige Ordnung, Festschrift für Jan Kropholler. Mohr Siebeck, Tübingen, pp 129–150
Kropholler J (2000) Der Renvoi im vereinheitlichten Kollisionsrecht. In: Gottwald P et al (eds), Festschrift für Dieter Henrich. Verlag Ernst und Werner Gieseking, Bielefeld, pp 393–402
Lagarde P (1986) Le principe de proximité dans le droit international privé contemporaine. Recueil des Cours 196:9–238
Leible S (2004) Parteiautonomie im IPR—Allgemeines Anknüpfungsprinzip oder Verlegenheitslösung? In: Mansel HP et al (eds), Festschrift für Erik Jayme. Sellier. European Law Publishers, München, pp 485–503
Leible S (2007) Der Beitrag der Rom II-Verordnung zu einer Kodifikation der allgemeinen Grundsätze des Europäischen Kollisionsrecht. In: Reichelt G (ed) Europäisches Gemeinschaftsrecht und IPR. Manzsche, Wien, pp 31–54
Leible S (2009) Rom I und Rom II: Neue Perspektiven im Europäischen Kollisionsrecht. Zentrum für Europäisches Wirtschaftsrecht, Bonn
Mance J (2007) Is Europe aiming to civilise the common law? European Business Law Review 18:77–99

Mankowski P (2004) Kulturelle Identität und Internationales Privatrecht. IPRax 24:282–290
Mansel HP (2003) Das Staatsangehörigkeitsprinzip im deutschen und gemeinschaftsrechtlichen Internationalen Privatrecht: Schutz der kulturellen Identität oder Diskriminierung der Person? In: Jayme E (ed) Kulturelle Identität und Internationales Privatrecht. C.F. Müller Verlag, Heidelberg, pp 119–154
Martiny D (2007) Objectives and values of (private) international law in family law. In: Meeusen J et al (eds) International Family Law for the European Union. Intersentia, Antwerpen, pp 69–99
McEleavy P (2008) The new Hague maintenance convention. ICLQ 984–996
McGlynn C (2000) A family law for the European Union? In: Shaw J (ed) Social law and policy in an evolving European Union. Hart Publishing, Oxford, pp 224–241
Meeusen J (2006) Op weg naar een communautair internationaal familie(vermogens)recht? Enkele Europeesrechtelijke beschouwingen. In: Mededelingen van de Nederlandse Vereniging voor Internationaal Recht Europees internationaal familierecht. T.M.C. Asser Press, Den Haag, pp 1–70
Meeusen J (2007) What has it got to do necessarily with the European Union?: International family law and European (economic) integration. The Cambridge Yearbook of European Legal Studies 2006–2007, pp 329–355
Michaels R (2006) EU Law as private international law? Re-conceptualising the country-of-origin principle as vested rights theory. Duke Law School Legal Studies
Mills A (2009) The confluence of public and private international law. Cambridge University Press, Cambridge
Moran RT, Harris PR, Moran SV (2007) Managing cultural differences, 7th edn. Elsevier/Butterworth-Heinemann, Boston
Pataut E (2008) International jurisdiction and third states: a view from the EC in family matters. In: Malatesta A et al (eds), The external dimension of EC private international law in family and succession matters. CEDAM, Milan, pp 123–148
Pertegás M (2007) Beyond nationality and habitual residence. Other connecting factors in European private international law in family matters. In: Meeusen J et al (eds) International family law for the European Union. Intersentia, Antwerpen, pp 319–340
Pocar F (2008) The "communitarization" of private international law and its impact on the external relations of the European Union. In: Malatesta A et al (eds), The external dimension of EC private international law in family and succession matters. CEDAM, Milan, pp 1–15
Poillot-Peruzzetto S (2005) Les enjeux de la communautarisation. In: Fulchiron H, Nourissat C (eds) Le nouveau droit communautaire du divore et de la responsabilité parentale. Dalloz, Paris, pp 13–37
Poillot-Peruzzetto S, Marmisse A (2001) Le droit international privé communautaire de la famille. Revue des Affaires Européennes, pp 460–468
Pontier JA (1997) Conflictenrecht: grondslagen, methoden, beginselen en belangen (diss. Amsterdam). Ars Aequi Libri, Nijmegen
Pontier JA (2005) Europees conflictenrecht. Een complexe geschiedenis in vogelvlucht. Vossiuspers UvA, Amsterdam
Reichelt G (2007) Zur Kodifikation des europäisches Kollisionsrecht–am Beispiel des ordre public. In: Reichelt G (ed) Europäisches Gemeinschaftsrecht und IPR. Manzsche, Wien, pp 5–11
Rüberg S (2005), Auf dem Weg zu einem europäischen Scheidungskollisionsrecht (diss. Konstanz), Available at http://www.ub.uni-konstanz.de/kops/volltexte/2005/1694/pdf/Rueberg.pdf
Rühl G (2008) Rechtswahlfreiheit im europäischen Kollisionsrecht In: Baetge D et al (eds), Die richtige Ordnung. Festschrift für Jan Kropholler zum 70. Geburtstag. Mohr Siebeck, Tübingen, pp 187–209
Sanada Y (1989) The cultural bases of the Japanese as a key to the myth of the reluctant litigant in Japan: a prelude to the understanding of the Japanese legal culture. In: The Institute of Comparative Law (ed) Conflict and Integration: Comparative Law in the World Today. Chuo University Press, Tokyo

Santer J (1999) Préface. In: Rodríguez Iglesias GC et al (eds) Mélanges en hommage à Fernand Schockweiler. Nomos, Baden-Baden, p 15

Sauveplanne JG (1990) Renvoi. In: International encyclopedia of comparative law, Private international law, Chapter 6, vol. III. Mohr Siebeck, Tübingen

Schack H (2001) Das neue Internationale Eheverfahrensrecht in Europa. RabelsZ 65:615–633

Schaub R (2005) Grundlagen und Entwicklungstendenzen des europäischen Kollisionsrechts. Juristen Zeitung 60:328–337

Schulz A (2007) The accession of the European community to the Hague conference on private international law. ICLQ, pp 939–949

Siehr K (2005) Auf dem Weg zu einem Europäischen Internationalen Privatrecht. Zeitschrift für Europarecht, pp 90–100

Siehr K (2008) Die Kodifikation des Europäischen IPR—Hindernisse, Aufgaben und Lösungen. In: Jud B et al. (eds), Kollisionsrecht in der Europäischen Union. Jan Sramek Verlag, Wien, pp 77–95

Sonnenberger H J (2008) Randbemerkungen zu, Allgemeinen Teil eines europäisierten IPR. In: Baetge D et al (eds) Die richtige Ordnung, Festschrift für Jan Kropholler. Mohr Siebeck, Tübingen, pp 227–246

Spamann H (2001) Choice of law in a federal system and an internal market. Jean Monnet working paper 8/2001

Susanti I (2008) The conflict rules on the protection of migrant workers. Hephaestus, Groningen

Symeonides SC (1993) Private international law codification in a mixed jurisdiction: the Louisiana experience. RabelsZ 57:460–516

Symeonides SC (2001) Material justice and conflicts justice in choice of law. In: Borcher PJ, Zekoll J (eds) International conflict of laws for the third millennium, Essays in honor of Friedrich K. Juenger. Transnational Publishers, Ardsley, pp 125–140

Symeonides SC (2009) The conflicts book of the louisiana civil code: civilian, American or original? Tulane Law Review 82:1042–1081

Symeonides SC (2010) American federalism and private international law. Hellenic Journal of International Law, available at http://ssrn.com/abstract=1612949.

Ten Wolde MH (2004) Will professionals in other countries be able to rely on a European Certificate of Inheritance for all purposes? In: Les Successions Internationales dans l'UE. Perspectives pour une Harmonisation. Deutschen Notarinstitut (DNotI), Würzburg, pp 503–514

Ten Wolde MH (2009) Inleiding Nederlands en Europees Internationaal Privaatrecht, Deel A Algemeen deel en materieel IPR Personen-, familie- en erfrecht. Hephaestus, Groningen

Ten Wolde MH, Knot JG (2006) European international law of succession. Hephaestus, Groningen

Thoma I (2007) Die Europäisierung und die Vergemeinschaftung des nationalen ordre public. Mohr Siebeck, Tübingen

Thue H (1996) Connecting factors in international family law. In: Lowe N, Douglas G (eds) Families Across Frontiers. Kluwer Academic Publishers, The Hague/Boston/London, pp 53–62

Tomasi L, Ricci C, Bariatti S (2007) Characterisation in family matters for purposes of European private international law. In: Meeusen J et al (eds) International family law for the European Union. Intersentia, Antwerpen, p 374

Traest M (2003) De Europese Gemeenschap en de Haagse Conferentie voor het Internationaal Privaatrecht. Maklu, Antwerpen/Apeldoorn

Uhle A (2004) Freiheitliche Verfassungsstaat und kulturelle Identität. Mohr Siebeck, Tübingen

Van Loon J H A (2006) Over de verhouding tussen het Europees Gemeenschapsrecht en De Haagse Conferentie voor het internationaal privaatrecht. Tijdschrift@ipr.be, pp 100–102

Van Loon JHA, Schulz A (2008) The European community and the hague conference on private international law. In: Martenczuk B, van Thiel S (eds) Justice, liberty, security: new challenges for EU external relations. VUBPress, Brussels, pp 257–299

Van den Eeckhout V (2008) The promotion of fundamental rights by the Union as a contribution to the European Legal Space (III): the role of European private international law. Available at http://refgov.cpdr.ucl.ac.be

Vigand S (2005) La construction de l'espace de liberté, de securité et de justice: vers un droit international privé communautaire de la famille. (diss. Panthéon-Assas, Paris II)

Vischer F (1999) Connecting factors. In: international encyclopedia of comparative law, Private international law, vol III. Mohr Siebeck, Tübingen, pp 3–33

Vlas P (2009) Alimentatie uit Brussel met een Haags randje. WPNR 6794:293–295

Vlas P (2003) Naar een EG-Verordening Erfrecht? WPNR 6533:393

Vonken APMJ (2006) De internationale beslissingsharmonie nader beschouwd. Tijdschrift voor Privaatrecht 43:9–125

Weber A (2004) Die Vergemeinschaftung des internationalen Privatrechts (diss. Frankfurt am Oder). TENEA, Berlin

Zweigert K (1948) Die dritte Schule im Internationalen Privatrecht. Zur neueren Wissenschaftsgeschichte des Kollisionsrechts. In: Raape L et al (eds), Festschrift für Leo Raape. Rechts- und staatswissenschaftlicher Verlag, Hamburg, pp 35–52

Zweigert K (1973) Some reflections on the sociological dimensions of private international law or what is justice in conflict of laws? University of Colorado Law Review, pp 283–299

Appendix 1: Brussels II*ter*-Proposal

Proposal for a Council Regulation amending Regulation (EC) No 2201/2003 as regards jurisdiction and introducing rules concerning applicable law in matrimonial matters, Brussels 17 July 2006, COM(2006) 399 final.

The Council of the European Union [...]

(1) The European Union has set itself the objective of maintaining and developing the European Union as an area of freedom, security and justice in which the movement of persons is ensured. For the gradual establishment of such an area, the Community is to adopt, among others, the measures relating to judicial cooperation in civil matters needed for the proper functioning of the internal market.

(2) There are currently no Community rules in the field of applicable law in matrimonial matters. Council Regulation (EC) No 2201/2003 of 27 November 2003 sets out rules on jurisdiction, recognition and enforcement of judgments in matrimonial matters and matters of parental responsibility, but does not include rules on applicable law.

(3) The European Council held in Vienna on 11 and 12 December 1998 invited the Commission to consider the possibility of drawing up a legal instrument on the law applicable to divorce. In November 2004, the European Council invited the Commission to present a Green Paper on conflict-of-law rules in divorce matters.

(4) In line with its political mandate, the Commission presented a Green Paper on applicable law and jurisdiction in divorce matters on 14 March 2005. The Green Paper launched a wide public consultation on possible solutions to the problems that may arise under the current situation.

(5) This Regulation should provide a clear and comprehensive legal framework in matrimonial matters in the European Union and ensure adequate solutions to the citizens in terms of legal certainty, predictability, flexibility and access to court.

N.A. Baarsma, *The Europeanisation of International Family Law*,
DOI: 10.1007/978-90-6704-743-2,

(6) With the aim of enhancing legal certainty, predictability and flexibility, this Regulation should introduce the possibility for spouses to agree upon the competent court in proceedings for divorce and legal separation. It also should give the parties a certain possibility to choose the law applicable to divorce and legal separation. Such possibility should not extend to marriage annulment, which is closely linked to the conditions for the validity of the marriage, and for which parties' autonomy is inappropriate.

(7) In the absence of choice of applicable law, this Regulation should introduce harmonised conflict-of-law rules based on a scale of connecting factors to ensure legal certainty and predictability and to prevent "rush to court". Such connecting factors should be chosen as to ensure that proceedings relating to divorce or legal separation be governed by a law with which the marriage has a close connection.

(8) Considerations of public interest should justify the possibility in exceptional circumstances to disregard the application of the foreign law in a given case where this would be manifestly contrary to the public policy of the forum.

(9) The residual rule on jurisdiction should be revised to enhance predictability and access to courts for spouses of different nationalities living in a third State. To this end, the Regulation should set out a harmonised rule on residual jurisdiction to enable couples of different nationalities to seise a court of a Member State with which they have a close connection by virtue of their nationality or their last common habitual residence.

(10) Article 12 of Council Regulation (EC) No 2201/2003 should be amended to ensure that a divorce court designated pursuant to Article 3a has jurisdiction also in matters of parental responsibility connected with the divorce application provided the conditions set out in Article 12 of the same Regulation are met, in particular that the jurisdiction is in the best interests of the child.

(11) Regulation (EC) No 2201/2003 should therefore be amended accordingly.

(12) Since the objectives of the action to be taken, namely to enhance legal certainty, flexibility and access to court in international matrimonial proceedings, cannot be sufficiently achieved by the Member States and can therefore, by reason of scale, be better achieved at Community level, the Community may adopt measures, in accordance with the principles of subsidiarity as set out in Article 5 of the Treaty. In accordance with the principle of proportionality, as set out in that Article, this Regulation does not go beyond what is necessary to attain these objectives.

(13) This Regulation respects the fundamental rights and observes the principles recognised in particular by the Charter of Fundamental Rights of the European Union as general principles of Community law. In particular, it seeks to ensure full respect for the right to a fair trial as recognised in Article 47 of the Charter.

(14) [The United Kingdom and Ireland, in accordance with Article 3 of the Protocol on the position of the United Kingdom and Ireland annexed to the Treaty on European Union and the Treaty establishing the European Community, have given notice of their wish to take part in the adoption and application of this Regulation.]

(15) Denmark, in accordance with Articles 1 and 2 of the Protocol on the position of Denmark annexed to the Treaty on European Union and the Treaty establishing the European Community, is not participating in the adoption of this Regulation, and is therefore not bound by it nor subject to its application.

Has adopted this Regulation: [...]

(2) the following Article 3a is inserted:

"Article 3a *Choice of court by the parties in proceedings relating to divorce and legal separation*

1. The spouses may agree that a court or the courts of a Member State are to have jurisdiction in a proceeding between them relating to divorce or legal separation provided they have a substantial connection with that Member State by virtue of the fact that

   (a) any of the grounds of jurisdiction listed in Article 3 applies, or
   (b) it is the place of the spouses' last common habitual residence for a minimum period of three years, or
   (c) one of the spouses is a national of that Member State or, in the case of the United Kingdom and Ireland, has his or her "domicile" in the territory of one of the latter Member States.

2. An agreement conferring jurisdiction shall be expressed in writing and signed by both spouses at the latest at the time the court is seised."

(3) In Articles 4 and 5, the terms "Article 3" are replaced by the terms "Articles 3 and 3a".

(4) Article 6 is deleted;

(5) Article 7 is replaced by the following:

"Article 7 *Residual jurisdiction*

Where none of the spouses is habitually resident in the territory of a Member State and do not have a common nationality of a Member State, or, in the case of the United Kingdom and Ireland do not have their "domicile" within the territory of one of the latter Member States, the courts of a Member State are competent by virtue of the fact that:

(a) the spouses had their common previous habitual residence in the territory of that Member State for at least three years; or

(b) one of the spouses has the nationality of that Member State, or, in the case of United Kingdom and Ireland, has his or her "domicile" in the territory of one of the latter Member States."

(6) In Article 12 (1), the terms "Article 3" are replaced by the terms "Articles 3 and 3a".

(7) The following Chapter IIa is inserted:

"CHAPTER IIa
Applicable law in matters of divorce and legal separation

Article 20a *Choice of law by the parties*

1. The spouses may agree to designate the law applicable to divorce and legal separation.The spouses may agree to designate one of the following laws:

   (a) the law of the State of the last common habitual residence of the spouses insofar as one of them still resides there;
   (b) the law of the State of the nationality of either spouse, or, in the case of United Kingdom and Ireland, the "domicile" of either spouse;
   (c) the law of the State where the spouses have resided for at least five years;
   (d) the law of the Member State in which the application is lodged.

2. An agreement designating the applicable law shall be expressed in writing and be signed by both spouses at the latest at the time the court is seised.

Article 20b *Applicable law in the absence of choice by the parties*

In the absence of choice pursuant to Article 20a, divorce and legal separation shall be subject to the law of the State:

(a) where the spouses have their common habitual residence, or failing that,
(b) where the spouse had their last common habitual residence insofar as one of them still resides there, or failing that,
(c) of which both spouses are nationals, or, in the case of United Kingdom and Ireland, both have their "domicile", or failing that,
(d) where the application is lodged.

Article 20c *Application of foreign law*

Where a law of another Member State is applicable, the court may make use of the European Judicial Network in civil and commercial matters to be informed of its contents.

Article 20d *Exclusion of renvoi*

The application of a law designated under this Regulation means the application of the rules of that law other than its rules of private international law.

Article 20e *Public policy*

The application of a provision of the law designated by this Regulation may be refused only if such application is manifestly incompatible with the public policy of the forum."

Appendix 2: Council Draft on the Brussels II*ter*-Proposal of 23 May 2008

Proposal for a Council Regulation amending Regulation (EC) No 2201/2003 as regards jurisdiction and introducing rules concerning applicable law in matrimonial matters, Document No. 9712/08 JUSTCIV 106.

The Council of the European Union [...]

(1) The **Community** has set itself the objective of maintaining and developing (...) an area of freedom, security and justice (...). For the **progressive** establishment of such an area, the Community is to adopt (...) measures relating to judicial cooperation in civil matters **with cross-border implications to the extent necessary** for the proper functioning of the internal market.

(1a) According to Article 65, point (b) of the Treaty, these measures are to include those promoting the compatibility of the rules applicable in the Member States concerning the conflict of laws and of jurisdiction.

(1b) The European Council at its meeting in Vienna on 11 and 12 December 1998 requested that the possibility of drawing up a legal instrument on the law applicable to divorce be considered within five years of the entry into force of the Treaty of Amsterdam and, at its meeting in Tampere on 15 and 16 October 1999, it endorsed the principle of mutual recognition of judgments and other decisions of judicial authorities as the cornerstone of judicial cooperation in civil matters and invited the Council and the Commission to adopt a programme of measures to implement the principle of mutual recognition.

(1c) On 30 November 2000, the Council adopted a joint Commission and Council programme of measures for implementation of the principle of mutual recognition of decisions in civil and commercial matters. The programme identifies measures relating to the harmonisation of conflict-of-law rules as those facilitating the mutual recognition of judgments.

N.A. Baarsma, *The Europeanisation of International Family Law*,
DOI: 10.1007/978-90-6704-743-2,

(2) There are currently no Community rules in the field of applicable law in matrimonial matters. Council Regulation (EC) No 2201/2003 of 27 November 2003 sets out rules on jurisdiction, recognition and enforcement of judgments in matrimonial matters and matters of parental responsibility, but does not include rules on applicable law.

(3) The European Council **held in The Hague on 4 and 5 November 2004 invited the Commission to submit in 2005 a Green Paper on the conflict of laws relating to divorce (Rome III)**.

(4) In line with its political mandate, the Commission presented **on 14 March 2005** a Green Paper on applicable law and jurisdiction in divorce matters. The Green Paper launched a wide public consultation on possible solutions to the problems that may arise under the current situation.

(5) This Regulation should provide a clear and comprehensive legal framework in **matters of divorce and legal separation** in the European Union and ensure adequate solutions to the citizens in terms of legal certainty, predictability, flexibility and access to **justice**.

(5a) Should the Community adopt the proposal for a Regulation on jurisdiction, applicable law, recognition and enforcement of judgments and cooperation in matters relating to maintenance, the substantive scope and the provisions of this Regulation should as far as possible be interpreted consistently with it, having in mind the different context of the two instruments.

(…)

(5c) In several provisions the Regulation refers to nationality as the connecting factor. The question of how to deal with cases of multiple nationalities should be left to national law.

(6) **Increasing mobility of citizens requires more flexibility on the one hand and more legal certainty on the other hand. Therefore, this Regulation should strengthen party autonomy in matters of divorce and legal separation.** With the aim of enhancing legal certainty, predictability, flexibility **and access to justice**, this Regulation should introduce the possibility for spouses to agree upon the competent court in proceedings for divorce and legal separation. It should **also** give the parties a certain possibility to choose the law applicable to divorce and legal separation. **This should be particularly useful in cases of divorce by mutual consent**. Such **a** possibility should not extend to marriage annulment, which is closely linked to the conditions for the validity of the marriage, and for which **party** autonomy is inappropriate.

(6a) Although this Regulation should cover only international cases, this should not prevent the spouses from choosing in their agreement a court in a Member State or the courts of a Member State in general.

(6b) **Certain safeguards should be introduced to ensure that the spouses are aware of the consequences of their choice. As a minimum the agreement on the choice of court or the agreement on the choice of applicable law should be made in writing, signed and dated by both parties. However, if the law of the Member State where both spouses are habitually resident provides for additional formal requirements, those requirements should be respected. For example, such additional formal requirements may exist in a Member State where the agreement is inserted in a marriage contract.**

(9) **Article 6 of Regulation (EC) No 2201/2003 should be deleted. The deletion of Article 6 should not change the exclusive nature of the provisions on jurisdiction.**

(9-0-a) **Article 7 of Regulation (EC) No 2201/2003 should be replaced by a harmonised rule on subsidiary jurisdiction to enhance predictability and access to courts for spouses living in a third State and who do not have a common nationality of a Member State. This rule should enable couples (...) to seise a court of a Member State with which they have a close connection by virtue of the nationality of one of the spouses or their last common habitual residence.**

(9a) **For specific exceptional cases this Regulation should provide a *forum necessitatis*. The *forum necessitatis* should be aimed at providing a forum in those cases where the courts of a Member State which have jurisdiction in accordance with the Regulation could not grant a divorce for specific reasons. Only in such specific exceptional cases should the spouses have the possibility to apply for divorce in the Member State where their marriage was concluded or of which one of them is a national. However, the court of the Member State whose law does not provide for divorce or does not recognise the marriage in question for the purposes of pronouncing divorce should not be required to determine which other court has jurisdiction. Furthermore, the term "authority" as stipulated in Article 7a should not refer to a specific body but rather to the general legal system of the Member State concerned.**

(9b) **Where the Regulation refers to the fact that the applicable law does not provide for divorce, this should be interpreted in such a way that the applicable law does not know the concept of divorce at all.**

(10) Article 12 of Council Regulation (EC) No 2201/2003 should be amended to ensure that a divorce court designated pursuant to Article 3a [and 7] has jurisdiction also in matters of parental responsibility connected with the divorce application provided that the conditions set out in Article 12 of the said Regulation are met, in particular that the jurisdiction is in the best interests of the child.

(10a) **The spouses should be able to choose as the law applicable to divorce and legal separation the law of a country with which they have a special connection or the law of the forum. The formal requirements for such a choice should be the same as those provided in the Regulation for the choice of court. However, where the spouses designate the law applicable before the court in the course of proceedings, it is sufficient that such designation is recorded in court in accordance with the law of the forum and paragraphs 2 and 3 of Article 20a do not apply**.

(10b) **(ex 7)** In the absence of choice of applicable law, this Regulation should introduce harmonised conflict-of-law rules based on a scale of connecting factors to ensure legal certainty and predictability and to prevent "rush to court". Such connecting factors should be chosen **so** as to ensure that proceedings relating to divorce or legal separation **are** governed by a law with which the **spouses have** a close connection.

(10b-1) **In certain situations the law of the forum should apply; in particular where the applicable law does not provide for divorce, where it does not grant one of the spouses because of his or her gender equal access to divorce or legal separation or where the court is seized in accordance with Article 7a(a) or (b). This, however, should not prejudice the public policy clause (*ordre public*)**.

(10c) **When determining the law applicable on the basis of nationality, it should be respected that certain States with a common law system have the concept of "domicile" instead of "nationality" as connecting factor in matters of divorce or legal separation**.

(10d) **(ex 8)** Considerations of public interest should justify **giving the courts of a Member State** the possibility, in exceptional circumstances, to disregard the application of the foreign law in a given case where this would be manifestly contrary to the public policy of the forum.

(10e) **When a court has to apply the law of another Member State it may make use, in particular, of the European Judicial Network in Civil and Commercial Matters in order to obtain information on the content of that law**.

(10f) **The Commission will make a proposal concerning the procedures and conditions according to which Member States would be entitled to negotiate and conclude on their own behalf agreements with third countries in individual and exceptional circumstances, concerning the sectoral matters covered by this Regulation**.

(11) Regulation (EC) No 2201/2003 should therefore be amended accordingly.

(12) Since the objectives of **this Regulation** (…) cannot be sufficiently achieved by the Member States and can therefore, by reason of **the** scale

and effects of this Regulation, be better achieved at Community level, the Community may adopt measures, in accordance with the principles of subsidiarity as set out in Article 5 of the Treaty. In accordance with the principle of proportionality, as set out in that Article, this Regulation does not go beyond what is necessary to attain these objectives.

(13) This Regulation respects the fundamental rights and observes the principles recognised in particular by the Charter of Fundamental Rights of the European Union as general principles of Community law. In particular, it seeks to ensure full respect for the right to a fair trial as recognised in Article 47 of the Charter.

(14) **In accordance with Articles 1 and 2 of the Protocol** on the position of the United Kingdom and Ireland annexed to the Treaty on European Union and the Treaty establishing the European Community, **and without prejudice to Article 4 of the said Protocol, the United Kingdom and Ireland have not taken part in the adoption of this Regulation and are not bound by it or subject to its application**.

(15) In accordance with Articles 1 and 2 of the Protocol on the position of Denmark annexed to the Treaty on European Union and the Treaty establishing the European Community, **Denmark does not take part** in the adoption of this Regulation and is (…) not bound by it nor subject to its application.

Has adopted this Regulation: […]

(7) The following Chapter IIa is inserted:

CHAPTER IIa Applicable law in matters of divorce and legal separation

Article 20a

Choice of ***applicable*** *law by the parties*

1. The spouses may agree to designate the law applicable to divorce and legal separation **provided that it is** one of the following laws:

   (a1) the law of the State where the spouses are habitually resident[1] at the time the agreement is concluded, or

   (a) the law of the State **where the spouses were last habitually resident**, insofar as one of them still resides there[2] **at the time the agreement is concluded**, or

   (b) the law of the State of the nationality of either spouse [or, in the case of **a State which has the concept of "domicile" as connecting factor in matters of divorce and legal separation,**

[1] Note for the translators: See Article 3(1)(a), 1st indent, of Regulation 2201/2003.

[2] Note for the translators: See Article 3(1)(a), 2nd indent, of Regulation 2201/2003.

of the "domicile" of either spouse] **at the time the agreement is concluded, or**

(c) **(...)**

(d) the law of the **forum**.

2. **Without prejudice to paragraph 4 an agreement designating the applicable law may be concluded and modified at any time, but at the latest at the time the court is seized.**

3. **Such agreement** shall be expressed in writing, **dated** and signed by both spouses. **Any communication by electronic means which provides a durable record of the agreement shall be equivalent to "writing".**[1]
However, if the law of the Member State where both spouses have their habitual residence at the time the agreement is concluded provides for additional formal requirements for such agreements, (...) those requirements (...) have to be satisfied. If the spouses are habitually resident in different Member States and the laws of those Member States provide for different formal requirements, the agreement is formally valid if it satisfies the requirements of either of those laws.

4. **If the law of the forum so provides, the spouses may also designate the applicable law before the court in the course of proceedings. In such a case, it is sufficient that such designation is recorded in court in accordance with the law of the forum**[2].

Article 20b

Applicable law in the absence of choice by the parties

In the absence of **a** choice pursuant to Article 20a, divorce and legal separation shall be subject to the law of the State:

(a) where the spouses **are habitually resident at the time the court is seised**[3] or, failing that,

(b) where the spouse**s were last habitually resident provided that that period did not end more than one year before the court was seised** insofar as one of them still resides there[4] **at the time the court is seised** or, failing that,

---

[1] Note to translators: see Article 23(2) of Regulation (EC) No 44/2001.

[2] Note for all translators: "record" should be translated within the meaning of "take note for its record." Note for FR translators: in FR please translate "record" as "donner acte."

[3] Note for the translators: See Article 3(1)(a), 1st indent, of Regulation 2201/2003.

[4] Note for the translators: See Article 3(1)(a), 2nd indent, of Regulation 2201/2003.

(c) of **the nationality of** both spouses[1] (…)**,** [or, in the case of **a State which has the concept of "domicile" as connecting factor in divorce and legal separation matters, of the** "domicile" **of both spouses,] at the time the court is seised** or**, failing that,**

(d) where the **court is seised**.

(…)

Article 20b-1
The application of the law of the forum

1. **Where the law applicable pursuant to Article 20a and 20b does not provide for divorce or does not grant one of the spouses because of his or her gender equal access to divorce or legal separation, the law of the forum shall apply**.
2. **Notwithstanding Article 20b where the court is seised pursuant to Article 7a (a) or (b), the law of the forum shall apply**.

Article 20c
Application of foreign law

(deleted)

Article 20c-1
Universal application

The law designated by this Regulation shall be applied whether or not it is the law of a Member State.[2]

Article 20d
Exclusion of renvoi

The application of a law designated under this Regulation means the application of the rules **(…) in force in that State** other than its rules of private international law.[3]

---

[1] Note for the translators: See Article 3(1)(b) of Regulation 2201/2003.

[2] Note for the translators: See Article 3 of the Rome II Regulation (No 864/2007).

[3] Note for the translators: See Article 15 of the 1980 Rome Convention (mutatis mutandis).

Article 20e
Public policy

The application of a provision of the law designated by this Regulation may be refused only if such application is manifestly incompatible with the public policy (***ordre public***) of the forum.[1]

Article 20e -1
Differences in national law

Nothing in this Regulation shall oblige the courts of a Member State whose law does not provide for divorce or does not recognise the marriage in question for the purposes of divorce proceedings to pronounce a divorce by virtue of the application of this Regulation.

Article 20f
States with two or more legal systems[2]

1. **Where a State comprises several territorial units, each of which has its own rules of law in respect of divorce and legal separation, each territorial unit shall be considered as a State for the purposes of identifying the law applicable under this Regulation.**
2. **A Member State within which different territorial units have their own rules of law in respect of divorce and legal separation shall not be required to apply this Regulation to conflicts solely between the laws of such units.**

[…]

Article 1a
Transitional provisions

1. **This Regulation shall apply to legal proceedings instituted, and to agreements referred to in Articles 3a and 20a concluded after the date of application in accordance with Article 2.**
2. **However, an agreement on the choice of court or on the choice of applicable law concluded in accordance with the (…) law of a**

[1] Note for the translators: See Article 26 of the Rome II Regulation (No 64/2007).

[2] Note for the translators: See - mutatis mutandis - Article 25 of the Rome II Regulation (No 864/2007).

Member State before the date of application of this Regulation (...) shall also be given effect, provided that it fulfils the conditions set out in the first subparagraph of paragraph 3 of Articles 3a or 20a.

3. **This Regulation does not prejudice agreements on the choice of applicable law concluded in accordance with the (...) law of the Member State of the court seised before the date of application of this Regulation.**

Appendix 3: Resolution of the European Parliament on the Brussels II*ter*-Proposal

European Parliament legislative resolution of 21 October 2008 on the proposal for a Council regulation amending Regulation (EC) No 2201/2003 as regards jurisdiction and introducing rules concerning applicable law in matrimonial matters (COM(2006)0399—C6-0305/2006—2006/0135(CNS)), [2010] OJ C15E/128.

[...]

Text proposed by the Commission	Amendments by Parliament

Amendment 38

ARTICLE 1, POINT 7
Article 20a, paragraph 1, introductory part (Regulation (EC) No 2201/2003)

1. The spouses may agree to designate the law applicable to divorce and legal separation. The spouses may agree to designate one of the following laws:	1. The spouses may agree to designate the law applicable to divorce and legal separation ***provided that such law is in conformity with the fundamental rights defined in the Treaties and in the Charter of Fundamental Rights of the European Union and the principle of public policy***. The spouses may agree to designate one of the following laws:

N.A. Baarsma, *The Europeanisation of International Family Law*,
DOI: 10.1007/978-90-6704-743-2, © T.M.C. ASSER PRESS, The Hague,
The Netherlands, and the author 2011

Amendment 18
ARTICLE 1, POINT 7
Article 20a, paragraph 1, point -a (new) (Regulation (EC) No 2201/2003)

	(-a) the law of the State in which the spouses have their habitual residence at the time when the agreement is concluded;

Amendment 19
ARTICLE 1, POINT 7
Article 20a, paragraph 1, point a (Regulation (EC) No 2201/2003)

(a) the law of the State of ***the last common*** habitual residence of the spouses insofar as one of them still resides there;	(a) the law of the State of habitual residence of the spouses insofar as one of them still resides there ***at the time when the agreement is concluded***;

Amendment 20
ARTICLE 1, POINT 7
Article 20a, paragraph 1, point b (Regulation (EC) No 2201/2003)

(b) the law of the State of the nationality of either spouse, or, in the case of United Kingdom and Ireland, the "domicile" of either spouse;	(b) the law of the State of the nationality of either spouse, or, in the case of United Kingdom and Ireland, the "domicile" of either spouse ***at the time when the agreement is concluded***;

Amendment 21
ARTICLE 1, POINT 7
Article 20a, paragraph 1, point c (Regulation (EC) No 2201/2003)

(c) the law of the State where the spouses have ***resided*** for at least ***five*** years;	(c) the law of the State where the spouses have ***previously had their habitual residence*** for at least ***three*** years;

Amendments 22 and 23
ARTICLE 1, POINT 7
Article 20a, paragraph 1, point c a (new) (Regulation (EC) No 2201/2003)

(ca) the law of the State in which the marriage took place;

Amendment 24
ARTICLE 1, POINT 7
Article 20a, paragraph 2 (Regulation (EC) No 2201/2003)

2. An agreement designating the applicable law shall be expressed in writing and be signed by both spouses at the latest at the time the court is seised.

2. An agreement designating the applicable law shall be expressed in writing and be signed by both spouses at the latest at the time the court is seised.

However, if the law of the Member State in which one of the spouses has his or her habitual residence at the time when the agreement is concluded stipulates additional formal requirements for such agreements, those requirements must be met. If the spouses have their habitual residence in different Member States whose respective laws stipulate additional formal requirements, the agreement shall be valid if it meets the requirements of the law of one of those Member States.

If the agreement forms part of a marriage contract, the formal requirements of that contract must be met.

Amendment 25
ARTICLE 1, POINT 7
Article 20a, paragraph 2 a (new) (Regulation (EC) No 2201/2003)

	2a. Should the law indicated pursuant to the first paragraph not recognise legal separation or divorce or do so in a form that is discriminatory as regards one of the spouses, the lex fori shall apply.

Amendment 27
ARTICLE 1, POINT 7
Article 20b, point a (Regulation (EC) No 2201/2003)

(a) where the spouses have their ***common*** habitual residence, or failing that,	(a) where the spouses have their habitual residence ***at the time when the jurisdiction is seised,*** or failing that,

Amendment 28
ARTICLE 1, POINT 7
Article 20b, point b (Regulation (EC) No 2201/2003)

(b) where the spouse had their ***last common*** habitual residence insofar as one of them still resides there, or failing that,	(b) where the spouse*s* had their habitual residence insofar as one of them still resides there ***at the time when the jurisdiction is seised***, or failing that,

Amendment 29
ARTICLE 1, POINT 7
Article 20b, point c (Regulation (EC) No 2201/2003)

(c) of which both spouses are nationals, or, in the case of United Kingdom and Ireland, both have their "domicile", or failing that,	(c) of which both spouses are nationals, or, in the case of *the* United Kingdom and Ireland, ***in which*** both ***spouses*** have their "domicile" ***at the time at which the jurisdiction is seised***, or failing that,

Amendment 30
ARTICLE 1, POINT 7
Article 20b, subparagraph 1 a (new) (Regulation (EC) No 2201/2003)

Should the law indicated pursuant to the first point not recognise legal separation or divorce or do so in a form that is discriminatory as regards one of the spouses, the lex fori shall apply.

Amendment 31
ARTICLE 1, POINT 7
Article 20e a (new) (Regulation (EC) No 2201/2003)

Article 20ea
Information from the Member States
1. By … at the latest[1]***, the Member States shall notify the Commission of their national rules concerning the formal requirements applying to agreements relating to the choice of competent jurisdiction and of the applicable law.***

The Member States shall notify the Commission of any subsequent change to those rules.

2. The Commission shall make available to the public the information which has been notified to it pursuant to paragraph 1 by means of appropriate measures, in particular the European Judicial Network in civil and commercial matters.

[1] Three months after the date on which this Regulation comes into force.

Table of Cases

Court of Justice of the European Union

Case 26/60 *Van Gend en Loos* [1963] ECR 1
Case 6/64 *Costa* v. *ENEL* [1964] ECR 585
Cases 90 and 91/63 *Commission* v. *Luxembourg and Belgium* [1964] ECR 625
Case 14/68 *Walt Wilhelm and others* v. *Bundeskartellamt* [1969] ECR 1
Case 22/70 *Commission* v. *Council* [1971] ECR 263
Case 7/71 *Commission* v. *France* [1971] ECR 1003
Case 24/71 *Meinhardt* v. *Commission* [1972] ECR 269
Case 13/73 *Angenieux* et al. v. *Hakenberg* [1973] ECR 935
Case 12/76 *Tessili* v. *Dunlop* [1976] ECR 1473
Case 120/78 *Rewe Zentral* [1979] ECR 649
Case 138/79 *SA Roquette Frères* v. *Council* [1980] ECR 3333
Case 139/79 *Maizena GmbH* v. *Council* [1980] ECR 3393
Case 272/80 *Criminal proceedings* v. *Frans-Nederlandse Maatschappij voor Biologische Producten BV* [1981] ECR 3277
Case 283/81 *Cilfit Srl* et al. v. *Ministry of Health* [1982] ECR 3415
Case 267/83 *Diatta* v. *Land Berlin* [1985] ECR 567
Case 294/83 *Les Verts* v. *European Parliament* [1986] ECR 1339
Case 205/84 *Commission* v. *Germany* (German Insurance) [1986] ECR 3755
Case 59/85 *State of the Netherlands* v. *Reed* [1986] ECR 1283
Case C-297/89 *Rigsadvokaten* v. *Ryborg* [1989] ECR I-1943
Case C-339/89 *Alsthom Atlantique* v. *Compagnie de Construction Mécanique Sulzer SA* [1991] ECR I-107
Cases C-6 and 9/90 *Francovich* et al. v. *Italy* [1991] ECR I-3365
Case C-76/90 *Säger* [1991] ECR I-42221
Case C-168/91 *Konstantinidis* [1993] ECR I-1191
Case C-305/92 *Albert Hoorn* v. *Landesversicherungsanstalt Westfalen* [1994] ECR I-1525
Case C-452/93 *Fernández* v. *Commission* [1994] ECR I-4295
Case C-55/94 *Gebhard* [1995] ECR I-4165
Case C-214/94 *Ingrid Boukhalfa* v. *Bundesrepublik Deutschland* [1996] ECR I-2253
Case C-85/96 *Martínez Sala* [1998] ECR I-2691
Case C-90/97 *Swaddling* v. *Adjudication Office* [1999] ECR I-1075
Case C-212/97 *Centros* [1999] ECR I-1459
Case C-430/97 *Johannes* [1999] ECR I-3475

N.A. Baarsma, *The Europeanisation of International Family Law*,
DOI: 10.1007/978-90-6704-743-2, © T.M.C. ASSER PRESS, The Hague,
The Netherlands, and the author 2011

Case C-7/98 *Krombach* v. *Bamberski* [2000] ECR I-01935
Cases C-122/99P and C-125/99P *D and Sweden* v. *Council* [2001] ECR I-4319
Case C-184/99 *Grzelczyk* [2001] ECR I-6139
Case C-413/99 *Baumbast and R.* v. *Secretary for the Home Department* [2002] ECR I-7091
Case C-208/00 *Überseering BV* v. *Nordic Construction Company GmbH* [2002] ECR I-9919
Case C-167/01 *Inspire Art* [2003] ECR I-10155
Cases C-187/01 and C-385/01 *Gözütok and Brügge* [2003] ECR I-1345
Case C-491/01 *R* v. *Secretary of State for Health, ex parte British American Tobacco (Investment) Ltd.* [2002] ECR I-11453
Case C-27/02 *Engler* v. *Janus Versand GmbH* [2005] ECR I-481
Case C-116/02 *Erich Gasser* v. *Misat* [2003] ECR I-14693
Case C-148/02 *Garcia Avello* [2003] ECR I-11613
Case C-159/02 *Turner* v. *Grovit* [2004] ECR I-03565
Case C-224/02 *Pusa* [2004] ECR I-5763
Case C-281/02 *Owusu* v. *Jackson* [2005] ECR I-01383
Case C-372/02 *Adanez-Vega* v. *Bundesanstalt für Arbeit* [2004] ECR I-10761
Case C-411/03 *Sevic* [2005] ECR I-10805
Case C-443/03 *Leffler* [2005] ECR I-9611
Case C-154/04 *R (Alliance for Natural Health)* v. *Secretary of State for Health* [2005] ECR I-6451
Case C-406/04 *De Cuyper* [2006] ECR I-6947
Case C-353/06 *Grunkin-Paul* [2009] ECR I-07639
Case C-499/06 *Nerkowska* [2008] ECR I-03993
Case C-68/07 *Sundelind Lopez* v. *Lopez Lizazo* [2007] ECR I-10403
Case C-98/07 *Nordania Finans and BG Factoring* [2008] ECR I-1281
Case C-523/07 *A* [2009] ECR I-02805
Case C-66/08 *Kozłowski* [2008] ECR I-06041
Case C-135/08 *Rottmann* v. *Freistaat Bayern* [2010] ECR (not yet reported)
Case C-168/08 *Laszlo Hadadi (Hadady)* v. *Csilla Marta Mesko, married name Hadadi (Hadady)* [2009] ECR I-06871
Order of the ECJ in Case C-278/09 *Olivier Martinez and Robert Martinez* v. *MGN Ltd.* [2009] ECR I-11099
Opinion 1/94 of 15 November 1994, *WTO* [1994] ECR 5267
Opinion 1/03 of 7 February 2006, *Lugano* [2006] ECR I-1145

Court of First Instance of the European Union

Case T-43/90 *José Miguel Diaz Garcia* v. *European Parliament* [1992] ECR II-2619
Case T-85/91 *Khouri* v. *Commission* [1992] ECR II-2637
Case T-298/02 *Herrero Romeu* v. *Commission* [2005] ECR II-4599

European Court of Human Rights

ECtHR 18 December 1986, *Johnston and Others* v. *Ireland,* Application No. 9697/82

France

Cour de Cassation 17 April 1953, *RCDIP* 1953, p. 412.
Cour de Cassation - Première chambre civile, 14 December 2005

Germany

Bundesverfassungsgericht 12 October 1993, BVerfGE 89, 155 *(Maastricht-Urteil)*

The Netherlands

Hoge Raad (Supreme Court)

HR 13 December 1907, *Boon v. Schmidt, W.* 8636.
HR 9 December 1965, *NJ* 1966, 378
HR 23 February 1973, *NJ* 1973, 366
HR 28 November 1975, *NJ* 1976, 547
HR 27 May 1977, *NJ* 1977, 600
HR 4 May 1979, *NJ* 1979, 547
HR 9 February 1979, *NJ* 1979, 546 and *AA* 1979, p. 268
HR 9 June 1995, *NJ* 1995, 617
HR 6 October 1995, *NJ* 1997, 257
HR 6 December 1996, *NJ* 1997, 189
HR 26 January 1996, *NIPR* 1996, 179
HR 4 June 1999, *NJ* 1999, 535
HR 12 May 2000, *NIPR* 2000, 172
HR 9 November 2001, *NIPR* 2002, 2
HR 21 December 2001, *NIPR* 2002, 77 and *NJ* 2002, 282
HR 15 February 2002, *NIPR* 2002, 148 and *NJ* 2003, 371
HR 12 March 2004, *NIPR* 2004, 97

Hof (Court of Appeal)

Hof Arnhem 5 March 1985, *NIPR* 1986, 265
Hof Amsterdam 15 August 1988, *NIPR* 1988, 503
Hof Amsterdam 5 October 1992, *NIPR* 1993, 76
Hof Amsterdam 15 February 1993, *NIPR* 1993, 403
Hof Amsterdam 29 September 1994, *NIPR* 1995, 203
Hof Amsterdam 6 October 1994, *NIPR* 1995, 204
Hof 's-Gravenhage 28 July 1995, *NIPR* 1996, 58
Hof Amsterdam 11 April 1996, *NIPR* 1997, 189
Hof 's-Gravenhage 6 March 1998, *NIPR* 1998, 273
Hof Amsterdam 14 January 1999, *NIPR* 2000, 260
Hof 's-Hertogenbosch 26 January 2000, *NIPR* 2000, 97
Hof 's-Gravenhage 10 March 2000, *NIPR* 2000, 173
Hof Amsterdam 20 July 2000, *NIPR* 2002, 82
Hof Amsterdam 25 January 2001, *NIPR* 2001, 91
Hof 's-Gravenhage 17 January 2001, *NIPR* 2003, 76
Hof Amsterdam 21 February 2002, *NIPR* 2004, 207
Hof 's-Hertogenbosch 9 December 2004, *NIPR* 2005, 220.
Hof Amsterdam 11 August 2005, *NIPR* 2006, 10
Hof 's-Gravenhage 18 October 2006, *NIPR* 2007, 5
Hof 's-Gravenhage 25 March 2009, *NIPR* 2009, 260
Hof 's-Gravenhage 15 April 2009, *NIPR* 2009, 183

Rechtbank (District Court)

Rb. Amsterdam 29 January 1970, *NJ* 1970, 188
Rb. 's-Gravenhage 8 November 1983, *NIPR* 1985, 330
Rb. Amsterdam 23 May 1984, *NIPR* 1985, 110
Rb. 's-Gravenhage 15 November 1988, *NIPR* 1989, 209
Rb. 's-Gravenhage 2 October 1990, *NIPR* 1991, 79
Rb. Alkmaar 20 June 1991, *NIPR* 1991, 322
Rb. 's-Gravenhage 17 September 1991, *NIPR* 1991, 356
Rb. 's-Gravenhage 27 January 1992, *NIPR* 1992, 185
Rb. 's-Gravenhage 14 July 1992, *NIPR* 1992, 346
Rb. 's-Gravenhage 14 July 1992, *NIPR* 1992, 347
Rb. 's-Gravenhage 27 October 1992, *NIPR* 1993, 89
Rb. 's-Gravenhage 23 March 1993, *NIPR* 1993, 242
Rb. 's-Gravenhage 11 May 1993, *NIPR* 1993, 246
Rb. 's-Gravenhage 1 December 1993, *NIPR* 1994, 97
Rb. 's-Gravenhage 29 December 1993, *NIPR* 1994, 102
Rb. 's-Gravenhage 29 November 1995, *NIPR* 1996, 197
Rb. 's-Gravenhage 10 April 1996, *NIPR* 1996, 215a
Rb. 's-Gravenhage 25 September 1996, *NIPR* 1997, 78
Rb. 's-Gravenhage 27 November 1996, *NIPR* 1997, 83
Rb. 's-Gravenhage 20 March 1998, *NIPR* 1998, 187
Rb. 's-Gravenhage 22 October 1999, *NIPR* 2000, 15
Rb. 's-Gravenhage 7 April 2000, *NIPR* 2000, 182
Rb. 's-Gravenhage, 26 January 2001, *NIPR* 2001, 100
Rb. Roermond 29 March 2001, *NIPR* 2001, 188
Rb. Haarlem 30 October 2001, *NIPR* 2003, 87
Rb. 's-Gravenhage 15 April 2002, *NIPR* 2002, 174
Rb. 's-Gravenhage 19 June 2002, *NIPR* 2002, 242
Rb. 's-Gravenhage 7 March 2003, *NIPR* 2003, 246
Rb. 's-Gravenhage 23 April 2003, *NIPR* 2003, 173
Rb. 's-Gravenhage 27 August 2003, *NIPR* 2003, 253
Rb. 's-Gravenhage 27 October 2003, *NIPR* 2004, 11
Rb. 's-Gravenhage 10 December 2003, *NIPR* 2004, 119
Rb. Haarlem 20 January 2004, *NIPR* 2004, 125
Rb. 's-Gravenhage 23 February 2004, *NIPR* 2004
Rb. 's-Gravenhage 12 May 2004, *NIPR* 2004, 234
Rb. 's-Gravenhage 20 September 2004, *NIPR* 2005, 16
Rb. 's-Gravenhage 13 October 2004, *NIPR* 2005, 18
Rb. Alkmaar 7 July 2005, *NIPR* 2005, 314
Rb. Alkmaar 26 January 2006, *NIPR* 2006, 106
Rb. 's-Gravenhage 3 May 2006, *NIPR* 2007, 16
Rb. 's-Gravenhage 10 May 2006, *NIPR* 2007, 18
Rb. 's-Gravenhage 17 May 2006, *NIPR* 2007, 19
Rb. 's-Gravenhage 5 July 2006, *NIPR* 2006, 282
Rb. 's-Gravenhage 22 September 2006, *NIPR* 2007, 109
Rb. Alkmaar 28 September 2006, *NIPR* 2006, 271
Rb. Maastricht 28 March 2007, *NIPR* 2007, 118
Rb. Alkmaar 15 November 2007, *NIPR* 2008, 16

Index

N.A. Baarsma, *The Europeanisation of International Family Law*,
DOI: 10.1007/978-90-6704-743-2,

Printed by Printforce, the Netherlands